HUMANITY HAS BEEN A HOLY THING

Toward a Contemporary Feminist Christology

Ellen K. Wondra

Colgate Rochester Divinity School/Bexley Hall
Crozer Theological Seminary
Rochester, New York

UNIVERSITY
PRESS OF
AMERICA

Lanham • New York • London

Copyright © 1994 by
University Press of America®, Inc.
4720 Boston Way
Lanham, Maryland 20706

3 Henrietta Street
London WC2E 8LU England

Library of Congress Cataloging-in-Publication Data
Wondra, Ellen K.
Humanity has been a holy thing : toward a community feminist
christology / Ellen K. Wondra.
p.   cm.
Originally published as the author's thesis (Ph.D.)—University of
Chicago, 1991.
Includes bibliographical references and index.
1. Jesus Christ—Person and offices.   2. Feminist theology.
I. Title.
BT205.W596   1994   232'.082—dc20   93–48363 CIP

ISBN 0–8191–9438–7 (cloth : alk. paper)
ISBN 0–8191–9439–5 (pbk. : alk. paper)

Table of Contents

iv

PART II: THE RELATION OF WOMEN'S EXPERIENCE TO
CHRISTOLOGY

PART   III: TOWARD   A   CONTEMPORARY   FEMINIST
CHRISTOLOGY

PREFACE

Humanity Has Been a Holy Thing was written as my doctoral dissertation, and I present it without substantial revision. Since I finished writing at the very end of 1990, a number of other works have appeared that address some of the same concerns I have raised here. The work of womanist theologians is of particular importance. Entering into dialogue with that work requires significant revision of much of my own preliminary constructive project as it is presented here. I look forward to this next phase, but here I have only hinted at some of the issues and questions involved.

Any book, like any human life, is constituted relationally. This book has benefitted enormously from the many relations in which I participate. I would particularly like to thank the following individuals who have willingly and eagerly been involved in this project.

Numerous members of the faculty at the University of Chicago Divinity School have been generous in their advice and constructive criticism. Anne E. Carr and Brian A. Gerrish, my readers, provided valuable assistance throughout. And David Tracy has been of inestimable and constant assistance and support as my advisor, conversation partner, and friend.

Also at the University of Chicago I had the privilege of working with many students, individually and in groups. I wish particularly to thank the Women's Dissertation and Pot-luck Society, the Dissertation Support Group, and Carol Anderson, Sandra Dixon, Gary Zimmerman, and Randy Newman for their conversation and companionship.

At Colgate-Rochester Divinity School/Bexley Hall/Crozer Theological Seminary, James Evans, James Poling, Thomas Troeger, and Han van den Blink have been exemplary colleagues in their support of my work on this and many other projects, and in their conviction of the importance of feminist theology. Bill Petersen encouraged and supported my interest in F.D. Maurice and other topics. Ralph H. Elliott and Shirley Jones generously arranged for a reduction in my duties to enable the completion of this project. The library staff tirelessly sought out rare copies of sources. Mary Ann Lawrence and Wendi Bishop helped with the technicalities with endless good cheer. Elizabeth Waller, Evelyn Kirkley, and Lesley Adams demonstrated time and again the strength of sisterhood. Liz Zivanov, Jeanette Tweedy, and numerous other students listened to me think out loud, told me jokes, and graced me with their own thoughts and work. George Joseph helped me reschematize a number of the chapters of this work and solve some technical problems, as well as providing friendship, sympathy, and encouragement. Rebecca Fox and Bill Green were always there with ready ears and helpful suggestions.

Liz Zivanov and Catherine Oliver were also indescribably generous with their editorial skills in the preparation of the manuscript. The idiosyncracies of expression and the neologisms remain despite their best efforts.

My family, Gerald, Elizabeth, and Janet Wondra and Jeff Walker, have supported me emotionally and materially over the duration of all my educational programs. Shekinah, Portia, Grace, Nathaniel, Franklin, Eleanor, Cindy Lou, and Josephine reminded me of the necessities of food, affection, and a warm lap.

The name of the demons which beset a project such as this is legion. I am ever thankful that the angels are legion as well. This book is dedicated to all who have been my companions along the way.

Part I

The Feminist Christological Problem

Chapter 1

Introduction

"But who do you say that I am?" Jesus' question to his followers is but one version of the Christological question, the question of the ideal intimate relation of human and divine incarnate in the Christ. In Mark's Gospel (8:27ff.), the question arises from the midst of impassioned and public consideration of the manner in which God's saving presence and activity might take form in the contemporary world. No less in any age, religious belief in the presence of God challenges and is challenged by the world in which that belief is set. In the late twentieth century, the challenge to both faith and world often comes particularly from the margins of human existence, from those whose experience has been suppressed and silenced even when their very existence has not been threatened. The established correlations between the human situation and the affirmations of faith are rent by the interruption of radically different human situations characterized by struggles for liberation, and by the resulting explicit revisions of the affirmations of faith.

Feminism stands as one, highly significant voice at the margins, critically analyzing the relegation of women to the status of alien and subjugated Other, and using that very "otherness" as the foundation of new construals of all aspects of human existence. [1] Within Christianity, feminist theologians subject every area of Christian belief, tradition, thought, and practice to critical scrutiny in order to uncover the explicit misogyny of Christianity, and to disclose the pervasive distortions of unconscious androcentrism. [2]

But feminist theology is more than critique. It is also critical and self-critical reflection on women's religious experience, leading to the reconstruction of every aspect of Christianity to give adequate and integral expression to that reflection. This constructive moment in feminist theology suggests the possibility of alliance with other forms of contemporary theology that seek to find a credible articulation of the relation of Christian faith to the world in which believers live. It is one purpose of this book to examine how a number of white North American feminist theologians engage the specifically Christological task as part of their ongoing project of reconstruing Christian theology so that it moves toward reflecting *all* of human experience, and not just the experience of a powerful minority.

As is already evident, I understand the feminist theological task to be one of correlation between the human situation as experienced by women and the affirmations of faith. [3] That this is a *critical* correlation is evident from the relentless suspicion directed by all forms of feminism to every aspect of life in patriarchal[4] culture. That feminist theology is a *mutually* critical correlation between human situation and religious belief is indicated by the ongoing attempts of feminist theologians to give expression to the religious experience of those who find both meaning and truth in the often apparently conflicting claims of contemporary feminism and some form of Christianity informed by Christian traditions. [5] Reflection on this experience asserts an often positive connection between Christian belief and women's experience of authentic liberation, while in no way dismissing the depth and extent of the connection between Christianity and the suppression and subjugation of women's lives and experience.

The centrality of the Christ to Christianity establishes the importance of Christology in any Christian theological reflection. The key tenet of Christian faith, and a key focus of Christian theology, is the belief that the true relation between the divine and the human, and so the true natures of both divine and human, are somehow particularly manifested in Jesus of Nazareth whom Christians call the Christ. Therefore, feminist Christian theology must at some point and with some care consider Christology if it is to be *Christian* theology rather than, for example, feminist theism.[6] At the same time, traditionalist theologies' formulation of Christology is inadequate in our contemporary situation to the extent that traditionalists fail to address and/or inadvertently perpetuate the ongoing destructive history of effects of the misogyny of patriarchal religion and the androcentric distortions of core Christian symbolism. But the scathing critique of Christianity and especially Christology advanced by post-biblical feminist thought indicates that what is at stake for feminist theologians in any feminist construction of Christology is more than a simple restatement of familiar liberal views. The import of this post-biblical critique is that the effects of patriarchy and androcentrism are so pervasive in both scope and depth--affecting the deep structures of human consciousness as well as ideas, institutions, and practices--as to cast a pall of suspicion over even the best-intentioned efforts at reconstruction. Feminist theologians themselves must face the possibility that their attempts to retrieve and reconstruct those liberating facets and impulses of Christianity which are part of their feminist and religious experience are unwittingly also an apologetic that benefits the very patriarchal practices and orientations from which they seek liberation.[7]

Christian feminist theologians have become a problem to ourselves. And this problematic is made evident by the conjunction of three sometimes-conflicting types of experience, each of which contributes to liberation: personal conviction, Christian faith, and feminism. This book addresses this problematic not in order to dissolve it, but to indicate the generative possibilities it contains for a Christology that responds adequately to all three areas of challenge.

These possibilities emerge through a frank and thoughtful conversation.[8] But the possibility of fruitful conversation depends upon establishing the contexts from which the participants emerge and to which they return, as well as the context of the conversation itself. And fruitful dialogue depends on recognizing both the existing areas of acknowledged common concerns and points of agreement, *and* the exact areas where initial significant conflicts are to be found. The plan of this book, then, is first to establish the contexts and terms of the discussion. In Part One, that will be done by a further elaboration of the problematic for white feminist Christology from the perspective of theology and from the perspective of white feminism. This elaboration will indicate what methodological approaches and criteria for evaluation are appropriate to this particular conversation. These will be discussed in Chapter 3.

Part Two will begin with the examination of narrative texts which give concrete evidence that women's religious experience can be construed as resistance to domination and as re-encounter with the divine. I will establish some common ground among the white feminist theologians discussed subsequently, by developing the key category of women's experience specifically as religious response to situations of oppression. First, I will define experience in light of one contemporary feminist understanding of the nature of human experience and its epistemological components. I will then discuss how this experience-based epistemology is applicable to situations of resistance to oppression, and how an epistemology modified in this way moves from its existential base to metaphysical and ethical claims about the structure of human existence in relation to ultimate reality. Next, I will turn to a typology of religious experience that will help bring into focus how the various Christologies discussed in the later chapters are expressive of religious experience in general and white Christian women's religious experience in particular. Then I will show how this view of religious experience relates to tradition in the formulation of Christology. This will allow a fuller elaboration of three criteria of adequacy appropriate for evaluating the specific Christological proposals to which I will then turn in Part Three.

The first of these proposals, presented by Rosemary Radford Ruether, construes Christology on a prophetic-eschatological model that emphasizes proclamation about the divine rather than the divine's self-manifestation. My analysis of Ruether's Christology in light of her criticism of Christian tradition, theology, and practice and of her construction (particularly of Christian anthropology) will bring to light the strengths of this particular model while also indicating how her de-emphasis of the pole of manifestation finally leaves her Christology inadequate to both tradition and contemporary women's religious experience.

The next four chapters examine three Christologies that focus on the self-manifestation of the divine through the Christ. A comparative discussion of the Christologies of Patricia Wilson-Kastner, Marjorie Hewitt Suchocki, and Carter Heyward will illumine how each has reconstructed the Wisdom-Logos strand of Christological tradition to render it usable for feminist liberation theology. Again, my analysis will show the particular strengths of this model while also indicating its inadequacies.

Finally, I will conclude by offering a sketch of a feminist liberation Christology that attempts to maintain the tensions between the two models. I will indicate how the epistemology and metaphysics of resistance delineated in the fourth chapter are of significant assistance in this task. I will end by restating the feminist Christological problem in a manner that will place it in conversation with a differing contemporary Christology grounded in women's experience: that emerging from the analysis and reflection of African-American womanist[9] theologians.

Notes

1. With Elisabeth Schüssler Fiorenza, I understand feminism to be "a women's liberation movement for social and ecclesiastical change" and a "theoretical worldview" which addresses the full range of patriarchal domination and the struggles to overcome it. (Elisabeth Schüssler Fiorenza, *Bread Not Stone: The Challenge of Feminist Biblical Interpretation* [Boston: Beacon Press, 1984], 5.) Related to,

but distinguishable from, feminism is womanist thought and practice. The term *womanist*, first used by the poet and essayist Alice Walker, is used by African-American theologians to refer to women of color whose commitment to women's liberation encompasses issues of race and class as well as gender, something white feminism has all too often failed to do. For more on this, see "The Difference Difference Makes" in Chapter 4, and "Broadening the Conversation: Womanist Christologies" in Chapter 12.

2.   Androcentrism "takes *man* as the paradigmatic human being" while making women "invisible and marginal." "The mind-set promotes the view that women's experiences and cultural contributions are less valuable, less important, or less significant than men's." (Schüssler Fiorenza, *Bread Not Stone*, 2.)

3.   Mary Daly and others argue for a method of liberation rather than correlation. (See, e.g., Mary Daly, *Beyond God the Father: Toward a Philosophy of Women's Liberation* [Boston: Beacon Press, 1973], 8.)

4.   "Patriarchy defines not just women as the 'other' but also subjugated peoples and races as the 'other' to be dominated. It defines women, moreover, not just as the other of men but also as subordinated to men in power. . . " Patriarchy, then, is a "pyramidal system and hierarchical structure of society in which women's oppression is specified not only in terms of race and class but also in terms of 'marital' status." (Schüssler Fiorenza, *Bread Not Stone*, 5.)

5.   By "traditional" here I mean Christianity that claims definitive and in some sense normative continuity with some form(s) of Christian tradition. I intend no distinction at this point on the basis of, for example, the relative normative weighting of Scripture, tradition, reason, and experience.

6.   Schubert M. Ogden, "Problems in the Case for a Pluralistic Theology of Religions," *Journal of Religion* 68 (1988): 499.

7.   Elisabeth Schüssler Fiorenza, *In Memory of Her: A Feminist Theological Reconstruction of Christian Origins* (New York: Crossroad, 1983), 21.

8.   On conversation, I am following David Tracy, *Plurality and Ambiguity: Hermeneutics, Religion, Hope* (San Francisco: Harper and Row, 1987), 17-27 and throughout; and F. D. Maurice. See my discussion of conversation in Chapter 3. See also David Lochhead, *The Dialogical Imperative: A Christian Reflection on Interfaith Encounter* (Maryknoll: Orbis, 1988).

9.   On the use of this term, refer to note 1, above.

Chapter 2

The Feminist Christological
Problem

As many theologians have noted, it is Christology that stands at
the center of Christian theology, because it is through the
doctrine of Christ that understandings of God, humanity,
salvation, and every other element of Christian faith and practice
are clarified and elaborated. The New testament does not contain
a fully developed consistent Christology; nor has the Christian
tradition ever spoken with but one voice in answering the
question "Who do you say that I am?" However, the consensus
has been that it is in the Christ that Christians encounter the
fullness of God and the fullness of humanity; and that in Jesus
of Nazareth, Christians encounter the Christ. It is the precise
meaning of statements like these that has been under discussion
for two millennia.

Until the Enlightenment, the Chalcedonian formulation
provided the summary definition of how divinity and humanity
are united in one person "recognized in two natures, without
confusion, without change, without division, without
separation.[1] But since the Enlightenment, the Chalcedonian
affirmation has been subject to revision. Its basic insight--that

in Christ humanity and divinity are united--has been maintained. But the terms of this expression have been changed to express modern understandings of human personhood as constituted not by substance but by consciousness. This has meant a shift from "impersonal, static, metaphysical categories of substance, essence, and nature toward personal, dynamic, moral categories."[2] This shift once again raised the question of the meaning of statements that one individual can have two natures. In its modern and contemporary forms, this question cannot be addressed without also looking at the historical character of human existence, and the historicity of the texts which provide Christians with basic information about the one they follow as the Christ. [3]

For Christian feminists, the development of Christology from the early church to the contemporary period has another aspect as well. For, as white feminist thinkers as diverse as Mary Daly, Rosemary Radford Ruether, and Patricia Wilson-Kastner have documented, the development of Christology cannot be extricated from the continuation and development of Christianity as a specifically patriarchal religion whose core symbols and texts center on a God with attributes associated with human males in patriarchal society. The white feminist Christological task begins, then, with an assessment of the effect of patriarchal distortion on this key doctrine.

As Patricia Wilson-Kastner helpfully indicates, the feminist Christological problem is shaped by the conjunction of two negative judgments on the possibility of feminist Christianity with the positive experience of those who find feminism and Christianity integrally connected. [4] The two negative judgments are rendered by groups which otherwise have little in common: traditionalists (or "Biblical and doctrinal fundamentalists" as Wilson-Kastner names them)[5] and post-biblical feminists.

Each of these judgments, different in their presuppositions while agreeing in their conclusions, stands in stark contradiction to the judgment arising from feminist Christians' experience: that Christianity has been and is a major source and inspiration for women's liberation from oppression. Christian feminists make this judgment even while acknowledging that Christianity is, also and at the same time, a contributor to women's subjugation, marginalization, and silencing. As Marjorie Hewitt Suchocki says, "if the question to be raised is, 'Can a woman be both feminist and Christian,' then it is precisely we women who identify ourselves as both who are in question. We do not simply raise the question; we *are* the question."[6] That question can be neither denied nor avoided. Instead, feminist Christians must attempt to reconstruct Christianity to reflect their experience of its liberating and transforming possibilities, and must at the same time engage the feminism that has made ever more pressing the desire for liberation.

Traditionalist and Androcentric Christology

The essential position of the Biblical and doctrinal fundamentalists is that the subordination of women to men in Christian thought and practice and in Western culture, and the gender differentiation which accompanies it, are both acceptable and normative.[7] Appeals to Scripture, tradition, reason, and experience, and to some aspects of non-theological thought (including some schools of psychology and social theory) support a complex of arguments that understand the subordination of women as a reflection of the natural inferiority of women as part of the divine order from creation;[8] as a consequence of women's descent from and resemblance to Eve, who sinned first and traduced Adam;[9] or as otherwise reflecting God's will or plan.[10] Other proponents of the traditionalist position argue that women are spiritually equal, but should remain socially unequal until the end of time.[11] Yet others argue that, because church and society are two different orders or "kingdoms," acceptable arguments for social equality cannot analogously be made for ecclesial equality.[12] Some forms of these arguments, on the bases of their own principles, methodologies, and/or sources, patently lack internal coherence and consistency. But others are in fact fully coherent and consistent on these same terms.

That is, these views of "woman's place" are based in and warranted by arguments from classical natural theology, which finds the essence and development of human social relations to be an expression of divine creativity or will; from the primary or incontestable authority of Scripture as divinely inspired or normative; and from religious and ecclesial tradition as apostolically descended expressions of divine redemptive activity in the midst of a fallen or secularized world. In other words, what is at issue here between traditionalist and feminist claims is not differing applications of the same philosophies, principles, or methods, but a profound and basic disagreement at this presuppositional level. The significance of the location of the dispute must not be understated, or the breadth, scope, and depth of the conflict will be missed.

Accurate analysis of the ground of conflict has shaped the feminist critique of Christianity in important ways. As Elisabeth Schüssler Fiorenza has perceptively demonstrated, there has been a development in feminist biblical and theological hermeneutics away from an apologetic approach which understands as anomalous explicitly misogynist texts, traditions, and practices. With this has come movement toward both a dialogical-hermeneutical interpretive model with roots in neo-orthodox theology (which seeks a generalizable principle or core tradition within the Bible and Christian practices), and a liberation theology model with roots in sociology of knowledge and critical theory (which recognizes the thoroughgoing androcentric character of *all* texts and traditions and locates revelation in contemporary communities of struggle).[13] This shift is associated with a shift in analysis from consideration of misogyny to disclosure of androcentrism.[14] In other words, it is the very fact of internal coherence and consistency within traditionalist arguments that indicates that the problem lies at the level of first principles, primary methodological commitments, and grounding world views.

The traditionalist arguments briefly summarized here, then, tacitly or explicitly judge feminism and Christianity to be radically incompatible, because they see feminism as overthrowing social arrangements that are divinely established, revealed, and sanctioned. Feminist Christianity is, therefore, a contradiction in terms.

But the traditionalist position is not the only source of inner-Christian dismissal of the possibility of feminist Christianity. The androcentrism that pervades Christianity is apparent in moderate, liberal, and even political and liberation theologies as well, which often either fail to take into account women's experience, or continue the suppression of that experience in their interpretations of texts and traditions. Two examples will suffice.

Jürgen Moltmann's explication of the theology of the cross in *The Crucified God* sharply contrasts the radicality of the scandal and folly that the crucifixion presents in human history with the radical freedom that the crucified and risen Christ offers his followers. [15] The Passion narratives' accounts of the shattering effect of Jesus' suffering and death on his disciples and their consequent flight contrast with their return to following Jesus after his resurrection. The disciples' abandonment and return reveals the meaning of Jesus' crucifixion and resurrection. The behavior of the disciples is paradigmatic, even normative: "Even the disciples of Jesus fled from their master's cross. Christians who do not have the feeling that they must flee the crucified Christ have probably not yet understood him in a sufficiently radical way." [16]

These formulations are called into question, however, when one notes that the accounts in the Passion narratives themselves are less starkly absolute and completely contrasting than Moltmann makes them appear. Quite simply, not all the disciples fled. The women (and, in Luke and John, some of the men) remained at the foot of the cross. Of their decision to stay Moltmann offers only the implicit explanation inferable from the normative claim about flight quoted above. Moltmann is otherwise conscientious in bringing to bear critical theory in his project of developing a political theology that judges all ideologies in the light of the radical claims of God in Christ. His selective reading here, then, is uncharacteristic and indicative of the larger problem for and in contemporary theology of androcentric definition of the content of human experience.

In his monumental study *Jesus: An Experiment in Christology*, Edward Schillebeeckx also emphasizes the behavior of the male disciples at the time of Jesus' crucifixion, when the disciples "let him down," [17] but return to following him after the resurrection. Schillebeeckx explicitly recognizes the presence of the women in the accounts of the crucifixion and resurrection. However, he interprets Mary Magdalene's encounter with the risen Christ quite differently from Peter's: her encounter re-establishes intimacy; [18] but it is Peter whose initiative reconverts the other disciples.

Schillebeeckx's handling of the texts which describe Jesus' women disciples is uncharacteristically literalistic and apologetic in light of his general use of a rigorous historical-critical method to get at the "hard core of the tradition." He refuses to break the silence of the text about the ecclesial role of Mary Magdalene, and uses the reports of her post-resurrection encounter with Jesus to ground "'lay' experiences within the Christian community." [19] But "Peter is . . . the first Christian confessor to arrive at a Christological affirmation." [20]

Both Moltmann and Schillebeeckx--one a political theologian, the other a reconstructionist--are vulnerable to criticism of the adequacy and consistency of their arguments. Each, in the different ways I have suggested, uses Scripture to support anthropological claims; and each uses Scripture selectively in a way which devalues accounts of the presence and participation of women. [21]   These claims are then closely related to Christological arguments. With both, Christology is centered in an experience of faith that emphasizes striking contrast between human and divine activity, throwing a very harsh light on human frailty, wavering loyalties, and fallibility. Jesus, now revealed as the Christ, is on the other hand constant, faithful, benevolent, forgiving; in other words, everything his frail, fleeing human followers are not. But however much the Scriptural narratives may support this kind of formulation, they also challenge it. Frailty and failure of faith and loyalty cannot be posited as universal if some of the disciples did not flee.

Furthermore, the exclusion of the women disciples (in Moltmann) or the inadequately argued limitation of their role (in

Schillebeeckx) is evidence of the exclusion of the experience of women in general from the anthropological considerations so crucial to Christologies "from below." As has been cogently argued by feminist theorists in various disciplines (including feminist theology), women's experience (including their religious experience) cannot be easily or accurately characterized using the sharp contrasts found in these Christologies and elsewhere.[22] From this critique, it is evident that a quite different understanding of human experience is needed.

For this present work, the significance of the defense or tacit acceptance of the subordination of women is not just that it has in part provided the context of struggle and transformation from which feminist theology continues to spring. It has also shaped the self-understanding of feminists who consider themselves Christian. As shall become evident in my discussion of the critical and constructive arguments advanced by the white feminist theologians considered in this book, the problematic for feminist theologies is set in part by this acceptance or support of subordination, as feminist theologians present critical analyses and evaluations of elements of the conservative position, and then develop correctives and constructive alternatives to it.

Post-Biblical Feminist Critique

The second challenge to the possibility of a feminist Christology comes from another direction. Some feminist philosophies, theologies, and social theories carry the analysis of androcentrism and misogyny further to argue that Christianity itself is irredeemably and inherently patriarchal and therefore inevitably harmful to women as a group, regardless of the benefits it may have brought to some women. Feminist attempts to reform Christian thought and practice may in fact perpetuate the very patriarchal domination they are meant to correct. Chief among those presenting this view are Mary Daly, Carol Christ, and Daphne Hampson, joined in their argument (though not in all of their conclusions) by Rita Nakashima Brock.[23]

As Marjorie Hewitt Suchocki has rightly noted, it is Daly's analytic and constructive work that has brought many Christian women to the project of feminist theology in the first place. [24] The author of one of the earliest detailed discussions of explicit Christian sexism, [25] Daly initially argued that misogynist Christian traditions identifying women as the Alien Other were the result of external influences on basic or core doctrine. Inner-Christian resources could be discovered for the renewal of anthropology and practice for which Daly called. But in *Beyond God the Father*, Daly shifted her identification of the location of sexism from statements *about* women to the exclusion *of* women from Christian thought and practice. Her analysis of three mutually dependent elements--the systematic exclusion of women, the history of effects of concrete images or symbols, and the reciprocal legitimating functions and interdependence of religion and society--led Daly to conclude that Christianity is so deeply and thoroughly patriarchal that it must be rejected outright and its influences exorcised, not only for the liberation of women, but for the salvation of the planet. [26] In particular she identified Christology--Christolatry in her discussions--as the area of theology where the essential patriarchal character of Christianity and its consequences are most pronounced.

Daphne Hampson argues that Christianity is at its core a historical religion. That is, it relies on reference to the acts of God in history, and to one act in particular, and cannot retain its identity without such reference. That this reference is to a set of past events, in whom a unique male is crucial, in a history which is patriarchal, raises insuperable difficulties for attempts to connect Christianity and feminism. Only by distancing itself from these past events could Christianity become conducive to feminism; but were Christianity to do so, it would reduce its historical claims to pure myth. And there is no reason feminists should embrace a patriarchal myth. Instead, Hampson contends, feminists need to develop a new theism which is nonanthropomorphic, using from Christianity and other religions only what is useful in developing a religion that can adequately express women's encounter with the divine. [27]

Feminist thealogian Carol Christ agrees with Daly's conclusions, but gives her analysis two emphases that differ slightly from Daly's. [28] Christ's attention is directed to the nature and function of symbols, and to the effects of the conjunction of particularity and universality that is characteristic of Jewish and Christian monotheism. For Christ, Christology reflects the core problem, which is theology proper--the construal of the divine.

Rita Nakashima Brock locates the problem with classical Christology in yet another area: the identification of one being outside the self as "the prime source for love and action." [29] Whether divine savior or divine hero, the individual exemplar blocks self-awareness, relationality, and mutual empowerment, all of which Brock considers essential to social and personal well-being.

These four feminist critics of the possibility of a feminist Christology focus on three areas: Implicit and explicit gender and characterological elements of Christianity's core symbolism; the structural location of women's identity and salvation outside of women's existence and experience; and the kind of exemplar or model that Jesus provides, whether he is seen as divine or human. The first two of these concerns are structural as well as material; the third focuses on how Christianity understands the person Jesus.

For all four critics, the problem originates in the way in which patriarchal culture and religion understand women. Following Simone de Beauvoir's classic discussion in *The Second Sex*, Daly argues that the identification of a concrete group--women-- as the Alien Other is expressed and perpetuated in Judaism and Christianity in the myth of the Fall and its misnaming of the mystery of evil "into the distorted molds of the myth of feminine evil." [30] The multiple consequences of this misnaming and the sexual hierarchy it sanctifies include misogyny, female self-hatred, the identification of God with the male and the male with God, and religion's "original sin" and Fall of prostituting itself to patriarchy. [31] Patriarchal symbols and myths function to disguise and distort historic reality by portraying it as divinely or supernaturally given, formed, and ordered. [32]

Specifically, Christianity's core symbolism of God the immutable, omnipotent Father, Christ the Son, and the (male) Holy Spirit discloses the essential character of the religion at the same time that it continues the misnaming of historical reality. [33] As Christ argues, since religious symbols "give meaning, that is objective conceptual form, to social and psychological reality both by shaping themselves to it and by shaping it to themselves," [34] theological qualification or reflective interpretation of religious symbols has little effect on their basic import. [35] Therefore, even if God the Father is understood as self-sacrificial or kenotic, or as Liberator, Redeemer, or brooding hen, the patriarchal imagery is still primary, and distorts both non-sex specific and even female imagery. [36] God is still and primarily a patriarch even if benign. And faith in this God necessarily supports patriarchal domination. The core itself must be changed, if patriarchal domination is to be overcome. [37] Yet, Hampson argues, Christianity cannot change this core and still retain its identity: it will always of necessity be a patriarchal religion. [38]

Daly argues that the suppression of women's experience is accomplished by a core symbolism, which reframes human life into a Looking Glass world whose true arrangements are masked under a series of interrelated reversals that deny female reality and participation in human existence and that justify women's degradation by co-opting unto exclusively male competence spiritualized and disembodied versions of primary female functions. [39] Identifying God as male distorts female relation to transcendent power. Female power is directly connected to the transcendent only when it is abstracted from concrete female identity: women can be "like God" only if they are no longer women, only if they deny their own religious, bodily, and social experience. [40] Brock argues that Christianity proclaims to women that their value and their salvation is determined by their connections to a male savior, even as their ordinary existence is defined by their relationships to men. [41] Classical Christianity, rather than redeeming women from the patriarchy that enslaves them and denies them their identity, instead sanctifies their oppression. [42] As Christ concludes, for women the dilemma is quite specific: "Women have lived in the interstices between inchoate experiences and the shapings given to experience by the stories of men. In a very real sense, women have not experienced their own experience." [43]

For Carol Christ, the problem with Judaism's and Christianity's patriarchal symbols is not just that they present male reality as normative. At issue is also the kind of reality they present. From earliest Jewish tradition on, a key metaphor for God has been drawn from tribal warfare, which Christ links with alienation of human from human, community from community, and humanity from nature. [44] Concretely, this warfare was often between the Israelites and those who understood the divine in polytheistic and female terms. [45] Consequently, reinterpretation of Biblical traditions--including those liberation traditions that draw on the prophets--cannot be adequate for feminist religious expression. For both Daly and Christ, the patriarchal and misogynist nature of this core symbolism is sufficient reason to reject Christianity as providing any indication of the truth of human reality. But even were this not sufficient to compel such a rejection, Daly argues, the history of effects also makes rejection necessary.

> Defenders of [a] method [of reconstruction] argue that the symbol "can be used oppressively" or that it "has been used oppressively" but insist that it need not function in this way. This kind of defense is understandable but it leaves a basic question unanswered: If the symbol *can* be "used" that way and in fact has a long history of being "used" that way, isn't this an indication of some inherent deficiency in the symbol itself? [46]

In painful and comprehensive detail, Daly describes the multifarious concrete ways in which patriarchy and particularly patriarchal religions have sought to destroy women in mind, body, and soul. "The medium is the message"; the message has been and continues to be heeded; and the outcome is murderous intentions and actions toward women. [47]

Daly argues that the distortion of concrete imagery about God that pervades Christianity in its symbol systems and in its history of effects is particularly evident in Christology. This core set of symbols idolatrously sets up in the place of the power of Be-ing a limited, distorted, and destructive image drawn from the reality of patriarchal domination, names that image "God," and insists it be worshiped. [48]

There are two primary problems with Christolatry in Daly's view. The maleness of Jesus has been used to confirm the inferiority of the female as the "inferior sex" even as it sanctifies male dominance. Thus, even when God is understood in gender-neutral terms, the fact of an indisputably male divine savior confirms the essentially patriarchal character of divinity. [49] In Christ's view, Christology is but one instance of the more basic problem of identifying "God/He" as explicitly and characterologically male. [50] This problem is simply rendered more intense by Jesus' being indisputably, historically, unavoidably male: appeal to him as an exemplar necessarily lends support to patriarchy. Jesus is not and never can be a figure with whom women can fully and healthfully identify. [51] Hampson concurs with these assessments, raising the question as to whether or not Christianity's central figure can ever be inclusive of all humanity. [52] For Brock, the problem is not Jesus' maleness *per se*, but the construction of maleness as normative for humanity in Western patriarchal culture. [53]

The classical Christian claim that Jesus as the Christ is the *unique* Son of God compounds the problems inherent in Christology, in the view of these four feminist critics. For Daly and Hampson, the uniqueness of the incarnation denies the presence of "the power of Being in all persons" [54] and adds weight to the claims that have been made about the maleness of Jesus. Although built on response to the historical Jesus and his "charismatic and revelatory" *human* power, [55] Christolatrous symbolism thus disguises human potential as the power of a hypostatized and essentially male god. Moreover, the uniqueness claim of Christolatry preserves a disempowering orientation toward the past at the expense of the present and the future. [56] On all counts, the symbol of the unique male Christ perpetuates dualisms that ground other forms of domination and threaten the continuation of the life of the planet. [57]

For Carol Christ, the conjunction of particularism and universality claims associated with Jewish and Christian monotheism "spawn," sanction, and "countenance" destructive intolerance of other ways or forms of salvation and the peoples who profess them. [58] Universal monotheism, regardless of the explicit or implicit gender identification of its god, will, Christ thinks, always have this effect.

For Brock, the problem with Christology resides primarily in the identification of *one* person other than the self as "the prime source for love and action." *Any* external exemplar pulls attention away from self-awareness, and away from relationality and mutual empowerment. [59] Hero-worship--the location of an ideal in a single individual--masks the fact that erotic, generative power resides in connectedness; instead, power is understood hierarchically. [60] Further, the emphasis on individuals seen in isolation conceals the role of social and cultural factors in events. [61] Structurally speaking, Jesus--or anyone else--in the role of individual heroic human exemplar is, in Brock's view, as problematic as Jesus in the role of divine savior.

For Daly, Hampson, Christ, and Brock, then, the reliance of Christology and Christianity on a core symbolism that is patriarchal in content and structurally hierarchical and exclusive means that feminists must reject these symbols as irredeemable for feminist religious belief and thought. [62] Not to do so is to continue the power of patriarchy, with its destructive effects for women, men, and the world as a whole. The way in which symbols function in human existence demonstrates this, as does the destructive history of effects of the use of these symbols. As Daly concludes,

> Under the conditions of patriarchy the role of liberating the human race from the original sin of sexism would seem to be precisely the role that male symbol *cannot* perform. The image itself is one-sided, as far as sexual identity is concerned, and it is precisely on the wrong side, since it fails to counter sexism and functions to glorify maleness. [63]

What, then, of the possibility that a fully and only human Jesus might serve as an exemplar or human model, if not a divine savior? Hampson agrees that Jesus may serve as one exemplar, but if that is all he is, the profession which so claims him is not Christian. [64] Daly rejects the possibility of Jesus as exemplar because the use Christology has made of the particularities of Jesus' human life further damages women's well-being, in that these particularities are used to support a double-standard ethic of individualism (for men) and self-sacrifice (for women). Jesus' role as "mankind's most illustrious scapegoat," [65] the ultimate willing victim, is powerfully directed through the mechanism of projection toward those who are considered Other--women, in particular. [66] The effect is to foster what women have internalized as false humility or self-deprecation, [67] reinforcing women's tendencies to accede to patriarchy's identification of women as scapegoats who must sacrifice themselves to atone for the "original sin" of being female in a patriarchal world. [68]

But Jesus was an *innocent* victim who offered himself for the sins of others; the message of the myths that fund patriarchy is that women are never and can never be innocent. Only a male savior--whether Jesus or some other--can lift the blame to which women are subject. [69] The conclusion is plain: The use of the *human* Jesus as any kind of model or exemplar for women at all reinforces the essential messages of patriarchy about women's essential defectiveness as human beings.

Brock's concern with the way in which the human Jesus is portrayed begins with the classical understanding of his perfection. His static perfection is taken to be what shows divine presence incarnate in him. [70] But in both qualities he is profoundly *un*like other humans; he is, therefore, not really exemplary of human possibility. Second, Jesus' perfection is demonstrated by his being a passive victim of evil forces, who is unable to save himself and must rely on an omnipotent deity for deliverance. Such idealization of victimization must be rejected on a number of grounds, according to Brock. It slows or blocks the search for justice for victims while at the same time immobilizing the oppressed and denying their legitimate anger. And the idealization of victimization upholds selflessness and self-sacrifice, with the same effects Daly describes of encouraging internalization of dominant views and nurturing self-hatred and projection of responsibility onto others. [71] The fact that Jesus is a hero--a lone, ideal figure--combines with his characterization as victim to work against relationality.

Finally, the fact that Jesus is saved from his passive victim's fate by abstraction into a supernatural existence affirms the desire for "an unmoving place to stand, an absolute principle we use to act for justice," a desire that removes the ambiguities that characterize lived existence and ultimately becomes a demand for totalitarianism. [72]

> In Christology the use of the cosmic Christ has functioned to muffle the cry of the human person in our presence. We are convinced we hear, instead of the person before us, the voice of Christ, and that conviction becomes a shield against our deepest hearing. [73]

Jesus' humanity, as it is classically portrayed, conceals real human needs and possibilities, and thus works against rather than for human well-being.

The conclusion reached by Daly, Hampson, and Brock is that even the human Jesus cannot serve as an exemplar for women seeking liberation and healing in a patriarchal world. [74] Instead, women must seek their liberation and healing in their own experience.

Brock consequently redefines the feminist Christological task so that Christology is "part of a community self-naming process"[75] in which the figure of Jesus is affirmed as one individual among many who together respond to "God's loving graciousness. . . to become active agents of our own becoming, searching and listening for God's loving presence in our midst."[76] No longer at the center, Jesus is a figure from the past, "a distant partner who participates in our search for life whole and healed."

> The feminist Christian commitment is not to a savior who redeems us by bringing God to us. Our commitment is to love ourselves and others into wholeness. Our commitment is to a divine presence with us here and now, a presence that

works through the mystery of our deepest selves and our relationships, constantly healing us and nudging us toward a wholeness of existence we only fitfully know. That healed wholeness is not Christ; it is ourselves. [77]

Brock believes, then, that Christology can be reformulated without Christ at the center. [78] Instead, the center is held by Christa/community as the incarnation of the erotic power of connectedness driving toward wholeness. And Jesus is "a remarkable man for his time," nothing more. [79]

Daly and Hampson, on the other hand, find it better to reject the symbol of Christ altogether rather than reconstruct it. Because of the centrality and necessity of the symbol of Christ to Christianity, rejection of Christolatry perforce means rejection of Christianity as well.

And with this conclusion Carol Christ heartily concurs. What feminists need, Christ concludes, and what feminists are finding and consciously developing, are explicitly female symbols drawn from women's concrete experience. [80] Only by moving in the direction of affirmation of their own experience and recognition of its resonance with the divine will feminists surpass the crippling and destructive impoverishment of spirit and imagination that has been women's and men's lot with patriarchal religions. [81] The rising symbol of the Goddess(es) expresses the power that women are finding and affirming in their own experience. [82]

The challenge issued by feminist critics to Christology is apparently finally comprehensive. Not only are the core and indispensable symbols explicitly male to the exclusion of women, the character of the beings portrayed in these symbols is drawn from patriarchy, with its exaltation of individualism, idealism, and static perfection. The equation of this patriarchal ideal with divinity not only excludes the female from the Godhead; it sanctifies patriarchal maleness, with massively destructive historical effect. This is devastating also for understanding what it means to be human, for salvation is attained through the acceptance of passive victimization and coerced self-sacrifice, precisely what patriarchy demands of women who are defined as less than fully human.   There is, that is, no element of Christology that is left untouched.

The challenge issued to feminist Christian theology is straightforward:

> A serious Christian response to [feminist] criticism of the core symbolism of Christianity either will have to show that the core symbolism of Father and Son do not have the effect of reinforcing and legitimating male power and female submission, or it will have to transform Christian imagery at its very core. [83]

The Challenge of Feminist Christian Religious Experience

The third challenge that contributes to the formulation of feminist Christian theology is the religious experience of feminist Christians themselves.   This experience is frankly ambiguous: Christian faith and practice have at one and the same time taught feminist Christians to hope for liberation and transformation, and to recognize the ways in which Christianity has itself contributed to an oppressive historical existence that cries out for that same liberation and transformation. Feminist Christian theologians recognize significant elements of truth in both challenges sketched above. Traditionalists are correct in appealing to Christian tradition and the presuppositions that support it; for this tradition has been persistent if not universal in its subjugation of women and women's experience. Post-biblical feminists are correct in their claim that patriarchal distortion has affected the depths of Christian theology and practice. But given the central location of women's experience as a source in contemporary theology and feminist theory and practice, [84] feminist Christian theologians find it imperative to consider their own experience in formulating their constructive proposals.   This experience stands in contrast to both the challenges discussed above. On the one hand, feminist Christian experience indicates that the subjection and marginalization of women perpetuated by patriarchal Christianity is contrary to the freedom for which Christ has set humanity free. On the other, feminist Christian experience indicates that that freedom is integrally connected, personally, socially, and historically, with specifically Christian faith.

"We do not simply raise the question; we *are* the question." [85] That question can be neither denied nor avoided. Instead, feminist Christians must attempt to reconstruct Christianity to reflect their experience of its liberating and transforming possibilities, and must at the same time engage the feminism that has made ever more pressing the desire for liberation.

The post-biblical feminist challenge must be met head-on. This does *not* mean a point-by-point refutation of Daly's direct evidence, which in any event is compelling and often convincing to most feminist Christian theologians. Instead, feminist Christian theologies begin, as I have noted above, with an historical and theological critique which follows from Daly's own, even when it does not appeal to her work directly. Indeed, the various ways in which theologians such as Rosemary Radford Ruether, Elisabeth Schüssler Fiorenza, and Carter Heyward have appropriated various post-biblical arguments indicate growing feminist Christian awareness of the inadequacy of many of even the best attempts at apologetic reform.

Specifically in the area of Christology, the post-biblical feminist analysis challenges feminist Christian theologians to take on at least two tasks. First, we must address the problem of the unique male savior. This problem, I have indicated, has two aspects--uniqueness and maleness--which post-biblical feminists see as related but to some extent distinct. Thus, even once Christology demonstrates that the maleness of Jesus is not central to his salvific work, the task remains to indicate how Christology fosters rather than diminishes the human realization of authentic human possibility. This task is, of course, in addition to demonstrating how Christianity's claims can be made in a world of plural religious truth.

Second, post-biblical feminist analysis sets the task of accounting for the historical effects of Christian symbolism and practice. As I have indicated, the details of Daly's evidence cannot be refuted. However, as the work of Elisabeth Schüssler Fiorenza and others indicates, the evidence can be rendered more complete; and its overall shape can be recast. Christianity in symbol and practice has more than one tradition, and the "suppressed voice" of the subjugated aspects of tradition have been carried forward even while kept marginalized. Nor are these subjugated aspects uniformly silenced, as Daly herself recognizes.

In sum, then, the post-biblical feminist challenge to Christian feminist theologians is that we take seriously the extent and centrality of the misogynist characteristics of patriarchal religion, that we demythologize and deideologize such religion absolutely and without remainder. This means that we must face squarely into the ways in which feminist Christian theologians are a problem to ourselves in our willing if unconscious consent to symbol systems that are oppressive, a consent manifested by reformist approaches that fail to be fully critical and so leave some symbols and their related ideas in a privileged position.

Further, it means that we must examine closely what we mean and desire as salvation, and how we experience salvation as both reality and possibility in our lives. A thorough critique of the symbols and concepts we already use to express this experience is part of such an examination.

Finally, it means that we must account for the past, present, and likely future effects of such an expression. Post-biblical feminism's tacit imperative here is that if reality is a human construct with consequences, those offering alternative constructs have a responsibility to assess the consequences as part of the constructive task.

In the midst of a substantive or material challenge, post-biblical feminism is, then, also making a formal challenge by suggesting three criteria for adequacy. Two of these are already familiar to contemporary theology: adequacy to experience and to tradition, here presented as the history of effects of tradition. Post-biblical feminism also can be taken to be offering a third: adequacy to the creation of a viable future. [86] The challenge which post-biblical feminism presents to feminist Christian theologies--and therefore to this book--is finally two-fold, both material and formal. It is a challenge that is understood differently by the feminist theologians whose work I am considering here, a point to which I shall necessarily return.

Context in Contemporary Christology

Identifying the challenge facing feminist Christian theologians as three-fold places feminist Christologies squarely within the contemporary discussion of Christology. In that discussion, two themes predominate. One focuses on the search for authentic freedom in situations of massive injustice, suffering, and oppression. The question of liberation hinges not only on present struggle, but also on future hope. Therefore liberation Christologies look toward a transformed future where the reign of God announced by the Christ is fulfilled. Eschatological vision joins with present experience of oppression and liberation and the traditions of the past in Christological formulations. [87]

The other theme is focused through the question of meaning and truth. Whereas liberation theologies argue that meaning and truth are discovered in concrete socio-historical struggle, revisionist and narrative theologies press the question of how human persons discover the meaning of their existence through experience, and know that the meaning they discover there is true. Here experiential epistemology must be connected with metaphysics in order to establish some correspondence between human consciousness (and unconsciousness) and the transcending reality toward which such consciousness ceaselessly strives. [88]

Feminist Christian theologies are engaged in both these pursuits in their considerations of the nature and meaning of women's experience of oppression and liberation. With other liberation theologians, feminist Christian theologians such as Rosemary Radford Ruether and Carter Heyward insist that the *praxis* of liberation--and for them specifically the *praxis* of the liberation of oppressed women--gives rise to an eschatological vision which pulls the transforming future into the present. And with other revisionist theologians, feminist Christian theologians such as Patricia Wilson-Kastner and Marjorie Hewitt Suchocki argue that reflection on experience--and for them specifically women's experience--is part of the human drive toward transcendence, which links humanity with the divinity that is its source and goal. The promise of feminist Christian theology, in part, lies in its contribution to the expansion of contemporary theological discussion so that it increasingly reflects the actual diversity of lived human experience.

Summary: The Feminist Christological Task

As one voice in the contemporary discussion of Christology, feminist Christian theology addresses the themes of liberation and of truth and meaning from the vantage point of women's experience. That experience has been problematized by three factors: the long-standing and powerful Christian tradition which has been pervasively distorted by patriarchal thought and practice; the comprehensive critical assessment given by post-biblical feminists of the extent of Christian misogyny and androcentrism; and feminist Christians' own ambivalent experience of Christianity as the source of both oppression and the hope for liberation.

The task facing feminist Christological considerations, then, is multi-fold. Each of these challenges must be addressed critically, appreciatively, and courageously. The problem of pervasive androcentrism and misogyny in tradition and current thought and practice must be investigated, with the dual intent of discovering the extent of patriarchal distortion and disclosing alternative traditions and practices that have resisted such distortion, and/or that assist resistance today. The post-biblical feminist critique must be evaluated for the extent of its validity, and new formulations developed that answer its legitimate challenges. In all this, feminist Christians' own experience must be subjected to critical and respectful reflection. Constructive proposals for Christology must be developed that at the same time reconstruct those elements of Christian tradition which drive toward liberation or resist domination, which respond critically to the contemporary context of Christian faith and feminist commitment, and which move toward a liberated and transformed future.

The risks as well as the challenges of this venture are great. On one side of the way to a feminist Christian theology lies the possibility of grafting onto Christianity elements which finally are incompatible with its central insights and claims. On the other lies the possibility of perpetuating its oppressive elements to the destruction of future generations. And always there is uncertainty about the outcome of constructive efforts.

> [T]he results of our journeying, spinning, weaving cannot be foretold. We might look to what we hope might happen, but we cannot assure that it can or will happen. To parallel Daly's journey [away from patriarchy] is to risk the question, to risk ourselves, for the genuineness of any question is that we do not know the answer. . . . the journey has no map, and the journey has no end. [89]

Notes

1.   Council of Chalcedon, Actio V. Mansi, vii. 116f., in *Documents of the Christian Church*, ed. Henry Bettenson, 2d ed. (Oxford: Oxford University Press, 1963), 51-52.

2.   Kenneth Cauthen, *Systematic Theology: A Modern Protestant Approach* (Lewiston, Ontario: Edwin Mellen Press, 1986), 245.

3.   Schubert M. Ogden, *The Point of Christology* (San Francisco: Harper and Row, 1982), 7-10.

4.   Patricia Wilson-Kastner, *Faith, Feminism, and the Christ* (Philadelphia: Fortress Press, 1983), 1-3.

5.   Ibid., 2. For a discussion of Wilson-Kastner's use of this term, see the discussion of her work in Chapter 6, below.

6.   Marjorie Hewitt Suchocki, "The Challenge of Mary Daly," *Encounter* 41 (1980): 307.

7.   The literature both supporting and critiquing this traditionalist view is voluminous. Not coincidentally, much of it has emerged in the context of ecclesial debates about the role of women in the churches, and in response to shifts in the culture in which Christianity is set (such as the rise of the influence of feminism). In addition to the material cited in this discussion, see the many well-researched and -

documented collections of overtly misogynist statements; the many anthologies on the role of women in the churches; and bibliographies on the debates surrounding the ordination of women within virtually every Christian denomination.

8. See John Chrysostom, *Quales Ducendae Sint Uxores*, 4; Augustine of Hippo, *De Genesi contra Manichee* 2:11; and Thomas Aquinas, *Summa Theologiae* 1:92, 1 ad. 1 and 2-2:26, 10c. (Cited in Daly, *The Church and the Second Sex*, 86, 87, and 91, respectively.)

9. Tertullian, *De Cultu Feminarum*, libri duo 1:1. (Cited in Daly, *The Church and the Second Sex*, 87).

10. See, for example, Karl Barth, *Church Dogmatics* 3.2 and 3.4. (Cited in *Women and Religion: A Feminist Sourcebook of Christian Thought*, ed. Elizabeth Clark and Herbert Richardson [New York: Harper and Row, 1977].) Daphne Hampson gives extended quotes from contemporary Anglican, Roman Catholic, and Orthodox theologians who make similar claims. (Daphne Hampson, *Theology and Feminism* [Oxford and Cambridge: Basil Blackwell, 1990], 66-71.)

11. This position is often related to the argument from the descent from Eve. See Jane Dempsey Douglass, "Women and the Continental Reformation," in *Religion and Sexism: Images of Women in the Jewish and Christian Traditions*, ed. Rosemary Radford Ruether (New York: Simon and Schuster, 1974), 299ff.

12. Therefore, one can argue for expanded roles for women in society without also supporting expanded roles for women in the church. For the general shape of this argument, see Karl Barth, *Church Dogmatics* 3.1, 3.2, and 3.4. (Cited in Clark and Richardson, *Women and Religion*.)

13. Schüssler Fiorenza, *In Memory of Her*, Chapter 1.

14. "Misogyny" refers to statements indicating a dislike of women. "Androcentrism" (defined in fn. 2 of Chapter 1) refers to a generally unconscious, pervasive bias that defines things associated with maleness as normative, relegating the female to the margins.

15. Jürgen Moltmann, *The Crucified God: The Cross of Christ as the Foundation and Criticism of Christian Theology*, trans. R. A. Wilson and John Bowden (New York: Harper and Row, 1974).

16. Ibid., 37-38.

17. Edward Schillebeeckx, *Jesus: An Experiment in Christology*, trans. Hubert Hoskins (New York: Vintage Books, 1981), 325.

18. Ibid., 345-6.

19.   Ibid., 345. It would seem reasonable to suspect that here the text is being used in service of a contemporary doctrinal discussion, without that discussion being directly acknowledged.

20.   Ibid., 389. Note that this claim can also serve to protect the foundation of the church "on this rock" without relying on the historically more dubious confession at Caesarea Philippi.

21.   That Moltmann is well aware of this problem and has subsequently attempted to address it is clear in his more recent "The Motherly Father: Is Trinitarian Patripassianism Replacing Theological Patriarchalism?" trans. G. W. S. Knowles, in *God as Father*, ed. J. Metz and E. Schillebeeckx (Eng. lang. ed. Marcus Lefebure) (Edinburgh: T. and T. Clark, 1981).

22.   See, among many possibilities, Valerie Saiving, "The Human Situation: A Feminine View," *Journal of Religion* 40 (April 1960): 100-112, reprinted in Carol Christ and Judith Plaskow, eds., *Womanspirit Rising* (New York: Harper and Row, 1979); Judith Plaskow, *Sex, Sin, and Grace: Women's Experience and the Theologies of Reinhold Niebuhr and Paul Tillich* (Lanham, MD: University Press of America, 1980); Daphne Hampson, *Theology and Feminism*; Carolyn Walker Bynum on medieval women mystics and the ritual theory of Victor Turner; the work by Carol Gilligan in psychology; and so on.

23.   Mary Daly, a former Roman Catholic, holds advanced degrees in both theology and philosophy, and used to teach Christian theology. Carol Christ holds advanced degrees in religious studies, with a focus on the Hebrew Bible and on religion and literature. Daphne Hampson, a British scholar, holds doctorates in church history and in systematic theology. While still a Christian, she wrote many of the theological position papers supporting the ordination of women in the Church of England. Rita Nakashima Brock's training is in theology.

24.   Suchocki, "The Challenge of Mary Daly," 307.

25.   Mary Daly, *The Church and the Second Sex* with a new Feminist Postchristian Introduction (New York: Harper Colophon Books, 1968 and 1975).

26.   Daly, "Autobiographical Preface" to the Colophon Edition of *The Church and the Second Sex*, 5-14; and *Beyond God the Father*. Mary Knutsen, ("'This Terrible Battle for Meaning': A Critical Interpretation of Mary Daly's Radical Feminist Critique of Christianity" [Unpublished paper, University of Chicago, 1982]) identifies the three elements of Daly's methodological shifts and

discusses each in great detail. I am deeply indebted to her paper for my discussion here. Alone among commentators on Daly, Knutsen provides an incisive analysis of Daly's appeal to a consensus theory of truth.

27. Hampson, *Theology and Feminism*, throughout.

28. Christ defines the term *thealogy* (which she credits to Naomi Goldenberg) as "reflections on the meaning of the Goddess" which are drawn from the reflector's experience. Thealogy has as its two foci nature and "the interpretation and celebration of women's experiences." The suppression of much of the history and worship of goddesses places thealogians in the position of having to retrieve and reconstruct traditions from minimal and often hostile sources, and of using their own imaginative capacities. For Christ's discussion of thealogy, see Carol Christ, *Laughter of Aphrodite: Reflections on a Journey to the Goddess* (San Francisco: Harper and Row, 1987), ix-xvii and passim.

29. Rita Nakashima Brock, "Beyond Jesus the Christ: A Christology of Erotic Power," (unpublished paper presented to the Currents in Contemporary Christology Section of the American Academy of Religion, November 1987), 1. Cf. Rita Nakashima Brock, *Journeys by Heart: A Christology of Erotic Power* (New York: Crossroad, 1988), 52-53.

30. Daly, *Beyond God the Father*, 47.

31. Ibid., 47-48. See also Christ, *Laughter of Aphrodite*, 139-140.

32. Daly's understanding of the nature and function of symbols reflects the influence of Paul Tillich on her thought. Like Tillich, Daly believes that symbols grow organically out of their context; they are not entirely susceptible to conscious production. Symbols also resemble their referents. (However, unlike Tillich, Daly believes that the symbols of Christianity refer to patriarchy--a human product--rather than to the divine.) The organic connection between symbol, referent, and context means that symbols hold real power to shape conscious and unconscious beliefs, behaviors, and attitudes. Therefore, the use of patriarchal symbols will inevitably reinforce the power of patriarchy. And the use of feminist symbols will inevitably reinforce the power of feminism.

33. Daly, *Beyond God the Father*, 13-31, 47. By "historical," both Daly and Christ understand life in history. However, Hampson has a different meaning, which is crucial to her argument: Christianity is a historical religion in that "Christianity proclaims there to have been

a revelation of God in history. Therefore that time and that particular history in which the revelation is deemed to have taken place become integral to the religion. Christianity cannot lose its reference to that history." And that history is also in some sense normative, because it is the locus of divine revelation. (Hampson, *Theology and Feminism*, 7f. Cf. Daphne Hampson and Rosemary Ruether, "Is There a Place for Feminists in a Christian Church?" *New Blackfriars* 68 no. 801 [January 1987]: 7-24.)

34.   Christ here follows anthropologist Clifford Geertz, who defines religion as "a system of symbols which acts to establish powerful, pervasive, and long-lasting moods and motivations in men [*sic*] by formulating conceptions of a general order of existence and clothing these conceptions with such an aura of factuality that the moods and motivations seem uniquely realistic." (Clifford Geertz, *The Interpretation of Cultures: Selected Essays* [New York: Basic Books, 1973], 90) For Christ, symbols arise out of a social context, which they reflect and legitimate; but the symbols do not necessarily have a referent other than the context. In other words, symbols are human creations and--for Christ even if not for Geertz--they are *only* that. Christ seems more confident than Daly that the creation and rejection of symbols can be a fully conscious activity.

35.   Christ, "The New Feminist Theology: A Review of the Literature," *Religious Studies Review* 3 (1977): 204. Hampson states this view even more strongly: the patriarchal character of Christian symbols "is necessarily present, and present as central to the religion. Even if at a conscious level people think that of course that was a patriarchal age, and we now live in certain respects in a more enlightened age, the metaphors and symbols which are present will be impressed on people's minds." (*Theology and Feminism*, 9.) Therefore, argue both Hampson and Christ, recourse to so-called inclusive language in fact increases the distortion by further covering over the essentially patriarchal character of the root imagery. This is one of many points where Ruether agrees with Daly, Christ, and Hampson. (Rosemary Radford Ruether, *Sexism and God-Talk: Toward a Feminist Theology* [Boston: Beacon Press, 1983], 60-61.)

36.   See, for example, Hampson, *Theology and Feminism*, 155. It is noteworthy that Hampson has published this conclusion after the publication of Ruether's kenosis proposal, discussed in Chapter 5, below.

37.   Correlate with this point in Christ's argument is her insistence
that who and what is invoked in worship is of great importance.   Thus,
she points out, Rosemary Radford Ruether's indication that the name
"God/ess" cannot be spoken ultimately undercuts naming divine power
in this way. (Christ, *Laughter of Aphrodite*, 275.) In general, Christ
finds any revision of liturgical language that stops short of refusal to
attribute male characteristics to the divine and of explicit attribution of
female characteristics to the divine laudable but finally inadequate.
(Ibid., 112-113.)

38.   Hampson, *Theology and Feminism*, 9. Cf. Hampson and
Ruether. Hampson is quite explicit that symbols do refer: "It is not
simply a construct in language; . . . To affirm that the word 'God'
refers is however not necessarily to believe that the word refers to a
kind of entity, one which could be distinguished from all else that is."
The grounds for this conviction are in religious experience, and
especially in prayer: "The word God names what one concludes must
be the case, the other level of reality which one believes to exist. If
it were not that prayer is effective, I cannot see what grounds there
could be for using the word God." (*Theology and Feminism*, 169-
170.) Patriarchal symbols name this experience in terms of the age in
which they emerged (ibid., 43). But the character of our age and ages
to come need not and indeed must not continue to be patriarchal. This
Hampson identifies as an ethical a priori, which seems to her to be an
adequate foundation for theistic claims. (Ibid., 29f. and passim.)

39.   "That language for millennia has affirmed the fact that Eve
was born from Adam, . . . [Adam's priest-sons] devised a sacramental
system which . . . lifted from women the onerous power of childbirth,
christening it 'baptism.' Thus they brought the lowly material function
of birth, incompetently and even grudgingly performed by females, to
a higher and more spiritual level. . . . Feeding was elevated to become
Holy Communion. Washing achieved dignity in Baptism and Penance.
Strengthening became known as Confirmation, and the function of
consolation, which the unstable nature of females caused them to
perform so inadequately, was raised to a spiritual level and called
Extreme Unction." (Daly, *Beyond God the Father*, 195.) Daly goes
on to extend this analysis to cover all of Christianity and secularized
Western culture.

40.   Christ, "Why Women Need the Goddess" in Christ and
Plaskow, 275; Christ, *Laughter of Aphrodite*, 138, 141. Cf. Daly,
Beyond God the Father, 62, 77. Cf. Hampson, *Theology and
Feminism*, esp. 50-80. Feminist historian Gerda Lerner makes the

same point at greater length in *The Creation of Patriarchy* (New York and Oxford: Oxford University Press, 1986).

41.   "Essential to that ancient dominant-submissive rape ritual are the rules that give no power and authority to women except through our connections to male institutions and our relationships of submission to men.   In Christianity, are women therefore redeemed and legitimated by our reconciliation to the saving efficacy of a male savior?" (Rita Nakashima Brock, "The Feminist Redemption of Christ," in *Christian Feminism: Visions of a New Humanity*, ed. Judith L. Weidman [San Francisco: Harper and Row, 1984], 56.) See also Brock, "Beyond Jesus the Christ," 1.

42.   Brock, "The Feminist Redemption of Christ," 69; Rita Nakashima Brock, "A Feminist Consciousness Looks at Christology," *Encounter* 41 (1980): 327.   Here Brock explicitly follows Daly.

43.   Christ, "Spiritual Quest and Women's Experience," in *Womanspirit Rising: A Feminist Reader in Religion*, 228.

44.   Christ, "New Feminist Theology," 211; idem, *Laughter of Aphrodite*, passim.   Following Ruether, Christ argues that the characteristics attributed to God arise from male alienation and its expression in dualistic thought and social structures which express alienation.   (Christ and Plaskow, "Introduction" in *Womanspirit Rising*, 5; Christ, *Laughter of Aphrodite*, 5, 142, 217.)   This point about the symbolic expression of male alienation leads Christ to reject the feminist Christian argument that Christian doctrines of the Incarnation overcome the dualistic split between life and death and finitude and infinity.

45.   Christ, *Laughter of Aphrodite*, 78-79.

46.   Daly, *Beyond God the Father*, 72.

47.   Daly's exhaustive and exhausting catalogues of the history of effects of patriarchy are found throughout *Beyond God the Father* and *Gyn/ecology: The Metaethics of Radical Feminism* (Boston: Beacon Press, 1978).

48.   Daly, *Beyond God the Father*, 19 and passim.

49.   Ibid., 70.

50.   In this, Christ differs from Daly, but does not disagree with her.   Daly's argument is that the identification of the male Jesus with God validates patriarchal and radical feminist claims that the God of Christianity is male.   Christ's argument is that the gender of God is already quite apparent from Judaism; the incarnation really adds nothing new to patriarchal symbolism, either in terms of gender identification and character, or in terms of the symbolic and

psycho-social subjugation of women and women's experience. (Christ, *Laughter of Aphrodite*, 217.)

51. Christ, *Laughter of Aphrodite*, 147.
52. Hampson, *Theology and Feminism*, 51.
53. Brock, "The Feminist Redemption of Christ," 60; cf. idem, *Journeys by Heart*, xii-xiii.
54. The quoted phrase is from Daly, *Beyond God the Father*, 71. Cf. Hampson, *Theology and Feminism*, 8; and Hampson and Ruether, 11.
55. Daly, *Beyond God the Father*, 70.
56. Ibid., 74. Cf. Hampson, *Theology and Feminism*, 51: "the problem here is not that Jesus was a man, but that this man has been considered unique, symbolic of God, God Himself . . . The Godhead, or at least Christology, then appears to be biased against women. . . . The question which feminists are raising then strikes at the very core of Christology. For it is being questioned whether a symbol which would appear to be necessarily male can be said to be inclusive of all humanity."
57. Daly, *Beyond God the Father*, 71-72, 78-79; Christ, *Laughter of Aphrodite*, 79; Brock, "The Feminist Redemption of Christ," 60.
58. Christ, *Laughter of Aphrodite*, 7-9, 79, 83. Again, Christ is significantly influenced by Ruether (primarily, on this point, in *Faith and Fratricide: The Theological Roots of Anti-Semitism*, with an Introduction by Gregory Baum [New York: Seabury, 1974]). Christ places greater emphasis than does Ruether on the roots of Christian claims to universality (and consequent Christian anti-Judaism) and Jewish claims to special status as the chosen people.
59. Brock, "Beyond Jesus the Christ," 1.
60. Ibid., 7.
61. Ibid., 8. In Brock's analysis, this carries over to the interpretation of Jesus' relations with those with whom he has healing contact. With Elisabeth Schüssler Fiorenza, Brock understands the stories of both the hemorraghing woman and the Syro-Phoenician to concern their exercise of power which divests Jesus of his patriarchal power by breaking through barriers of "male privilege and status that separated them." "The point is not Jesus' sole possession of power, but the revelation of a new understanding of power that connects members of the community. The power reversal comes from those perceived as weak who reveal the divine way of power, erotic power." (Ibid., 11, 13.)

62. Hampson gives less imperative force to this point than do the other three. Nevertheless, she seems quite baffled by the desire of feminists to continue as Christians, and sees efforts at Christian feminist theology as attempts to make it possible for women to continue to be Christian, rather than as reflections on contemporary women's religious experience. See, for example, *Theology and Feminism*, 39-41.

63. Daly, *Beyond God the Father*, 72.

64. "Christianity is also a belief--if the salt is to retain its saviour--in Christ. Christianity proclaims the revelation of God in history, the belief in the uniqueness of Christ, and the inspiration of the literature which tells us of these things. There lies the nub of the problem." (Hampson, *Theology and Feminism*, 4.)

65. Daly, *Beyond God the Father*, 75, quoting Thomas Szasz.

66. Ibid., 76.

67. Ibid., 53-54. Daly points out that if the "original sin" of patriarchy is its false naming of the source of evil, the "original sin" of women is our internalization of blame and guilt for being scapegoats for misogyny. (Ibid., 49.) See also Valerie Saiving's classic article, "The Human Situation: A Feminine View," reprinted in Christ and Plaskow, *Womanspirit Rising*; and Judith Plaskow's longer treatment in *Sex, Sin, and Grace*.

68. Daly, *Beyond God the Father*, 77. Cf. Hampson, *Theology and Feminism*, 121-126.

69. Daly, *Beyond God the Father*, 72.

70. Brock, "The Feminist Redemption of Christ," 60.

71. Ibid., 60.

72. Ibid., 62.

73. Ibid., 62.

74. Brock writes, "Jesus Christ need not be the authoritative center of a feminist Christian faith," either as savior or exemplar. ("The Feminist Redemption of Christ," 68.) Cf. *Journeys by Heart*, xiii-xiv and 52-53.

75. Brock, "The Feminist Redemption of Christ," 312.

76. Brock, "A Feminist Consciousness Looks at Christology," 312.

77. Brock, "The Feminist Redemption of Christ," 69.

78. Ibid., 69.

79. Brock, "Beyond Jesus the Christ," 8-9. This is the constructive argument Brock elaborates in *Journeys by Heart*. Brock identifies her constructive proposal as feminist Christian, despite her radical

decentering of Jesus of Nazareth. Brock writes that "christology, broadly defined, is the logical explanation of Christian faith claims about divine presence and salvific activity in human life." (*Journeys by Heart*, 51.) "Christian theology," she argues, "claims that the divine incarnation in human life redeems the human condition and reveals the true nature of God (or as I prefer, God/dess) as love. . . . By expanding Christ beyond Jesus of Nazareth, we can find the power of the redemption of human life revealed in the life-giving power of community." (Ibid., xii-xiii.) "Christ is what I am calling Christa/Community. Jesus participates centrally in this Christa/Community, but he neither brings erotic power into being nor controls it. He is brought into being through it and participates in the co-creation of it." (Ibid., 52.) While I find Brock's work interesting and provocative, I do not think it adequate as Christian theology, because it does not understand Jesus of Nazareth as particularly revelatory of the true relation between the human and the divine.

80.   Christ, *Laughter of Aphrodite*, 136ff.

81.   "The creation of new symbolisms in art, literature, music, religion, and ritual will make feminist goals easier to achieve. Instead of a discontinuity between symbols in the deep mind and desired social change, there will be a continuity and reciprocal reinforcement. If a feminist symbol system were created, then feminists might be able to overcome the feeling we sometimes have that we are struggling against the tide of nature and history, against, as it were, the 'general order of existence.'" (Ibid., 139.)

82.   Ibid., 154; and "Why Women Need the Goddess" in *Womanspirit Rising*. Cf. Hampson, *Theology and Feminism*, 136f., and 150ff. Hampson is interested in feminist religion that has "no anthropomorphically conceived God, yet a theistic sensibility." (Ibid., 168)

83.   Christ, "The New Feminist Theology," 205. Christ underscores the seriousness of this point in her claim that if she, Daly, and others making similar claims are correct in their analysis of religious symbolism in general and Christian symbolism in particular, then Christianity is facing a reformation like in scope and kind the Reformation of the sixteenth century. (Christ and Plaskow, "Introduction" in *Womanspirit Rising*, 10.) Hampson argues that feminism is a revolution that will reshape all theology (*Theology and Feminism*, 1-3). She also notes that no Christian feminist theology has yet answered Daly's challenge. Nor does she think it can be answered as long as feminists use the Bible. (Ibid., 108.)

84.   Chapter 4 deals with women's experience in detail.

85.   Suchocki, "The Challenge of Mary Daly," 307.

86.   Anne Carr makes this important point [Anne E. Carr, "Is a Christian Feminist Theology Possible?" *Theological Studies* 43 (June 1982): 292-293], which, unfortunately, has gone unnoticed except by Mary Knutsen, "This Terrible Battle for Meaning." See also Anne E. Carr, *Transforming Grace* (San Francisco: Harper and Row, 1988), 154-155.

87.   See, among many possibilities, Jürgen Moltmann, *The Crucified God*; and Jon Sobrino, *Christology at the Crossroads: A Latin American Approach*, trans. John Drury (Maryknoll: Orbis, 1984).

88.   See, for example, David Tracy, *The Analogical Imagination: Christian Theology and the Culture of Pluralism* (New York: Crossroad, 1981); and Schubert M. Ogden, *The Point of Christology*.

89.   Suchocki, "The Challenge of Mary Daly," 316-317.

Chapter 3

Toward an Adequate Feminist Christology: Methodology and Criteria

Methodology: Conversation

Given the multiple concerns and challenges facing the feminist Christian discussion of Christology, the appropriate method for engaging these concerns and challenges is conversation or dialogue. When dialogue is understood as at the same time mutually appreciative and mutually critical, it provides the possibility of full engagement with alternative views and positions that may contribute to the search for truth and transformation.[1] It "give[s] in to the movement required by questions worth exploring. The movement in conversation is questioning itself . . . It is a willingness to follow the question wherever it may go."[2]

Conversation or dialogue is a method entirely appropriate to any feminist theological pursuit. For one of the core insights and greatest contributions of feminist theory thus far has been its insistence that the human person be understood first, foremost, and always as relational.[3] That is, every human person is always already engaged with others; and it is that very engagement that constitutes the person *as* a person. The life of dialogue--to borrow the phrase aptly applied to Martin Buber--is simply the life that consciously and conscientiously embraces constitutive engagement with others, seeking both mutuality and justice in that engagement.[4]

But dialogue or conversation is not easy.

> Conversation is a game with some hard rules: say only what you mean; say it as accurately as you can; listen to and respect what the other says, however different or other; be willing to correct or defend your opinions if challenged by the conversation partner; be willing to argue if necessary, to confront if demanded, to endure necessary conflict, to change your mind if the evidence suggests it.[5]

These descriptive rules assume certain socio-historical preconditions, such as the equality and freedom of the partners and the absence of coercion--preconditions that can be at best only approximated in any given situation.[6] Understanding conversation or dialogue requires acknowledging the extent to which it is always affected by disparities and similarities of the parties' positions, power relative to each other, and interests. Conversation, that is to say, is always also coalition, with all the conflict, distress, and danger--and all the possibility--that term implies. "You don't go into coalition because you just *like* it. The only reason you would consider trying to team up with somebody who could possibly kill you, is because that's the only way you can figure you can stay alive."[7] For feminist theology, this insight is crucial. Feminist theology arises out of the crucible of domination and suppression, out of the marginalization of differing "others," and out of the desire and drive to resist and overcome such suppression. In such a situation, conversation partners are not equals, and they are not equally free. And they may often be competitors or adversaries. The conversation in which feminist theology is engaged is also a struggle to change the conditions in which the conversation is taking place.

This means that this conversation or dialogue also requires a thorough and unflinching disclosure of underlying, often deeply concealed presuppositions, orientations, and assumptions--one's own, and those used by others with whom one is engaged directly and indirectly--for these elements arise out of, shape, and are shaped by the conditions under which conversation occurs. As Audre Lorde has forcefully insisted, "The master's tools will never dismantle the master's house."[8] Feminist theory, embracing as it does a hermeneutics of suspicion, is necessarily engaged in searching out the deeply hidden presuppositions that continue to fund patriarchal domination of thought and practice to the suppression and destruction of those long defined as Alien Other. Such feminist suspicion is also self-critical in its recognition of the extent to which women have internalized the patriarchal assumptions in which women have been well schooled.[9]

Mutuality of engagement, appreciation of difference, rigor of thought and expression, challenge, conflict, criticism, and self-criticism: these are the minimal elements involved in engaging any question worth exploring. But how do these insights become a theological methodology?

In this matter I find the work of nineteenth century Anglican theologian F.D. Maurice instructive.[10] Living in a time of remarkable theological and social turmoil and transition, Maurice resisted the path taken by many of his contemporaries in erecting barriers against new forms of knowledge, massive shifts in philosophical, political, and theological presuppositions, and widespread religious pluralism and doubt.[11] Instead, Maurice developed an approach to theology that recognized the partial truth held by each of many differing contending positions, and sought a primary unifying principle that underlay and gave rise to apparently contradictory or mutually exclusive views.[12]

I will consider each of these opinions; I will attempt to show how and wherein each seems to have denied the truth of the others. I will attempt to show how that which each really prizes, that which he feels he cannot part with, will unite in a principle--larger, deeper, more satisfactory, than any of the three, yet freed from the perplexities and contradictions which each has felt in the opinions of the others, and occasionally in his own. [13]

The differences among positions arise from the emphases each group places on the principles most relevant to that group's historical circumstances. It is these very circumstances and the insights that arise from them that make each position indispensable to the rest. [14] Yet it is, ironically, these same circumstances and insights that lead each group to deny the truth of views held by others. [15] Ultimately, it is the same set of principles that forms the foundations under all positions. [16] The point of analysis, then, is appreciation, not conversion.

Maurice developed and used this method for a number of reasons. Theologically, it seemed to him required by the fact that God is One, perfect Charity. By definition, love is communicative, reciprocal, and other-directed; [17] therefore, it is the ground of all truth and goodness, and finds correspondence in that which it issues--that is, in creation. So unity or communion with that One is the source, end, and foundation of historical existence. At the same time, God is Trinity, inherently interrelated, dynamic, and diverse; and this relationality and diversity are likewise an inherent and good part of historical existence. [18] Humanity in all its diversity is created in the image of this dynamic relational love.

Humankind is also in constant union with the complete self-expression of that love, the Christ, who reveals the loving character of God *and* the true constitution of humanity as a race that is rightly related to God in trust. [19] "In Him we find how humanity has been a holy thing, though each man felt himself to be unholy. . . . In Him it is proved that man is meant to have his dwelling with God; . . ." [20] That is to say, humanity has been created to be in communion with its creator. [21] In the Incarnation, that creator is fully manifest also as Deliverer. And in the Incarnation, the relation of humanity to divinity is both restored and vindicated from its anomalous separation from God through sin.

Overall, while human persons created *in imago dei* have, by nature, the ability to desire, seek out, and discover elements of the truth, this capacity is fragile and easily damaged or distorted.

So critical analytic methods must proceed with care, detaching the argument that supports disbelief from "all the truths with which it is intertwined. . . . these truths stand firm without the denial which accompanies them, nay, will never stand firm till it be removed." [22]

Maurice's theological method grows out of these primary theological affirmations of love, relationality, and diversity, and of his sense of how these are distorted and concealed by sin. His method is a historicized version of the *coincidentia oppositorum*,[23] which, with the Romantics, he embraced because it deals with the "feast of contradiction" [24] found in the "multeity and dynamism" of living organisms by leading to that "from which all dynamism sprang and through which all unity was achieved." [25] The coincidence of opposites discloses the active and generative relationship of heart, mind, imagination, feeling, action, the physical world, and eternal principles. [26]

The opposites to be reconciled are models of construing thought as well as types of thought itself. Maurice and some of his contemporaries understood the processes of thought as at once organic and dialectic, two kinds of activity and creativity.[27] Thought moves toward an "ever-evolving, ever-richer coherence," which is fostered not only by explanation or exposition, but also by dynamic appropriation of external material; ideas are a "dynamically evolving absolute." [28]

On this basis, Maurice could perceive and affirm that theological or religious controversialists are trying to defend "the living principle embodied and expressed in" the various institutions, practices, and beliefs with which they are involved, though they may not be aware of this motivating element of their attempt.[29] This living principle is entwined with and even expressed through falsehood and the partiality caused by the limitations of historical existence. The fullness of the truth must be disentangled from these distortions, misrepresentations, and limited apprehensions. [30] These particularities must be treated with the same earnestness accorded to that which belongs to all ages.[31] And conflicting particularities must be put in a dialectic relation to each other, so that the tension between them may drive the analyst to a more profound, over-arching, and comprehensive truth. [32]

Within this dialectic, what is disclosed is both meaningful and true when it meets two criteria: it appeals to human reason; [33] and it is confirmed by the help and consolation it offers to the suffering and struggling, rather than by the delight it affords to the self-righteous and the conceited. [34] Maurice can appeal to these two criteria because they arise from and reflect the ground of the universe, which is the source of all good, goodness, truth, and beauty. In other words, human experience that is both reasonable and merciful is reliably connected with the divine, and so provides "hints" of both meaning and truth. [35]

In fact, Maurice (like Coleridge) was attempting a modified Socratic or dialogical method that poses problems as polarities or dualities related as thesis and antithesis, which join in a unified "higher third." [36] The truth lies at both poles; the task is to find a way to the reconciliation of opposites. [37] The tone of appreciation built into this method works toward allowing each party in a controversy to retain its own insight, while honing and deepening it and coming to a new recognition of its necessary and desirable relation to other positions. The critical moments in this process are directed not at a position itself, or at its undergirding principles, but at the distortion occasioned by narrowness, intolerance, and over-reliance on notions "appended" to the principles. [38]

Maurice's method, then, is profoundly dialogical or conversational. It involves critical appreciation of and engagement with the views held by differing others, assessment of tradition in light of contemporary experience, and an insistence that meaning and truth have not been perceived unless and until they are also accessible to those placed at the margins of human existence historically understood. Theologically, Maurice's method hinges on his affirmation of divine love as the source and end and ever-present inspiration of human desire and seeking. It is precisely Maurice's dialogical approach and its grounding in this theological affirmation that make it suggestive for feminist Christian theology.

Nevertheless, Maurice's method requires modification if it is to be helpful in the context in which contemporary feminist liberation theology is developed. Maurice's application of his method and his theological insights to concrete situations is problematic. As has been widely noted, both his social ethics and his practice denied positive significance to social conflict, which he viewed as unnecessarily divisive. [39] A more thorough analysis of the depth and pervasiveness of distortion and alienation and a consequently greater appreciation of conflict as potentially generative of both truth and justice are needed.

Therefore, in this book I have sought to follow Maurice's methodological guidelines by setting in conversation differing (and sometimes opposing) points of view. I have sought to disclose their underlying presuppositions and principles, assess the arguments associated with each position in relation to its own presuppositions, and evaluate it both appreciatively and critically on its own grounds first and foremost. I have also sought to identify the underlying concerns held in common by the positions in order to generate a new synthesis to which the multiple positions examined can contribute. But I have also taken seriously the coalitional and conflictual aspects of the contemporary discussions through the use of critical theory and social analysis, from the conviction that the remaining conflicts indicate problems more profound than Maurice recognized and less susceptible to theoretical resolution. In this sense, my approach is more eschatological than Maurice's, for, with contemporary liberation and political theologies, I am convinced that the theoretical resolutions that systematic theology constantly seeks will arise from ongoing *praxis* reaching toward the present embodiment of a transformation that lies finally in the future. [40]

Criteria of Adequacy

In describing as three-fold the Christological challenge facing feminist Christians, I have also suggested three criteria for assessing the adequacy of feminist Christological proposals. These criteria have to do with adequacy to Christian traditions, to contemporary women's experience, and to struggles for a liberated future. I will fully explain the rationale for each of these at the end of the next chapter. Here, the criteria themselves can be summarized in a preliminary fashion.

Christian theology appears always to have required some form of adequacy to tradition, and especially to Scripture. It is therefore incumbent upon feminist Christian theology to attend to the tradition if it wishes to participate in the contemporary theological discussion. Of equal import, however, are the specific challenges facing feminist theology. As I have indicated, traditionalists and post-biblical feminists alike argue that feminist Christian theology (and so Christology) cannot meet a criterion related to Christian tradition, because that tradition supports patriarchal domination both explicitly and systemically. The evidence for this argument, mustered from both the texts of the tradition and from the history of effects, is sufficiently compelling to require address. As Carol Christ has indicated, feminist Christian theology will either have to show that Christianity's patriarchal core symbols do not contribute to structures of domination and subjugation, or it will have to transform that core symbolism. [41]

Responding to this challenge does not, however, necessarily mean refuting it. Instead, feminist Christians recognize that the dominant strands of Christian thought and practice *are* patriarchal, misogynist, and androcentric. Continuing the concealment of this fact is not in the interest of liberation and transformation. [42] Instead, at least three elaborations of tradition are appropriate.

First, the history of Christian thought and practice must be more thoroughly explored to disclose the presence and participation of women, which have been suppressed and silenced for two millennia. As Rosemary Radford Ruether, Elisabeth Schüssler Fiorenza, and others have convincingly argued, this means exploring marginal traditions--including those deemed heretical-- and religious traditions associated with but not part of Christianity as part of the task of recovering a fuller history of Christian thought and practice. [43]

Second, such exploration broadens the basic understanding of what is meant by the term *Christian tradition*, thereby raising anew the question of what may be meant by adequacy to it.

Third, the exploration of the full range of Christian history in its full historical context addresses the roots of contemporary Christian feminism, by bringing to light the various heritages that shape contemporary women's religious experience.[44] A criterion of adequacy to tradition, then, entails adequacy to the texts and history of effects of Christianity *as those are reconstructed to reflect the presence and participation of women*.

Feminist theory and practice have as a central focus women's experience, for reasons to be explored more fully in the following chapter. In its emphasis on women's experience, feminist theology also has considerable affinity with other forms of contemporary theology, which focus on human experience as a source for theology as part of its Enlightenment heritage and its interaction with its contemporary context. However, as the subsequent discussion will indicate, not just any view of experience is adequate for the feminist theological discussion. What is required of feminist theology is adequacy to *women's* experience *in the struggle for liberation from patriarchy*.

First, this more precise definition of this criterion of adequacy rises from the ambiguity of women's experience itself, which recognizes that even as they continue to suffer patriarchal conditions, women also discover their own authenticity as full human persons in their quest for liberation from those conditions. Second, specifying the criterion of experience in this way also recognizes both the historical and continuous reliance of all forms of theology on human experience as a source, and the marginalization of women's experience in particular in that reliance.[45] Finally, the feminist theological emphasis on women's experience in the struggle for liberation explicitly requires theological accountability to the *full* range of human experience by drawing attention to the "lowest of the low," who, in patriarchal situations, are women.[46] The second criterion of adequacy for feminist theological proposals, then, is adequacy to women's experience in the struggle for liberation from patriarchy.

The third criterion--adequacy to a liberated future--is less familiar, in theological circles at least. As Christian and post-biblical feminists alike have argued, Christianity has apparently been more interested in continuing its past than in attending to the future of the world in which it is set.[47] This neglect of effects and consequences, these critics claim, has contributed to making Christianity as much a peril as a hope for human existence. Part of the challenge facing feminist theology, then, is demonstrating how feminist Christianity contributes to a *viable* future, which is to say, a liberated future for women as the lowest of the low.

Such a demonstration serves two other purposes as well. First, it responds to the post-biblical feminist analysis of the history of effects of Christianity by indicating how those effects may be expected to change in the future.[48] Second, it indicates the affinity between feminist theology and some other contemporary theologies that recognize the importance of the future (in the form of eschatology) to Christian thought and practice.[49] These theologies also recognize the interdependence of theory and practice, and identify the influence of Christian belief on human life as one indicator of the validity (here, both meaningfulness and truth) of Christian faith.[50] The specific emphasis of feminist Christian theology on a *liberated* future for women as the lowest of the low focuses both eschatology and pragmatism around the concrete situation of domination and liberation--a situation that characterizes the contemporary world and threatens the very future that this criterion attempts to help safeguard.

These three criteria of adequacy as preliminarily defined here serve to assess the appropriateness of feminist theological claims. Each of these criteria responds to the three-fold challenge facing feminist Christian theology. Each also indicates how feminist theology is a constructive contributor to the contemporary theological discussion. Further elaboration will make clearer precisely how these criteria are to be applied to the proposals for a feminist Christology examined in this book.

Toward an Adequate Feminist Christology

Formally, then, an adequate feminist Christology must meet criteria related to tradition broadly understood, to women's experience in the struggle for liberation as indicative of the fullness of human experience, and to a liberated future for women as the lowest of the low, reflecting the fullness of human liberation under the conditions of historical existence.

What is the substance of such a feminist Christology? As I shall demonstrate, there are two types of proposals currently available. One, focusing on the prophetic and the eschatological, emphasizes Jesus as a partial exemplar of the liberated humanity which is still to come, but sees the fullness of humanity as still lying in the future. Jesus-as-human represents the kenosis of patriarchal privilege and the emergence of a humanity characterized by relations of equality of service and engagement with the whole of creation. Jesus reveals the divine life by representing the kenosis of patriarchalized divinity, and re-establishing human perception of divinity as the source and inspiration of human historical authenticity. This authenticity is understood from the context of struggles for liberation from patriarchal dualism, and movement toward existence which is simultaneously limited and self-transcendent. The full revelation *and* the full realization of both liberated humanity and the liberating face of the divine lie in the future.

The second type focuses more directly on the historical manifestation of a relationship that has always existed between humanity and divinity, but that has been both distorted and concealed under the conditions of human existence. This type is a contemporary reconstruction of the Wisdom-Logos trajectories of Christology. Here, Jesus fully manifests the divine-human relation; and this manifestation partially re-establishes this relation in history, while promising its full restoration for all creation in a transformed future. In himself, Jesus embodies right relationship between human and divine, thereby indicating the true nature of both divinity and humanity. Human authenticity is found in relationality; and this authenticity participates in the divine life, which is itself primarily relational. Human exemplars in addition to Jesus are exemplary in that they, too, embody relationality characterized by mutuality and justice.

I will argue that each of these types of Christology moves toward an adequate feminist Christology, but each is inadequate alone. The prophetic-eschatological type emphasizes the kenotic aspects of the revelation given by Jesus to a degree that leaves unclear how, for Christians, Jesus is a decisive paradigm of the future humanity. Also less than adequately clear is how Jesus' relation to the divine is decisively paradigmatic of all future human relation to the divine. In other words, this type finally diverges from the central affirmation of Christian theology that, for Christians, Jesus is decisive in a manner unlike any other paradigmatic figure; that is, that Jesus is *the* Christ. Nevertheless, the emphasis in this type on both present historical existence and a liberated and eschatologically transformed future provides significant movement toward a more adequate feminist Christology.

The Wisdom-Logos type helpfully emphasizes present possibilities for wholeness, harmony, and reconciliation in human existence, and indicates how these are directly connected with the gracious presence of the divine. Jesus is the decisive re-presentation of the only liberating relationship humans can have with the divine. But the centrality of a single figure mitigates against a thorough focus on relationality, and at least tends toward the confusion of historical reality and ultimate reality. Moreover, as has often been the case in Christian theology, one element of the past--in this case, the manifestation of the divine in one decisive figure--tends to obscure the importance of the future, if not of the present. This approach alone, then, is also not sufficient as a feminist Christology.

The constructive proposal with which I will conclude the book will argue that a more nearly adequate feminist Christology can be developed out of the conversational interaction of the two types of Christology I shall analyze. I will therefore sketch such a Christology by drawing on the fruitful elements of each type, understanding (as Maurice did) that the less fruitful elements of each approach undergird the strengths of the other approach. In that proposal, I will argue that the experience of the victims of domination in history indicates that the struggle against the fragmentation, distortion, and domination that characterize much of human existence allows victims to know that they are unnecessarily afflicted yet nevertheless able to participate in the alleviation of their affliction and the transformation of its causes.[51]

When this experience is taken as normative, the anthropological theme of authentic humanity disclosed and discovered in resistance connects with the notion that it is in Christ that Christians find this experience both vindicated and connected directly with the existence of God. This is the case because the life, death, and resurrection of Jesus the Christ reveal the possibilities of transformative struggle in human existence and disclose the presence of God in those struggles. Thus, Jesus the Christ manifests "the only liberating relationship a person can have with God"[52] *and* the presence and activity of the only God who saves. In the Christ, redemption of all existence is accomplished in principle, but actualized only fully in the future. Thus, the incarnation of God in Jesus the Christ is simultaneously the revelation of what has always been the case, the vindication of this reality, and the promise of its greater future fulfillment.

In sum, then, I will propose a Christology that shows clear preference for the Wisdom-Logos type in its understanding of Jesus Christ as the definitive manifestation of both divinity and humanity. I will endeavor to maintain the imperative force and insights of the prophetic-eschatological type by using an anthropological theme that relies on the full historicity of human existence for its properly theological or metaphysical claims. I understand this proposal as provisional, subject not only to further study and elaboration of its components, but also to developments in the various conversations from which it springs. I shall conclude my discussion, therefore, with a brief look at one of the major conversations in which feminist theology is involved: African-American womanist theology.

Notes

1.　Tracy, *Plurality and Ambiguity*, 20. On conversation, see 1-27 in particular.

2.　Ibid., 18.

3.　The full implications of this insight are more profound than are often thought. The understanding of the human as relational will be discussed more fully in the next chapter, and will recur in its theological form throughout this book.

4.　See, for example, the various writings of Carter Heyward, discussed at length in Chapter 6 of this work.

5.　Tracy, *Plurality and Ambiguity*, 19.

6.　On this, see particularly the work of Jürgen Habermas on communicative competence; and Tracy, *Plurality and Ambiguity*, 26.

7.　Bernice Johnson Reagon, "Coalition Politics: Turning the Century," in *Home Girls: A Black Feminist Anthology*, ed. Barbara Smith (New York: Kitchen Table: Women of Color Press, 1983), 356-357.

8.　Audre Lorde, "The Master's Tools Will Never Dismantle the Master's House," in *Sister Outsider: Essays and Speeches* (Freedom, CA: The Crossing Press, 1984), 112.

9.　Lerner, *The Creation of Patriarchy*, 212-229 and throughout, provides a sound and helpful recent discussion of the problems of internalization as they affect women's thought, as well as a generally credible and convincing discussion of the development of patriarchy as a social and cultural system.

10.　The life of Frederick Denison Maurice (1805-1872) in many ways exemplified the trials and preoccupations of Victorian Christianity. Maurice was the son of a Unitarian minister and a mother who (with her elder daughters) converted to Calvinism, although the mother thought she was not among the elect. After an agnostic young manhood at the University of Cambridge--which he left without a degree because he would not subscribe to the Church of England's Articles of Religion--Maurice was converted to Christianity in part through the deathbed of yet another of his sisters. He served as Chaplain of Guy's Hospital in London, working there among the poor; and then became Chaplain at Lincoln's Inn, a position he held while also teaching theology at King's College, London. He was dismissed from this position because of his arguments on the nature of eternal life, set forth in his *Theological Essays* (originally published in 1853).

He had already excited controversy through his leadership of the Christian Socialist movement and his friendship with Charles Kingsley. Maurice also taught at the Working Men's College, helped found Queen's College (for women), and was active throughout his life in various educational, organizational, and journalistic endeavors on behalf of the poor. He ended his life as Knightsbridge Professor of Casuistry, Moral Theology, and Modern Philosophy at the University of Cambridge.

Maurice was a prolific writer. His principal books include *The Kingdom of Christ* (1838 and 1842), *The Lord's Prayer* (1848), *Theological Essays* (1853), *The Doctrine of Sacrifice* (1854), *What is Revelation?* (1859, in response to H. L. Mansel's Bampton Lectures), *The Conscience* (1868), and *Social Morality* (1869), as well as theological commentaries on virtually every book of the Bible. Maurice was actively and publicly involved in the major religious and social controversies of his day, and published widely on many of them. His son Frederick's *The Life of Frederick Denison Maurice, Chiefly Told in His Own Letters* (1884) is indispensable to understanding the man's theology as well as his life. In his excellent unpublished dissertation on Maurice, William H. Petersen gives an excellent short biography and classification of Maurice's writings, indeed the best such discussion with which I am familiar. ("Frederick Denison Maurice as Historian: An Analysis of the Character of Maurice's Unsystematic Theology, Attempting to Disclose a Method Capable of Reconciling Secular and Ecclesiastical Historiography" [Ph.D. diss., Graduate Theological Union, 1976].)

It had originally been my intention to include a separate chapter on Maurice's method and Christology. However, since his direct role in this project is more methodological than substantive, I have chosen to present an appreciative reconstruction of Maurice's method at this juncture of the larger argument.

11.   On the crises in Victorian culture and religion, see, for example, Walter E. Houghton, *The Victorian Frame of Mind*, 1830-1870 (New Haven: Yale University Press, 1957); and Charles D. Cashdollar, *The Transformation of Theology, 1830-1890: Positivism and Protestant Thought in Britain and America* (Princeton, N.J.: Princeton University Press, 1989).

12.   By "unifying," Maurice meant not uniformity, but fellowship. See, for example, Frederick Denison Maurice, *The Kingdom of Christ: or Hints to a Quaker Reflecting the Principles, Constitution,*

and Ordinances of the Catholic Church (London: Darton and Clark, 1838), 1:186-187; hereafter referred to as *Kingdom of Christ* 1838.
    13.   Maurice, *Kingdom of Christ* 1838, 1:75. Maurice's language not surprisingly reflects the androcentric use of masculine pronouns; unless otherwise noted, I have maintained his original language throughout.
    14.   "I wish to make each one of your parties perceive," Maurice wrote to the Quakers, "that it has hold of a principle, that it must not for all the world abandon; and I wish them to show you by what means only you can uphold each of these principles without mutilation, with real power, and in harmony with the rest. In plain words, I wish not to unquaker you in order to make you churchmen, but to teach you how to be thorough Quakers, that you may be thorough churchmen." (*Kingdom of Christ* 1838, 1:13.)
    15.   This partial character may be shown in the position's orientation to *either* Bible, church, or conscience (Robert T. Hall, "The Unity of Philosophy, Theology, and Ethics in the Thought of Frederick Denison Maurice" [Ph.D. diss., Drew University, 1967], 161). Or it may be indicated by a position's inability to take into account the past, the current context, or the future. (*Kingdom of Christ* 1838, 1:xxi-xxii.) It is not historical circumstances *per se* as much as human attempts to address them separate from the larger truths to which they are related which accounts for the distortions and limitations found in any one expression of insight into truth. (*Kingdom of Christ* 1838, 1:7.) Therefore, Maurice concludes, while each position is right in asserting its own measure of truth, it is most likely wrong in denying the truth of perceived by others. (*Kingdom of Christ* 1838, 1:75) This extends to Christianity itself, vis a vis "other" religions: Other religions are possessed of a measure of truth; but Christianity has been given a greater and clearer measure by its foundation in the one who makes fully manifest the nature of God and God's relation to creation. (See Frederick Denison Maurice, *The Religions of the World and Their Relation to Christianity Considered in Eight Lectures Founded by Hon. Robert Boyle* [London: Macmillan and Co., 1877] and elsewhere.)
    16.   Maurice, *Kingdom of Christ* 1838, 1:8.
    17.   Maurice, *Theological Essays*, with an Introduction by Edward F. Carpenter. From the second edition originally published in 1853 (London: James Clarke & Co. Ltd., 1957) 419, 426; Maurice, *Life*, 1:413f; Maurice, *The Doctrine of Sacrifice*, 101f.

18. For all his apparent Platonism, Maurice differs from earlier
Christian Platonists in seeing diversity as a positive, integral part of
creation, and not an indication of its fall from perfection. Diversity
does not *necessarily* mean fragmentation. Therefore, diversity *per se*
is not something that must be overcome as part of redemption. Nor is
it a hindrance or flaw in philosophical or theological discussion.

19. Maurice, *Social Morality* , 231, 378; idem, *The Epistles of
St. John* (London: Macmillan, 1867), 24-25, 31, 65-66; idem,
Christmas Day and Other Sermons (London: Macmillan 1892), 7-10;
idem, *The Unity of the New Testament*, 1st American ed. (Boston:
Lee and Shephard, 1879; London: Macmillan and Co., 1884), 2:60;
idem, *Sermons preached in Lincoln's Inn Chapel* (New ed.; 6 vol.;
London and New York: Macmillan and Co., 1891-1892), 3:251-252;
and passim.

20. Frederick Denison Maurice, *The Epistle to the Hebrews;
Being the Substance of Three Lectures Delivered in the Chapel of
the Honourable Society of Lincoln's Inn, on the Foundation of
Bishop Warburton, with a Preface containing a Review of Mr.
Newman's Theory of Development* (London: John W. Parker, 1846),
29-30.

21. Maurice describes this communion as "the resemblance of
[God's] character, the fulfillment of his commands, . . . the condition
where we can behold His countenance and live, in which we can
receive from Him all the power to will and to do." (*Kingdom of
Christ* 1838, 1:269; *Kingdom of Christ* 1959, 1:182. Maurice refers
to this as "the Sacramental idea of a holy constitution, and of all evil
as a departure from it." (*Kingdom of Christ* 1838, 1:295-6.)

22. Maurice, *Kingdom of Christ* 1838, 1:69. The desire for truth
in matters of controversy is inseparable from general human
well-being. Moreover, the discovery of a group's principles and the
removal of elements contradicting them restores the original power of
attraction the group's view held. (*Kingdom of Christ* 1838,
1:163-164 and 1:186-187.) Maurice's intense interest in these matters,
apparent particularly in the 1838 version of Kingdom of Christ, was
sparked by the ongoing controversy, unrest, and dis-ease attendant on
various efforts at church reform. (See *Kingdom of Christ* 1838, 1:1-
7, for example.) It is remarkable that Maurice, unlike the Oxford
divines grouped around E. B. Pusey and J. H. Newman, called not for
the fortification of the Church of England's position, but for pluralism
and for the recognition of the commonalities and complementarities

among the Protestant "sects" and with the Established Church (with all its warring parties).

23.   See David Newsome, *Two Classes of Men: Platonism and English Romantic Thought* (London: J. Murray, 1984), entire, but especially Chapter 3, "Opposites and Contraries." The significance of the *coincidentia oppositorum* in Maurice is also noted (though not appreciatively) by Julia Wedgwood (*Nineteenth Century Teachers and Other Essays*. [London: Hodder and Stoughton, 1909], 58-59), Otto Pfleiderer (*The Development of Theology in Germany since Kant, and its Progress in Great Britain since 1825* [London: Swan Sonnenschein and Co., 1890], 328-329), and Houghton, *The Victorian Frame of Mind*, 178f.

24.   The phrase is Benjamin Jowett's, quoted in Newsome, 17.

25.   Newsome, 17, 49.

26.   Newsome, 17ff. and passim. Indeed, Maurice expressed great admiration for the philosophical theology--as well as the church diplomacy--of Nicolas of Cusa, "the seeker of unity," who recognized that "THE ONE for which he is inquiring . . . is not the negation of plurality. It must be that in which all things find their meeting point. The greatest and the least must be included in it. If you speak of it as the highest, you must speak of it also as the lowest.   You seek it through all contradictions; it harmonizes all. . . . Is not the One the living God?" (*Moral and Metaphysical Philosophy*, 2 vols. [London: Macmillan, 1890], 2:53-54.) There is some suggestion in Maurice's ten-page discussion of Nicolas of Cusa that Maurice saw more than a few similarities between Nicolas' historical situation and theological convictions and his own.   What Nicolas failed to appreciate fully, according to Maurice, is the importance of the conscience. But, he added, "who had or who has?" (57-58.)

27.   As Coleridge and Maurice were aware, modeling ideas as analogous to organisms places certain limitations that are neither necessary nor desirable.   "[T]he growth of an organism demands a steady diet without too many shocks; the growth of the mind depends on the mastery of variety. (Stephen Prickett, "Coleridge, Newman, and F. D. Maurice: Development of Doctrine and Growth of the Mind," *Theology* 76 [July, 1973]: 345-346.) Coleridge and Maurice added a second model: thought as dialectic, that is, thought as subject to "constant dialectical modification by the new and unpredictable." (Prickett, 346.) Prickett indicates that Maurice found this more nearly analogous to human growth than the analogy with organic development.

28.   Prickett, 344-3455.   Prickett's article, and the longer book from which it seems to be drawn (*Romanticism and Religion: The Tradition of Coleridge and Wordsworth in the Victorian Church* [Cambridge and New York: Cambridge University Press, 1976]), looks closely at Maurice's *The Epistle to the Hebrews*, which includes a 128-page review of John Henry Newman's *Essay on Development*. Prickett examines the effect Maurice's review had on Newman's revision of the *Essay*, and also shows a connection between Maurice's Preface and his lectures on the Epistle.

29.   Maurice, *Kingdom of Christ* 1838, 1:9. For the roots of this in Maurice's controversy-ridden childhood, see his biographer son's reflections, *Life* 1:127.

30.   Maurice learned from the Bible that it is the concrete particularities of history that both bridge historical differences (*Kingdom of Christ* 1842, 2:177.) and form a ladder to transcending reality. (Kingdom of Christ 1838 2:50.)

31.   Maurice, *Life* I:271.

32.   This is the kind of relation Maurice attempts to establish between the views of High Church and Evangelical parties within the Church of England, and between Roman Catholicism and Protestantism. On the former, see *On Right and Wrong Methods of Supporting Protestantism* (London: John W. Parker, 1843), 19 (cited in Michael C. Busk, "F. D. Maurice's Trinitarian Theology: An Historical and Constructive View" [Ph.D. diss., University of Chicago, 1984], 176); and on the latter, Frederick Denison Maurice, *Three Letters to the Rev. W. Palmer on the Name "Protestant"; on the Seemingly Ambiguous Character of the English Church; and on the Bishopric at Jerusalem, with an Appendix* (London: G. Rivington, 1841), 16; Frederick Maurice, *Life* 1:320; and Frederick Denison Maurice, *Sermons Preached in Lincoln's Inn Chapel*, 2:33 (where the tension inherent in this understanding of comprehensiveness is apparent).

33.   Hall, 65.

34.   Theological Essays, 3rd, 141f. Maurice's insistence on this criterion comes from the conjunction of his pastoral work, his theological reflection, and his examination of his own conscience. See, for example, *Life* 1:236.

35.   Maurice insists on these same grounds that the truth of Scripture is confirmed by daily experience, particularly the experience of suffering.   On the relation of revelation and experience in general and in relation to the authority of Scripture, see Busk, 34-40.

36.   Newsome, 52.   This method modified the Socratic, which poses questions in a manner so contradictory that "argument . . . proceeds by a succession of blind alleys." (Newsome, 43.)

37.   Julia Wedgwood says of Maurice, "it was to his mind a mark of truth to contain an apparent contradiction, and he seems to have felt always as if a contradiction were explained when both its members were distinctly stated." Wedgwood notes that contradiction is no more certain a test of truth than it is of error.   But she also observes that "What made his whole drift hard to follow was that, sooner or later, his reader or hearer had to surrender for a time the belief that logical coherence was the test of truth.   There is always in any sustained reasoning of his, a gap to be crossed, where no logical bridge is possible, and his follower must trust to the wing of his strong, imaginative faith."   (58)   This, I would suggest, is exactly what Maurice intended.

38.   Maurice, *Kingdom of Christ* 1838, 1:7.

39.   For example, Maurice refused to support the burgeoning labor movements of his time, preferring small-scale workers' production collectives to widespread systemic reform of industrial capitalism.   His abhorrence of conflict as part of social reform is at odds with his engagement in the religious controversies of his day, which was frequent, and occasionally inexplicable to his opponents and supporters alike.   On his social policy, see the finally unsympathetic work of Torben Christensen (*The Divine Order: A Study in F. D. Maurice's Theology* [Leiden: E. J. Brill, 1973] and *Origin and History of Christian Socialism: 1848-1854* [Universitetsforlaget I Aarhus, 1962]); on the latter, see, for example, the discussions of his controversy with Mansel in William H. Petersen's dissertation.

40.   It may be worth noting here that I am not the only theologian significantly influenced by Maurice to make these modifications. This is the same manner, I think, in which Carter Heyward has also reconstructed Maurice in her work, which is heavily influenced by him. (See my discussion of Heyward in Chapter 6.)

41.   Christ, "New Feminist Theology," 205.

42.   Schüssler Fiorenza, *Bread Not Stone*, passim.

43.   See Rosemary Radford Ruether, *Sexism and God-Talk*, and idem, *Womanguides: Readings Toward a Feminist Theology* (Boston: Beacon Press, 1985) and Schüssler Fiorenza, *In Memory of Her*.

44.   See the Epilogue to Mary Pellauer's "The Religious Social Thought of Three U. S. Woman Suffrage Leaders: Toward a

Tradition of Feminist Theology" (Ph.D. diss., University of Chicago, 1980).

45. Ruether, *Sexism and God-Talk*, Chapter 1, "Feminist Theology: Methodology, Sources, and Norms," 12-46.

46. The validity of this statement hinges on understanding patriarchy as an interstructured system of differentiation of power and privilege on the basis of race/ethnicity and class as well as gender. This statement can also be supported on theological terms of a Johannine sort, as Maurice does in his frequent appeals to ideal-typical figures, such as the bed-ridden woman, the working man, and the young man at Cambridge. (See, for example, *The Epistle to the Hebrews*, lxv; *Life* 1:86-87 and 2:470.)

47. Daly, *Beyond God the Father*, 46, 74; Brock, *Journeys by Heart*, xviii, 54; Hampson and Ruether, *passim*.

48. See Carr, "Is a Christian Feminist Theology Possible?," 292-293.

49. See, for example, Moltmann, *The Theology of Hope*; Schillebeeckx, *God the Future of Man*; and McFague, *Models of God*.

50. See, for example, Tracy, *Blessed Rage for Order*; and Ogden, *The Reality of God* and *On Theology*.

51. The groundwork for this argument will be laid in Chapter 4, "Women's Experience in Feminist Theology."

52. Isabel Carter Heyward, *The Redemption of God: A Theology of Mutual Relation* (Washington: University Press of America, 1982), 200.

Part II

The Relation of Women's Experience to Christology

Chapter 4

The Construction of Women's Experience in Feminist Theory and Theology

Introduction

As I indicated in the Introduction to this book, feminist theology subjects every area of Christian belief, tradition, thought, and practice to critical scrutiny in order to disclose the pervasive distortions of androcentric thought and patriarchal practice. Feminist theology also seeks to reconstruct what it has criticized in order to bring to light the presence and contributions of women as fully human persons. As I argued in Chapter 2, these tasks are made problematic by the conjunction of three judgments concerning the possibility of feminist Christian theology. Two of the judgments--those of post-biblical feminist criticism and traditionalist androcentric theology--agree that Christian feminism is impossible; but proponents of each view reach the same conclusion through radical disagreement about the truth, meaning, and value of patriarchal religion. The third judgment contradicts the other two: on the basis of reflection on their own concrete experience, Christian feminists find in Christianity an important source for the birth and nurturance of the hope for liberation which is in them. Nevertheless, Christian feminists concur with post-biblical feminists in finding Christianity profoundly patriarchal; and they also concur with traditionalists in finding in Christianity the truth, meaning, and value of human existence. Thus, Christian feminists find themselves in a problematized situation.

In Chapter 3, I argued that conversation is the method appropriate to such a situation. In that chapter, I defined conversation as "a willingness to follow the question wherever it may go."[1] A conversational method recognizes and insists that, in situations of conflict, distress, danger, and possibility, it is important to understand conversation as also coalitional--that is, as dialogue where disparities of power and knowledge threaten not only the conversation itself, but also the very survival and well-being of the participants in the conversation. In such a situation, it is imperative to recognize the limitations circumscribing each view. A conversational and coalitional method nevertheless acknowledges that each view, however partial, does contain some measure of the truth of the matter at hand. Truth, then, is generated out of the conflict and coincidence of opposites, through a process of disentanglement from distortions, misrepresentations, partialities, and particularities. Truth, in other words, is always mediated by the context in which it is disclosed, concealed, and recognized.[2]

In this chapter, I shall argue that, like truth itself, human experience is never unmediated or entirely direct. Rather, its apparent immediacy is always in fact mediated by the structures, processes, and contexts in which experience occurs. As this chapter shall argue, experience is "a complex of habits resulting from the semiotic interaction of 'outer world' and 'inner world,' the continuous engagement of self or subject in social reality."[3] Human consciousness is "interpreted or reconstructed by each of us within the horizon of meanings and knowledges available in the culture at given historical moments."[4]

Therefore, as consciousness changes, so does experience.

Women's Religious Experience in Narrative Form

The argument of this chapter begins with four narrative texts, which provide an evidentiary basis for my later discussion of the structural character of human historical experience, of religious experience, and of the relation of both to tradition and to Christology. I have chosen these texts because they are representative of the range of feminist and womanist description of religious experience in their expression of certain tensions and themes that are considered in different forms in the expository reflections found in feminist and womanist theological formulations.[5] These themes include alienation, resistance, and longing for and movement toward wholeness. As the following narratives indicate, these themes are related interactively.

Throughout Part Two of this book, I shall elaborate the meaning of these themes in expository and theoretical terms, arguing that an interactive or relational view of the structure of experience, given substantive content in a particular understanding of resistance, provides a description of women's experience that is relatively adequate for feminist and womanist theology.[6] In Chapter 5 I will also discuss religious experience as such, using a phenomenological and dialectical approach that links concrete human experience as distanciation and participation to the proclamation and manifestation of the divine. In Chapter 6 I shall discuss the relation of experience and tradition to each other and to Christology, and conclude with a revisiting of the criteria of adequacy proposed in Chapter 3.

The first of the narrative texts that provide evidentiary examples of women's religious experience is an oft-cited passage from Alice Walker's prize-winning novel *The Color Purple*. Here, Walker writes imaginatively of the effects of gender and race domination on the human spirit, and the possibilities of transformation:

> Ain't no way to read the bible and not think God white, [Shug] say. Then she sigh. When I found out I thought God was white, and a man, I lost interest. . . . Here's the thing, say Shug. The thing I believe. God is inside you and inside everybody else. You come into the world with God. But only

them that search for it inside find it. And sometimes it just manifest itself even if you not looking, or don't know what you looking for. Trouble do it for most folks, I think. . . . It ain't a picture show. It ain't something you can look at apart from anything else, including yourself. I believe God is everything, say Shug. Everything that is or ever was or ever will be. And when you can feel that, and be happy to feel that, you've found it. . . . it is like Shug say, You have to git man off your eyeball, before you can see anything a'tall.[7]

The second narrative is from Carol Christ, a post-Christian feminist thealogian whose expository work was examined in Chapter 2:

[W]hen I was completing my dissertation on Elie Wiesel's stories, I found myself engaged in a dialogue with God inspired by Wiesel's story of God and Man changing places, the epilogue to *The Town beyond the Wall*. As I retold Wiesel's story from a woman's point of view, I changed places with God and began to reproach him for allowing women's voices to be silenced in history, and in churches and synagogues called his. I asked him why he hadn't sent a messiah or at least a prophet to relieve our sufferings, our beatings, our rape. My energy spent, I fell silent in my room. After a bit, I heard, what I described as a "still small voice" saying, "In God is a woman like yourself. She shares your suffering. She too has had her power of naming stolen from her. First she was called an idol of the Canaanites, and then she ceased to exist as God." In retrospect, I would name that night as the beginning of my initiation into the Goddess.[8]

The third narrative is from Carter Heyward, a feminist Christian theologian who is also one of the first women priests in the Episcopal church. Heyward's expository work will be examined in a later chapter.

It was in the spring of 1971, while working toward my master's degree at Union [Theological Seminary], that I was "born again," compelled by the power of the Holy Spirit to open my eyes wide to the movement of God in my own life and in the lives of people throughout human history who have been inspired, sparked, and awakened to God's will that *all* women and men on this earth be created truly equal. . . . the women's liberation effort called me into the heart of the Christian faith I had professed from childhood, and, for the first time, I looked straight into the eyes of my sisters and brothers and met there the compelling eyes of God. . . . Washed, cleansed, and made new by the power of God, many of my sisters and I, knowing full well the extent of our own brokenness and participation in sins of lovelessness, selfishness, and arrogance, made a common commitment to spend the rest of our lives in efforts to build a world both more fully human and fully divine. [9]

The fourth story is reported by Rosemary Radford Ruether, from a class on violence against women that Ruether taught with Susan Brooks Thistlethwaite:

One woman in the class recounted her experience of being raped in a woods. During the rape she became convinced that she would be killed and resigned herself to her impending death. When the rapist finally fled and she found herself still alive, she experienced a vision of Christ as a crucified woman. This vision filled her with relief and healing, because she knew that "I would not have to explain to a male God that I had been raped. God knew what it was like to be a woman who had been raped." [10]

Each of these is a narrative of conversion, away from a strong sense of alienation between the female narrator and God. The elements of alienation are most explicit in the passages from Walker and Christ; but they may be assumed in Heyward's account (and are explicated elsewhere in her work). [11] It is also appropriate to assume some alienation in any account of rape, a violent act where the very being of the victim is assaulted. In all four accounts, alienation is caused by the effects of patriarchy on these women's relation to the divine and to the human community.

Each of these narratives also contains forceful use of traditional language and categories to describe the narrator's relation with God: the Bible as a whole in *The Color Purple*, the Jewish tradition of contention between human and divine in Christ's story, the power of the Holy Spirit in Heyward's account, the image of the Crucified One in Ruether's retelling of a woman's rape. In each case, it is some element of tradition that provides the framework for understanding these experiences of intensified distanciation and participation. [12]   In some measure, the experience of nonparticipation and distanciation is in relation to the framework of tradition itself.   That is, it is *over against* the mediating power of tradition that the experience occurs.   And this experience issues in a proclamatory corrective response to that mediating power. [13]

The four narratives also speak of conversion toward a new sense of self and a new sense of the divine, which express a sense of and longing for wholeness, connection, and participation. This sense is conveyed most explicitly in Walker's statement that "God is everything . . . Everything that is or ever was or ever will be" and in Heyward's naming of the divine as movement toward "a world both more fully human and more fully divine."   But this sense also undergirds the cry out of alienated silence in Christ's story and the experience of relief and healing in Ruether's account. [14] In all four accounts, the longing for wholeness involves renewed connection with the divine and transformed participation in the human community.

The intensification of participation occurs as the divine is encountered anew as liberating force in the midst of the suffering occasioned by domination: as a self who is fellow sufferer (in Christ and in the story of the woman's rape), who is inspirer and empowerer (in Heyward), who is surprising and unexpected presence (in Walker).   The context of this intensified participation is contemporary engagement in struggle against the forms of subjugation particular to women under the conditions of patriarchy: violent and life-threatening rape, a lifetime of domination and abuse, academic study and spiritual formation in male-dominated educational and ecclesial institutions.   Yet the terms through which the meaning and significance of struggle are conveyed are, in Heyward and Ruether and by implication in Walker, traditional as well as contemporary: the presence of the divine as Holy Spirit, the vision of human and divine suffering as crucifixion. In the midst of women's struggles for survival and liberation, mediated by them and by ambiguous traditions that both support domination and provide hope for liberation, the divine self is newly encountered. And this encounter ruptures the dominating powers of the mediating factors. [15]

These narratives indicate that what is experienced is a partial rending of a veil which conceals the divine and fragments and alienates human existence. But the veil is not human existence *per se*. It is, rather, patriarchy and its symbols of the divine, the human, and the relation between the two. Indeed, it is precisely in the context of deliberate, conscious resistance to patriarchal domination that these encounters occur. These narratives of the ordinary stuff of women's lives under patriarchy--of political and personal struggle for equality, of the recognition of the depth and duration of patriarchal domination, of the aftermath of terrorizing violence such as rape, of the long-term effects of racism and sexism--are tales of resistance. [16] In standing against the patriarchal framework of their lives, these female subjects in patriarchy insist on "the maintenance . . . of a shred of humanity." [17] Their resistance runs against the logic and the fact of the depredation and destruction that is patriarchal domination. These women's resistance is the basis of further resistance. It is also, these narratives reveal, an occasion for powerful and persuasive encounter with the divine, for conversion toward hope and meaning *in the midst of* contexts that threaten or rob women's lives of these qualities. As Rosemary Radford Ruether put it in her 1984 address to the American Academy of Religion,

> The patriarchal distortion of all tradition, including Scripture, throws feminist theology back upon *the primary intuitions of religious experience itself, namely, the belief in a divine foundation of reality which is ultimately good, which does not wish evil nor create evil, but affirms and upholds our autonomous personhood as women, in whose image we are made. . . .* [Feminist theology] is engaged in a primal re-encounter with divine reality and, in this re-encounter, new stories will grow and be told as new foundations of our

identity. . . . It allows the divine to be experienced in places
where it has not been allowed to be experienced before. [18]

These narratives give evidence that, in addition to criticizing
patriarchy and making a critical correlation between theology and
our historical situation, feminist religious thought is struggling
to articulate a new kind of religious experience out of the life
experience of women who have broken through at least some of
the mediation imposed by patriarchal religious traditions. In so
doing, some of these women have encountered an ultimate which
is other than themselves, something indicative of the whole.
They have encountered something they find meaningful,
gracious, trustworthy, and profoundly true, something which
stands with them against their subjugation and for their
transformation. This new encounter yields an experience of
conversion toward God as well as toward self and others, a
vision of the very nature of the Holy, and an experience of
gracious acceptance.   Far from indicating an idolatrous
divinization of the self, these experiences issue in "a faith
response of an individual" that is "at once highly personal and
irrevocably communal." [19]

The examples I have quoted disclose only partial change in
what mediates immediate experience.   Many of the images,
constructs, concepts, and symbols are necessarily drawn from
what is available for use in reflecting on and expressing
immediate experience.   Feminist theory has attended fairly
carefully to the inadequacy of available images, concepts,
symbols, and language to express women's experience of any
sort. [20] Feminist theorists have also stressed the importance of
imagination and the creation of new images. [21] But, for feminist
Christian thinkers, both new concepts and imaginative constructs
arise within the constraints of patriarchal traditions, both because
these traditions have contributed to the construction of women's
experience, and because as *Christian* thinkers, these feminists
are committed to some measure of continuity with the Christian
tradition in all its ambiguity. Nevertheless, all of these concepts
and images, in developing new ways or reviving or
reconstructing old ways of imaging the divine, interrupt and

decrease the mediatory power of patriarchal texts, traditions, and histories of effects, and open new ways not only for persons to speak about their religious experience, but actually to encounter the divine in all its graciousness.

What twentieth century feminist religious experience presents theologians is, I believe, a genuine *novum*: "a new midrash or a third covenant. . . . a new beginning, in which the personhood of woman is no longer at the margins but at the center, where woman is not defined as object, but defines herself as subject."[22] In this new beginning, women encounter an ultimate that is both other and whole in a new experience which gives rise to a new consciousness.[23]

In what follows, I will argue that all human consciousness must be understood as fluid, interactive, and complex, yielding a view of experience as common in its structures but varying in its content. I will then argue that tradition--an important constitutive element of contemporary experience and consciousness--must similarly be understood as complex and interactive. Insofar as it is misleading to define "common human experience" as singular in its empirical elements (such as pride, for example), it is likewise misleading to characterize any tradition in universal or singular empirical terms.[24] Nevertheless, it is possible to thematize experience and tradition within metaphysically and empirically sustainable frameworks. I will suggest that women's experience can be so thematized under the rubric of resistance, which I understand as the maintenance of a shred of humanity in situations of massive dehumanization. I will propose that the theme of resistance to dehumanization encompasses suffering, struggle, liberation, and transformation.

I will further suggest not only in these chapters but in the detailed studies that follow that the feminist appeal to women's religious experience as resistance both critiques and recovers a variety of traditions. This process of critique and recovery embraces strands within Judaism and Christianity which represent encounters with a gracious, self-manifesting, and destabilizing presence, thereby keeping feminist Christian theology within the historic traditions of Christianity while also

meeting the feminist requirement of taking fully into account the
struggles of women against dehumanizing subjugation and for
liberation into an emerging full humanity.

Women's Experience Defined

Feminist theology gives central importance to women's
experience,[25] beginning with the critical recognition that the
extent and character of women's experience of existence and
transcendence and women's ongoing contributions to the
existence of others are largely suppressed, silenced, and negated
by misogynist and androcentric definitions of the human, the
rational, and the divine.[26] Women's experience may then serve
as a norm or criterion by which other sources--notably sources
from religious tradition, including Scripture--are both evaluated
and reconstructed.[27]

In seeking to redress androcentric suppression, feminist
theology also appeals to women's experience as a primary source
of subject matter and for theory.[28] A clear understanding of the
meaning of the term "women's experience" and its
epistemological and methodological functions within feminist
religious thought is, therefore, as necessary as is a preliminary
notion of its referents or contents. The purpose of this section
is to provide a formal definition of women's experience. The
view of experience I will present has significant affinities with
the revisionist approaches of Ogden and Tracy in its emphasis on
the structure of experience as prior to any specification of
content. As I will present it here, my view modifies the
revisionist approach by rendering more explicit the processes and
elements by which experience is constituted. Such an emphasis
is advantageous in that it resists any easy moves to concrete
content as particularly exemplary of what is structurally
common.

The Shape of Human Experience

Contemporary revisionist theologians such as David Tracy and Schubert Ogden argue that truth and meaning claims are grounded in essential structures of human existence and in the epistemology that can be deduced from such structures. [29] For these theologians, this structural experiential epistemology is related to primary affirmations about the divine as both utterly transcendent and universally immanent. [30] But the accompanying empirical or existential content of descriptions of "common human experience" often presents a falsely universalized and in fact androcentric view of the concrete and historical range of human existence. Valerie Saiving demonstrated this more than thirty years ago, concluding:

> It is clear that many of the characteristic emphases of contemporary theology--its definition of the human situation in terms of anxiety, estrangement, and the conflict between necessity and freedom; its identification of sin with pride, will-to-power, exploitation, self-assertiveness, and the treatment of others as objects rather than persons; . . . --it is clear that such an analysis of man's dilemma was profoundly responsive and relevant to the concrete facts of modern man's existence. . . . As a matter of fact, however, this theology is not adequate to the universal human situation. . . . For the temptations of woman *as woman* are not the same as the temptations of man *as man*, and the specifically feminine forms of sin . . . have a quality which can never be encompassed by such terms as "pride" and "will-to-power." They are better suggested by such items as triviality, distractibility, and diffuseness; . . . dependence on others for one's own self-definition; tolerance at the expense of standards of excellence; . . . --in short, underdevelopment or negation of the self. [31]

In other words, while the metaphysical structures of experience may be common, the explicit empirical characterizations of the content of that experience abandon this structural commonality to focus on one particular group: powerful men in dominant cultures. [32]

Nor is a mere modification of the posited content of putatively universal experience (pride, for example) necessarily adequate to address this problem. For, as feminists of color have long noted[33] and white feminists increasingly acknowledge, white feminist theory and theology have also inadvertently posited their own false empirical universal: the experience of white women--and generally of educated, middle-class white women--has been the normative (even if not the only) concrete women's experience to which white feminist thought and practice has appealed. This failing suggests that experience must be understood in a manner that mitigates against the suppression of difference.

Feminist theory identifies Woman--i.e., the putative essential female human being--as a cultural concept rising from patriarchal systems and structures. Under patriarchy, "the construction of women's experience has never been adequate." [34] How, then, is the female subject to be conceptualized? [35] In patriarchal society, a conceptualization based on what women *do* (including what they think and feel) cannot stand: all practices are pervaded and distorted by multivalent and interstructured systems of domination. But biological or philosophical essentialism (what women *are* as such) runs the risk of obviating real, experiential differences between women on the basis of race and class, as well as continuing to define women by their bodies. [36] Furthermore, essentialism often posits a new universal human experience in the same way as the theologies that white feminism critiques: the experience of a (relatively) more powerful group is taken as universal, to the exclusion and suppression of the experiences of less powerful differing groups. [37]

One of the primary constructive tasks of feminist theory, then, is to provide an adequate articulation of women's experience, a project that "modifies or fractures the constructs that left [women's] lives out of account"; [38] that is, that modifies theory itself. Among the elements of theory modified or fractured are the definitions of subjectivity, consciousness, and experience, all of which arise out of and reflect patriarchal, androcentric practices and modes of thought.

The corporate, critical, and self-critical exploration of and reflection on women's concrete lives that is described as consciousness raising [39] provides significant epistemological bases for new, interactive and processive understandings of the human subject, of consciousness, and of human experience. The epistemological claim inherent in the practice of consciousness raising is that reliable knowledge arises out of a corporate situation of mutual engagement, struggle, and transformation in which women "hear each other into speech," corporate reflection, and analysis. [40] The knowledge emerging in this way is taken to be reliable, even while subject to modification through further reflection and analysis. [41] A second claim is that even the deep-seated effects of domination and suppression may be overcome within just such a corporate context of critical reflection and action. [42]

This epistemology is, in turn, based on a complex view of the human subject. On the view developed by feminist theorist Teresa de Lauretis, subjectivity is fundamentally grounded neither in some human core or essence unaffected by the changes and chances of existence, nor in subjects' material conditions (including their relations to structures of domination). Rather, subjectivity is constituted "by one's personal, subjective engagement in the practices, discourses, and institutions that lend significance (value, meaning, and affect) to the events of the world." [43] Experience is then defined as "a complex of habits resulting from the semiotic interaction of 'outer world' and 'inner world,' the continuous engagement of self or subject in social reality." [44]

The human subject is thus understood to be socially and historically constituted, and human consciousness develops and changes within the limits of historical identity and concrete situation. The subject's agency within her situation reconstructs both the situation itself and her consciousness of it.

> [C]onsciousness is not the result but the term of a process . . . , a particular configuration of subjectivity, or subjective limits, produced at the intersection of meaning with experience. . . . In other words, . . . different forms of consciousness are grounded, to be sure, in one's personal history; but that history--one's identity--is interpreted or reconstructed by each of us within the horizon of meanings

and knowledges available in the culture at given historical
moments, a horizon that also includes modes of political
commitment and struggle. . . . Consciousness, therefore, is
never fixed, never attained once and for all, because
discursive boundaries change with historical conditions. [45]

Obviously, then, the many particular dimensions of the
subject's situation have formative significance and produce great
varieties of experience. But any subject's commonality or
solidarity with other subjects as well as her differences from
them likewise arise out of both the situation and her experience
of it.

From the perspective of this particular feminist theory, human
experience is understood as common in its processes and
structures rather than its content. Each and every human subject
is constituted by the interaction of internal and external worlds;
what differs is the concrete elements of those worlds. Under the
terms of this view of experience, the subject is historically and
contextually formed, conscious, and critically and self-critically
reflective. And the subject exists as a subject within a
community that is likewise formed. At the same time, this
definition of experience accounts for the mediation provided by
linguistic structures and conventions, and for the responsible
agency of human subjects.

The concrete content of *women's* experience, writes de
Lauretis, can be sought "in that political, theoretical,
self-analyzing practice by which the relations of the subject in
social reality can be rearticulated from the historical experience
of women." [46] This specifically feminist experience is the
appropriate source for feminist theory and practice because, as
ongoing critical and self-critical process, feminist experience
breaks the silences and suppressions that are a consequence of
patriarchy in order to interrupt patriarchal domination, disclose
the participation of women in all areas of human existence, and
reveal the social and historical construction of all experience. [47]

On the view of experience I have presented here, posited
commonality need not resort to a potentially biased substantive
universal, such as pride, anxiety, or even dehumanization.
Because the interactive social structures and processes that

constitute experience are what is common, it is possible for differing persons to understand and learn from each other's concrete experience without reducing the differences, conflicts, and perhaps incompatibility of their historical existences. To put it another way, conceptualizing human experience as an interactive process *in principle* "defends the other's capacity to remain alien and opaque and yet share in the same rights and claims" reserved for one's own group.[48] And on this feminism insists, by taking an approach that exhibits "a stubborn generosity toward divergent opinions."[49]

Feminist theology, while standing in agreement with this general view of the structure of experience, attends as well to its specifically religious elements. Religious experience is never unmediated or entirely direct. Rather, its immediacy is always mediated by the structures, processes, and contexts in which religious experience occurs.[50] Therefore, as consciousness changes, so does religious experience. As the four narratives at the beginning of this chapter evidence, women's understandings of their own humanity and their hopes for liberation are prompted, distorted, suppressed, reinforced, and transformed by their encounter with the divine as that is mediated through the many dimensions of their existence, including the spiritual, ecclesial, and theological. The experience of liberation decreases the mediation of patriarchal symbols and structures--both traditional and contemporary--and opens up the possibility of a re-encounter with the divine that validates feminist experience of conversion from alienation and transformation toward wholeness.

The Difference Difference Makes

Defining women's experience in the manner I have indicated has the distinct advantage of opening into the emerging discussion of difference as a central issue for feminist (and for all) theology. Recently, Susan Brooks Thistlethwaite has convincingly argued that, given the propensity of white feminists to recapitulate the tendencies of patriarchy to suppress differences of race and class, white feminist theology must begin with difference, rather than with the presumption of commonality.[51]

To begin with difference is to recognize that the varieties of women's experience are irreducibly interstructured on the basis of gender, race, and class; and that the fundamental characteristic of this interstructuring is domination and subordination. When patriarchy is understood as that system of domination and subordination which constructs race and class as well as gender on hierarchicalized lines, it becomes evident that, while women may have in common some elements of experience on the basis of gender, their experience as women will also differ as their race/ethnicity and class locations differ. [52]

In theology, a growing number of African-American womanist scholars have noted the difference such differences make in the construction of theology from the vantage point of women's experience. In Christology, for example, Jacquelyn Grant and Kelly D. Brown have noted that white feminist theologians have often assumed that *all* women's experience is like white middle-class women's experience. [53] Consequently, white feminist Christologies have assumed that sexism is the only problem that Christology must address; racism and classism are not deemed significant.

Womanist theology, in contrast, addresses the double and often triple oppression of African-American women and other women of color, who are subjugated not only by sexism and the construction of gender, but also by systems of race and class domination. This different experience is evident in emerging womanist Christologies. As Brown writes, "A Christ with a womanist consciousness will confront the interpretations of Jesus which have aided and abetted the oppression of Black women, and affirm women's faith that Jesus has identified with them in their struggles to be free." [54] Constructive womanist Christologies--which I shall discuss in the final chapter of this book--emphasize the importance of survival and of liberation that affects the entire community. Christ, then, is affirmed as "unambiguously committed to the survival and liberation of the oppressed."[55]

Emerging womanist theology recognizes that human experience is constructed differently as social locations based on gender, race, and class differ. Yet, as I have indicated and as these womanist theologians recognize, different experience nevertheless is common in its structures, and is interlocked or interstructured across lines of difference. Neither difference nor commonality can be eliminated; neither actual universality nor complete fragmentation is possible.[56] Yet in this situation of differing and often conflicting experiences that constitute human existence as social, some thematization is necessary. To that thematization I now turn.

Notes

1.   Tracy, *Plurality and Ambiguity*, 20.
2.   Tracy, *Analogical Imagination*, 201 and throughout.
3.   Teresa de Lauretis, *Alice Doesn't: Feminism, Semiotics, Cinema* (Bloomington, IN: Indiana University Press, 1984), 182.
4.   Teresa de Lauretis, "Feminist Studies/Critical Studies: Issues, Terms, and Contexts," in *Feminist Studies/Critical Studies* (Bloomington, IN: Indiana University Press, 1984), 8.
5.   Three of these narratives come from the work of women whose expository works are considered at length elsewhere in this book. Walker, not considered as extensively elsewhere in this work, is greatly influential in womanist theology; and this particular text from *The Color Purple* has had great influence on many white feminist religious thinkers. Therefore, I have included her narrative here. For other narratives of feminist religious experience, see *The Stories We Hold Secret: Tales of Women's Spiritual Development*, ed. Carol Bruchac, Linda Hogan, and Judith McDaniel (Greenfield Center, NY: Greenfield Review Press, 1986); *Inheriting our Mothers' Gardens: Feminist Theology in Third World Perspective*, ed. Katie Geneva Cannon et al. (Philadelphia: Westminster Press, 1988); *Speaking of Faith: Global Perspectives on Women, Religion, and Social Change*, ed. Diana L. Eck and Devaki Jain (Philadelphia: New Society Publishers, 1987); *With Passion and Compassion: Third World Women Doing Theology*, ed. Virginia Fabella and Mercy Amba Oduyoye (Maryknoll: Orbis, 1988); *Sacred Dimensions of Women's*

Experience, ed. Elizabeth Dodson Gray (Wellesley, MA: Roundtable Press, 1988).

6.   The term "womanist" is used by African American women to refer to their distinctive approach to the full humanity of women. Following Alice Walker, Jacquelyn Grant defines the term thus: "A womanist is one who has developed survival strategies in spite of the oppression of her race and sex in order to save her family and her people." (Grant, *White Women's Christ and Black Women's Jesus*, 205) The major works in womanist theology in print thus far include Grant's book and numerous articles in journals and anthologies; numerous essays by Delores Williams as well as her forthcoming book; Katie G. Cannon's *Black Womanist Ethics* and numerous articles; Kelly D. Brown's "'Who Do They Say that I Am?' A Critical Examination of the Black Christ"; and numerous other articles, essays, and sermons (the last published, among other places, in *Those Preachin' Women*, Ella Mitchell, ed.).

7.   Alice Walker, *The Color Purple* (New York: Washington Square Press, 1982), 177-179.

8.   "Reflections on the Initiation of an American Woman Scholar into the Symbols and Rituals of the Ancient Goddesses," in *Journal of Feminist Studies in Religion* 3 no. 1 (1987): 58.

9.   Carter Heyward, *Our Passion for Justice: Images of Power, Sexuality, and Liberation* (New York: Pilgrim Press, 1984), 154-155.

10.   Rosemary Radford Ruether, "The Future of Feminist Theology in the Academy," *Journal of the American Academy of Religion* 53 no. 4 (Dec 1985): 710-711.

11.   See particularly Heyward's autobiography, *A Priest Forever*.

12.   For an exposition of the intensification of distanciation and participation and its relation to encounter with the divine, see the section "Religious Experience as Participation and Distanciation" in Chapter 5.

13.   For an exposition, see the section "The Relation of Experience and Tradition" in Chapter 6.

14.   This notion of a sense of wholeness or totality which precedes individual existence is not, of course, unique to feminist theology. On the importance of this in the process philosophy of Alfred North Whitehead, see Schubert M. Ogden, "Present Prospects for Empirical Theology," in *The Future of Empirical Theology*, ed. Bernard E. Meland (Chicago: University of Chicago Press, 1969), 82ff. This sense of totality provides Ogden with one basis of his notion of common human experience.

15. On the significance of rupture for ontic, ontological, and ethical understandings of reality, see my discussion of Emil Fackenheim's post-Holocaust Jewish thought in "The Experience of Victims as the Ground for Metaphysics and Ethics" in Chapter 5.

16. See the fuller exposition of this point in "Metaphysics and Ethics from Women's Experience" in Chapter 5.

17. Emil Fackenheim, *To Mend the World: Foundations of Future Jewish Thought* (New York: Schocken Books, 1981), 225.

18. Ruether, "Future of Feminist Theology," 710-711; emphasis added.

19. Tracy, *Analogical Imagination*, 320.

20. See, among many possibilities, Cheris Kramarae, ed., *The Voice and Words of Women and Men* (Oxford: Pergamon Press, 1980); Roberta W. Caldie, *Dominance and Language: A New Perspective on Sexism* (Washington, D.C.: University Press of America, 1981); Carol Gilligan, *In a Different Voice: Psychological Theory and Women's Development (Cambridge, MA: Harvard University Press, 1982)*; and Sally McConnell-Ginet, Ruth Borker, and Nelly Furman, eds., *Women and Language in Literature and Society* (New York: Praeger Publishers, 1980).

21. See, for example, the work of Mary Daly, Carol P. Christ, Starhawk, Elisabeth Schüssler Fiorenza, Rosemary Radford Ruether, Dorothee Soelle, and Carter Heyward.

22. Ruether, "Future of Feminist Theology," 711.

23. Not is it only the more outspoken advocates of feminist theology who recognize the radically new in feminist religious experience. The most conservative opponents to feminism have recognized right along that, for example, once women are ordained, the church and its theology will be irrevocably changed. See, for example, William Oddie, *What Will Happen to God? Feminism and the Reconstruction of Christian Belief* (London: SPCK, 1984); and Theodore P. Letis, "Feminine Spirituality: Eve Shakes an Angry Fist at YAHWEH, But He Triumphs Through the *Son*," in *The Journal of Christian Reconstruction* 9 (1982-1983): 182-200.

24. For example, the direction of my detailed studies of contemporary feminist Christologies is toward the maintenance of tension between two types of interpretations of Christian tradition, one of them oriented by prophetic and eschatological insights, and the other by participation in present manifestations of the divine. While my own preference is for the latter type, I will contend that a tension must be maintained between the two if feminist theology is to be adequate to

both tradition and contemporary experience. Identifying a single "core" or principle--be it prophecy or wisdom--is not adequate on either account. Nor will it serve visions of future liberation and transformation.

25. See, for example, Rosemary Radford Ruether, "Feminist Theology: Methodology, Sources, and Norms," chapter 1 in *Sexism and God-Talk*; Carter Heyward, "Feminist Theology: The Early Task and Beyond" and "Introduction to Feminist Theology: A Christian Feminist Perspective," chapters 2 and 25, respectively, in *Our Passion for Justice*; Anne E. Carr, *Transforming Grace: Christian Tradition and Women's Experience* (San Francisco: Harper and Row, 1988), 30-36, 118-123, and passim; and Pamela Dickey Young, *Feminist Theology/Christian Theology: In Search of Method* (Minneapolis: Fortress Press, 1990).

26. See particularly the following: Valerie Saiving, "The Human Situation: A Feminine View" in *Womanspirit Rising: A Feminist Reader in Religion*, edited by Carol P. Christ and Judith Plaskow (San Francisco: Harper and Row, Publishers, 1979), pp. 25-42 (originally published in *The Journal of Religion* [April, 1960]); Judith Plaskow, *Sex, Sin and Grace: Women's Experience and the Theologies of Reinhold Niebuhr and Paul Tillich* (Lanham, MD: University Press of America, 1980); and Elisabeth Schüssler Fiorenza, *Bread Not Stone: The Challenge of Feminist Biblical Interpretation* (Boston: Beacon Press, 1984) and *In Memory of Her: A Feminist Theological Reconstruction of Christian Origins* (New York: Crossroad, 1983).

27. See Ruether, *Sexism and God-Talk*, 20-45; and Schüssler Fiorenza, *Bread Not Stone*, 58-63 and passim. It should be noted that neither Ruether nor Schüssler Fiorenza considers women's experience *alone* to be normative; rather, experience and tradition are dialectically related, shaping and interpreting each other. Cf. Young, 19.

28. Cf. Young, 19.

29. In showing its basic affinity with credible philosophy, theology can in this manner re-secure its threatened credibility as a system of thought. See Tracy, *Blessed Rage for Order*, 3-21; Ogden, "Present Prospects for Empirical Theology"; idem, "The Reality of God," in *The Reality of God: And Other Essays* (San Francisco: Harper and Row, 1963, 1977); and the verification-falsification debate of the 1950s and early 1960s.

30. Ogden, "Present Prospects for Empirical Theology," 73; cf. Tracy, *Blessed Rage for Order*, passim; and idem, *Analogical Imagination*, passim.

31. Valerie Saiving, "The Human Situation: A Feminine View," in *Womanspirit Rising*, 35, 37; italics in the original. (Saiving has discussed this early article in "A Conversation with Valerie Saiving," *Journal of Feminist Studies in Religion* 4 no. 2 [1988]: 99-115.) Further, the characterizations of experience take place in a context in which Woman is defined by deviations from a male norm. As Pamela Dickey Young writes, "Whether 'universal' theological concepts such as those of sin and salvation really applied to women in the same way they applied to men was not considered. Yet women were assumed to be those most prone to sin and temptation, and here Eve was usually cited as the prime example." (Young, 16.) While Saiving's study discusses Nygren and Niebuhr, I have given in Chapter 2 examples of how late twentieth century theologians also continue this androcentric bias.

32. For authors who discuss this problem, see note 26, above. See also my discussion of Moltmann and Schillebeeckx in Chapter 2.

33. See the sources cited in note 6 of this chapter, and in the concluding section of Chapter 12.

34. Nannerl O. Keohane et al., eds., *Feminist Theory: A Critique of Ideology* (Chicago: University of Chicago Press, 1982), vii.

35. Some feminists--notably the French post-structuralists-- challenge the notion that it is either possible or desirable to conceptualize female subjects at all. For the theological problems with this view, see Susan Brooks Thistlethwaite, "Experience in White Feminist Theory," chapter 1 in *Sex, Race and God: Christian Feminism in Black and White* (New York: Crossroad, 1989); and Carol P. Christ, "Embodied Thinking: Reflections on Feminist Theological Method," in *Journal of Feminist Studies in Religion* 5 no. 1 (Spring 1989): 7-16.

36. For example, in her recent book Pamela Dickey Young argues that experience is always produced by reflection; that is, it is a form of knowledge rather than something unmediated. Yet she presents basic characteristics of women's bodily experience (menstruation, sexuality, childbirth) as if uninfluenced and unconstructed by social, historical, and individual factors. (53ff.) Thus women's bodies are immutable definers of women's being.

37. See, among many possibilities, Jacquelyn Grant, "A Black Response to Feminist Theology," in *Women's Spirit Bonding*, edited by Janet Kalven and Mary I. Buckley (NY: Pilgrim Press, 1984), 117-124; Delores S. Williams, "Womanist Theology: Black Women's Voices," in *Weaving the Visions*, Judith Plaskow and Carol P. Christ,

eds. (San Francisco: Harper and Row, 1989), 179-186; Katie Geneva Cannon, "The Emergence of Black Feminist Consciousness," in *Feminist Interpretation of the Bible*, Letty M. Russell, ed., (Philadelphia: Westminster, 1985), 30-40; as well as Jacquelyn Grant, *White Women's Christ and Black Women's Jesus: Feminist Christology and Womanist Response* (Atlanta: Scholars Press, 1989); and Kelly Delaine Brown, "'Who Do They Say that I Am?' A Critical Examination of the Black Christ" (Unpublished dissertation, Union Theological Seminary, 1988.). Thistlethwaite and Spelman discuss these issues from their perspective as white women.

38. Keohane et al., vii.

39. Consciousness raising, "the essential first step" of feminist theory (Keohane et al., vii.) is at the same time a technique of "analysis, structure of organization, method of practice, and theory of social change." (Catharine A. MacKinnon, "Feminism, Marxism, Method, and the State: An Agenda for Theory," in Keohane et al., 5.) This method "anchor[s] women's power and account[s] for women's discontent in the same world they stand against." It is "within yet outside the male paradigm just as women's lives are." (MacKinnon, 20-21) Consciousness raising brings about "the collective critical reconstitution of the meaning of women's social experience, as women live through it. . . The process is transformative as well as perceptive, since thought and thing are inextricable and reciprocally constituting of women's oppression." (MacKinnon, 29.)

40. The quoted phrase is generally attributed to Nelle Morton.

41. The claim that such knowledge is reliable or valid while transitory arises from philosophical pragmatism, in that validity is measured by effectiveness in present and future reflection and action. See Sharon D. Welch, *A Feminist Ethic of Risk* (Minneapolis: Fortress, 1990), 158, 196 n.13.

42. MacKinnon, 21.

43. de Lauretis, *Alice Doesn't*, 159. De Lauretis, it should be noted, does not discuss the role of religion or metaphysics in the formation of experience. That dimension will be bracketed, therefore, in those parts of my discussion which draw on her work directly. I will return to the religious dimension in the next chapter.

44. Ibid., 182. De Lauretis here follows Lacan, Eco, and Peirce.

45. de Lauretis, "Feminist Studies/Critical Studies: Issues, Terms and Contexts," 8.

46. de Lauretis, *Alice Doesn't*, 186.

47. Feminist experience serves as one norm for feminist theology as well, because feminist theology's explicit commitment to the liberation of women from patriarchal oppression derives in the first instance from women's experience in exactly this struggle. See, for example, Schüssler Fiorenza, *Bread Not Stone*, 44 and *passim;* Heyward, *Our Passion for Justice*, ch. 2, 25; Ruether, *Sexism and God-Talk*, ch. 1; and Young, 62ff.

48. Jürgen Habermas gave this definition of an unbiased universal at a symposium on public theology held at the Divinity School of the University of Chicago in October, 1987. This insistence on safeguarding the rights and claims of the differing other may, at first glance, seem at odds with the stated bias upon which feminist discourse also insists. Many feminist theorists insist that *all* human experience is partial and limited. What is necessary, then, is for the stance of any formulation to be rendered evident, and its pretenses to substantive universality to be set aside. (See, for example, Schüssler Fiorenza, *Bread Not Stone*, xv, 44ff., 61ff.; and *In Memory of Her*, *passim*; and Ruether, *Sexism and God-Talk*, ch. 1.) Feminism's explicit stating of the bias or privilege that is in fact present shows a profound commitment to a dialogical or conversational approach, in that feminism identifies its interests, intentions, and presuppositions at the outset, making them available for questioning, criticism, and (in principle) modification. Far from obviating the claim of "others" for fair treatment, feminism's statement of its intentions protects this claim at the same time it works to guarantee its application within that group historically identified and dominated as alien other: women living in patriarchal social systems.

49. This is how Jean Lambert identifies a major characteristic of feminist biblical methodology. ("An 'F Factor'? The New Testament in Some White, Feminist, Christian Theological Construction," in *Journal of Feminist Studies in Religion* 1, no. 2 [1985]: 93-113; see, e.g., 111.)

50. In other words, like human experience in general, religious experience is "a complex of habits resulting from the semiotic interaction of 'outer world' and 'inner world,' the continuous engagement of self or subject in social reality." (de Lauretis, *Alice Doesn't*, 182.) Religious consciousness, like all consciousness, is "interpreted or reconstructed by each of us within the horizon of meanings and knowledges available in the culture at given historical moments, . . . " (de Lauretis, "Feminist Studies/Critical Studies: Issues, Terms, and Contexts," 8.)

51. Thistlethwaite, *Sex, Race, and God*, throughout.
52. See my discussion of Rosemary Radford Ruether's early and significant formulation of interstructuring in Chapter 7, which summarizes Ruether's work in *New Woman/New Earth* (especially Chapter 5, Between the Sons of White and the Sons of Blackness: Racism and Sexism in America," 115-130).
53. Grant, *White Women's Christ and Black Women's Jesus*; Brown, "'Who Do They Say that I Am?'"
54. Brown, 193.
55. Ibid., 201.
56. The pragmatic implications of interstructured analyses are at least as important as the theoretical ones: analyses which assume that different historical existences are either uniform or unconnected one with another conceal the interdependencies of individuals and groups, masking and diminishing responsibility and effective agency. See Welch, *A Feminist Ethic of Risk*, Part One, "Cultured Despair and the Death of Moral Imagination."

Chapter 5

Resistance and Transformation
as Religious Experience

In the preceding chapter, I developed a formal or conceptual description of women's experience--indeed, of human experience--as fluid, social, plural, interactive, and intersubjective. I described human experience as relational in two senses. First, its content emerges through contact with others--human persons, the environment of human existence in the world, and with the divine. Second, experience is formally constituted by the interaction of social, historical, psychological, symbolic, physical, and ideological systems and structures of meaning, understanding, and activity. This complex description of experience suggests how it is possible for differing persons to understand and learn from each other's experience (a reflective project, after all) without reducing the difference and perhaps incompatibility of their historical existences.

Feminist religious thought insists that historical existence also has a transcendent element. Support of this claim requires, first, indication of how historical experience may be connected with transhistorical, transcendent reality. This connection may then be typified in specifically religious and theological terms.
be typified in specifically religious and theological terms.

Elisabeth Schüssler Fiorenza, Rosemary Radford Ruether, Carter Heyward, and others have specified women's experience in the struggle for liberation as an appropriate source and norm for feminist theological reflection. [1] That experience can be understood concretely as resistance to dehumanizing oppression, a characterization which requires further elaboration. Furthermore, the connection between the concrete experience of resistance to oppression and transcendent reality can be delineated by using a careful philosophical and theological examination of the import of experience itself. One fruitful resource for this discussion is the work of post-Holocaust Jewish philosopher Emil Fackenheim, who has exactingly argued precisely such a connection. [2]

The Experience of Victims as the Ground for Metaphysics and Ethics

Fackenheim's argument presumes that all modern philosophical thought must begin from experience, and that experience contains a transcendent element which makes possible both thought and moral existence. That transcendent element comes through confronting, grasping, and enduring concrete human historicity and finitude. [3] But the possibility of such an authentic existence is radically ruptured by the Holocaust, whose logic and effect is precisely to render such existence impossible.

The problem presented by the Holocaust is also religious. Modern religious thought relies on "a modern committing testimony" in which "thinking aris[es] from a committed existence." [4] On this view, revelation takes place in an independent world created by a "far" (or transcendent) God who is always moving toward "nearness" (or immanence). What experience reveals is the present love of God, a love which is as strong as death. [5] Revelation is found in "present experience," and confirmation of its transcendent element comes through the prayer-life of those whose relation with this God precedes their experience. [6] But revelation is negated when God is experienced as entirely absent, or when the love of God is overwhelmed by massive dehumanizing death; when prayer is silenced and the logic of death itself hinges on the very fact of birth into relationship with God. [7]

Thus the Holocaust, in pressing these questions in stark and inescapable form, ruptures both philosophical and religious thought. It radically and relentlessly refutes the presuppositions and primary orientations of both thought and faith by exposing those flaws and deficits in both which render them incapable not only of preventing such a horror, but even of comprehending it. [8]

After such an inexplicable event, thought and faith are paralyzed, and the impossibility of either looms large. What offers the hope of overcoming this paralysis and challenges this impossibility is only one thing: Thought and life are possible here and now, because thought and life were a reality there and then through the resistance of the victims to the logic of destruction with which they were assaulted. [9] The *novum* of paralyzing horror is met by a *novum* of resistance.

Within this world *in extremis*, resistance is properly defined as "the maintenance by the victims of a shred of humanity." [10] To retain, to recreate a shred of humanity in the midst of the radical, systemic dehumanization of the Holocaust world is itself an act of resistance by those who felt themselves "under orders to live" in the midst of confronting the overwhelming horror which entrapped them. [11] Such resistance is an Ultimate beyond will or nature; it is a way of being indistinguishable from life itself. [12]

This resistance is an ontic reality. But it is also an ontological category: this phenomenon in history also indicates something essential and inescapable about the nature of human being itself. [13] Authentic thought after the Holocaust is also resisting thought: it confronts the whole horror of dehumanizing assault, grasps its meaning despite the logic of destruction which conceals that meaning, and appropriates that experience in order to struggle against it. The tension of grasping and resisting drives thought beyond itself into "overt, flesh-and-blood action and life." It confronts and endures finitude in its most extreme form, and so is also transcendent. [14] In the structure of thought, there is, therefore, an ontological category which drives toward an imperative for future thought and action. [15]

At the same time, resistance is an imperative found in relation to the limitations placed on action by the exigencies of historical existence. Human persons have the capacity and the drive to resist dehumanization; but the forces of dehumanization are themselves such that such resistance may not always be possible. [16]

Resistance--the maintenance of a shred of humanity--is also evident in the words and actions of those who consciously opposed the Nazi state, whether for philosophical, humanitarian, or religious reasons. [17] This form of resistance points to the possibility of mending the philosophical and religious ruptures produced by the Holocaust. And the possibility of mending the ruptures moves the ontological category of resistance into an imperative for life.

Both forms of resistance--that of being and that of doing-- demonstrate that the mending of thought, religion, and life itself is possible now because it was actual during the event itself. Such a mending necessarily involves not only the brokenness of history, but the brokenness of any experience of the presence or nearness of the divine as authentically connected with historical experience. For the appeal of the resisters is often precisely to this divine presence and historical-existential revelation; so the appeal itself recreates the possibility of such an appeal now. [18] And if it is possible, it is mandatory: ought still implies can, particularly for a mended faith which turns toward a God who aids human power. [19]

Third--and not the least important--this mending by resistance continues the resistance of the victims *by remembering them*. This remembrance is a refusal, like the victims' own refusal, to give the executioners any victories. [20] Were a mending not possible, the Holocaust world would triumph: thought, life, faith would be irremediably ruptured in their continuity with the pre-Holocaust world, and in the possibility of their authenticity and historicity.

Resistance, then, Fackenheim urges, is the key to confronting and mending the rupture of the world produced by the

Holocaust. Through resistance to massive dehumanizing destruction, the possibility of authentic human life, of thought, and of faith are recreated within historical existence, neither denying the possibility of transcendence nor escaping history into an ideal (and false) transcendent realm where history--and so its victims--have no import.

Metaphysics and Ethics from Women's Experience

How is Fackenheim's elaborate and passionate argument fruitful for feminist Christian religious thought and practice? More precisely, how can feminist Christian religious thought legitimately and respectfully appropriate Fackenheim's reconstruction of epistemology and metaphysics? [21]

Other histories of subjugation need not duplicate in each particular the elements characteristic of the Holocaust to be helpfully illumined and interpreted by understanding the Holocaust as rupture. Indeed, no other history can. But there *are* analogues--similarities and differences--elsewhere in the history of subjugation and massive dehumanization and destruction, often spread over centuries, and finally perpetuated even in the absence of any advantage to the dominant group. [22]

The history of women is one case in point. For women have been subjected to comprehensive dehumanization and attempts at their destruction as individuals and as a group solely on the grounds of their being women, not just on the grounds of what they have done. [23] The primary motivation of patriarchy in regard to women has been the desire to define and control women's humanity through the construal of women as Alien Other, in some critical way less fully human than men. Physical destruction and social isolation have been the instruments of this dehumanization. Yet the dehumanization of women has always subverted the survival of patriarchy, in that women are the only human childbearers, and have always been needed participants in the production as well as the reproduction of life. [24]

Every instance of dehumanization and destruction is horrifying; yet no two cases are identical. Fackenheim's argument serves, finally, to provide a new phenomenology and philosophy that allow thought to confront massive suffering, respecting the particularities of its victims without denying the suffering of others. The Holocaust stands as a *novum* not only on the basis of the ways in which it is unique or unprecedented. More, it constitutes a break of monumental proportions in the previously posited continuity and progressive development of Western civilization. [25] The particularities of scope, severity, intent, and philosophical rationalization of this event starkly force on consciousness as perhaps never before what has been the case all too often in human history, in different but similar manner. In other words, reflection on the character of the Holocaust's horrors forces thought to recognize aspects of human being that Western civilization has not previously faced, notably hithertofore unexercised aspects of human evil, and the human capacity to resist and so transcend that evil. The *novum* in human history is not only the event, but also the rupture of thought it produces.

But also possible is a responsive *novum* of deliberate attempt to confront, grasp, and mend this rupture. This is possible now, because it was actual then--in the Holocaust, and in other acts of resistance, such as those by women under patriarchy, or by peoples of African descent during slavery and subsequently. This mending entails, among other things, recognizing the status of resistance as an ontological category that describes and even constitutes the human, and does so with imperative force. Only now--in the face of this *novum*--is it possible to see how this resistance and mending have been the case analogously but not identically also at other junctures of human history.

When this single event of rupture and mending is understood as a *novum* in this way--as singular but with similarities to other events and historical patterns--the importance of Fackenheim's discussion of resistance becomes greater. Through his insistent use of the victims' experience and his thematization of that experience as resistance, Fackenheim reconstrues the history of domination and dehumanization in a manner which *at one and the same time* acknowledges the depth, scope, and tragedy of unjust suffering *and* illumines the continued humanity even of those most dehumanized. Under the theme of resistance, it is possible to see the victims as both drastically limited in their capacities as agents and as active agents nevertheless. The theme of resistance makes it clear that the appropriate question is not "Why did so many succumb?" but "How did even one survive?"[26]

The importance of this becomes clearer when resistance is contrasted with other possible themes. Suffering, endurance, survival, or triumph no doubt accurately thematize aspects of the experience of some of the victims, some of the time. But each of these also conventionally contains a dualized view of human agency or responsibility. Suffering, endurance, and survival often connote only passive response to unchangeable circumstances, while triumph implies only activity that overthrows these circumstances. As has been demonstrated by womanist scholars, the fundamental anthropological presumption in these categories is one of untrammeled choice, a situation which is real for only a privileged few (if even for them). [27] With such a presupposition in place, the question of victims' collusion or collaboration with their own fate often arises. But this question presumes the validity of a definition of agency that is grounded outside of the systemic and systematic dehumanization which is characteristic of domination and subjugation.[28] To begin from resistance understood as the maintenance of a shred of humanity in situations of massive dehumanization is to begin from what may be possible *for the victims themselves*, not for those whose situations are less extreme.

Moreover, beginning from resistance gives more weight to agency than to passivity. [29] Resistance illumines not only the continued humanity of those assaulted with forces of dehumanization; it also indicates how their suffering, when confronted, may be an occasion through which the possibility of meaning is grasped and recreated, not only for the sufferers, but for their successors. Beginning from resistance renders the memory of the victims of history subversive and dangerous to the forces of dehumanization, denying the executioners posthumous victories. [30]

The value of the theme of resistance to feminist historical thought is great, in that it provides a construal of history that begins from the suppressed, the silenced, and the marginalized.[31] It construes history from the position in which women under patriarchy have lived and died. And it makes this construal on the basis of the experience of the silenced. This beginning point actively asserts that the silenced in fact significantly formed the very history whose recording excludes them--a key point for feminist historical criticism and reconstruction--and they did so in a manner which changed the meaning of history itself as well as the course of its events. This meaning may have been largely lost at the time; but it is recoverable now. And its recovery vindicates the lives and deaths of those who produced it. Further, beginning from the experience of the victims itself energetically resists even tacitly blaming the victims for their own fate, a fault often apparent in such construals as fail to question the themes by which experience is rendered.

But of even greater value, particularly for feminist theologians, is the explicit connection which Fackenheim demonstrates between resistance and transcendence. This is a connection at least some feminist religious thinkers have presumed;[32] but to my knowledge, none have worked out an epistemology or metaphysics which in fact fully explicates this presumption.[33] It is, however, an important question, for precisely the reasons Fackenheim indicates. In the modern period, the connection between experience and revelation (or the conviction of the factual nature of transcendence) has been fragile. This connection is frayed even further in the several hermeneutics of suspicion, which reasonably question the bases on which particular definitions and events of experience, revelation, and encounter with the transcendent are granted authority and authorization. What remains is experience itself. Yet, even understood in the complex manner I have indicated previously in this chapter, *that* there is an experience *deemed* transcendent is clear enough, but precisely how this experience actually *has a* transcendent element--that is, the factuality of the experience--is unclear.

Fackenheim's achievement in this area is to indicate not only the historic importance of the experience particular to the dominated and dehumanized, but to indicate how this experience in fact is connected with transcendence. Ontic reality discloses ontological ultimacy; human being is malleable, shaped by historical events into new being. [34] Therefore, new experience-- here, the experience of the victims in particular--reconstitutes human being and Being itself. So resistance to dehumanization has ontological, metaphysical standing. To use religious terms, it is revelatory and transformative of the constitution of human being. And its operations--similar in form to all other ontological operations--drive from historical being to Being itself; that is, they drive from the human to the divine. In situations of massive dehumanization, maintaining a shred of humanity--resistance--*is* being. Resistance mends the rupture in the cosmos created by the human evil found in massive, systemic dehumanization; it reconnects being with Being itself.

By following Fackenheim's lead, then, feminist thought can indicate how the historical resistance of women to the dehumanization of patriarchy both constitutes and is revelatory of the constitution of human existence as past reality and present and future possibility. Further, resistance as moral imperative indicates one way in which the experience of those who have gone before can be appropriated in the shaping of current and future life as the continued struggle for liberation--a struggle which involves resistance as an ongoing activity of thought and life. Far from being marginal to human existence, dominated women are central to it, and central to thought about it.

Religious Experience as Participation and Distanciation

In the last chapter, I developed a formal or conceptual description of experience as fluid, social, plural, and interactive; that is, as relational. In the first section of this chapter, I indicated how ontic, historical experience may be connected with ontological and transcendent reality. In this section, I will render that connection in specifically religious and theological terms. When theology is understood as reflection on human experience in relation to religious traditions, a description of religious experience as such is clearly necessary. I will present here an interpretation of religious experience as a dialectic between human experiences of participation and nonparticipation in which the divine is encountered through manifestation and proclamation. I shall indicate throughout the remainder of this book how this interpretation assists both in analyzing the constructive Christologies emerging from feminist thought, and in placing those proposals in a relation that will generate further constructive work. [35]

Working from the studies of historian of religion Mircea Eliade, philosopher Paul Ricoeur and theologian David Tracy posit a phenomenological dialectic of manifestation and proclamation that is designed to thematize religious experience as such without minimizing religions' particularities and differences of content and concrete location in human history. [36] Both Ricoeur and Tracy understand the religious phenomena of manifestation and proclamation to be dialectically related. Each is indispensable to the other if a full account of religious experience is to be attained. The necessary relationship of the two poles is not complementary as much as generative. Particular religious traditions or accounts of religious experience may express a preference for or emphasis on one more than the other; but the less emphasized pole remains. Further, interpretation of both manifestation and proclamation is shaped by the historical situation and projects of the interpreters, so that praxis-based theologies (such as political and liberation theologies) understand and use both themes differently than do revisionist philosophies and theologies (such as those presented by Ricoeur and Tracy).

Ricoeur's study casts the polarities of manifestation and proclamation as antinomies whose conflictual relationship makes clear their distinctive individual traits. In the experience of manifestation, the sacred is encountered "as awesome, as powerful, as overwhelming," not susceptible to complete articulation in speech. [37] In addition, the experience of encounter is expressed through "the productive imagination" [38] and through *act*, ritual and behavior that reiterates the efficacity or power of the sacred in human ways of being in the world. Through this range of expression, human persons see themselves as participants in the power of the sacred. "To see the world as sacred is at the same time to *make* it sacred, to consecrate it." [39]

On the other hand, proclamation opposes manifestation in the first instance by giving the word or "certain fundamental discourses" primacy over and against the numinous from which these emerge. [40] The logic of proclamation is "the logic of limit-expressions," where redescription explodes, bursts, or otherwise disrupts ordinary meaning through intensifications and reversals which challenge the conventional. [41] Proclamation, that is, is discourse that pushes toward the extremes, toward "limit-experiences" of crisis, distress, decision, and culmination. [42]

Proclamation, then, explodes out of the sacred, overcoming participation with distanciation, myth with kerygma, coherence and correspondence with paradox and extravagance. But, Ricoeur contends, the sacred is neither annihilated nor unchanged by proclamation. Instead, the poles of manifestation and proclamation are transformed and transmuted.

> The word . . . breaks away from the numinous. . . . But there would be no proclamation if the word, too, were not powerful; that is, if it did not have to power to set forth the new being it proclaims. A word that is addressed to us rather than our speaking it, a word that constitutes us rather than our articulating it--a word that speaks--does not such a word reaffirm the sacred just as much as abolish it? [43]

The explosive discourse of proclamation functions only because it reactivates the ancient and "primary symbolism" which corresponds with faith. [44] So as much as proclamation may contain within it a drive toward demythologization, it also contains a drive toward remythologization and resacralization which is nevertheless a development rather than a return. And this drive for recovery itself is necessary to preserve the genuine power of proclamation. [45]

In his use of this dialectic of manifestation and proclamation within Christian theology, David Tracy begins with the basic human experience of intensification understood as encounter with the sacred or divine. Intensification always has two moments, participation and distanciation, in that every "event of disclosure" both discloses the whole, but never does so adequately or fully, and so is also an event of concealment.[46] The experience of intensification tends in two directions: participation, which is correlated with encounter via manifestation; and distanciation, which is correlated with encounter via proclamation. Yet the two directions are dialectically related: every event of disclosure-concealment is an event of intensification of particularity which "releases" itself positively toward both participation and distanciation. Thus every encounter belongs to a wider reality *and* expresses that experience to others.[47]

Yet in expression, each encounter with the divine demands an expression where one moment of the dialectic predominates.[48] Thus, religious experience and the expressions to which it gives rise yield two related and corresponding ideal types.[49]

When intensification tends toward participation, "the religious expression will be named 'manifestation,'" as in the mystical, priestly, metaphysical, and aesthetic elements of Christianity. Here, the sacred is sensed to be radically immanent, numinous, immediately powerful, the enveloping ground which is always already present.[50] The human self is understood as belonging to and participating in a sacred cosmos, divinized by that participatory contact with the sacred.[51] Within this type, Christologies tend to emphasize fundamental trust in humanity, history, and cosmos, in which God is present as love and in which existence is gifted. The Christ is then understood to be the incarnated manifestation of the true nature of both human and divine, as, for example, "the decisive re-presentation" of God and of the authentic character of human existence.[52] And the kind of human existence which is manifested in the Christ is understood to be always already possible.[53]

When the intensification of particularity tends toward nonparticipation, "the religious expression will be named 'proclamation,'" as in the prophetic, ethical, and historical.[54] Here, the sacred or divine is encountered as a power that shatters, defamiliarizes, or stands over against the human as the radically other which is nonetheless like a self. The human self is ambiguous, in relation to the sacred both "essentially good, [and] existentially estranged," finite and limited.[55] Christologies within the proclamation paradigm tend to emphasize Christ's cross and prophetic-eschatological message. The Christ is taken as a disclosure of the need for reform, for refusal to comply with the structures and forces of sin, for protest, suspicion, and conflict or struggle against the present human condition.[56] The focus here is on the fact that the life commanded by Christ is not yet actualized, at least in part because of human nonacceptance of the divine reality and love.

Within Christianity, Tracy argues, the dialectic of manifestation and proclamation develops in such a way that the divine is experienced as like a self: "the transcendent, unnameable Other" disclosed through manifestation is one who speaks as well as acts. God is manifest in the word as one who discloses its ownmost particularity as both participation and distanciation.[57] And this manifestation via proclamation is what also discloses the human self as participant and nonparticipant in world and history, both of which are both affirmed and disconfirmed or shattered by religious experience.[58]

On this reading, the dialectic of manifestation and proclamation must be maintained within contemporary understandings of Christianity, if these are to be authentic.[59] These "types," then, serve as a descriptive and classificatory schema which can indicate the relation between more concretely described particular religious experiences. And it is in exactly this way that I will recur to this description a number of times during the course of this book.

Moreover, in Tracy's formulation, as in Ricoeur's, the dialectic is not static. Tracy indicates how Christian understandings of manifestation and proclamation are themselves transformed by historical action which is a response to a contemporary situation.[60] There are, then, identifiable "trajectories" of the "routes" of both manifestation and proclamation, two of which are of particular relevance to the present work.

First, among the trajectories of the route of manifestation is that provided by the mediation of the ordinary.[61]   For theological formulations located on this trajectory--including contemporary feminist religious thought[62]--intensification comes through the everyday, the conventional shape of which is shattered by the "shocking, lovable, real otherness of all concrete others" as these are sensed to be related to the sacral power of the whole comprising God, self, and (both historical and natural) world.[63]

The second relevant trajectory in response to the contemporary situation transforms the dialectic of manifestation and proclamation by action in history and consequent reflection on the primacy of praxis.   For theologies developing this synthesis--which include contemporary feminist theologies understood from the perspective of a liberation focus--"we are primarily neither hearers of the word nor seers of a manifestation. But because we have seen and have heard, we are freed to become doers of the word in history."[64]   Liberating praxis transforms the paradigm of manifestation by recasting its characteristic emphases on the giftedness of existence in creation and on incarnation as manifestation of the divine as the forces grounding prophetic, eschatological urgency and the imperative for social-historical action.[65] Liberating praxis transforms the paradigm of proclamation by recasting *its* characteristic emphases on the cross and on the prophetic-eschatological direction of religious life so they address alienating and oppressive structures of social existence as those affect the socially-constituted individual.

What is significant about both these trajectories is their very expansion of the dialectic.   That is, intensification of the everyday and of praxis constitutes a historical and phenomenological development *beyond* the relation of manifestation and proclamation which both Ricoeur and Tracy have described.   Here the "journey of intensification" often begins with either proclamation or manifestation (and, as Tracy indicates, the beginning point continues to provide emphases as the journey progresses), [66] but the nature and direction of the intensification is substantially transformed by "fidelity to the concrete," by the reality of conflict, suffering, and liberation as constitutive of human experience, and by eschatological and prophetic strands of Christian tradition. Indeed, the very structure of this dialectic may be undergoing an expansive transformation effected by liberation theologies' reference to everyday experience in the struggle for liberation as the concrete locus of specifically religious experience. If this is the case, the dialectic of religious experience may be more accurately described as three-fold: the divine is encountered via manifestation, proclamation, and liberating action.

The point of considering at some length the dialectic schemas of Ricoeur and Tracy is that the thematization of religious experience in terms of a dialectic of manifestation, proclamation, and liberating action contributes to the complex account of the shape of "common human experience" as a source in contemporary theology which Part Two of this book is developing. The divine is encountered in experiences in which the particularity of the human subject is intensified, and the sacred is experienced as overwhelmingly powerful. The subject describes the encounter in terms of disclosure or manifestation *of* the sacred, *and* in terms of concealment or interpretive proclamation *about* the sacred which stands at some distance from and over against the experiencing subject.

In both moments, the subject produces the expression, which is to say that there is always an interpretation of the experience which arises out of the subject's reflection on it. [67] However, the extent of this interpretive reflection differs between the two poles of manifestation and proclamation. In the former, the expression is symbolic and "bound"; it corresponds with and adheres to the elements used symbolically. But in the latter, the "labor of language" and the "free invention of discourse" come into play more powerfully, as proclamation stands at greater distance from the experience of encounter than does manifestation. Nevertheless, in both moments, encounter with the divine is mediated by the manner in which the interpretive and reflective capacities of the experiencing subject are employed in construing the experience.

This means that the contexts of human experience and of reflections on them provide significant mediation of encounters with the divine in a manner which effectively shapes participation in and distanciation from them. Thus, the very possibility of encounter with "a divine foundation of reality which is ultimately good, which does not wish evil nor create evil, but affirms and upholds our autonomous personhood" [68] is both enabled and suppressed by the conditions and particularities of human existence.

The accounts of religious experience with which I began Chapter 4 of this work illustrate this conclusion. In each case, the mediating power of the patriarchal context of these women's lives constitutes an alienation and fragmentation of the subjects' relations with the divine itself. Yet this relation persists, albeit in distorted form which both conceals and discloses the fact of that relatedness. The subjects continue to long for wholeness; and in their explicitly feminist experience, they are enabled to break through the negative mediations of patriarchy and discover validity and meaning in their longing for wholeness and connection.

Thus, the emergence of feminist consciousness contributes to a conversion experience: the divine is newly encountered via manifestation as fellow sufferer of violent suppression and degradation;[69] as "Everything that is or ever was or ever will be";[70] as movement and power that awakens, sparks, and inspires.[71] These manifestations then are expressed in a combination of images drawn both from the subjects' feminist experience, and from the context in which that experience occurs and is subjected to reflection. These images are ambiguous in at least two ways. First, they utilize traditional symbols which have been linked with both oppressive and liberating proclamation. Second, they both disclose and conceal the authentic novelty of the encounter, in that the use of customary symbols continues to evoke familiar responses as well even as it transforms. Yet in the midst of this ambiguity, feminist reflection on "primal re-encounter with divine reality" and "the primary intuitions of religious experience"[72] expresses and empowers liberating action which itself further reduces the distorting mediations of the patriarchal contexts of human life and experience.

In other words, women's subjugation by and resistance to patriarchy has specifically religious importance and imperative force which are reflected in and furthered by the critical and reconstructive tasks of feminist theology. Finally, these tasks are aimed not only at interpretation, but at the actual reconstitution of the human subject. And without such reconstitution, those factors of domination which distort human consciousness and experience have significant effect on human capacity authentically to encounter the divine itself in the midst of human existence.

Notes

1.   See, for example, Schüssler Fiorenza, *Bread Not Stone*, 44 and *passim;* Heyward, *Our Passion for Justice*, ch. 2, 25; Ruether, *Sexism and God-Talk*, ch. 1; and Young, 62ff.

2.   My discussion here relies particularly on *To Mend the World: Foundations of Future Jewish Thought*, in which Fackenheim seeks out the connection between revelation and historical existence, particularly when such existence must be characterized as "murder and manslaughter," [*Mord und Totschlag*] as it must after the Holocaust and in situations of ongoing massive unjust suffering. Fackenheim defines post-Holocaust thought as "not only located temporally after the Holocaust but also affected by it." (*To Mend the World*, 13 n.3.) Fackenheim's considerations focus on remembrance of the event and particularly the witness of its silenced and murdered victims, who are otherwise rendered absent from history as the record of human being. I am indebted to Gary Zimmerman for many discussions which have influenced my thought in this section.

3.   Here Fackenheim is following Heidegger's understanding of being as being-toward-death which participates in the history of the actualities of authentic being. (Ibid., 147-166 and passim.) This understanding of being is consistent with the description of consciousness and experience I have given in the preceding section.

4.   Ibid., 74.

5.   Ibid., 75-77, 87-90.

6.   Fackenheim is here following Franz Rosenzweig's *The Star of Redemption*, which distinguishes two covenants, and relates Judaism and Christianity on the basis of birth (in the first case) and baptism (in the second). Each of these requires the other to understand the revelation accorded it. (*To Mend the World*, 69ff. is an extended discussion of *The Star of Redemption*.)

7.   The Holocaust world of massive dehumanization and destruction was directed at human persons on the basis of their being rather than their doing; that is, it was directed at the Jews *simply and only* because they were Jews by heritage and by birth. (This phenomenon has considerable import for any feminist analysis of history, that is, on any analysis of history which recognizes the suppression and silencing of women and women's experience on the basis of their gender.) The point of this massive assault was not only the death of the victims, but also their complete dehumanization, indeed their visible self-transformation

8.   Entering the Holocaust world and confronting its logic of destruction discloses a *novum*, an unprecedented event of shattering import which redefines existence in completely dehumanized terms, both for the victims--particularly the *Muselmänner* and the burning children--and for those implicated solely by their *not* being victims. (Ibid., 201-215.) The world-shattering impact of the Holocaust comes from its scope, its character, and its inexplicability.   As Soren Kierkegaard wrote, "Is then the inexplicable explained by saying that it has occurred only once in the world? Or is not this the inexplicable, that it did occur? And has not this fact, that it did occur, the power to make everything inexplicable, even the most explicable events?" (*Either/Or* [New York: Anchor, 1959], 2:344ff; quoted by Fackenheim, *To Mend the World*, 134-135 and passim.)

9.   "Astoundingly, the world of the Holocaust, paralyzing our thought long after, did not succeed in wholly paralyzing, even as the world held total sway, some of those most exposed to it. . . ." (Ibid., 23-24.) This statement, with modifications, is Fackenheim's constant refrain.

10.   Ibid., 225.

11.   As survivor Pelagia Lewinska writes: "At the outset the living places, the ditches, the mud, the piles of excrement behind the blocks, had appalled me with the horrible filth. . . . And then I saw the light! I saw that it was not a question of disorder or lack of organization but

that, on the contrary, a very thoroughly considered conscious idea was in the back of the camp's existence.

. . . They wished to abase us, to destroy our human dignity, to efface every vestige of humanity, to return us to the level of wild animals, to fill us with horror and contempt toward ourselves and our fellows. But from the instant that I grasped the motivating principle . . . it was as if I had been awakened from a dream. . . . I felt under orders to live. . . . And if I did die in Auschwitz, it would be as a human being. . . . And a terrible struggle began which went

12. Ibid., 223-224.

13. Fackenheim here follows the lead of Heidegger; see *To Mend the World*, 162-166.

14. Ibid., 239.

15. "The Idea of Man can be--has been--destroyed, for humanity can be--has been--destroyed. But because humanity itself *has been* mended--*in* some men and women *by* some men and women--the Idea of Man *can* be mended." (Ibid., 276.) The concept of mending--*Tikkun*--as Fackenheim uses it comes from the rituals of kabbalistic Judaism. See ibid., 252ff.

16. This conclusion is necessitated particularly by the phenomenon of the *Muselmänner*, defined by Primo Levi as "the drowned, [who] form the backbone of the camp, an anonymous mass, continuously renewed and always identical, of non-men who march and labour in silence, the divine spark dead within them, already too empty really to suffer. One hesitates to call them living; one hesitates to call their death death." (*Survival in Auschwitz*, 82; quoted in Fackenheim, *To Mend the World*, 99-100.)

17. Ibid., 250-294. This form of resistance differs from that of the victims: it is one based in doing (opposition) rather than being (survival); that is, it is one where resisting thought might be distinguished from unremitting struggle between life and death.

18. Ibid., 276 and passim.

19. In this regard, Fackenheim cites Gershom Scholem: "The impulse below calls forth an impulse above." (*Major Trends in Jewish Mysticism* [New York: Schocken, 1965], 27, 260ff., 232 ff., and passim; quoted in Fackenheim, ibid., 253.) Christians might now--as then--appeal to the power of prayer; see ibid., 290ff.

20. See Fackenheim's essay "The Commanding Voice of Auschwitz," in *God's Presence in History: Jewish Affirmations and Philosophical Reflections* (New York: New York University Press, 1970), 71-93.

21.   This question presses in part because of Fackenheim's construal of the Holocaust as unique and unprecedented, in some manner unlike any other events of massive human suffering. Feminist thought, on the other hand, identifies the ongoing suffering of women under patriarchy not as event (if that word implies a specifiable period within the whole of history), but as a constant in recorded history and-- in the view of some--as the foundation of much of that history. I am indebted to Gary Zimmerman, Janet MacLean, and Jennifer Brown for a number of the elements of this discussion.

22.   Elements like these in the Holocaust are, I take it, the decisive ones for Fackenheim's designation of it as a rupture. For discussion of the history of resistance in varying situations, see Welch, *A Feminist Ethic of Risk*, 8 and passim. See also the various histories of subjugation which reflect on the peculiarly American institution of slavery and racism, on imperial conquest throughout the world, and on ethnic and tribal warfare in the Twentieth Century.

23.   Catharine MacKinnon argues that women have been subjugated or objectified most fundamentally around their sexuality. (MacKinnon, *passim.*) MacKinnon's interpretation, it seems to me, arises from her legitimate desire to indicate how women have always also been actors or agents in human history. It will be my argument that construing history under the rubric of resistance (as Gerda Lerner promises to do in a second volume to *The Creation of Patriarchy*) has the precise value of understanding all victims as also agents. This, in turn, allows a more profound assessment of the subjugation of women; that is, one that does not artificially isolate one element of being as the target of oppressive ideologies and practices.

24.   The murderous intent directed toward women by patriarchy is different in kind from that directed toward the Jews, then, because the situation of women *vis a vis* the dominant culture is different. Some women have also benefitted in some ways from the very system which has also sought their dehumanization, through the derivative status and privilege conferred on some women because of their relations with powerful or privileged men and male groups. Thus, the subjugation, degradation, dehumanization, and destruction of some women is less severe than that of others--but only because of class and race differences, not because of some modification in misogyny itself. At the same time, other women are subjected to even greater degrees of oppression. This differentiation also divides women as a group against themselves, mitigating against the identification by women of the common elements in their situations, and so diminishing the likelihood

and scope of their organized resistance. See Ruether, *New Woman/New Earth*, ch. 5; and the final chapter of Lerner, *The Creation of Patriarchy* (where Lerner summarizes her study in precisely these terms).

25. To understand the Holocaust in this way does not mean that never before have massive dehumanization and destruction occurred. For example, the Middle Passage of Africans into slavery in the Americas ought also to be widely recognized as an event of massive dehumanization and accompanying resistance, with the same rupturing power and need for mending as Fackenheim has so carefully explored in the Holocaust of the Europeans Jews.

26. See Fackenheim on the *Muselmänner*, *To Mend the World*, 217.

27. Katie Geneva Cannon, *Black Womanist Ethics* (Atlanta: Scholars Press, 1988), 2-3. See also Welch, *A Feminist Ethic of Risk*, Chapter 2, "The Ethic of Control."

28. For example, prior to his full elaboration of resistance as reality and category, Fackenheim often finds it necessary to address the question of the adequacy of Jewish resistance to the Holocaust. The persistence of this question is one reason 'for Fackenheim's insistence that

29. As Fackenheim notes, this means also recreating the notions of the agency and passivity of the executioners and those who failed to act on behalf of the victims. See *To Mend the World*, 225-240. Welch cogently argues that resistance "incorporates both the accommodation necessary to survival and the creative defiance that lays the groundwork for change in the future." (*A Feminist Ethic of Risk*, 77.)

30. See Fackenheim on the imperative arising from Auschwitz; Moltmann, *The Crucified God*, passim; and Welch, *A Feminist Ethic of Risk*, passim.

31. That women's history can legitimately be construed precisely under the rubric of resistance is ever more amply demonstrated by the many excellent historical projects of feminist historians. See, for example, Lerner's *The Creation of Patriarchy* and Fox-Genovese's *Within the Plantation Household: Black and White Women of the Old South*.

32. For example, Ruether presumes such a connection in her conclusion that feminist theology "is engaged in a primal re-encounter with divine reality," a claim illustrated and discussed in the previous chapter, where the entirety of Ruether's statement can be found.

33.   The feminist theologian who most nearly does so is Patricia Wilson-Kastner, whose epistemology and theology are discussed at length below.   Sharon Welch's recent *A Feminist Ethic of Risk* deliberately and explicitly eschews transcendence for immanence (168-169; 172-180.)

34.   Fackenheim, *To Mend the World*, 162-166.

35.   Religious experience overall and in its various aspects can be thematized or typified in a wide variety of ways. I have selected the typology developed by Paul Ricoeur and David Tracy (discussed in this section) because it provides a heuristic device which is more appropriate than are other candidates to the feminist Christologies I am studying. All four of the Christologies studied in this book seem to fall within H. Richard Niebuhr's "Christ transforming culture" type. More recently, George Rupp has classified Christologies according to four types; but the approaches of these Anglo-American feminists seem to combine what he designates as realist-transactional and nominalist-transactional types.   (George Rupp, *Christologies and Cultures: Toward a Typology of Religious Worldviews* [The Hague and Paris: Mouton, 1974]) Eugene TeSelle's emphasis on the humanity of Christ has much in common with all four of the feminist authors I have studied; but his move to a Logos type does not provide an adequate framework for the prophetic-exemplar approach taken by Ruether, nor for the less pronounced emphasis on the prophetic in the other three. (Eugene TeSelle, *Christ in Context: Divine Purpose and Human Possibility* [Philadelphia: Fortress Press, 1975]) Conversely, the discussion of Christ as Word in Peter C. Hodgson's *Jesus--Word and Presence: An Essay in Christology* (Philadelphia: Fortress Press, 1971) will not account for the recovery of the Wisdom-Logos strand effected by Wilson-Kastner, Suchocki, and Heyward. In addition, the manifestation-proclamation typology of Ricoeur and Tracy is also particularly suited to an examination of the importance of human experience in shaping Christology in a way not found in these other studies.

36.   Paul Ricoeur, "Manifestation and Proclamation," in *Journal of the Blaisdell Institute* 12 (Winter 1978): 13-35; Tracy, *Analogical Imagination*, Chapter 5 ("The Religious Classic: Manifestation and Proclamation") and Chapter 9 ("Christian Reposes in the Contemporary Situation: Family Resemblances and Family Quarrels").

37.   Ricoeur, 14.

38.   Ibid., 15.

39. Ibid., 16-17. These traits can be gathered in a logic of correspondence which is bound by symbolism drawn from nature requiring only "a minimal hermeneutics." These natural symbols are not (like metaphors) "free invention[s] of discourse" the understanding of which "brings into play a labor of language." (Ibid., 19-20.) According to Ricoeur, "nature speaks of the depth from which its order has emerged and toward which chaos it may always regress." (Ibid., 18) These symbols adhere to and derive their force from the elements they use; and they are "legitimated by the immediate liaison between the appearance and its meaning." (Ibid., 16-17)

40. Idols (as expressions of hierophanies) are opposed by a "theology of the Name"; ethics is opposed to aesthetics; and proclamatory ritual is the expression of "a fundamentally historical vision of reality" where the human environment is desacrilized. (Ibid., 22-23.)

41. Ibid., 23-26.

42. Ibid., 27-28.

43. Ibid., 32.

44. Ibid., 34.

45. "In truth, without the support and renewing power of the sacred cosmos and the sacredness of vital nature, the word itself becomes abstract and cerebral. Only the incarnation of the ancient symbolism ceaselessly reinterpreted gives this word something to say, not only to our understanding and will, but also to our imagination and our heart; in short, to the whole human being." (Ibid., 35.)

46. Tracy, *Analogical Imagination*, 201.

47. As Tracy writes, the particular self of the experiencing subject is first freed "into a sense of a real participation in, a belonging to, a wider and deeper reality than the self or the community" and then "positively distanced from the original experience in order to express the meaning of that experience . . . to others who may not now share it, but can share its meaning through experiencing the now-rendered expression." (Ibid., 199-200.)

48. Further, Tracy notes, expressions of encounter with the divine are transformed and transmuted not only by the internal dialectic manifestation-proclamation, but also by the mediations of historical existence.

49. These are emphases only: just as the dialectic between participation and distanciation is found within any particular event of disclosure-concealment, so elements of manifestation will and must be found in even the most emphatically proclamatory religious expression.

This fact mitigates against "overclaims" in favor of either emphasis. (Ibid., 203-4, 212.)
 50. Ibid., 215, 218.
 51. Ibid., 208.
 52. Ogden, *Point of Christology*, 82f. and passim (on representation of God), and 17 and passim (on authenticity).
 53. Tracy, *Analogical Imagination*, 330-331.
 54. Ibid., 203.
 55. Ibid., 208.
 56. Ibid., 311.
 57. Ibid., 211. "The Christian religion is one in which the word does negate any claim to a mode of participation which logically approaches identity or existentially relaxes into complacency" in its understanding of the relation between God, self, and world. (Thus, Christianity's radical rejections of idolatry.) But Christianity also "includes and demands genuine manifestation"; and thus its doctrines of creation, which identify nature as a manifestation of God's power. (Ibid., 214.)
 58. Ibid., 209.
 59. In Tracy's view, the dialectic relation between proclamation and manifestation within Christianity is that between focal power and enveloping ground which affect each other through defamiliarization and transformation. The interlocking of prophetic, ethical, and historical strands with mystical, metaphysical, and aesthetic ones demonstrates the adequacy of this analysis. (Ibid., 215.) And the rooting of these strands in the central, "classic event and person of Jesus Christ as true word *and* decisive manifestation" grounds Christianity "in the dialectics of an enveloping always-already manifestation" seen in doctrines of creation and incarnation, manifestation which is "constantly transformed by a defamiliarizing, often shattering, not-yet proclamation" of cross and eschaton. (Tracy uses this typology at a later point to analyze the contemporary development of Christology [*Analogical Imagination*, 307-338]; and I will have recourse to this discussion in my own discussions of Christology, below.) Yet "both Christian manifestation and proclamation are ultimately rooted in that God whose radical otherness in freedom posits itself to us as the radical immanence of an all-pervasive, defamiliarizing, shattering, enveloping love in cosmos, in history, in the self." (Ibid., 218.)
 60. Ibid., 371.

61. Other mediators Tracy identifies are critical-philosophical reflection (377-379) and the extraordinary (382-384).
62. See my discussion of the Wisdom-Logos Christologies of Patricia Wilson-Kastner, Marjorie Hewitt Suchocki, and Carter Heyward, below. Intensification of the everyday is also characteristic of the post-biblical feminism of Mary Daly and Carol P. Christ, among others.
63. Tracy, *Analogical Imagination*, 380-382. As Carol Christ and Judith Plaskow note, "For feminists, *experience* refers simply to the fabric of life as it is lived." ("Introduction: Womanspirit Rising," in *Womanspirit Rising*, 6.) As is clear from my discussion of experience earlier in this book, I would take issue with the designation of this understanding as "simple." But Christ and Plaskow's emphasis on dailiness, concreteness, and the ordinary is an accurate understanding of the bent of feminist thought.
64. Ibid., 390.
65. Ibid., 390.
66. It is important to note that political theologies' explicit "eschatological proviso" or insistence on the proleptic character of contemporary Christian experience does not automatically or facilely locate these theologies only within the ideal type of proclamation. That is, the experiences associated with manifestation--participation, the graced nature of all of existence, the revelatory or disclosive power of creation--are significantly present at the root of some of these formulations. (Tracy mentions, in this category, the work of Metz and Gutierrez. As I shall argue later, Heyward, Suchocki, and Wilson-Kastner, among the feminists I will study in detail here, also belong in this group.)
Also noteworthy is that the understanding of proclamation is substantially altered not in its focus on the challenge provided by distanciation or alienation, but in its emphasis on the social and political rather than internal and personal aspects of this experience. (Tracy here mentions Moltmann and Cone, among others and, among feminist theologians, Ruether.) When the transformation effected by the primacy of praxis is understood as precisely that--a transformation of a dialectic which nevertheless continues to be present--both the actual shape and interests of these theologies and their relation to other theologies both traditional and contemporary become more readily evident. That this is helpful to any approach to theology which wishes to be genuinely conversational is surely

67.   Recall, again, the four narratives at the beginning of Chapter 4.

68.   Ruether, "The Future of Feminist Theology," 710f.

69.   Christ and Ruether; see Chapter 4.

70.   Walker; see Chapter 4.

71.   Heyward; see Chapter 4.

72.   Ruether; see Chapter 4.

Chapter 6

The Relation of Women's Experience to Christology

The purpose of the second part of this book is to provide a framework within which the feminist Christological problem described in Part One can be addressed. That problem emerges from the dilemmas of Christian feminist experience, which finds in Christianity both a major contributor to the patriarchal subjugation of women *and* an indispensable source of hope for liberation and transformation leading to wholeness for women and for the world.

In order to account for this phenomenon, feminist theology appeals to women's experience. Yet the precise meaning and status of that appeal has all too often been unclear. In Chapter 4, I began to develop a notion of experience which I judge to be a relatively adequate elaboration of that appeal. Narratives of women's feminist religious experience lend themselves to an analysis of experience as structurally complex and relational, constituted by reflection arising out of consciousness that is formed by the interaction of social, psychological, symbolic, historical, and systemic aspects of existence. I have argued that the view of experience that I developed can account for significant commonalities and differences in concrete experience. I have also suggested that attention to structural analysis can itself resist the tendency to take particular concrete experiences as universal, a tendency that continues the very history of domination and suppression against which feminist and womanist theory and practice are directed.

In Chapter 5, I related this notion of experience as historically and relationally constituted to the perennial question of the relation of history and transcendence. In exploring and expanding the religious thought of Emil Fackenheim, I argued that beginning from the experience of the victims of history provides a fruitful avenue for mending and transforming the ruptures of history and its relation to transcendence that situations of massive dehumanization engender. With Fackenheim, I argued that the phenomenon of resistance--understood as the maintenance of a shred of humanity in the midst of massive suffering--is a transformative event with metaphysical and ethical importance. Because resistance is both possible and actual, it serves to mend the ruptured relation between concrete being in history and transcendent Being.

I then turned to a phenomenological description of religious experience as such, using a dialectical typology to show how human experiences of encounter with the divine through participation and distanciation express relation to the divine as both manifested and proclaimed in human existence. I modified that typology by suggesting that a third element--liberating action in the midst of daily life--also has revelatory power. I concluded by suggesting that the narratives of feminist religious experience, when understood in light of the multi-faceted descriptions of experience that I have developed, suggest a specific and urgent religious importance to the tasks of feminist theology.

In this chapter, I will relate my discussion of experience to the problems facing Christology in the contemporary period. This relationship has three aspects that will be discussed in this chapter. Because contemporary theological formulations correlate contemporary experience with Christian tradition, an explicit discussion of the problems of such correlation in feminist theology is necessary; and such discussion will form the first part of this chapter. Second, I will turn once again to the work of F. D. Maurice to suggest how Christology may connect human experience (formed by interactions of tradition and contemporary existence) to God. With Maurice, I will suggest that Christology gives expression to a two-fold revelation of the relation of God to humankind, and of human persons to each other and to God. Next, I will restate the criteria of adequacy initially stated in Chapter 3. I will then conclude this part of the book with a restatement of the feminist Christological problem and a preliminary overview of the approaches to Christology found in contemporary feminist theology.

The Relation of Experience and Tradition

In contemporary theological method, the adequacy of theological formulations is assessed relative to two factors: contemporary human experience, and Christian tradition (with emphasis on the earliest traditions as these are found primarily in Scripture). Thus far in this book, I have focused my discussion on the nature of human experience. This has been the case because feminist theologies rely on women's experience as a (if not the) primary source and norm. I have also suggested that Christian tradition is problematic for feminist theology because of its androcentric and misogynist orientation and content. It is this orientation and content, together with theology's commitment to adequacy to Christian tradition, that has led some feminists to forsake Biblical traditions and the religions they support in favor of spiritual and religious views that are less overtly patriarchal. [1] Carol Christ aptly summarizes the challenge of the post-biblical feminist critique in writing that

A serious Christian response to [feminist] criticism of the core symbolism of Christianity either will have to show that the core symbolism of Father and Son do not have the effect of reinforcing and legitimating male power and female submission, or it will have to transform Christian imagery at its very core. [2]

This challenge has been met in numerous ways: the search for a "usable" tradition (or set of traditions) that has always stood over against patriarchal domination; the retrieval and reconstruction of marginalized, suppressed, and distorted strands of Christian thought and practice that have afforded a measure of equality for women; the broadening of the notion of "tradition" beyond strands customarily deemed orthodox; and the subordination of tradition as a source and norm to the primacy of women's experience. [3]

It is not the purpose of this discussion to elaborate on and evaluate these options. Rather, I wish to address two matters, the first venturing a description of tradition that parallels my earlier discussion of experience, and the second briefly suggesting some persistent themes found in many strands of tradition that are useful to contemporary feminist theology.

The Shape of Tradition

In contemporary theological discussions, "tradition" as a category refers not to an external and immutable body of material which is given to current experience, but rather to the activities and beliefs of many, diverse historical communities over time. [4] These activities and beliefs, together with the structures and processes by which they are transmitted across time and space, form the preunderstanding that is a critical component of any religious experience understood to be constituted by the complex interaction of many factors. [5] This body of belief and practice is interpreted, formed, and re-formed to construct the community's self-understanding in continuity with its constitutive history and beliefs. [6] The authority of the tradition is, then, in part the authority of the community: the tradition and the community--currently as well as historically-- both author and authorize each other, whatever other source(s) of authority they may have. [7]

Tradition and experience, then, are interlocked both in process and in content. In that tradition as a body of beliefs is the reflective product of a community over time, it is a body of cumulative experience.[8] At the same time, experience, because it takes place in community and in history, is shaped and given value by the community's sense of itself, which includes its reflections on its history, which is to say, its traditions. In other words, the meaning of any given experience will be determined in part by a community's judgment of it as authoritative, normal, or deviant; and that judgment is made in light of the historical and contemporary elements that form its identity.

This mutual interrelationship between tradition and experience is found not just at the level of manifest content, but also in those deep processes and structures which shape consciousness and self-understanding. Language, symbol, ritual, and other forms of individual and corporate expression shape the ways in which life may be experienced and understood. Thus, even new experiences are found to have an element of the familiar when they are understood.[9] Reciprocally, understanding of new experience often entails a reshaping or reinterpretation of the past, that is, a reshaping of history and tradition through development, correction, and confrontation.[10]

The importance of the interrelationship of tradition and experience is great, then, in that the two effect and affect each other at every level of human existence. Nor does the effective interrelationship of tradition and experience cease in the present. It is also projected into the future, the shape of which is imagined and, indeed, to some extent created on the strength of possibilities and imaginings in the present as those are shaped by the past.

It is important to note, however, that tradition and experience are related not only as enablers one of the other, but also as limiters. Tradition and experience are both always ambiguous.[11] For women, that ambiguity is located most compellingly in the fact that tradition and experience support both domination and liberation. Feminist analysis of the history of women's existence and experience indicates that the community that authors, authorizes, and is authorized by western religious traditions has been and is one of patriarchal domination as well as one of freedom. That is to say, whatever the process of transmission may disclose, it also conceals the significant participation of women. This patriarchal, androcentric character is pervasively embedded in the very languages, texts, and traditions that are used as sources and norms.

Furthermore, what is considered appropriate experience in the present--either understandable or permissible--is in significant measure limited by what is *rendered* understandable and *deemed* permissible by the tradition that shapes that experience. [12] Thus, the content of a particular tradition and the community-based process of transmission both shape and regulate experience related to that tradition.

Because of their patriarchal roots and androcentric character, most Christian traditions stand in some tension with contemporary experience in the struggle for liberation, even while that hope for liberation is itself in some measure rooted or grounded in the very events that tradition seeks to represent. That is, traditions are "frequent betrayer[s] of the very event[s] entrusted to [their] care." [13]   Therefore, unreconstructed traditions cannot be an adequate norm for feminist theology, even if they can (within some limits) serve as a source. [14]

In sum, then, "Christian tradition" may be taken to refer to a complex and fluid body of material that is constantly subjected to reinterpretation and reconstruction, rather than to a univocal and static corpus.   On this view, tradition is one of the constituters of experience, contributing to the shaping and reshaping of consciousness. But it is also shaped and reshaped *by* experience, from its origins in at-one-time contemporary events and through its subsequent reappropriations by the community that authorizes it.

The Recovery of Traditions of Wholeness and Freedom

It is important to note that, with other contemporary theologians, feminist theologians argue that critical evaluation and reconstruction of the Christian tradition as a whole is an act of fidelity to the Christian tradition itself, which contains self-critical and self-reformatory elements that press toward deideologization as well as demythologization. [15] These appeals rely on reference to a number of strands within the large body of Christian traditions, strands that can be broadly thematized under two headings: wholeness and freedom.

As is apparent from the narratives at the beginning of Chapter 4, and as will become more evident in Part Three, feminist religious experience and theological formulation express longings for and intuitions of a gracious whole that encompasses and informs human existence, inspiring and moving toward freedom and well-being within human existence and beyond it. This whole is experienced as a gracious and destabilizing power present with--yet other than--the experiencing subject.[16] Encounter with this power (variously named as God, God/ess, the Spirit, and so on) both gives meaning to and transforms present existence.

It is noteworthy that these elements are themselves significant strands in the very traditions that support domination as well as in the prophetic elements of Scripture, in the Wisdom traditions that connect daily lived experience with the presence of the divine, in the testimony of transformed lives of named and unnamed persons of faith throughout history, and in the eschatological hope for divine fulfillment of human longings and aspirations.

In other words, in feminist religious experience, the divine is encountered both as gracious manifestation of the possibility of authentic liberation, and as judge of historic and continuing distortion and suppression of such possibilities.[17] Profoundly present in these experiences is the transformation of the mediation of encounter with the divine that is part of the process of transmission of tradition, as well as the shifting of the mediations that contribute to the constitution of present experience.[18] Indeed, I would argue, it is feminist religious experience that renders a suspect tradition fundamentally trustworthy despite and even in the midst of the negative realties which that same tradition contains.[19]

Far from rejecting either the process of transmission as such, or the content that is transmitted, feminist theologians seek to criticize the narrowness and so the inadequacy of both, and to reconstruct both process and content to reflect the full diversity of all the communities, beliefs, and practices that form the pre-understanding not only of feminist experience, but also of religious experience taken as disclosive of the whole.[20] The relation of tradition and experience within feminist theology, then, is dialogical, the dialogue partners being feminist religious experience in the struggle for liberation (on the one hand), and (on the other) the many components that constitute that experience, one of which is traditions that drive ambiguously toward both domination and liberation.[21]

The Relation of Women's Experience to Christology

For feminist and womanist Christologies--to which I shall turn in the remaining chapters of this book--encounter with the divine is mediated not only by feminist experience in the midst of patriarchal domination. It is also mediated by understandings of Jesus as the Christ, that is, as in some sense for Christians the representation of the relation between humanity and divinity. For feminist Christology as for all Christology, Jesus the Christ is taken to disclose something decisive about the nature and activity of the ultimate or transcendent, and the connection of human experience with that ultimate.

The connection between the ultimate and the historical is, of course, a perennial philosophical and theological problem, one that has not become any easier to resolve over the centuries. Nor is it my intention to suggest a new resolution to this dilemma in this present work. Here, I will once again use the work of F. D. Maurice to indicate the avenue of resolution upon which my own work currently relies. This avenue is fruitful because it ties together some of the themes developed in these three chapters: the longing for connection and wholeness, resistance to dehumanization and fragmentation, and the confirmation (and reconstruction) of tradition by contemporary experience.

One of Maurice's root principles was that "all human beings constantly experience God, so that 'the whole truth, in all its substance, in all its juiciness, lies at the roots of our own being and sustains it.'"[22] That is, all human beings have a universal faculty that pervades all human experience and that in principle drives every human consciousness beyond itself to the transcendent, to God.[23] This faculty devolves upon humanity by virtue of humankind's creation by God and in God's image. And its presence in human persons is verified by the human sense of what we ought to be and to become.[24] Or, to put it another way, "we can know nothing of ourselves till we look above ourselves. We can see light only in God's light. The knowledge of man is possible, because the knowledge of God is possible."[25] Therefore, every aspect of human existence is a "hint" about the nature of humanity, of divinity, and of the unbreakable relation between the two.[26]

However, since human existence is distorted by the basic sin of presumed separation from God and by the concrete social and personal consequences of this sin--which, for Maurice as for contemporary feminists, includes structures of dehumanization--some revelation is needed to disclose this essential "fact" about human existence. For Christians, that revelation comes through recognition of Jesus as both Son of God and Son of Man. As Son of God, Christ reveals "God to men"; and as Son of Man, Christ reveals "men to themselves."[27] This two-fold revelation answers the human longing for vindication of the felt connection to the transcendent, and it does so by affirming that all persons are children of God who are called to "rise and go to the Father."[28] As Busk notes, "the Son of Man reveals that although we turn away from the Father through sin, we are related to him because he freely desires to re-establish that relation and lovingly accept us again as his child."[29]

God's desire for renewed relation with humanity is richly vindicated, in Maurice's view, by human resistance to evil and the associated longing for connection that is found in that resistance. For example, Maurice considers Job's relentless insistence that his suffering is unmerited to be causally connected to his affirmation that there is a living redeemer whom Job will encounter in the flesh.[30] That longing is met by God's answer to Job out of the whirlwind, which brings Job to a confession of his own humility and into the loving embrace of God.[31] This

Biblical model vindicates the experience of the poor and the afflicted that they are righteous, despite the fact that the present conditions of their existence may suggest otherwise. Conversely, the factuality of Scripture is "abundantly confirmed by daily observation" of human existence and reflection on that existence.[32]

For the Christian, every confirmation of both Scripture and experience is itself decisively confirmed by faithful encounter with Jesus the Christ, whose humbling of himself in identifying with humanity in the incarnation shows that "Christ's union with the Father is not an exception to what it means to be a human being but history's chief exemplification of it."[33] Thus, Maurice can write,

> The truth is that every man is in Christ; the condemnation of every man is, that he will not own the truth; he will not *act* as if this were *true*, he will not believe that which is the truth, that, except he were joined to Christ, he could not think, breathe, live a single hour.[34]

Or, "In [Christ] we find how humanity has been a holy thing, though each man felt himself to be unholy. . . . In Him it is proved that man is meant to have his dwelling with God."[35] Humanity has been created to be in communion with its creator; and it is the Christ who reveals this fact about human constitution and re-establishes the unity between human creatures and the divine creator and redeemer.

For feminist Christology, this means that recognition of the connection between one's understanding of Christ and resistance to dehumanization and the transformation that accompanies it provides both vindication of that resistance and affirmation of the presence of God in the midst of human struggles for liberation and transformation. Contemporary experience, that is, both validates and is clarified by the mediation that belief in Jesus as the Christ provides within the context of Christian feminism. Furthermore, this validation and clarification confirm the longing for something beyond the self in the present historical context. As Maurice would put it, contemporary experience of resistance and transformation provides a glimpse of eternal life, understood as "a kingdom of Heaven within--a kingdom of Heaven ever present with us now; different in kind from the visible world, but affecting it, and swaying its movements continually. . . ."[36] This sense of presence and promise grounds liberating action that transforms the present historical context and the experience of those living within it. Presence and transformation are both decisively re-presented for feminist Christians in their experiences and interpretations of Jesus as the Christ.

Criteria of Adequacy Revisited

In the preceding chapter, I proposed three criteria for the assessment of feminist proposals to give theological form to the claim that, for Christians, Jesus is the Christ. These criteria are adequacy to Christian traditions, adequacy to contemporary women's experience, and adequacy to a liberated future. The discussion of these three chapters makes it possible to elaborate these criteria more fully.

For feminist theology, women's experience serves as both source and norm. Yet the difficulties of defining the term "experience" are many. I have argued in Chapter 4 that it is necessary to understand experience as a complex and fluid process in which the many factors of human existence are understood to constitute the human subject and human consciousness relationally. These factors are social and psychological, historic and current, religious and "secular." The consciousness of the human subject is constructed by her engagement with and reflection on her social context; and her practice or agency in that context affects the context itself. Experience thus is to be understood as an interactive process whose content changes with location and time. If theology is to be adequate to experience, on this reading, it must attend to all of the many factors by which the human subject is constituted, and to the processes of interaction among them. Further, this attention must respect differences in subjects' experience, that is, among varying groups and over time. If, as I have argued, the processes of experience are common, attention to difference or particularity can still be framed within the notion of a single humanity,[37] but without the false universalism which has characterized much of contemporary theology to this point.

I have also argued that women's experience under the conditions of patriarchy can be thematized under the rubric of resistance, when resistance is understood as the victims' maintenance of a shred of humanity in situations of dehumanizing oppression. Resistance illumines the irreducible humanity of the dehumanized, and it does so on the basis of their own experience. Resistance may also be an occasion through which the possibility of meaning is grasped and recreated; it may be an occasion of transformation or mending. In other words, the concrete historical experience of resistance contains within it the possibility of transcendence; and that transcendence has the power to reconstitute the world.

Historical transcendence is, in religious terms, in some sense experienced as encounter with the divine. In elaborating a dialectic of manifestation and proclamation, I have characterized this encounter in terms of participation and nonparticipation. The intensification of participation that characterizes experiences of manifestation emphasizes continuity between the sacred and the ordinary, while the intensification of nonparticipation that characterizes experiences of proclamation emphasizes disruption and distanciation. These polarities are generatively related. And genuine religious expression always contains both moments, in mutually corrective tension, as my brief examination of four texts describing feminist religious experience indicates.

In order to approach relative adequacy in relation to experience, then, contemporary theology must not only attend to the complex social, cultural, and historical factors by which human consciousness is constituted and changed. It must also examine the relation between history and transcendence, as that is understood and effected in the concrete experience of human persons. These experiences open up not only into an expanded understanding of the human, but also into new understandings of the divine, who is encountered in the intensities and limits as well as in the ordinariness of human existence. My attention here to the experience of the marginalized and dehumanized suggests that the experiences of these groups in particular can be especially fruitful for contemporary theology: they capture what Ruether calls a "primary intuition," a "belief in a divine foundation of reality which is ultimately good, which does not wish evil nor create evil, but affirms and upholds our autonomous personhood . . ." [38]

I have argued that experience is to be understood relationally and interactively. The same holds true for tradition, which is, I have suggested, a body of cumulative experience that is related dialogically to contemporary experience, with each shaping and re-shaping the other. I have also indicated that, on the basis of women's experience, feminist theology both criticizes and reconstructs tradition to recover the suppressed and silenced presence and participation of women and to interrupt the structures and forces that have brought about that suppression. This reconstruction is an act in fidelity with the tradition itself. Reconstruction may also be understood as an indication that, despite the ambiguity for women of religious tradition, tradition nevertheless may come to be experienced as fundamentally trustworthy to the extent that it both discloses and is transformed by women's experience.

To be relatively adequate to this view, contemporary theology must grapple with the ambiguity of the Christian tradition as it relates to the subjection and liberation of women. This will necessarily include addressing the histories of reception and resistance that are inextricably interwoven in the many traditions that make up Christian thought and practice. This task also entails examining the many complex factors--including non-ecclesial and non-theological elements--that contribute to the shaping and transmission of Christian and related traditions, especially those in contradistinction to which the more prominent strands of Christian tradition have been formed. [39]

In Part II, I have said little explicitly about the importance of the future. In Part I, I indicated that Christian and post-Christian feminist critics alike have identified Christianity's orientation to its patriarchal past as a major problem for contemporary feminist religious thought. There I suggested that, to achieve relative adequacy, Christian feminist theology must demonstrate how feminist Christianity contributes to a viable, liberated future for women as the lowest of the low. Such demonstration will indicate how Christianity may contribute to a viable future for all of humanity, and for the earth itself. [40]

The vision of a liberated future toward which Christian feminism desires to move emerges out of both tradition and contemporary experience, as I shall indicate in the following chapters. In line with other eschatologically oriented theologies, Christian feminist theologies are interested in reconstructing both theology and ethics to aid in the liberation of those whose historical and current experience has been one of suppression and subjugation. For many of these peoples, there is no historic past of liberation and well-being to recreate. There are, however, moments and glimpses of partial liberation sufficient to nurture a vision of what may be yet to come. There are also many "red threads" of resistance to domination which can serve as a powerful and inspiring source for both present efforts and future vision. [41]

An adequate construction of such a vision will have to take into account the complex interweaving of historic forces and structures of domination and liberation, and the various movements and actions that have broken long-standing systems of domination. This vision ought also to draw on contemporary efforts for and visions of liberation, attending with some care to the ambiguities and provisionalities of such efforts and visions. Also important will be considerations of the responsibility for the future carried by theologians in the present. For, as my discussions of both tradition and experience suggest, while the future cannot be entirely bound by either present or past, it surely is *shaped* by both.

Although my considerations have focused primarily on feminist discussions concerning human experience and its religious components, how the experience of women is examined, analyzed, and thematized has bearing on the examination, analysis, and thematization of *all* human experience. For centuries, the dominant strands of Christian tradition have attempted to suppress and silence women's experience. But this patriarchal and androcentric suppression has never been entirely successful.[42] In the words of Sojourner Truth, "If the first woman God ever made was strong enough to turn the world upside down all alone, these women together ought to be able to turn it back, and get it right side up again! And now they is asking to do it, the men better let them."[43] Feminist religious experience and the theology arising from it renew this offer and convey this promise.

Notes

1.   See, again, my discussion of the post-biblical feminist critique in Chapter 2.

2.   Christ, "The New Feminist Theology," 205. Christ underscores the seriousness of this point in her claim that if she, Daly, and others making similar claims are correct in their analysis of religious symbolism in general and Christian symbolism in particular, then Christianity is facing a reformation similar in scope and kind to the Reformation of the sixteenth century.   (Christ and Plaskow, "Introduction" in *Womanspirit Rising*, 10.)   Hampson argues that feminism is a revolution that will reshape all theology (*Theology and Feminism*, 1-3). She also notes that no Christian feminist theology has yet answered Daly's challenge. Nor does she think it can be answered as long as feminists use the Bible. (Ibid., 108.)

3.   Schüssler Fiorenza (in *In Memory of Her* and *Bread Not Stone*) and Radford Ruether (in *Sexism and God-Talk* and *Womanguides*) provide lengthy critical discussions of each of these options.

4.   In a recent dictionary article, George H. Tavard writes that a consensus has emerged within the last thirty years that understands Tradition as "the process of transmission," tradition as "the content of what is transmitted," and traditions as "the distinctive inheritance of separate churches and movements." ("Tradition," in *New Dictionary of Theology*, Joseph A. Komonchak, Mary Collins, and Dermot A. Lane, eds. [Wilmington, DE: Michael Glazier, Inc., 1987], 1040. See also Mary McClintock Fulkerson, "Ecclesial Tradition and Social Praxis: A Study in   Theological Method" [Unpublished Ph.D. dissertation, Vanderbilt University, 1986].) I will have recourse to all three meanings in this discussion.

5. Tracy, *Analogical Imagination*, 243 n. 9. Cf. Ogden, "Present Prospects for Empirical Theology," 72: "No one can deny that any interpretation of the scriptural witness has to move within the hermeneutical circle by which all our efforts at understanding are circumscribed. There is always the possibility that the meaning one professes to read out of Scripture is really the meaning he first had to read into it in order even to understand it."

6. Here I am following primarily the discussions of David Tracy, *Analogical Imagination*, 234-240 and related footnotes (243ff.); and Schubert M. Ogden, "The Authority of Scripture for Theology," in *On Theology*, 45-68.

7. Jean C. Lambert, "An 'F Factor'?" 112; Smith, 49; and Ogden, "The Authority of Scripture for Theology," in *On Theology*, 45-68; idem, *The Point of Christology*, 102.

8. Ruether, *Sexism and God-Talk*, 12-18.

9. Edward Schillebeeckx, *Christ: The Experience of Jesus as Lord*, trans. John Bowden. (New York: Seabury, 1980), 40.

10. Tracy, *Analogical Imagination*, 240. Tracy correctly insists that the grounds for development or correction of--or confrontation with--tradition are appropriately "the authoritative expressions of the tradition itself," including its self-corrective, deideologizing prophetic elements.

11. Schillebeeckx, *Christ*, 38 and 66ff.; Tracy, *Analogical Imagination*, 66, 236 and passim.

12. See, for example, Wendy Martyna, "Beyond the 'He/Man/ Approach," in *Signs: Journal of Women in Culture and Society* 5, no. 3 (1980): 482-493; Andrea E. Goldsmith, "Notes on the Tyranny of Language Use," and Jeannette Silvera, "Generic Masculine Words and Thinking," both in *The Voice of Women and Men*, ed. Cheris Kramarae, (Oxford: Pergamon Press, 1980). See also the sources listed in fn. 20, below.

13. Tracy, *Analogical Imagination*, 321. Here, Tracy is referring to the church. I have made the quote plural in order to indicate both the plurality of the traditions that make up the churches, and the betrayal committed by other traditions as well.

14. As we have seen, some feminist religious thinkers (such as Mary Daly, Carol P. Christ, and Daphne Hampson) have rejected Christianity altogether. Others (such as the four Christian feminist theologians discussed in the next several chapters and myself) believe that Christianity is not irredeemably patriarchal, because there are strands and themes throughout Christianity's past which are usable in

a reconstruction of Christian thought and practice that fully incorporates the presence and participation of women.

15.   See, for example, Ruether's defense of the prophetic-liberating paradigm, discussed below. Elisabeth Schüssler Fiorenza argues that for feminist liberation hermeneutics, "The personally and politically reflected experience of oppression and liberation must become the criterion of 'appropriateness' for biblical interpretations." (*Bread Not Stone*, 60.) These arguments easily compare with the defense of deideologization found in Schubert Ogden's *Faith and Freedom* and *Point of Christology*. In those works, Ogden rings the changes on his earlier argument that the Scriptural witness to "the utterly transcendent one" as also one who is universally immanent is the basis of the Scriptural view of humankind as free and responsible. Thus, Ogden concludes that his empirical-existential approach to theology is "a necessary implication of the witness of the Christian faith." ("Present Prospects for Empirical Theology," 73-74.)

16.   See the section on women's religious experience, above.

17.   See my analysis of examples of these encounters, above. As Tracy writes, "Again, as in the general hermeneutical case, this tradition is retrieved as a classic tradition for the interpreter only through a realized experience of the event. Then tradition (and the classics it mediates) does not merely function as unacknowledged horizon of preunderstanding but is personally appropriated *as* tradition and, in that sense, *becomes* the interpreter's tradition." (*Analogical Imagination*, 243 n. 10.) Or, as F. D. Maurice put it, "all true words--the truest most of all--only speak *to* us when they speak *in* us." (*The Doctrine of Sacrifice: Deduced from the Scriptures*. [London: Macmillan and Co., 1879 (new edition)], 2.)

18.   To put this in more properly methodological terms, this experience transforms what is deemed appropriate *and* what is deemed intelligible.

19.   My emphasis here is rather different from that of Tracy's discussion of the tradition's trustworthiness (*Analogical Imagination*, 236 and related footnotes [243 n. 10, 244 n. 13, and 246 n. 26]). On my reading, Tracy appears to assume that theologians *begin* from a position of trust in tradition, and then discover elements of development and correction. I argue that feminist theologians, specifically as feminist, begin from a more ambiguous position, both recognizing the tradition's betrayal of women and their own experience of the tradition as one important source of the desire for liberation that sparks that same recognition.

20.   As Tracy writes, "the route to liberation from the negative realities of a tradition is not to declare the existence of an autonomy that is literally unreal but to enter into a disciplined and responsive conversation with the subject matter--the responses and, above all, the fundamental questions--of the tradition." (*Analogical Imagination*, 100.)

21.   I would agree with David Tracy that the collapse of problems of appropriateness and problems of intelligibility into each other generates confusion. (*Analogical Imagination*, 238.) This confusion is evident in Elisabeth Schüssler Fiorenza's critique of Tracy and Ogden in *Bread Not Stone* (49), which mistakes these revisionist theologians' concern for appropriateness to tradition as not fully critical. To the contrary, throughout their work, Tracy and Ogden both argue clearly and persuasively that any appropriate rendering of tradition must involve exhaustive use of all available critical methodologies, including the method of ideology critique on which Schüssler Fiorenza herself relies. On Schüssler Fiorenza's own failures to make full use of available historical-critical methods, see both Fulkerson and Young.

22.   Busk, 17, quoting *Life*, 1:247.

23.   Busk, 89, 96, and passim.   In 1837, Maurice wrote of a "universal faculty by which we converse with God, and which the learnedest and the poorest possess equally, superior to every other faculty, and the real characteristic of our humanity. . . ." (*Kingdom of Christ* 1838, 2:69. See also Maurice, *What is Revelation? A series of Sermons on the Epiphany; to which are added letters to a student of theology on the Bampton lectures of Mr. Mansel* (Cambridge: Macmillan, 1859), 290, 309-310.

24.   F. D. Maurice, *The Patriarchs and Lawgivers of the Old Testament*, second series (London: Macmillan, 1877), ii.

25.   F. D. Maurice, *What is Revelation*, 479. As was my practice earlier, I have left Maurice's androcentric language intact.

26.   Particularly important for Maurice is the experience of human relationality as both relatedness and difference.   "But since my brother is a being in himself, and not only a brother, since every father is a being in himself, and not only a father,--the actual relation, the living relation, drives us to seek for an Absolute, which lies beyond and behind the Relation." (*What is Revelation*, 276.)

27.   "The Use of the Word Revelation in the New Testament," in *Present-Day Papers on Prominent Questions in Theology*, second series, ed. Alexander Ewing (London: Strahan and Co., 1871), 14.

28. *Kingdom of Christ* 1842, 1:290. Maurice constantly uses variations on this Matthean notion throughout his writing. See, for example, the passage quoted in note 31, below.
29. Busk, 205.
30. "On the Sense of Righteousness in Men, and Their Discovery of a Redeemer," *Theological Essays* 1957, 54-67. Maurice writes, "when these two thoughts, the thought of a righteousness within him which is mightier than the evil, the thought of some deliverance from his suffering which should be also a justification of God, are brought together in his mind[, h]e exclaims, '*I know that my Redeemer liveth; in my flesh I shall see God*'. . . . It is not what this Redeemer may be or do hereafter he chiefly thinks of. He lives. He is with him now. Therefore he calls upon his friends to say whether they do not see that he has the root of the matter in him." (45-46; italics in the original.)
31. "When a man knows that he has a righteous Lord and Judge, who does not plead His omnipotence and His right to punish, but who debates the case with him, who shows him his truth and his error, the sense of Infinite Wisdom, sustaining and carrying out Infinite Love, abases him rapidly. He perceives that he has been measuring himself, and his understanding, against that Love, that Wisdom. A feeling of infinite shame grows out of the feeling of undoubting trust. The child sinks in nothingness at its Father's feet, just when He is about to take it to His arms." (Ibid., 48-49.)
32. Ibid., 50-51.
33. Busk, 211. Cf. F. D. Maurice, *The Gospel of St. John* (London: Macmillan, 1867), 297.
34. *Life*, 1:155; italics in the original. Maurice wrote this letter to his Calvinist mother in response to her conviction that she might not be among the elect.
35. Maurice, *The Epistle to the Hebrews*, 29-30.
36. *Life*, 2:242.
37. On the importance of the unity of humanity, see Patricia Wilson-Kastner, *Faith, Feminism, and the Christ*, discussed at length in the following chapter.
38. See Chapter 5, above.
39. In this area, the very important work of Rosemary Radford Ruether in *Faith and Fratricide* on the formation of traditions by suppression of distinctive "others" makes a significant contribution. (Rosemary Radford Ruether, *Faith and Fratricide: The Theological Roots of Anti-Semitism*. With an Introduction by Gregory Baum [New

York: Seabury, 1974].) This work is examined in the following chapter.

40.   On the connection between feminism and the well-being of the earth, see, for example, the discussions of women and nature in Rosemary Radford Ruether's *New Woman/New Earth* and *Sexism and God-Talk* (discussed in the next chapter), Sallie McFague's *Models of God*, and Carol P. Christ's "Why Women Need the Goddess" and other essays in *Laughter of Aphrodite*, as well as Susan Griffin's *Woman and Nature*.

41.   Gerda Lerner has been at some pains to identify this strand in *The Creation of Patriarchy*. The planned second volume of this work, still in preparation, will make this strand more explicit. Women of color have also made many useful and important contributions to tracing the history of resistance; and their theoretical as well as historical findings are of great value in generating present action and future vision.

42.   Ruether, *To Change the World*, 6.

43.   Sojourner Truth, "Ain't I A Woman," quoted in Grant, 220.

Part III

Toward a Contemporary Feminist Christology

Chapter 7

The Paradigmatic and Prophetic Christ

The Problem of Christology in White Feminist Theology

In the remaining chapters of this book, I will turn to four Christological proposals advanced by contemporary white feminist theologians. Christology is a central element in any systematic approache to theology. Women's religious experience in the struggle for liberation is a key element in the formulation of feminist theology. My considerations in these chapters have been shaped by bringing these two elements together. All four proposals rely on contemporary feminist experience as an interpreter of Christian traditions because that experience discloses both the collusion of those traditions with patriarchal domination and their irrepressibly liberating actuality and potential. A careful study of these proposals will then issue in a proposal of my own, in which the study of women's religious experience undertaken in Part II will be a significant component.

As I indicated in Part I, Christology poses a problem for white Christian feminists from two directions: feminist criticism, and traditional Christianity (or doctrinal fundamentalism, as Wilson-

Kastner terms it). Traditional Christian theologians argue that the subordination of women to men is part of a divine plan, validated by the incarnation of God in a male son. At the same time, post-Biblical feminists argue that no feminist Christian formulation can overcome the essential patriarchal character of core Christian symbols. Christology is, for some at least, the central doctrine that indicates the irretrievably patriarchal and misogynist character of Christianity.

To summarize briefly, feminist critics such as Mary Daly, Carol Christ, Rita Nakashima Brock, and Daphne Hampson point to three aspects of traditional Christology that render it destructive to women. First, the incarnation of God as a male in patriarchal society validates patriarchy as the divine order. It also reinforces the identification of women as the source of original and continuing sin. [1] Second, the central aspects of Jesus' life and death are problematic as well. He is an autonomous hero acting alone, not a person constructed by his relations. [2] And what makes him heroic is his self-sacrificial death, which is then held up as a model particularly for women, a model that is impossible for women to emulate successfully. Jesus, the model of self-sacrifice, in effect dooms women to an eternity of frustration. [3] Third, the designation of Jesus as the unique, once-for-all savior denigrates the religious insights of non-Christians, distances women from participation in divinity, and negates the meaning of history and historical developments. [4]

While most feminist critics can find some positive value in Jesus, they nevertheless agree that this male savior is not the savior contemporary women should seek. "The only thing a male savior can do is what the male savior, Jesus, has done, and that is to legitimize the oppression of women through the perpetuation of the 'myth of sin and salvation.' . . . Women must [instead] look for the New Being." [5]

Far from rejecting this criticism outright, white feminist Christian theologians (such as the ones included in this study) acknowledge the legitimacy of much of this feminist post-Christian critique of theology and Christology. While agreeing that Christianity and its theological formulations are profoundly patriarchal, white feminist Christian theologians continue to believe that the religious insights of Christianity have been of value to women and can be reconstructed to incorporate women's experience as central. As we shall see in this chapter and the next four, this reconstruction includes elements of critique, historical investigation, and constructive formulation. The result of this dialectic of criticism, investigation, and construction is full-blown feminist Christian theology, based in women's experience and in critical reconstruction of the Christian traditions that have been liberating as well as destructive for women.

The Christologies which are part of these emerging theologies have in common, first, their agreement with and appropriation of a core critique of patriarchy as dualistic; they see these dualisms as distorting every aspect of human existence, including religion.[6] Second, all insist on the central, constitutive role of human relationality to all theological and ethical formulations. Third, all agree that visions of liberating and redemptive historical possibilities and of future, transhistorical redemption arise in the context of historical struggles for liberation, nurtured by exemplary or paradigmatic figures in both the present and the past. Whoever else he may be, Jesus is one of these paradigmatic figures. Fourth, all agree that the problems facing feminist Christology are intensified by the patriarchal distortions in even the earliest Christian witnesses, and by the consequent reliance of feminist theology "upon the primary intuitions of religious experience."[7] Therefore, white feminist Christologies-- including the four examined here--rely on an interpretation of who Jesus *is*,[8] emphasizing Jesus' egalitarian relations with others, his identification with the lowest of the low (many of whom are women), his renunciation of any form of domination, his new understanding of service as mutual empowerment, and his trust in God. White feminist Christologies also view his death as the consequence of a life of mutuality and justice in a historical situation characterized by systems of domination, and they cast his resurrection as the vindication by God of such a life.

Despite these important similarities, white feminist Christologies differ significantly one from another. In addition to differences of interpretation or emphases of aspects of women's experience and of historical and theological traditions, the four white feminist theologies examined in this study also vary in their thematic casting of Christology, emphasizing either the prophetic and eschatological elements (as is the case with Ruether, discussed in this chapter) or the present Wisdom-Logos elements (as in Heyward, Wilson-Kastner, and Suchocki, discussed in the next chapters). This typological difference arises out of basic theological orientations, as well as out of each theologian's understanding of the problems in classical and contemporary Christological formulations, which make more problematic a feminist understanding of Jesus as the Christ. The manifestation-proclamation typology developed by Ricoeur and Tracy (and detailed in Chapter 5) assists in illumining both kinds of difference.

The white feminist Christologies that are the focus of Part III of this book both illustrate and modify this typology. Rosemary Radford Ruether presents a Christology that is primarily of the proclamation type. Jesus is the iconoclastic prophet who, by word and example, proclaims a new heaven and a new earth, in which idolatrous dualisms (or schisms) are overcome in a human existence characterized by mutual and just servanthood directed toward the whole of creation. God/ess is the matrix and inspiration of this liberating transformation. God/ess' prophet Jesus is radically misunderstood even by many of his followers, who are still enmeshed in systems of domination, both external and internalized. Yet the proclaimed new existence lives on, however partially, in those who take this prophetic model as exemplary. However, the full realization--the full manifestation--of the promised existence lies in the future, which is prefigured in proleptic, anticipated form in the prophetic Jesus and "in the form of our sister." [9] As I shall indicate, Ruether's Christology falls short of adequacy in its failure to indicate how this Jesus is also a full manifestation of God/ess.

The three Christologies examined in the following chapters are of the manifestation type. Patricia Wilson-Kastner, Marjorie Hewitt Suchocki, and Carter Heyward present an encounter with Jesus as the Christ who *is* a full manifestation or incarnation of the divine. In Heyward's words, Jesus is the representation of "the *only* liberating relationship" one can have with God. [10] That is, Jesus manifests the fullness of both humanity and divinity, in a relationship that has existed in principle from creation, that is partially available to all in the present, and that is promised to all as future transformation. While each of these Christologies relies to some extent on the prophetic elements of Jesus' life and work, finally their emphasis on the present reality of fulfillment and transformation loses some of the imperative force associated with the vision of a future realization of promises which, thus far, have been blocked by profound alienation and systemic distortion and domination. It is my contention, discussed in the final, constructive chapter of this work, that the two types taken together can lead toward a more adequate feminist Christology.

Christology

Introduction to Ruether's Christology

The Christ, says Ruether, is both redemptive person and Word of God. [11] Christ is "the model for this redeemed humanity that we have lost through sin and recover through redemption" [12] and "the manifest[ation] of the face of God/ess as liberator." [13] Christology, then, "should be the most comprehensive symbol of redemption from all sin and evil in Christian theology, the symbol that embraces authentic humanity and fulfilled hopes of all persons." [14]

But, Ruether notes, "Christology has been the doctrine of the Christian tradition that has been most frequently used against women"; [15] and it has virulent anti-Judaism as its left hand. [16] Along with the model of redeemed humanity and the liberating face of God/ess, Christology has presented a model of subjugation and a God who supports the dominant. The classical Christological question "From what must we be saved?" has been radicalized: "From what *in traditional Christology itself* must we be saved?" That is, Christology must be subjected to thorough critique and--if possible--reconstruction.

In Ruether's reconstruction, the Christ is the model or paradigm of redeemed humanity, present--but neither uniquely nor finally so--in Jesus of Nazareth, the iconoclastic prophet, *via* his relations with those around him. [17] Redemption is achieved both partially in, and fully only beyond, the conditions of human history. [18] Ruether's reconstruction draws on Scripture, Jewish and Christian religious traditions, and women's experience, all read through the double lens of the principle of the full humanity of oppressed women and the prophetic-liberating tradition found in the Bible.

The Character of Human Existence

Ruether describes the human condition as inherently and structurally dual, [19] as both transcendence (or aspiration) and existence. She sees this description as being in line with the basic structure of Christian theology, which describes Christian existence as a movement between human nature as imago dei and as fallen. Theology, as the mode of reflection on questions of ultimate meaning and value, "mediates between existence and the transcendent [and transforming] horizon of life." [20] Christian theology, in order to be adequate, must reflect the two dualities of human essence in contrast to human existence, and of authenticity and potentiality in contrast to historical actuality. [21] Human encounter with the divine is found in historical existence. That is where the transcendent breaks through all the distortions and limitations of finite existence. [22]

The finite and limited personal and social situation of the individual affects her conscious experience and the extent to which she may render that experience socially and religiously meaningful. [23] When human experience is distorted, limited, perverted, or suppressed--as it is under patriarchy--not only how human persons *understand* their relation to the divine is warped, but the very conditions for the possibility of *encountering* the divine in an authentic manner are distorted as well. Therefore, the concern voiced by Ruether over the denial of women's and others' authentic existence by patriarchal structures of thought and society must be understood as a concern for the possibility of divine activity in human history as well as a concern for justice. Patriarchal domination of women and of persons of color, of mind and heart as well as of body, of nature as well as of history, is evil and idolatrous as well as unjust: patriarchal domination is sin.

Patriarchal theology recognizes the inherently dual character of the human condition. But it resolves the troubling tensions and contradictions of the human condition by splitting dialectically related pairs--mind/body, spirituality/carnality, individual/community, being/becoming, truth/appearance, life/death--into dualisms where one aspect is identified as superior, and the other as inferior. [24] Furthermore, that valuation is defined as natural, even God-given. These dualisms are then the sources of the construction of "the world of alienation from which we seek liberation." [25]

The effects of structures of domination and subordination are multiple and pervasive. These structures and systems suppress the power and ability of the dominated to define themselves and the world. The possibility of relations of mutuality and intersubjectivity between individuals and groups is substantially reduced, if not eliminated. And oppression is both legitimated and further perpetuated by various forms of systemic violence and cultivated antagonisms, which conceal essential inter-relations among individuals and groups. [26]

For Ruether, the liberation and redemption offered by God/ess and found paradigmatically in the Christ entail the abolition of "falsifying dualisms" and the movement to the "dynamic unities" that characterize authentic human existence. [27] The dialectic interweaving of the personal, social, and systemic aspects of human existence requires that liberation and redemption address and affect all three areas. [28] But this task requires a complex analysis that specifies the concrete particularities of each social group's social and historical position as dominator and/or subjugated without ignoring similarities and commonalities among groups or the important fact that the primary dominant group is the same in each case. Ruether's discussion of forms of domination and subjugation as interstructured provides this analysis.[29]

Methodology for Liberation: Denunciation and Annunciation

Ruether argues that the sexual dualism--the equation of mind/body and superior/inferior with male/female[30]--that is the basis of male dominance and the subjugation of women is the original model of other systems of domination that favor white male elites, and disadvantage all women, and men (as well as women) of color, different ethnic groups, and lower economic and social classes and castes. The processes and effects of domination and subjugation are similar, regardless of which group is dominant and which is subjugated. But the concrete realities of subjugation vary from group to group and overlap in complex forms; that is, they are interstructured.[31] Therefore, liberation movements need an analysis of gender, race, and class in order to define human experience fully and accurately. This is certainly true of white feminist liberation struggles, which tend to continue the patriarchal practice of positing a universal norm on the basis of the valorization of the experience of a few at the expense of the experience of differing others.

Linked with social forms of domination, in Ruether's analysis, is human domination of nature, which has placed the natural order at the bottom of hierarchies of value and power. The concrete domination of nature relies on social-structural domination of the bodies and labor of workers, slaves, peasants, and women.[32] Humans can and must affect nature; but this is a fully historical project, not a mythical-romantic one, and it must be carried out in conjunction with other projects of liberation.[33]

Ruether's discussion of the interstructured character of oppression is foundational to her theological method, which reflects the dialectical character of human existence, with its moments of contradiction and harmony. This dialectic is one of negation and affirmation, or denunciation and annunciation.

This dialectical method in and of itself counters the oppositional character of dualistic thinking. [34] The analysis and critique of the distortions consequent upon patriarchal dualisms is developed out of an analysis of women's experience as oppressed. Denunciation of the system that produces such oppression is warranted by appeal to the prophetic-liberating principle of Biblical traditions, which also announces the full humanity of all persons as correlated with "original, authentic human nature." [35]

This movement of denunciation and annunciation both discloses *and generates* possibilities for authentic human existence in renewed form. Thus, Ruether's feminist liberation theology is based on three critical and constructive principles: the prophetic-liberating strands of tradition, women's experience as oppressed, and the ongoing promotion of full humanity (typified by the full humanity of oppressed women). [36] These three critical principles are interlocked: the promotion of the full humanity of oppressed women arises out of and is evaluated on the basis of women's experience, which is itself shaped by struggles for full humanity. These are both inspired and judged by prophetic-liberating religious traditions, whose own full potential is released when they are subjected to the critical and generative forces of experience in the struggle for liberation. [37]

Christology and Christian Anti-Judaism

Ruether's discussions of Christian anti-Judaism and Christian misogyny focus her critique of Christology and provide the groundwork for her reconstruction. It is through her critique of anti-Judaism that Ruether recovers the key tradition that also funds her feminist critiques and constructions.

Critique

Anti-Judaism, Ruether argues, is the "left hand of Christology ... the negative side of the Christian affirmation that Jesus was the Christ." [38] The credibility of the Christian proclamation of

Jesus as the divine fulfillment in history of Jewish messianic hopes has been thought to depend on the plausibility of the explanation proffered for Judaism's refusal to recognize its hopes as fulfilled in this way. [39] Otherwise, Christians would have to face the possibility that Jesus is the *failed* Messiah. Christian teachings of Jewish reprobation provide the required explanation. However, they also provide the basis for the millennia-long Christian and secular persecution of the Jews, culminating in the Holocaust of the European Jews between 1933 and 1945. After the Holocaust, Christian anti-Judaism poses even more of a threat to the validity of Christian teaching than does the possibility that Jesus failed as Messiah. [40]

Ruether is convinced that the core of Christological anti-Judaism is found in the incorporation into Christology of fulfilled messianism, which is the outcome of the dualization of history and transcendence. [41] This

> Realized eschatology converts each of the dialectics. . . [of] judgment and promise, particularism and universalism, letter and spirit, history and eschatology
> . . . into dualism, applying one side to the "new messianic people," the Christians, and the negative side to the "old people," the Jews. [42]

This particular application of these dualisms or schisms is carried throughout subsequent history, and has been brutally and nearly totally destructive of the Jews. [43]

But the application of these dualisms has served a function for Christians; this function, Ruether argues, must also be recognized if Christian anti-Judaism is to be eliminated at its roots. Christian origins in Judaism have made the Jewish rejection of Christ psychologically powerful as an ongoing challenge to Christian claims that Jesus is the Messiah who makes redemption a fulfilled reality. The suppression and destruction of the Jews is, psychopathologically, an attempt at the suppression and destruction of the fears aroused by the ongoing suffering and misery in the world, which contradict Christian views of redemption. "The Jews represent that which

Christianity must repress in itself, namely the recognition of history and Christian existence as unredeemed." [44]

Ruether proposes that Christian anti-Judaism can be rooted out only if the schisms involved are healed. This means revising Christology (and other aspects of Christian thought) so that Jewish particularity is valued on its own terms and on a par with Christian particularity. Such a revision means reinterpreting universality so that it "rests on the universality of God as Creator and Redeemer of mankind [sic] and the universe, not on the universality of [a] historical revelation and way of salvation." [45]

This necessary--though radical--revision is possible, Ruether thinks, only if Christianity gives up all explicit and implicit commitments to fulfilled messianism and instead understands past experiences and events as proleptic and anticipatory, as paradigmatic of the structure of human existence. [46] Then the demonization of others who do not find the same value in this particular past will not be necessary. [47] Moreover, the renunciation of fulfilled messianism allows Christianity to incorporate (rather than project) the self-critical element of Jesus' teaching as an inner-Jewish reformer. [48] Specifically, this means Christianity's recovering and reconstructing "the heritage of prophetic self-criticism" as necessarily connected with hope and promise. [49]

Corrective: The Prophetic Paradigm

Ruether argues that the "prophetic principle," "the prophetic-liberating tradition," or "the prophetic paradigm" is the norm by which Biblical faith critiques and renews itself. [50] Ruether describes four essential themes in this tradition:

> (1) God's defense and vindication of the oppressed; (2) the critique of dominant systems of power and their powerholders; (3) the vision of a new age to come in which the present system of injustice is overcome and God's intended reign of peace and justice is installed in history; and

(4) finally, the critique of ideology, or of religion, since ideology in this context is primarily religious. [51]

These themes, far from being a set of ideas whose content remains static over time, constitute a dialectic of covenant or promise, of salvation and judgment, of annunciation and denunciation. [52] The prophetic-liberating strand or tradition can, therefore, serve as a plumbline whose use produces assessments of differing ideas and practices across barriers of time and culture. [53] The principle also serves as an internal self-critique and corrective. [54]

However, it is not possible for feminist and other liberation theologies to appropriate wholesale or uncritically this prophetic-liberating tradition and paradigm. The tradition must be criticized and the paradigm reconstructed to take into account the domination of women and others--a domination which the tradition ignored and, at times, supported in its Biblical form. [55] "Analogical *midrash*," which recasts "ancient paradigms in the context of modern issues and modern consciousness" reconstructs these distorted traditions, using as its point of reference "the liberated future," to which this tradition has always pointed. [56] "Thus our own critique of scripture for failing to live up to its own prophetic promise reflects and is rooted in the self-criticism that goes on in and is basic to biblical faith itself." [57]

At the same time that feminist and other liberation theologies evaluate and reconstruct the prophetic-liberating tradition, that tradition necessarily does the same for these theologies. By insisting on the liberation of *all* the oppressed, the prophetic-liberating tradition militates, for example, against feminism's tendencies to imitate patriarchal claims to universalism and to establish new social and cultural hierarchies. [58] And it teaches that all movements for liberation are limited in vision and are prone to the seductions of power and privilege. [59] In other words, the prophetic-liberating tradition stands as a creatively self-critical force within the liberation movements that appropriate it. [60]

When the prophetic-liberating tradition of Scripture is reconstructed to correct its own shortcomings, it provides a powerful dynamic principle that rejoins criticism and self-criticism with hope for a future of liberation and transformation. And it does so on the basis of Biblical tradition. [61] The effect, for Ruether, is to recover a tradition which is useful for feminist liberation theology, not only because it corrects Christian anti-Judaism, but also because it establishes a Biblical basis for the full humanity of women who have been sinfully and unjustly oppressed. This principle, applied to Christology, provides the groundwork for a paradigmatic, proleptic view of the Christ who is known through Jesus in a significant but not complete way.

Christology and Christian Misogyny

Critique

The two primary dualities-become-dualisms Ruether finds at the basis of Christian anti-Judaism are those between history and transcendence, and between self and other. The process leading to these particular dualizations is modeled on the fundamental distortion of male related to female as superior is related to inferior. This most basic dualism is embedded in Christianity's most central complex of symbols, Christology.

> Women, of course, are still regarded as humble members of the Christian body, but their inability to represent Christ is sealed by the definition of Christ as founder and cosmic governor of the existing social hierarchy and as the male disclosure of a male God whose normative representative can only be male. . . . only the male represents the fullness of human nature, whereas woman is defective physically, morally, and mentally. It follows that the incarnation of the *Logos* of God into a male is not a historical accident but an ontological necessity. [62]

Patriarchal ideology, ideation, and dualism are enshrined in the Godhead itself, which is headed by God the transcendent Father. In the development of Christianity, symbols of divine immanence as feminine--e.g., Sophia--were eliminated by the appropriation of Sophia's other attributes to the Logos,[63] identified with the male Jesus as the Son and the Christ. There is, then, no female image within the doctrine of God; and the feminine is identified entirely with the creaturely.[64] "The female can never appear as the icon of God in all divine fullness, parallel to the male image of God."[65] The assumption that God is literally male undergirds the anthropological use of the maleness of Jesus to establish the inferiority of women. Reciprocally, the unquestioned and unquestionable maleness of the historical person Jesus supports the interpretation of images like "Father" and "Son" as literal presentations of primary realities about the divine.[66] The doctrine of the two natures of Christ, as formulated at Chalcedon, resolves "the duality between Jesus' historical existence and his mediation of eschatological presence" by sacrificing the humanity of the historical Jesus to the claim of the finality of Christ's mediating revelation of God.[67] Patristic theology's identification of women as an "inferior mix" of imago dei and fallenness,[68] and Scholastic theology's identification of women as defective because misbegotten[69] are but the culmination of centuries' long patriarchalization of Christology. But even the most patriarchal casting of theology cannot obscure an essential truth:

> [N]either masculinity traditionally defined nor femininity traditionally defined discloses an innately good human nature, and neither is simply an expression of evil. Both represent different types of alienation of humanity from its original potential.[70]

So, for Ruether as for other feminists, Christology faces enormous difficulties from symbolic, theological, historical, and contemporary angles.

> Must we not say that the very limitations of Christ as a male person must lead women to the conclusion that he cannot represent redemptive personhood for them? That they must emancipate themselves from Jesus as redeemer and seek a new redemptive disclosure of God and of human possibility in female form?[71]

There are two problems here: the maleness of the Christ, and the redemptive character of Jesus. The latter of these can be solved by demythologization of the tradition, and restoration of the presentation of Jesus in the Synoptic Gospels. The Synoptics' Jesus "can be recognized as a figure remarkably compatible with feminism. . . . [T]he criticism of religious and social hierarchy characteristic of the early portrait of Jesus is remarkably parallel to feminist criticism." [72] The Synoptics' Jesus is also closer to what Ruether takes to be the primary theme of the Biblical traditions, the prophetic. [73]

However, while the Synoptic Gospels' Jesus may be a "compatible figure" for feminism, he alone does not, *can* not manifest the Christ for women:

> This maleness of Christ still distances the woman from full representation in the new humanity. [Even] the male Christ with a 'feminine' personality does not liberate women but reinforces the identification of femininity with passivity. The woman today, increasingly distraught both by her sense of her personal repression and by the growing danger of world destruction through male, amoral technology, longs for an unrevealed redemptrix, a Christ who can affirm her own personhood as woman and can dismantle the systems of private repression and public violence. [74]

The Christological crisis for feminism that Ruether describes, then, can be attributed to the incorporation into classical Christological formulations of a number of basic dualisms that serve as false, schismatic resolutions of the dual character of human experience. The tension between the historical and the transcendent implied in the phrase "Jesus is the Christ" is dissolved into realized eschatology, which claims Jesus as the final and complete fulfillment of messianic expectation, whose reign will be established only outside and beyond history. The tension between particular experience and universal import is dissolved in the Christian polemic against Jewish and all other forms of particularism as the rejection of Christian universalism and its correlative religious, cultural, and political imperialism. The tension inherent in the diversity of male and female within one humanity, dissolved into the dualism of male superiority and female inferiority, is reflected in and perpetuated by the designation of the maleness of Jesus as both necessary and normative and the suppression of all female elements in the Godhead. In no case is the incorporation of these dualisms superficial; all sit so firmly at the foundations of classical Christologies that their removal risks destroying the Christological doctrine altogether.

Corrective: The Full Humanity of Women

One element of the corrective required to address the Christological crisis is reappropriation of the prophetic-liberating tradition, as we have seen. The second element is the promotion of the full humanity of oppressed women. This corrective is developed out of Ruether's analysis of women's experience.

In Ruether's work, "women's experience" means women's own critical reflection on and awareness of their plural and complex situation as one of subjugation in a patriarchal culture in which the dominance of male elites is a powerful and pervasive factor. [75] Women's experience reflects the alienation of women's existence under male dominance. At the same time, however, it explodes that dominance by empowering women to stand outside and against the sources of their alienation. Women's experience, then, is both critical force and "grace event," [76] liberating women from domination and releasing their potential. The process of exposing patriarchal distortion for what it is

> . . . throws feminist theology back upon the primary intuitions of religious experience itself, namely, the belief in a divine foundation of reality which is ultimately good, which does not wish evil nor create evil, but affirms and upholds our autonomous personhood as women, in whose image we are made. . . . It is engaged in a primal re-encounter with divine reality and, in this re-encounter, new stories will grow and be told as new foundations of our identity. [77]

That is, feminist consciousness reaches toward a transcendent grounding for women's identity and a new faith experience, which can provide the basis for theological reflection. [78]

The principle of the promotion of the full humanity of women is a response to that faith experience. This principle is not new in its essence, Ruether claims. It is, rather, a particular application of "the correlation of original, authentic human nature (imago dei/Christ) and diminished fallen humanity [which] provided the basic structure of classical Christian theology." [79] This application is warranted, in part, by the feminist perception that understandings of sin and paradigms of redemption have been distorted and contradicted by claims of normative status for maleness. [80]

The basic nature of sin, in Ruether's view, is the perversion or corruption of authentic human nature and potential, a corruption that is made concrete in the distortion and alienation of human relationality, both social and individual. [81] All sin indicates alienation also from the divine, who symbolizes fullness of relationality and whose own relationality is the matrix out of which all relations emerge. [82]

Western religious traditions and their social and political descendants are sinful in their sacralization of the primary historical sin of sexism by "making God and all religious symbols of the divine human relationship into sacred reiterations of male domination" [83] and by defining women as the source of sin and evil. [84] This being the case, the true primary sin of patriarchal religion is not pride, but idolatry of male dominance. [85] Patriarchal religion translates its idolatry into ethical and ecclesial systems of lordship and servility, defining as "redemptive" for women and other subjugated groups their voluntary submission to their own victimization. [86]

The principle of the promotion of the full humanity of *oppressed* women corrects and reconstructs the basic structure of Christian theology by taking into account all of humanity, and not just its historically dominant segment. Concretely, the principle of the full humanity of women calls for a reconstruction of Christology and soteriology that at the same time removes from Christology the justification of male dominance, and clearly presents the Christ as "the model for this redeemed humanity that we have lost through sin and recover through redemption" and "the face of God/ess as liberator" from all forms of oppression as well as the provider of transhistorical redemption.[87]

Christology Reconstructed

Reuther's proposals for a feminist liberation Christology attempt to heal the dualisms she finds to have given rise to both Christian anti-Judaism and Christian misogyny. She proposes eliminating fulfilled messianism from Christology, and replacing it with formulations that are, first, proleptic and anticipatory (rather than final and fulfilled) and, second, paradigmatic (rather than universal and absolute).[88] The outcome is her presentation of Jesus as an iconoclastic Jewish prophet who proclaims a new earth and a new heaven, and who embodies, in the living of his life and in his death, a new humanity that is still to come.

Jesus the Messianic Prophet

Formally, Ruether's Christology is typological rather than allegorical: it uses historical types in the past to point to still-future, more fully realized, yet still historical expressions.[89] A proleptic paradigm discloses both the authentic elements of present reality--always seen only in glimpses--and the future fulfillment that is longingly sought.[90] This Christology, Ruether thinks, is not anti-Jewish or otherwise nonpluralistic, because it does not require Jews, women, or others to renounce their own experience of divine redemption; and it does incorporate Jewish, women's, and other religious experiences as valid and fruitful elements. And it is not misogynist, because it does not, even implicitly, make maleness an element of salvation. At the same time, it represents the kenosis of patriarchy as a form of liberation. It also encourages the discernment of more than one image of Christ as the disclosure of "the gracious, redeeming face of God/ess." [91] It is, in short, more adequate to contemporary experience.

Christology comes out of a "re-encounter with the Jesus of the synoptic Gospels," but it is not an attempt to recover a "historical Jesus" portrayed there. [92]   It is a contemporary interpretation, a "normative statement about the Christian message to the world today."   Under the terms of Ruether's analysis of the Christological crisis and the necessity of refusing to equate any one historical individual with the Christ, Ruether looks at the Synoptics' Jesus in order to recover the experience of the figure who exemplified eschatological expectations and whose memory has been and is paradigmatic of

> that final hope which has not yet been accomplished, but still lies ahead of our present possibilities. This memory may then be reexperienced as a paradigm again and again, in that community which preserves this memory, providing the pattern for experiencing the eschatological in history. [93]

Ruether's search is for the prophetic paradigm of redemption. The Jesus who presents this paradigm is an iconoclastic Jewish prophet, who judged his own society and religion in light of his own "lively expectation of the coming of God's Kingdom." [94] Jesus' vision of the rapidly approaching Kingdom of God was prophetic and this-worldly: it would be a historical era of peace and justice. [95] The prayer that Jesus taught his followers makes this clear in its petitions for actual bread, remission of enmity and indebtedness, and the removal of temptation and evil: "The kingdom means conquest of human historical evil; the setting up of proper conditions of human life with God and one another here on earth within the limits of mortal existence." [96] Jesus the iconoclastic prophet understood that this Kingdom is God's, not his own: he is not the embodiment of that kingdom. He is, rather, a prophet of it. [97] He was an inner-Jewish reformer whose life and teachings attracted a group of followers who attempted to interpret his troubling death in light of his messianic message of liberation, right relationship, and hope, and in light of their experience of the continuing presence of his spirit, even after his death. [98]

Jesus can be seen as a liberator of others because he directed his attention to the roots of relations of domination and subjugation, rather than to their symptoms: he addressed himself to "the love of prestige, power and wealth that causes people to seek domination and lord it over each other," and to the transformation of these roles. [99] His attention to the structures of domination was concrete: he actively befriended and worked with the lowest members of his society, and used their social roles as the exemplary models for his radical redefinition of leadership. The examples of the lowest, the "last who shall be first," were often women--widows, prostitutes, particular Samaritan and Syro-Phoenician women--who were positioned "at the bottom of the present hierarchy" of class, caste, gender, and ethnicity. [100] Jesus' selection of these and other exemplars and his own relationships with them presented a model of liberation from hierarchical relations and for true mutuality, where all are "brothers-sisters of each other." [101]

Further, Jesus can be seen as the liberator (or redeemer) of others because he was himself liberated (or redeemed) by his encounters with others: notably by John when Jesus was baptized, and by the Syro-Phoenician woman when she challenged his exclusion of Gentiles from God's gracious reign. [102]

Jesus' presentation of God as *Abba* and of the Messiah as servant extends mutuality beyond relations between human persons to human relations with the divine. [103] God/ess is the liberator "who opens up a new community of equals." [104] The messianic prophet receives that liberation and is the liberated servant of others in aid of their liberation, even when such service leads to the prophet's death. [105]

What is new in Jesus' message is his model of mutual servanthood. Servanthood is not servitude, not service within a lord-servant relation. "By becoming servant of God, one becomes freed of all bondage to human masters. Only then, as a liberated person, can one truly become 'servant of all,' giving one's life to liberate others rather than to exercise power and rule over them." [106]

Such servanthood is fully mutual: none are masters, all are free, yet all serve each other. [107] The model comes from the lowest in society, and identifies divine redemptive activity with *their* daily activity, thereby signalling the transformation of both human and divine. [108] The coupling of the daily activity of the lowest with divine activity transforms the meaning of coerced servitude and overthrows structures of oppressive relationship. This transformation is iconoclastic and creative; it represents a new humanity in a new society not yet come fully into existence, the meaning of which cannot be known except through "the Christ, the messianic person, who represents a new kind of humanity." [109] Jesus' iconoclastic and transformative modeling of servanthood (including his use of women as exemplars) was at least as puzzling and troubling to his followers as it was to those with power: it was his followers who betrayed him, providing the opportunity for an apparent victory of the "principalities and powers" over him. [110]

But the apparent victory of the principalities and powers is not the full and final meaning of Jesus' death: his death is, rather, the victory of God/ess. [111] In his death, Jesus extends his abnegation of power and his identification with the outcast to the fullest by becoming one of the dead. [112] His followers, faced on the one hand with the shock of his death and the possibility of the failure of his mission, and on the other hand with their sense of the presence of his spirit among them, renounce their own betrayal and come to understand his death as redemptive and transformative. [113]

Jesus' death is redemptive and transformative because, like his life, it is both liberative and kenotic: it is a pouring out of self for the sake of others, especially the despised and rejected. His life and death signal the kenosis of God the heavenly ruler, who is now revealed as God the liberating transformer. [114] Jesus' life and death also disclose the kenosis of patriarchy, "the announcement of a new humanity through a lifestyle that discards hierarchical caste privilege and speaks on behalf of the lowly. . . . This system is unmasked and shown to have no connection with favor with God." [115]

Jesus, then, in his life and death discloses the patterns of right relationship, which are "transformatory and liberating" of individuals and of social structures. [116] His life and death are a paradigm of ongoing human hope. Encounter with this paradigm gives a proleptic foretaste of its full realization. [117] But the full realization of the hoped-for humanity and society lies in the future. So the absence of this full experience "keeps us ever searching and struggling, drawing us on to that 'still more' and 'not yet.'" [118]

The Iconoclastic, Prophetic Christ

Jesus the iconoclastic, messianic prophet is a paradigm of the Christ, but is not by himself fully the Christ. [119] What, then, does Ruether mean when she uses the term "Christ," both in relation to Jesus and in general?

> Christ, as redemptive person and Word of God, is not to be encapsulated "once-for-all" in the historical Jesus. The Christian community continues Christ's identity. As vine and branches Christic personhood continues in our sisters and brothers. In the language of early Christian prophetism, we can encounter Christ *in the form of our sister*. Christ, the liberated humanity, is not confined to a static perfection of one person two thousand years ago. Rather, redemptive humanity goes ahead of us, calling us to yet incompleted dimensions of human liberation. [120]

That is, while redeemed and liberated humanity is, for Christians, disclosed in Jesus, he is not the complete or final manifestation, even for Christians. [121]   Indeed, Ruether suggests, the memory of Jesus may be *more* paradigmatic when understood as partial, because it will no longer be subject to the distortions and perversions inherent in the absolutisms of finality and uniqueness, nor will it be forced to bear, alone, the full weight of human particularity. When Jesus is not the *only* Christ, the fullness of how he was and is *a* Christ will be more evident. [122] At the same time, understanding Christ as proleptic paradigm allows us to understand Jesus' existence, as well as our own, as standing between the "already" and the "not yet" of human existence and its fulfillment, thus keeping human hope, expectation, and creativity realistic and alive. [123]   In other words, when prophecy and hope are rejoined in paradigmatic figures, they may be rejoined in the rest of human existence in history.

The spirit of Jesus that his first followers experienced continues, and where this spirit is similarly manifest, the Christ is present. [124]   This continuing spirit initially was found in the network of relations of which Jesus was a key part, and this is where it is still found: *in relationship*. [125]   So for this reason as well, the Christ cannot be found in one person alone; the Christ is more nearly the spirit that exists in the midst of people in mutual relations that promote liberation from unjust structures and various other distortions of authentic human existence. [126] In other words, Ruether presents a Spirit Christology that is similar to its historic forebears in its affirmation of the appearance of the Christ in historical persons other than Jesus. [127]   But Ruether's Christology diverges from its precedents by also emphasizing the historical contexts--liberation from unjust structures--in which these paradigmatic figures live and die as prophets of the coming new humanity.

The Christ we encounter in the form of our sister, as well as in Jesus, points toward a final fulfillment that has yet to be achieved or even more than partially envisioned. The limitations of historical existence mitigate against the specification of any one historical (and so limited) vision as embodying the fullness that is yet to come. The diversity and variety of the many paradigmatic figures who together make up the Christ add to the richness of this vision of the new humanity on the way to liberation and redemption, and so move to surpass the limitations of existence. The Christ as paradigm is relative; the Christ is redemptive *for us*. [128]   A single paradigmatic figure such as Jesus may be taken to represent Christ; he may be paradigmatic for Christians, but he is not and need not be for others.

The relative character of the paradigm does not limit its power to redeem, however, because particularity and universality are not antitheses, although they have been put in dualistic relation. "True universalism must be able to embrace existing human pluralism, . . . Only God is one and universal. Humanity is finally one because the one God created us all. But the historical mediators of the experience of God remain plural." [129] The universal God redeems through the particular. The recognition of the particularity of any historical figure--including Jesus--restores the actual duality between history and transcendence that has been lost--perhaps particularly with Jesus--when the transcendent has been absolutized in the historical. Theologically, the recognition of historical particularity asserts that only God can be transcendent and universal; the historical is always contingent and limited, always particular. This is the basic structure of existence. [130]

Jesus is the Christ in that he repudiates the structures of domination, models liberation and redemption from these structures in his relations and in the totality of his life and his death, and imparts to his followers a spirit that leads them to do the same. Jesus saves by announcing the liberated humanity that is yet to come:

> [H]e models what it means to be authentically human. . . .
> As the model of redeemed humanity, he saves us from our sinful inclinations to distorted relationality, and points us toward our authentic potential as human beings--the potential we all have to live in mutual and reverent relationship with one another and the earth. Further, he saves us by challenging us to *save one another in his name*, that is, to continue his task and mission of making the Kingdom come more concretely on this earth. [131]

What is seen, always imperfectly, in these Christ-manifesting relations is a new humanity and a new age. But also manifest--and through these same relations--is the gracious, liberating face of God/ess, who is active in human history as original matrix and source of humanity, and as a force for liberation and the opening up of new possibilities. "Jesus discloses the transformatory and liberating patterns of relation to each other, and, through them, to God, . . ." [132]

Salvation as Liberation and Transformation

God/ess as Matrix and Liberator

Ruether envisions God/ess [133] in these terms:

> The God/ess who is the foundation (at one and the same time)
> of our being and our new being embraces both the roots of
> the material substratum of our existence (matter) and also the
> endlessly new creative potential (spirit). The God/ess who is
> the foundation of our being-new being . . . leads us to the
> converted center, the harmonization of self and body, self and
> other, self and world. [134]

The divine is what is "beneath and around" existence rather than "'up there' as abstracted ego. . . . That which is most basic, matter (mother, matrix), is also most powerfully imbued with the powers of life and spirit." [135] The God/ess of Ruether's formulations is the source of transformation and liberation, and is to be understood as dynamic rather than static. [136] Therefore, to affirm God/ess as founding matrix is also to embrace God/ess as the liberating source of "constant breakthrough that points us to new possibilities that are, at the same time, the regrounding of ourselves in the primordial matrix, the original harmony." [137]

Finally, understanding the divine as God/ess breaks and transforms the originatng dualism of patriarchy, that between male and female. God/ess is "both male and female, and neither male nor female," and thus points toward a "new heaven and earth" inhabited by an as-yet "unrealized new humanity," which is nevertheless grounded in existing human potential. [138] The image of God/ess, in whose image this new humanity is made, calls forth or inspires efforts toward new personal, social, and religious patterns and structures.

Ruether's image of God/ess locates liberation within historical existence and redemption beyond it, and affirms God/ess as the source of both. Reconciliation with God/ess means justice on earth, brought about through the revolutionizing of all human social and personal relations. [139] Because God/ess is not only the source of new being but also its founding matrix, God/ess' "liberating Word" must be understood as a call not to utopian escape from human existence, but to conversion within and to it.[140]

Conversion, Liberation, Transformation

Conversion, in Ruether's view, is a dialectical process that involves, first, comprehensive and profound renunciation of patriarchal ideology and practice and the privileges that go with it.[141] Conversion also involves the ongoing generation of new vision, arising both from patriarchalism and from its transformation.[142] Recognition of patriarchalism's "victim-blaming ideology of sin"[143] arises from feminist consciousness of the struggle within patriarchalism between women's full humanity (as both lost option and alternative future) and male dominance.[144] This consciousness produces a vision of conversion *from* the sin of domination and subjugation, and *to* the redemption offered by the full humanity of women.[145]

From what, then, need we be saved? Historically understood, we must be saved from patriarchalism's distortions and perversions of human existence, as sacralized in patriarchal religion--distortions and perversions which are themselves and in their effects comprehensive, pervasive, and often hidden and intractable. Religiously understood, we must be saved from idolatry, and reunited with the matrix of our existence.[146]

What, then, is salvation, and how are we to attain it? Ruether is careful to distinguish between historical liberation and final redemption or salvation, which she understands as transformation: Liberation may take place in history, but full redemption is necessarily beyond it.[147] Liberation and salvation are, however, closely related: God/ess is active in both, as is authentic human being as subject as well as object of both.[148] And the intent or goal of both is the same: the creation of new possibilities that are also "the regrounding of ourselves in the primordial matrix, the original harmony,"[149] that is, God/ess.

Liberation is a process of both conversion and transformation, and it effects *in history* a complex of breakthroughs into new possibilities, which are grounded in the "finite matrix of existence."[150] Conversion to original harmony, the center, the matrix, is related to transformative movement into new possibilities and the dismantling of all forms of distortion. Transformation must be understood as ongoing: the distortions present in human historical existence are pervasive and comprehensive in scope and depth, and continue to deform the capacity to imagine new possibilities.[151] Therefore, all human capacities and the social systems and structures that shape them all need to be transformed in order for a liberated, redeemed humanity to emerge.[152]

Along with social conversion and transformation must come the resurrection of the authentic self from under the alienated self.[153] For the oppressed, this resurrection is both the conversion to and the creation of that authentic, fully human self, which is denied, distorted, suppressed, and even destroyed by patriarchal domination.[154] The process involves externalization (or exorcism) of the internalizations of domination (such as self-hatred and self-destruction) so that liberation and self-esteem are possible.[155] Elements of the authentic, liberated self are already present, albeit always partially and in perverted or limited form, and these may be transformed and embraced.[156]

This conversion must not entail appropriation of the dominant definition of the normative human--the male. Instead, women "need to appropriate and deepen the integration of the whole self--relational with rational modes of thought--that is already theirs," both in their innate human capacities and in the way those capacities have been shaped--and distorted--culturally.[157] The process of conversion to the self also involves revaluation and transvaluation of androcentrically defined virtues and sins: the patriarchal sins of pride and anger and the virtue of self-abnegation must be revalued by the oppressed, so that anger and pride are seen as virtues in the struggle for liberation, while self-abnegation and self-sacrifice are understood as sins that serve to further subjugation.[158]

The ongoing process of liberation as conversion and transformation brings about the dissolution of false dualisms into dynamically and dialectically related dualities. Most fundamentally, liberation changes the relation between male and female, and so all other relations, since the subjugation of women is the basis of all domination-subjugation relations. [159]

The liberative transformation of the dualities of essence and existence, of possibility and actuality, is indicated theologically by the healing of the dualistic split between the world and the Kingdom or Reign of God in the midst of human existence, that is, neither fully achieved nor deferred until the end of history. [160] Discerning God's Reign is a matter of concrete reality, of recognizing the realities of bondage and the realities of liberation as they are taking place. [161] However, Ruether warns, God's reign can only be approximated in history; it cannot be fully achieved. [162] It is always both present and absent, even as it was during Jesus' ministry: no system, no society, no person embodies the reign of God entirely.

This view of God's Reign or Kingdom keeps a dynamic relationship between transcendence and history by indicating that there is reason to hope in and for history, but hope is restricted neither to an end-point nor to the transcendence of suffering and death. [163] This view also addresses and heals the dualism connected with "ambiguous historical existence and perfected messianic life." [164] Further, liberation means the transformation of the dualism of human (or history) and nature, which comes about by recognizing the way the ecological and the social are inherently interlocked. [165]

These processes of liberation also transform the dualism of particular and universal away from exclusivity and imperialism toward a recognition that only God is one (and therefore universal), while human existence is inherently pluralistic in form and in experiential content. [166] Liberation and salvation entail divine activity as constant breakthrough and as regrounding. [167] Human activity dismantles and transforms the distorted structures and elements of human existence. The divine and the human are reconciled; this means "the revolutionizing of human social, political relations, over-throwing unjust, oppressive relationship." [168]   Liberation anticipates--indeed, is paradigmatic of--salvation.   And the source of both liberation and salvation is God/ess.

The Shalom of God/ess

Because God/ess is both founding matrix and source of redemption, there will be some continuity between historical and transhistorical existence, such that images of return, of Shalom, and of a Jubilee (rather than eschatological end-point) metaphorically express what is hoped for and envisioned. [169]

> The scales begin to fall from our eyes, and all around us we see miracles. . . . The harmony is still there, persisting, supporting, forgiving, preserving us in spite of ourselves. Divine Grace keeps faith with us when we have broken faith with her. . . . To return Home: to learn the harmony, the peace, the justice of body, bodies in right relation to each other. The whence we have come and whither we go, not from alien skies but here, in the community of earth. Holy One, Thy Kingdom come, Thy will be done on earth. . . . The Shalom of the Holy; the disclosure of the gracious *Shekinah*; Divine Wisdom; the empowering Matrix; She, in whom we live and move and have our being--She comes; She is here. [170]

It is this vision of the Shalom of God/ess that inspires and drives struggles for liberation. The vision originates in God/ess as matrix and as liberator. And it is mediated in human history by paradigmatic figures whose response to God/ess brings forth a new humanity engaged in the creation of a new historical reality. For Christians, the paradigmatic figure is Christ, who can be encountered most significantly--but not exclusively--in Jesus. Jesus both proclaims and manifests the kenosis of patriarchy, and so assists in bringing to being God/ess' Shalom. He also thereby opens the way to new possibilities of new paradigms: Christ "in the form of our sister."

The Male Savior and the Kenosis of Patriarchy

Jesus represents both new humanity and the gracious and redeeming God/ess who is the matrix of harmony and unity. But does this representation of Christ in the form of our brother adequately address women's experience? Can a male savior--can *this* male savior--save women? [171]

The problem of the male savior is, I think, two-fold. The male savior, Jesus, historically has been and still is used against women, with brutal force and deadly consequences. And the ability of any male savior to disclose redemption from the perspective of women's experience is dubious at best. [172] Even if a male savior can be seen to disclose the redemption of human existence for women, there is the further question of what such a savior discloses about the divine. [173] Again, both the history of Christianity and the importance of women's experience focus the problem. Ruether puts the problem thus:

> The contemporary Christian woman is still taught to believe in a male Christ as the sole and unique expression of redeeming grace. This maleness of Christ still distances the woman from full representation in the new humanity. . . . Is it enough to claim that Jesus represents "generic humanity" or even was an antipatriarchal male, if he alone remains the exclusive face of the redeeming God and of our authentic humanity? As our perception of incompleteness changes with new sensitivities to racism, sexism, and European chauvinism, must not the image of Christ take ever new forms: as woman, as Black and Brown woman, as impoverished and despised woman of those peoples who are the underside of Christian imperialism? In what ways do women need such an appearance of a WomanChrist? Do men also need a WomanChrist. . . ? [174]

Ruether's Christology addresses these complex, interwoven questions by identifying Christianity's male savior as a historical figure who is the Christ only partially and incompletely. This historical figure is a male, but he is also a Palestinian Jew and a peasant: his maleness is one form of particularity among others, and all of them are interstructured. [175]

But it is Jesus' own life--his actions, his relations--rather than his maleness that makes him proleptically or paradigmatically Christ. He is paradigmatic because he is prophetic: he anticipates human liberation, fulfillment, and redemption by repudiating structures and relations of domination and subjugation.[176] This kenosis takes place in his relations and in his presentation of these relations to others as liberating models of an anticipated liberated humanity, which can be partially actualized within the limits of historical existence. The liberation of the lowest of the low in relation to Jesus enables them also to be paradigms of liberation and redemption for others.[177]

The maleness of Jesus is significant to his being the Christ only because of what it signifies historically. Because Jesus is a male who lives in a patriarchal society and who repudiates the privileges of maleness, he manifests the kenosis of patriarchy: he announces to men and women patriarchal existence's transformation into a new humanity and a new relation with the divine.[178] How Jesus understands his maleness--as a source of privilege to be emptied out--says much about him, and about God. But the biological fact has no cosmological significance.[179]

From the standpoint of our current existence within the partial confines of patriarchalism, then, Ruether's view of God/ess is best understood as kenotic of patriarchy itself, in that hierarchical privilege and power are deliberately emptied out of symbolic and social structures and conceptions.[180] God/ess, who transforms by "pointing us back to our authentic potential and forward to new redeemed possibilities," [181] risks much for the liberation and redemption of the cosmos. So Jesus' kenosis of patriarchy represents God/ess' kenosis as well: "God abandons God's power into the human condition utterly and completely so that we might not abandon each other." [182]

So, Ruether insists, *this* male savior--particularly--*can* participate in the salvation of women. But, she also insists, a male savior *alone* cannot save women *or anyone else*.

Particularity and limitation are basic to human existence, and they must be accepted and seen as dialectically related to the universality that is present only in the transcendent, only in God/ess. The need for many paradigmatic figures to present the fullest possible set of visions of redemption has, indeed, highly positive aspects for Ruether, not the least of which is the possibility of a WomanChrist who can "disclose the journey to redemptive personhood from women's experience." [183]

Summary and Evaluation: Prophetic Iconoclasm as Proclamation

In Ruether's Christology, Jesus is an iconoclastic, messianic prophet whose life and death provide a model of redeemed humanity. Jesus' model is, in itself, also an inspiration for others. The spirit of Jesus draws others into lives of liberating struggle and transformation of human existence. Not the least of Jesus' Christ-like characteristics is his passionate devotion to the Reign of God as something possible but not yet established in the midst of human history. The Shalom of God/ess brings all the disparate aspects of existence into harmony.

In his life and death, Jesus also shows the liberating face of God/ess; he is, in that sense, the Word of God that points to the fullness of God but is not itself the entirety of God. Jesus does not claim to be himself the One who is to come; he is, rather, a prophet of that One. And he shows how that One is drawing very near.

Jesus is the Christ, then, in that he discloses the new humanity that is coming into being, and he proclaims the Reign of the One who is to come. But, Ruether insists, he is not the only Christ. The Christ is known wherever the new humanity appears, and wherever the face of God/ess as liberator is shown. That is, we encounter Christ "in the form of our sister," as well as in the form of Jesus. Even for Christians, Jesus is not the only Christ. While he is paradigmatic of what it means to be the Christ, he also proclaims and even anticipates the possibility of further paradigms to come as the Shalom of God/ess unfolds in history.

The relativity of Jesus as the Christ even for Christians is necessary if the dualisms at the root of patriarchal domination are to be healed. And these dualisms must be healed if the fullness of both the new humanity and God/ess's Shalom are to come into being in human existence. For God/ess is dynamic: the matrix out of which all things come, the power and inspiration for liberation, and the final source of transformation. God/ess is the source of both being and new being. And for new being to emerge, ever new paradigms and proclamations are needed.

For Jesus to be the Christ, then, means for him *and for his followers* to recognize that he is not absolute and final; only God/ess is, and only beyond history. [184] Nor, then, is Jesus the absolute and final Christ. If the Christ is the model for a redeemed humanity that has yet to come into being, and if the Christ is also the face of God/ess as liberator in the midst of the movements of human historical existence, then no Christ can be unique and absolute if that means that no other Christ will ever be encountered. What it means to be the Christ is better understood in terms of fullness within historical conditions, complete authenticity in the midst of finite existence, and unswerving devotion to the source and power of history *precisely as* the source and power of history. The Christ stands as one who points beyond the self, beyond the human, to the true God who is the ground and power of all. When Jesus is understood to be *not* the only and final or complete embodiment of both humanity and divinity, both human and divine are set free for fuller expression of the range of possibilities inherent in both, different modes of being.

In his kenosis of patriarchy, Jesus empties out the power of human patriarchal domination to confine human possibility, to distort human existence, and to wreak havoc across the earth. Jesus also empties out the possibility that humans will believe that it is God who is the source of domination and subjugation. The God whom Jesus proclaims, and who inspires his life and his death, is not the heavenly ruler, but the historical liberator. The authentic human nature of Jesus as the Christ is quite evident in Ruether's formulations. It is how Jesus discloses the divine that is less clear.

Nor is this accidental. Ruether's primary critical concern--to overcome the dualisms of history and transcendence, and of particular and universal--convinces her that any attempt to render the transcendent in terms appropriate only to the finite and the historical will lead into the same difficulties that have produced the multiple crises facing Euro-American culture and religion, and so the world. [185] The fullness of God/ess is always beyond history, not fully poured out into history. It is the *Word* of God, the spirit of God, or the liberating face of God/ess that is present in history, and within the limits of historical forms and existence. Jesus' proclamation of God/ess and his authentically human life and death point accurately to where God/ess is to be found: at the source, and beyond.

Ruether's strong and powerful emphasis on the prophetic and eschatological elements of Christology has a number of benefits. First, this emphasis provides real drive, force, and grounding to the desire and need for liberation and transformation. The rejoining of criticism and hope and of history and transcendence in dialectic rather than dualized relation renders the struggle for authentic human existence realistic: real transformation is possible now, but its cost may be high. And Ruether's emphasis on the future as well as the past is especially helpful to those whose presence and participation has been largely distorted, suppressed, and silenced in records of the past. The fullness of truth and harmony lies ahead, says Ruether; there, all may participate in a way which, for all we know, has never been the case before. The possibility and promise of this future inspires those burdened not only by the unjust conditions of contemporary existence, but also by the further injustice of having no rooting in a heritage of full humanity.

But Ruether's emphasis on the prophetic and eschatological elements of Christology also has its problems. First, while Ruether emphasizes Jesus's kenosis of patriarchy--the old humanity--and judges that full and complete, she is also clear that the fullness of new humanity is not yet present in Jesus nor (by implication) even in the most liberated of the relations in which he is engaged. The new humanity lies ahead of him, even as it does of all other human persons. No more than any other prophet, before or since, does Jesus manifest the fullness of what it means to be human. Again, he points ahead and beyond, to the One who is to come.

Second, Ruether's recourse to a spirit Christology, reconstructed to be more historical and relational, leaves unclear how Jesus *as the Christ* is related to God *directly*. Jesus, inspired by God's spirit, proclaims the Word of God, and models something of the coming of God's Reign. But--again--no more than any other prophet does Jesus manifest the being of God/ess.

If a--and perhaps the--central affirmation of Christian faith is that Jesus is for Christians decisive in a way unlike other paradigmatic figures--perhaps the minimal way to state the contemporary meaning of the traditional affirmation "Jesus is the Christ"--then Ruether's portrayal of Jesus as *a* Christ rather than *the* Christ, even for Christians, falls short of full adequacy.

This shortcoming arises, I think, out of Ruether's inadvertent continuation of a dialectic-become-dualism of which she seems unaware in her own work: that of manifestation and proclamation.

As I have elaborated in Chapter 5, the dialectic of manifestation and proclamation begins from human encounter with the divine as experience of both participation in and distanciation from the whole. The pole of manifestation focuses the intensification of participation, and the immanent power of the divine as the enveloping ground which is always already present.[186] The Christ is understood to be the incarnated manifestation of the true nature of both human and divine, as, for example, the representation of "the only liberating relation one can have with God," that is, of the authentic character of human existence.[187] When this paradigm is transformed via liberating praxis, the giftedness of existence in creation is taken to be the force grounding prophetic, eschatological urgency and the imperative for social-historical action.[188]

The pole of proclamation focuses the intensification of distance and difference, where the divine is encountered as a radically other power that defamiliarizes. Christologies within the proclamation paradigm tend to emphasize Christ's cross and prophetic-eschatological message. The Christ is taken as a disclosure of the need for reform, resistance, protest, and struggle against the present human condition.[189] When this paradigm is transformed via liberating praxis, the emphases on the cross and on the prophetic-eschatological are reoriented to address alienating and oppressive structures of social existence that constitute the individual.

The point that Tracy is insistent on making is that the separation of these two poles into oppositions loses the experiential fullness of the human encounter with the divine. When the "always-already which is yet a not-yet" tension of religious experience is broken into dualism, the two separated poles are reduced to "'mere' symbols, mere ciphers of transcendence, simply examples of possibility."[190] The sense of the whole, in which the human participates through manifestation and from which the human is distanced for the sake of proclamation, is lost from expression of the experience of that whole.

The prophetic and the eschatological must, Tracy contends, stay in dialectical tension with the ongoing gracious presence of God manifest in history. For Christology, this means a maintained tension between cross, resurrection, and incarnation; between the Christ as the word of and about God, and the Christ as self-manifestation of God.[191] Although, Tracy notes, all theologians will place greater emphasis on one pole than on the other, and do so out of their own encounters with the divine, "Each emphasis . . . needs the other as a self-corrective moment in its own particular journey of intensification, not just as a merely external corrective or 'reminder' of the other aspects of the whole."[192]

Ruether's Christology does contain elements of both manifestation and proclamation, but it does so in rather dualistic terms. First, Jesus himself is a figure in which proclamation is substantially more evident than is manifestation, both relative to the Christ and relative to God/ess. That is, Jesus is prophetic of the eschatological fullness of Christ, which is yet to appear.

Nowhere is this clearer than in the concluding sections of *Womanguides*' section on redemption:

> Must not the Christ-image be ever projected on the new horizon of history that appears before us, leading us on to our yet unrealized potential? As our perception of our incompleteness changes with new sensitivities to racism, sexism, and European chauvinism, must not the image of Christ take ever new forms: as woman, as Black and Brown woman, as impoverished and despised woman of those peoples who are the underside of Christian imperialism? [193]

The kenotic Jesus empties out the power of patriarchy, but is not himself fully the Christ, because he does not embody the lowest of the low in the history of human existence to this point. He does not embody the new, liberated humanity.

Further, Ruether's description of the Christ correlates manifestation primarily with the new humanity and proclamation primarily with God/ess: Christ is "the model for this redeemed humanity"[194] and "the manifest[ation] of the face of God/ess as liberator."[195] In Ruether's view, the Christ may--but has not yet--disclosed the full humanity to be realized in the future. And the Christ manifests one aspect of God/ess: the liberating face, the word, the spirit. The full self-manifestation of God/ess as both matrix and the One who is to come lies in the trans-historical future. That One's *spirit* is present in history, as word and as inspiring power; but the fullness of God/ess remains concealed.

Ruether's Christology, then, tends toward dualism around the question of how the divine and the human are related in the Christ. In light of her own criteria for evaluating feminist liberation theological proposals, this tendency raises the question of the adequacy of her discussion of Christology. Ruether suggests as criteria the prophetic-liberating principle derived from Scripture, and the full humanity of women that emerges from struggles for liberation from oppression.

Ruether's reconstruction of the prophetic-liberating tradition heavily emphasizes denunciation of present reality and annunciation of the future, eschatological establishment of a different reality, in history and beyond it. Her primary interest is in the prophetic strand of the Hebrew Bible, and its continuity in the Synoptic Gospels. [196] Her interpretation of these Biblical materials focuses on the failings of human structures and institutions. When she speaks of God in relation to these failings, her interest is in God's intervention as vindicator of the oppressed. [197] Missing here is the sense of God's presence in the midst of human failings, as, for example, the comforter of the poor against whose afflictions God wreaks judgment. Ruether's reading of the prophetic-liberating principle captures major elements of the Biblical traditions; but it does not present the tradition in its fullness. When Ruether's principle is then applied to other areas, such as Christology, the same deficit is continued. This contributes to Ruether's not casting Jesus as "God with us," present in human suffering as much as ahead of it as liberator.

Ruether's second criterion is the full humanity of women, which she envisions arising out of women's historical situation as oppressed. And her source for construing women's situation is women's experience. Yet oddly missing from her Christology is the concrete experience of women of the presence of God through the Christ precisely in experiences of oppression. For example, in a published address, Ruether recounts the story told by a woman student of her rape and its aftermath:

> When the rapist finally fled, and she found herself still alive, she experienced a vision of Christ as a crucified woman. This vision filled her with relief and healing: "I would not have to explain to a male God that I had been raped. God knew what it was like to be a woman who had been raped." [198]

Yet the caption to the photograph in *Womanguides* of "The Crucified Woman" reads, "is she only a victim, or can women bring forth redemption from their sufferings on the cross of patriarchy?" [199] If this is an image of the WomanChrist, she is only human. Yet the account given by the woman who was raped is of the presence of *God*. Similar accounts by other women of their own experience of the presence of God through the suffering Christ are numerous. [200]

Within the framework of her own criteria, then, Ruether's Christology is lacking precisely at the point that her emphasis on the prophetic and the eschatological overshadows the present manifestation of God. The problems with her proposals are even more evident within the framework of the larger Christian theological discussion, which minimally claims that Jesus is the Christ in a way that is decisive or definitive *for Christians*.[201] In Ruether's view, the Christ is relative; any past or present Christ will be superseded by future Christs who provide models of the new humanity that are more appropriate to changed historical conditions. Neither is the one acclaimed as Christ in Christian communities--Jesus--himself fully a Christ, in that he does not embody the lowest of the low in his own circumstances. Jesus is not definitive even in his own time, and no single Christ can be definitive for all time.

This negative evaluation of the relative adequacy of Ruether's Christology does not mean her work is not both helpful and fruitful. Far from it. Rather, Ruether's feminist liberation theological formulations serve as one pole, which can be set in dialectical relation with another that puts greater emphasis on the manifestation of the divine through the human. Ruether's Christology contributes a powerful and necessary prophetic and eschatological focus. Her emphasis on prophecy, struggle, and breakthrough from the future has an imperative force, which militates against historical ideologization and idolatrous projection of human achievement onto the divine. Here, the relativization of Christology through eschatology is a forceful reminder of both the capacity of the divine to disrupt and transform human complacency and delusion, and of the capacity of the human to respond to such disruption by transforming the distortions and injustices of historical existence.

But more is needed to move toward a Christology that is relatively adequate to contemporary women's experience in the struggle for liberation, to these struggles as ongoing into the future, and to the fullness of Christian traditions in which the triumph of patriarchy has never been absolute.

Notes

1.   This is the core of Daly's critique.   It is important to
remember that with this incarnation comes a stripping away from
women of valued and specifically female functions, and the symbolic
(but nonetheless significant) assignment of these same functions to
men. See *Beyond God the Father*, 195. Hampson's argument is
slightly different, in that it is based on the ongoing power of
patriarchal symbols to reinforce patriarchy.

2.   This is Brock's criticism in *Journeys by Heart*.

3.   This is a second aspect of Daly's critique, although she would
take exception to my reference to eternity.

4.   Daly, Christ, Brock, and Hampson are all emphatic on this
point.

5.   Jacqueline Grant, *White Women's Christ and Black Women's
Jesus: Feminist Christology and Womanist Response* (Atlanta:
Scholars Press, 1989), 178-179.

6.   This critique is developed most fully by Rosemary Radford
Ruether, and is discussed at length in this chapter.

7.   Ruether, "The Future of Feminist Theology in the Academy,"
710-711.

8.   In his book *The Point of Christology*, Schubert M. Ogden
persuasively argues that the point of Christology is existential-
historical, that is, it is "not about the being of Jesus in himself, but
about the meaning of Jesus for us." (87; see also 56f., 59f., 64f.) My
point here is that white feminist Christologies, in less explicit form,
make the same argument in that they interpret Jesus through
contemporary women's experience in the struggle for liberation from
patriarchal oppression. As I shall indicate in this chapter and the next
four, the authors I discuss agree that Jesus means liberation from
oppression and transformation toward liberation, although the way this
meaning is elaborated varies among these white feminists.

9.   Ruether, *Sexism and God-Talk*, 131.

10.   Heyward, *Redemption of God*, 200; idem, *Our Passion for
Justice*, 46 and 178.

11.   Ruether, *Sexism and God-Talk*, 138.

12.   Ibid., 114.

13.   Ruether, *Womanguides*, 105.

14.   Rosemary Radford Ruether, "The Liberation of Christ- ology
from Patriarchy," in *Religion and Intellectual Life* 2 (Spring 1985):
116.

15. Rosemary Radford Ruether, *To Change the World: Christology and Cultural Criticism* (New York: Crossroad, 1983), 45.

16. Ibid., 31 and elsewhere.

17. Ruether, *Sexism and God-Talk*, 114.

18. Ibid., 114.

19. Note that this means that human existence is profoundly *relational*, on the model described in the earlier discussion of women's experience.

20. Rosemary Radford Ruether, *Liberation Theology: Human Hope Confronts Christian History and American Power* (New York: Paulist Press, 1972), 2, 5.

21. Ruether, *Sexism and God-Talk*, 93.

22. Thus, theology both legitimately and necessarily uses ideas and symbols current in its socio-historical context to disclose aspects of transcendence that speak to "new experiential needs," which arise from historical existence (Ruether, *Sexism and God-Talk*, 14). See also Daphne Hampson and Rosemary Ruether, "Is There a Place for Feminist in a Christian Church?", 16.

23. Ruether, *Sexism and God-Talk*, 13.

24. Rosemary Radford Ruether, *New Woman/New Earth: Sexist Ideologies and Human Liberation* (New York: Seabury, 1975), 74; and many other works. The exact terms for these most fundamental dualisms vary historically and in Ruether's many discussions of them. The list I have given here is that which is specifically related to feminist liberation theology.

25. Ruether, *Liberation Theology*, 16.

26. Judith Vaughn. *Sociality, Ethics, and Social Change: A Critical Appraisal of Reinhold Niebuhr's Ethics in the Light of Rosemary Ruether's Work* (Lanham, MD: University Press of America, 1983), 106.

27. Ruether, *Liberation Theology*, 5, 7.

28. Ruether, *Sexism and God-Talk*, 181. See also Ruether, *New Woman/New Earth*, passim.

29. This discussion is found in its most detailed form in *New Woman/New Earth*, 115-132. Ruether's discussion of the inter-structuring of gender, race, and class--its limitations aside--is a major contribution to the development of feminist theology as a theology of liberation.

30. Ruether, *Liberation Theology*, 19, 95. The process leading to these dualisms is largely but not exclusively one of the psychological projection onto others of feared elements of the self. This projection

is itself in turn reinforced by domination, which reciprocally rationalizes exploitation of the subjugated. The exploited, moreover, internalize their domination. Ruether develops this idea in *Faith and Fratricide*. See also Ruether, *Sexism and God-Talk*, 162.

31. For example, while it is the case that women in the United States "share a common condition of women in general (dependency, secondary existence, domestic labor, sexual exploitation, and the projection of their role in procreation into a total definition of their existence)," it is also the case that "this common condition takes profoundly different forms, as women are divided against each other by class and race." (Ruether, *New Woman/New Earth*, 125)

32. That is, "man's" domination of nature has been under the control of ruling-class males who dominate other persons as well (Ruether, *To Change the World*, 58-60).

33. Ruether, *Sexism and God-Talk*, 91.

34. Mary Hembrow Snyder, *The Christology of Rosemary Radford Ruether: A Critical Introduction* (Mystic, CT: Twenty-Third Publications, 1988): 15.

35. Ruether, *Sexism and God-Talk*, 18-19.

36. In Chapter 3, I suggested that three criteria are required to assess the adequacy of theological proposals: adequacy to religious traditions, to contemporary human experience, and to future use in concrete projects of liberation. Ruether's method is formally similar at this point. For discussion of the dialectic between tradition and liberation in Ruether, see Grant, *White Woman's Christ and Black Woman's Jesus*, 117.

37. In addition, the Biblical prophetic tradition and other parts of Scripture contain revelatory paradigms for the construction of a new world. Even patriarchal texts that silence and suppress women's voices and presence can be "sources for [reflection on] our own experience" now, because they indicate that patriarchy was never entirely successful in "defining what women actually were or did in past times." Therefore, engagement with patriarchal religious traditions can assist in creating "an enlarged memory" that gives voice to the silenced past, recovering moments of struggle for liberation, and generating constructive vision by placing in conjunction disparate, often conflicting traditions from within the same faith communities. (Ruether, *To Change the World*, 6.) See also Ruether, "Future of Feminist Theology," 707; and Mary McClintock Fulkerson, "Review of Rosemary Radford Ruether, *Womanguides*," *Journal of the American Academy of Religion* 54 [Fall 1986]: 607.

38.   Ruether, *To Change the World*, 31.   Therefore, Christian anti-Judaism cannot be dismissed as an accident, a "peripheral element," or an import from paganism; it is fundamental in Christian thought. Ruether's concern with Christian anti-Judaism is of long and continuous standing, and formative for all her other Christological criticisms and constructions, particularly her understanding of Jesus as a messianic prophet. *Faith and Fratricide* (1974) is Ruether's most exhaustive published presentation on this topic. Her unpublished "The Messiah of Israel and the Cosmic Christ: A Study of the Development of Christology in Judaism and Early Christianity" (1971) develops more fully the Biblical and historical arguments found in *Faith and Fratricide*. (See Snyder, passim, and Gregory Baum's Introduction to *Faith and Fratricide*, passim, for discussions of this work.)

Ruether's recent book *The Wrath of Jonah: The Crisis of Religious Nationalism in the Israeli-Palestinian Conflict*, co-authored with Herman J. Ruether (San Francisco: Harper and Row, 1989), traces Christian responses to Judaism and Zionism since 1967, as well as providing an analysis of the Israeli-Palestinian conflict. (For how the situation and so the response has changed since the publication of *Faith and Fratricide*, see *The Wrath of Jonah*, 206-207.)   The Ruethers believe that the "ethnocentric nationalism" they see in Israel's treatment of the Palestinians is contradictory to the teaching and prophecy toward justice that Jews have provided in Western societies (xiv), and of the prophetic principle that Judaism and Christianity share (238), which is the principle upon which Rosemary Ruether relies for the transformation of anti-Judaism, sexism, racism, classism, and so on. The plea in this book is for mutual acceptance and repentance, coupled with mutual criticism.

39.   Ruether maintains that Judaism rejected *all* messianic figures because they did not meet all expectations attached to the Messiah. The rejection of Jesus has to be seen in this light, as fidelity to messianic hope (Snyder, 35). Ruether notes that Jesus' claims about the inbreaking reign of God would have discredited him among his fellow Jews. "The fact that one can 'begin' to experience the dawning of this miracle [the presence of the reign of God] in no way alters the fact that no Jew, including Jesus, would have spoken of the Kingdom as 'already here' or the Messiah as having 'already come' as long as sin continued and the evil nations maintained their sway over Israel." (Ruether, "Messiah of Israel," 175; quoted in Snyder, 37.) See also *Sexism and God-Talk*, 119f. In *The Wrath of Jonah (197-199)*, the Ruethers extend the critique of realized Messianism to the view

advanced by Emil Fackenheim and others that the founding of the state of Israel marks "'the beginning of the dawn of our redemption.'"

40.   Ruether, *To Change the World*, 33. After the Holocaust, "The question for Christianity arises from Christian culpability for almost two millennia of anti-Semitism, which fed the hatred and indifference that made the Holocaust in 'Christian' Europe possible. . . . Christians must ask about the silence of 'man,' specifically Christians, who not only failed to act to save their Jewish neighbors but, in many cases, aided and abetted the violence." (Ibid., *The Wrath of Jonah*, 204.) See also Fackenheim, *To Mend the World*, 280ff.

41.   Ruether, *Faith and Fratricide*, 246. In Ruether's view, Christian anti-Judaism has three basic elements: (1) Christianity's failure as a prophetic-messianic inner-Jewish reform movement, and its designation as sectarian by Jewish authorities; (2) the "eschatological advent" interpretation of Jesus' failure to return soon; and (3) the anti-Jewish terms of Christian apologetics in the Greco-Roman world. (See Ruether, *Faith and Fratricide*, 94, 246-247; idem, *Disputed Questions: On Being a Christian*, [Nashville: Abingdon, 1982], 47.)

42.   Ruether, *Faith and Fratricide*, 246.

43.   Ruether's criticism of Zionism and the State of Israel in *The Wrath of Jonah* arises in part from the sense that Zionism has internalized these schisms. See particularly 217, 220-221, 232, and 244. See also Ruether, "Eschatology and Feminism" in *Lift Every Voice: Constructing Christian Theologies from the Underside*, ed. Susan Brooks Thistlethwaite and Mary Potter Engel (San Francisco: Harper and Row, 1990): 112.

44.   Ruether, *Faith and Fratricide*, 245.

45.   Ibid., 236.

46.   Ruether, "Messiah of Israel," 437; quoted in Snyder, 47.

47.   Ruether, *Faith and Fratricide*, 255-256.

48.   Ruether, *Disputed Questions*, 64.

49.   Ruether, *To Change the World*, 34.

50.   Ruether, *Sexism and God-Talk*, 22f; idem, "Feminism and Religious Faith: Renewal or New Creation?" *Religion and Intellectual Life* 3 (Winter 86): 13; idem, "Feminist Interpretation: A Method of Correlation," in *Feminist Interpretation of the Bible*, ed. Letty M. Russell, (Philadelphia: Westminster Press, 1985), 117.

51.   Ruether, *Sexism and God-Talk*, 24.

52.   Snyder, 17.

53. Ruether, *Sexism and God-Talk*, 27. What is in accord with the prophetic-liberating tradition in one era may very well not be in another. For example, the Biblical denunciation of the Canaanites when the Israelites were oppressed highlanders is a protest against injustice and oppression, and so in accord with the principle. However, the same denunciation when Israel was itself a kingdom is an ideological defense of national interest at the expense of another, competing group, and so in discord with the principle.

54. Indeed, Ruether argues, its critical application is appropriate *only* to self-criticism, not to criticism of "others" outside one's own culture or society. (Ruether, *Disputed Questions*, 34; and similar discussions in Ruether, *Faith and Fratricide*.) On this principle, the criticism of Jewish Zionism, of the State of Israel and of Jewish religious thinkers found in *The Wrath of Jonah* alongside the criticism of Christian thinkers is rather surprising. However, the Ruethers note, "Mutual criticism does not mean a competitive put-down but a concern of communities to help each other be truthful about their failures and to regain their prophetic voice. Thus Christian-Jewish solidarity today must include both a critique of Christian anti-Semitism and a concern to liberate the Jewish community to regain its prophetic voice toward its own system of power." (219.) The Ruethers' recent critique of both Jewish and Christian Zionism seems to be based on the assessment (found in *Faith and Fratricide*) that Christian anti-Judaism springs in large measure from Christian absolutization, revealed as error by Judaism's contrasting valuation of particularities as pointing to the sole absolute, God. The error of Zionism and of the State of Israel is a similar absolutizing of both suffering and redemption (*The Wrath of Jonah*, 199, 238, 244, and passim). Zionism is, therefore, a violation of the key Jewish tradition in Rosemary Ruether's analysis, and so is subject to critique by those who subscribe to that tradition, be they Jews or Christians.

55. Carol Christ and Elisabeth Schüssler Fiorenza criticize Ruether at this point because of the androcentrism of the content of the tradition, its transmission, and its use, which--Christ judges--is sufficiently central and foundational to make reconstruction of it impossible and the tradition itself unusable. (See Christ, "The New Feminist Theology," 207.) Schüssler Fiorenza, unlike Christ, believes that the tradition can be rendered usable through a feminist reconstruction; but she thinks Ruether has yet to accomplish this (Fiorenza, *In Memory of Her*, 17-18).

Ruether has responded to these criticisms by indicating that she has described a dynamic rather than a "timeless essence." Second, she has generalized (rather than abstracted) the characteristics typical of this dynamic as it is found in a number of historical instances. Third, she has explicitly recognized that the prophetic-liberating tradition fails to be fully critical. This failure occurs because the "subjects of this liberating *praxis*" are limited by their own historical position and its privilege: while they see their own oppression, they do not see whom they are oppressing (Rosemary Radford Ruether, "Review of Elisabeth Schüssler Fiorenza, *In Memory of Her*," *Horizons* 11 (Spring, 1984): 146-150; 147-149). Finally, Ruether judges, the prophetic strand, *as she has described it*, contains within it the seeds of its own correction, and these have borne fruit within the various historical liberation movements that have used this tradition (Ruether, "Re-contextualizing Theology." *Today* 43 (April 1986): 26; also Snyder, 17.)

However, the mode of Ruether's recent criticism of Zionist and Israeli Judaism would seem to validate the criticism put forward by Schüssler Fiorenza, Sheila Greeve Davaney, and Daphne Hampson that the prophetic tradition functions as a "core," "essence," or "golden thread" which is, finally, historically inviolable and immutable. (See Schüssler Fiorenza, loc. cit.; Sheila Greeve Davaney, "Problems with Feminist Theory: Historicity and the Search for Sure Foundations," in *Embodied Love: Sensuality and Relationship as Feminist Values*, ed. Paula M. Cooey, Sharon A. Farmer, and Mary Ellen Ross [San Francisco: Harper and Row, 1987]: 79-95; Hampson, *Theology and Feminism*, 28.) In *The Wrath of Jonah*, it is Zionism's abandonment of this tradition in favor of Western Christian absolutisms that is at the root of Israeli mishandling of the just claims of the Palestinian people.

56.   Ruether, "Feminism and Religious Faith," 13; idem, *Sexism and God-Talk*, 23, 33; idem, *Liberation Theology*, 7.

57.   Ruether, *To Change the World*, 5.

58.   Ruether, *Disputed Questions*, 34.

59.   Ruether, *Sexism and God-Talk*, 32.

60.   In Ruether's view, the Biblical prophetic-liberating tradition is the forerunner of all Euro-American liberation movements, including those that dismiss religion as inherently ideological (Ruether, "Recontextualizing Theology," 26).

61.   Therefore, Ruether can answer the claims of Daly, Christ, Hampson, and others that Christianity is inherently and irremediably patriarchal by saying "Christianity is not simply a culture of

domination. It is also deeply rooted in a culture of liberation. Christianity is rooted in the great insights of the Hebrew Bible that denounced systems of injustice that oppressed the poor. Prophetic faith included the critique of religion. The prophets and Jesus recalled faith to the work of justice and mercy, rather than sanctification of oppression." (Hampson and Ruether, 20.)

62. Ruether, *Sexism and God-Talk*, 125-126. Note here Ruether's general concurrence with Daly's and Hampson's analyses of Christology. "[T]he question of whether a male saviour can save women is not merely a provocative theoretical question. It is one on which many thousands of women have already voted with their feet by leaving the church and seeking alternative feminist communities." (Idem, *To Change the World*, 47.)

63. The concept of God as Logos was also linked to patriarchal social hierarchy by Eusebius' parallel between the Logos and the emperor; the Logos exercises social control over those defined as "other," as well as being the creative and ordering aspect of God. Thus, "Christology becomes the apex of a system of control." (Ruether, *Sexism and God-Talk*, 125.) Ruether cites as positive elements of Logos Christologies their combination of the liberating messiah (who stands over against worldly power) with the original creator and guider of the world. This combination prevents a dualistic split between creation and redemption. However, when the Logos comes to be seen as the foundation of the powers of the world, the liberating potential of Logos Christologies is suppressed in favor of the sanctification of the dominant social and religious order. (Idem, *Womanguides*, 109.)

64. Ruether, "The Female Nature of God: A Problem in Contemporary Religious Life," in *God as Father*, ed. Johannes-Baptiste Metz and Edward Schillebeeckx; Eng. lang. ed. Marcus Lefebure, (Edinburgh: T. & T. Clark, 1981), 63. That is, the symbolics of patriarchal theology assign the same roles to the feminine as women have played in patriarchal society and culture.

65. Ibid., 63. Ruether argues that religions presenting divinity as either the Goddess or a pairing of Goddess and God were prior to and often violently superseded by male monotheism. That is, she agrees with Daly, Christ, and others that the triumph of God in male monotheism includes the suppression of the Goddess. But she does not concur with their particular understandings of how the Goddess is to be recovered. See *Sexism and God-Talk*, Ruether's dialogue with Daphne Hampson, and elsewhere.

66. Ruether, *To Change the World*, 46; idem, *Sexism and God-Talk*, 67.
67. Ruether, *Faith and Fratricide*, 243.
68. St. Augustine, *De Trinitate* 7,7,10, indicates "the male generic character of the imago dei." See Ruether, *Sexism and God-Talk*, 93-94.
69. Ruether, *To Change the World*, 45, and *Sexism and God-Talk*, 126, where Ruether discusses Aquinas' *Summa Theologia* Part I Q 92, 1 and 2; Q 99,2; and Part 3, Supplement, Q 39,1. These and similar texts in Bonaventure are used currently in (Roman and Anglo-) Catholic rulings and discussions to prohibit or argue against the ordination of women.
70. Ruether, *Sexism and God-Talk*, 110.
71. Ibid., 135. See also Ruether, "The Liberation of Christology," 119.
72. Ibid., 135.
73. Ruether examines four alternative models of Christ as part of warranting her choice of "the prophetic, iconoclastic Christ" as the one most adequate to both Scripture and contemporary experience. (1) The "imperial Christ," who comes from Judaism's messianic-kingship tradition, supports hierarchy and subjugation against the vindication of the oppressed. (2) The "androgynous Christ"--found in some of early Christianity's gnostic Christologies, in Julian of Norwich, and in some Nineteenth Century Anglo-American sects--either desexualizes or valorizes the feminine without challenging male dominance--and without presenting any woman as the representation of full human potential. Thus, they continue to have an androcentric bias. (3) Spirit Christologies--found in the Joachite mystics as well as in some gnostic sects and some Nineteenth Century Anglo-American sects--affirm the appearance of the Christ in historical persons other than Jesus, but tend to "disembody" the spirit of Christ from concrete, historical persons and circumstances. This, in turn, supports sectarian withdrawal from engagement with the surrounding social order. (4) The "prophetic iconoclastic Christ" of Nineteenth Century Christian socialist movements and contemporary liberation theologies is the closest, Ruether finds, to the Jesus of the Synoptics in seeking not a reversal of the social order, but a new order altogether. Ruether's preferred model is, in fact, a combination of the prophetic model of the Synoptics with a Spirit Christology. See *Ruether, To Change the World*, 47-56; *Sexism and God-Talk*, 122-138; and my discussion of

Ruether's retrieval of Spirit Christologies, below. On all this, see also Brock, *Journeys by Heart*, 61-65.

74.   Ruether, *Womanguides*, 112.

75.   Because various systems of domination are interstructured, producing interlocking systems of domination and subjugation by race and class as well as gender, women's experience is necessarily pluralistic. Ruether insists that theory and practice drawn from women's experience are adequate only when they reflect this pluralism positively as "genuine variety and particularity," which is at the same time characterized by a set of experiential commonalities among women across lines of race and class (Ruether, "Feminist Interpretation," 113, 116; idem, "Future of Feminist Theology," 704). However, as Jacquelyn Grant and (subsequently) Susan Brooks Thistlethwaite helpfully point out, the juxtaposition of particularity and commonality in Ruether's and others' view of interstructuring tends to weigh more heavily on the side of commonality, risking the loss of the tension between varyingly marginalized groups, and tending to mask the reality of conflict (Grant, op. cit., 191). For this reason, Thistlethwaite, as a white woman struggling with racism, proposes that white feminists start not from commonality but from difference. (*Sex, Race, and God*, 11-26 and passim.)

76.   Ruether, "Feminist Interpretation," 113-115.

77.   Ruether, "Future of Feminist Theology," 710.

78.   The birth of feminist consciousness is thus itself a conversion experience in the religious sense. See, for example, Heyward, "Limits of Liberalism: Feminism in Moral Crisis," in *Our Passion for Justice*, 153-174.

79.   Ruether, *Sexism and God-Talk*, 18-19. The application of the feminist principle of promotion of the full humanity of oppressed women to theology hinges on establishing a correlation between this principle and principles found in theological traditions, particularly, for Ruether, the prophetic-liberating tradition.

80.   Ibid., 19.

81.   Ibid., 160-161. The social character of sin makes it necessary to describe variously the concrete manifestations of sin, in relation to the social placement of particular individuals and groups. That is to say, there is no universal primary sin. Socially, while each group may have a particular sin that arises from and characterizes its position, these types of sin are interstructured. "Women sin by cooperating in their own subjugation, by lateral violence to other women who seek emancipation, and by oppressing groups of people such as children and

domestic servants under their control. Women can be racist, classist, self-hating, manipulative toward dominant males, dominating toward children. But these forms of female evil cooperate with and help to perpetuate an overall system of distorted humanity in which ruling-class males are the apex." (Ibid., 180-181.)

82. Vaughn, 148.

83. Ruether, "Recontextualizing Theology," 24. The primary historical concretization of the structure of sin, in Ruether's view, is sexism, because "a most basic expression of human community, the I-thou relation as the relationship of men and women, has been distorted throughout all known history into an oppressive relationship that has victimized one-half of the human race and turned the other half into tyrants. The primary alienation and distortion of human relationality is reflected in all dimensions of alienation." (Ruether, *Sexism and God-Talk*, 161.)

84. Ruether, "Future of Feminist Theology," 707.

85. Ruether, *To Change the World*, 27. In disavowing pride as the primary human sin, Ruether stands in the line of feminist critique begun by Valerie Saiving in her classic essay, "The Human Situation: A Feminine View," in *Womanspirit Rising*, ed. Christ and Plaskow, 25-42.

86. Ruether, *Sexism and God-Talk*, 207; idem, "Future of Feminist Theology," 707. See the discussion of internalization, below.

87. Ibid., 138, 114.

88. Ruether, *Disputed Questions*, 71-72; Idem, *To Change the World*, 42-43. Ruether's insistence on a proleptic and anticipatory emphasis comes primarily from her analysis of Christian anti-Judaism; her insistence on paradigms rather than absolutes, while rooted in that analysis, is made all the stronger by her analysis of Christian misogyny and of the necessity of religious pluralism that affirms particularity in a context of mutual solidarity. On Christian misogyny, see my discussion, above. On religious pluralism, see (among many possibilities) Ruether, *The Wrath of Jonah*, 244-246, "Feminism and Jewish-Christian Dialogue: Particularism and Universalism in the Search for Religious Truth," in *The Myth of Christian Uniqueness: Toward a Pluralistic Theology of Religions*, John Hick and Paul F. Knitter, eds. (Maryknoll, NY: Orbis Books, 1988). See also the review article by Schubert M. Ogden, "Problems in the Case for a Pluralistic Theology of Religion," 493-507.

89. Ruether, *Sexism and God-Talk*, 116-138.

90.   "The fullness of redeemed humanity, as image of God, is something only partially disclosed under the conditions of history. We seek it as a future self and world, still not fully achieved, still not fully revealed. But we also discover it as our true self and world, the foundation and ground of our being. When we experience glimpses of it, we recognize not an alien self, but our own authentic self. We experience such glimpses through encounters with other persons whose own authenticity discloses the meaning of such personhood. By holding the memory of such persons in our hearts and minds, we are able to recognize authenticity in ourselves and others." (Ruether, *Sexism and God-Talk*, 114.) Or, as Snyder aptly summarizes Ruether's position, "When Ruether says, therefore, that 'Jesus is the Christ,' she is making a claim about the ongoing possibilities inherent in being human." (Snyder, 48.)

91.   Ruether, *Womanguides*, 105.

92.   Ruether, *Sexism and God-Talk*, 135.   The difference is important: Ruether certainly recognizes that a reconstruction which is yet another quest for the historical Jesus is theologically problematic whether or not it is historically practicable. At the same time, Ruether, as a Christian theologian, and as a historian who understands the formative effect of the past on the present, does not wish to jettison the past, no matter how patriarchal.   Ruether therefore presents a "re-encounter," which is informed most particularly by the Synoptic Gospels (which Ruether understands as the record of the earliest witnesses rather than as a transcript of Jesus' sayings) reread through the lens of contemporary women's experience in the struggle for liberation. On the formation of the Synoptics, see *Sexism and God-Talk*, 123.

93.   Ruether, *Faith and Fratricide*, 248.   Ruether is also convinced that this kind of memory of Jesus is the most faithful: since Jesus did not present himself "as God's 'last word' and 'once-for-all' disclosure of God," Christianity's insistence on doing so is a repudiation of "the spirit of Jesus and . . . the position against which he himself protests." (Ruether, *Sexism and God-Talk*, 122.)

94.   Ruether, *Faith and Fratricide*, 248.

95.   Thus, Ruether insists that the original messianic idea in Jesus' time was *both* spiritual and social. "Reconciliation with God means the revolutionizing of human social, political relations, over-throwing unjust, oppressive relations." (Ruether, *To Change the World*, 11, and throughout the first essay.) See also Ruether, "Eschatology and Feminism," 116-121, for Ruether's recent discussion of the

development of eschatology. Jesus understood as messianic prophet stands in line with the aspect of eschatology which Ruether finds the most promising for our times and situations.

96. Ruether, *To Change the World*, 14-15. Ruether thinks that the Lord's Prayer is the most nearly original of Jesus' sayings we have.

97. "Jesus does not think of himself as the 'last word of God,' but points beyond himself to 'One who will come.'" (Ruether, *Sexism and God-Talk*, 121.) See also Ruether's recent comments on The Gospel of John's presentation of Jesus as a paradigmatic figure who brings a "foretaste of the truth" in Hampson and Ruether, 17.

98. Ruether, *Faith and Fratricide*, 68f; Hampson and Ruether, 15.

99. Ruether, *To Change the World*, 15; idem, *New Woman/New Earth*, 64f. Cf. Matt 20:25-27.

100. Ruether, *To Change the World*, 55. Ruether insists that the selection of women as exemplars is not because they were female *per se* (i.e., a biological rather than a social group), but because of what being female means in patriarchal society: women are the oppressed of the oppressed in a hierarchical and patriarchal social order of interstructured relations of class, gender, and race.

101. Ruether, *Sexism and God-Talk*, 136.

102. Ibid., 136 and 138. Grant notes that it is this redeemed-redeemer movement in Jesus the paradigm that allows others to serve as paradigms of redemption. Thus, the "once-for-all" status of Jesus as the Christ is left behind. (Grant, op. cit., 143-144.) Grant's argument is contrary to Brock's criticism that Ruether's Christology is inadequate to a relational paradigm. Brock's criticisms spring in part from her judgment that "Missing from Ruether's position is the crucial presence of members of Jesus' community as embodying God/dess and having a transforming impact on him." (Brock, *Journeys by Heart*, 66.)

103. Ibid., 136.

104. Ibid., 69.

105. Ibid., 121.

106. Ibid., 121.

107. Ibid., 5, 121; idem, *To Change the World*, 54; idem, *Womanguides*, 108.

108. Ruether, *Sexism and God-Talk*, 121.

109. Ruether, *To Change the World*, 54.

110. The Romans and the Jewish elites "acted from the perspective of their political expediencies. In this sense, the only people who really could betray Jesus were his own disciples, for only they really heard and acknowledged his authority. The gospels tell us that indeed the disciples did betray him, . . . all the disciples whose hearts continued to be fixed on dreams of power over their enemies." (Ruether, *To Change the World*, 17-18.) Ruether is careful in her treatment of the crucifixion to leave no room for Christian anti-Judaism. This interpretation emphasizes the primacy of self-criticism within the Christian community over criticism of any "others" (although she extends this criticism to Zionism and the State of Israel in *The Wrath of Jonah*). Her Scriptural warrants for criticism of Christian religious elitism come through her frequent invocation of Matthew 20:25-27. See, for example, Ruether, *New Woman/New Earth*, 66.

111. Ruether, *To Change the World*, 29.

112. Ibid., 17-18.

113. Ruether, *Sexism and God-Talk*, 122; idem, *Faith and Fratricide*, 66.

114. Ruether, *Sexism and God-Talk*, 11; idem, *Womanguides*, 108. One of the effects of Jesus' death is to call into question the model of God as "omnipotent sovereign." (Idem, *To Change the World*, 29.)

115. Ruether, *Sexism and God-Talk*, 137-138.

116. Ruether, *To Change the World*, 7.

117. Ruether, *Faith and Fratricide*, 250. "In Jesus, then, we have the symbol of flesh and blood of what will happen in the future, revealing the destiny of the human race, and making known the transformation by which men [*sic*] shall enter into their destiny." (Baum, "Introduction," *Faith and Fratricide*, 18.) See also Hampson and Ruether, 17.

118. Ruether, "Christian Origins and the Counter Culture," *Dialog* 10 (Summer 1971), 199; quoted in Vaughn, 159.

119. "If Jesus is to serve as our paradigm of [the human], then he must not be seen simply as a finalization of an ideal, but one who reveals to us the structure of human existence as it stands in that point of tension between what is and what ought to be. We might say that Jesus is our paradigm of hoping, aspiring [humanity], venturing his life in expectation of the Kingdom, and Christ stands as the symbol of the fulfillment of that hope. Jesus Christ, then, stands for that unification of [humankind] with [its] destiny which has still not come,

but in whose light we continue to hope and struggle." (Ruether, "Messiah of Israel," 436 [unpublished manuscript], quoted in Snyder, 47.

120. Ruether, *Sexism and God-Talk*, 138; italics in the original. Ruether's description of the Christ we may encounter "in the form of our sister" comes from what Ruether designates a Spirit Christology text. (Ibid., 131.)

121. Therefore, Ruether's Christology cannot be deemed adequate for Christian theology--so argue both Schubert M. Ogden and Daphne Hampson--because Ruether does not make some form of the essential Christian affirmation that Jesus is the Christ, that is, that Jesus is related to God in a unique way. (Ogden, "Problems in the Case for a Pluralistic Theology of Religions," 499-500. Ogden defines the "christological assertion" as one "that asserts [in some manner] his decisive significance for human existence by asserting that it is through him that the meaning of God for us . . . is decisively re-presented." [Ogden, *The Point of Christology*, 41-42]. See also Hampson, *Theology and Feminism*, 65.)

122. Ruether, *Sexism and God-Talk*, 114-115.

123. Ruether, *Faith and Fratricide*, 19-20. "In his name we continue to proclaim that hope, and also to begin to experience its presence. But, like Jesus, we also do that under the cross of unresolved human contradictions. The final point of reference for the messianic advent still remains in the future. Its unambiguous arrival still eludes us." (Ruether, *To Change the World*, 42.)

124. Ruether, *Sexism and God-Talk*, 122. The spirit, more precisely, is "the iconoclastic and prophetic vision of Jesus." (Ibid., 123.) See also Hampson and Ruether, 17.

125. Ruether, *To Change the World*, 55. Ruether suggests that some of these relations were redeeming *for Jesus*, not just for others: "The redeemer is one who has been redeemed, just as Jesus himself accepted the baptism of John. Those who have been liberated can, in turn, become paradigmatic, liberating persons for others." (Idem, *Sexism and God-Talk*, 138.)

In light of these clear statements, Brock's criticism of the adequacy of Ruether's movement from "a nonrelational paradigm to a relational one" seems forced. Brock writes, "In placing Jesus' fullest relationship to God/dess within a prophetic context, the world to which Jesus subsequently preaches and ministers becomes the objective proof of his private relationship with God/dess. . . . The oppressed function, in Ruether's scheme, as victims to be acted upon. The world is not described as constitutive of Jesus' personal awareness of God/dess or as a source of his power. Jesus is the hero and liberator." (Idem, *Journeys by Heart*, 65.) However, as is evident even from the summary reading of Ruether which I have provided, Ruether deliberately reconstructs the prophetic tradition away from a lone hero orientation, and into one characterized by mutual relations: neither during his life nor after it is Ruether's Jesus the *sole* liberator. Ruether also makes it clear that Jesus views the oppressed as agents whose agency has been unjustly and systemically denied them, hardly as the passive or powerless victims that Brock seems to have in mind. Finally, Ruether is little interested in Jesus' personal awareness--she is no "New Quester." Her insistence on Jesus' this-worldly orientation is, if anything, overstated.

126. On this basis, Ruether constructs what she calls a liberation ecclesiology on the basis of Mary's Magnificat in the Gospel of Luke. "As a woman, specifically a woman from among the poorer classes of a colonized people under the mighty empire of Rome, she represents the oppressed community that is to be lifted up and filled with good things in the messianic revolution. . . . If women of the oppressed classes and social groups represent the poorest of the poor, the most despised of society, then such women can become the models of faith and their liberation becomes the special locus of the believing and liberated community." The Mary of the Magnificat thus is the model for a church that joins God in the preferential option for the poor. (Ruether, *Sexism and God-Talk*, 157.)

127. Paul W. Newman discusses the Biblical and subsequent developments of Spirit Christologies and proposes a reconstruction of this strand in *A Spirit Christology: Recovering the Biblical Paradigm of Christian Faith* (Lanham, MD: University Press of America, 1987). In the Preface to this book, he names Ruether as the foremost among those "who have read the manuscript and given criticisms and encouragement." For Ruether's own discussion of the development of this Christological strand, see *Sexism and God-Talk*, 130-134. Ruether's key phrase "Christ in the form of our sister" is drawn from a text that Ruether uses as exemplary of Spirit Christologies. (Ibid., 131.) "This kind of spirit Christology does not separate out a past perfect historical Christ from the ongoing Spirit. Rather it sees Christ as a power that continues to be revealed in persons, both male and female, in the present. Christ is located in a new humanity that discloses the future potential of redeemed life. The reality of Christ

is not completed in the past but continues to be disclosed in the present." (Ibid., 131.)

128. Ruether, *Faith and Fratricide*, 250, and elsewhere.

129. Ruether, *To Change the World*, 39. See also Ruether, *Faith and Fratricide*, 236.

130. Ibid., 239. For an application of this to some forms of Judaism, see Ruether, *The Wrath of Jonah*, 199, 217-218 and passim.

131. Snyder, 101.

132. Ruether, *To Change the World*, 5.

133. In *Sexism and God-Talk* and elsewhere (but not consistently), Ruether uses the neologism *God/ess* as "a written symbol intended to combine both the masculine and feminine forms of the word for the divine while preserving the Judeo-Christian affirmation that divinity is one." The word is unpronounceable. For Ruether, this fact helps this symbol point toward "that yet unnameable understanding of the divine that would transcend patriarchal limitations and signal redemptive experience for women as well as men." (*Sexism and God-Talk*, 46.) In other words, the term is eschatological. Furthermore, its use is appropriate to signify a deity whose fullness is finally unknowable in human history: God/ess is "I am who I shall become," nameable through apophatic statements as accurately as kataphatic ones. I take Ruether's parallel with the Hebrew name YHWH to be deliberate. (*Sexism and God-Talk*, 71.)

134. Ruether, *Sexism and God-Talk*, 70-71. This complex of images of God/ess overcomes the dualisms of matter and spirit and immanence and transcendence (Ibid., 85). Judith Vaughn helpfully notes that "God/ess is inseparably, (1) a community which serves as the matrix for the interrelations of all other entities, and (2) the inter-relation of those entities." This implies co-creatorship between divinity and humanity (Vaughn, 158-159).

135. Ruether, *Sexism and God-Talk*, 49. Ruether notes that her view that "Spirit and matter . . . are the inside and outside of the same thing" is based on and coherent with contemporary scientific discussions on the relation between matter and energy. (Ibid., 85.)

136. The dynamism of God/ess also supports genuine religious pluralism, in that God/ess at any given moment is nonabsolute (Ruether, *Disputed Questions*, 67; idem, *To Change the World*, 39).

137. Ruether, *Sexism and God-Talk*, 71. Here, liberation is understood as "encounter with our authentic selves resurrected from underneath the alienated self." (Ibid., 71.)

138. Ruether, "Female Nature of God," 66.

139. Ruether, *To Change the World*, 11.

140. Ruether, *Sexism and God-Talk*, 254-258.

141. Renunciation must encompass philosophical, theological, social, political, and psychological structures, systems, ideas, and practices. Additionally, renunciation must include the privilege of "the security of bondage," as difficult for the subjugated to give up as is the privilege of domination for the dominant (Ruether, *Womanguides*, 82).

142. The dialectic relation between the elements of sin, freedom, and alternative vision means that consciousness of sin and evil originates in conversion, which is also a choice to disaffiliate from certain realities. Our future vision is shaped by--and so in this central sense arises from--the concrete historical context of domination and subjugation. But this context cannot produce a fully alternative vision; it only recapitulates the problem. This context must be transformed, and its transformation engenders a new vision which surpasses the old.

143. Ruether, "Future of Feminist Theology," 707.

144. Ruether, *Disputed Questions*, 19; idem, *Sexism and God-Talk*, 214.

145. Because this vision is linked to transformation as well as to the ambiguities of human existence, it is always emergent, its content never static.

146. These distortions and perversions are evidenced in the interstructured but differing social systems of sexism, racism, and classism. *Patriarchalism*, thus, refers not only to male dominance of the female, but also to those forms of hierarchical dualism which result in the dominant position of one historical group. In her public speech, Elisabeth Schüssler Fiorenza uses the term *kyriocentrism* to describe the status accorded "the lords of history."

147. The strength of Ruether's insistence on distinguishing liberation and salvation is no doubt intensified by her critique of eschatology as the collapsing of apocalypticism into history. The separation in apocalyptic of the historical era and the eschatological era tends, Ruether thinks, to retain the political character of messianism, which is lost in eschatology. (See Snyder, 30ff. Snyder discusses Ruether's unpublished work "Messiah of Israel," which is, apparently, her most comprehensive treatment of the Jewish origins of Christianity.) Ruether is also critical of traditional Christianity's tendency to locate liberation with ultimate redemption, that is, out of history and so out of the realm of human responsibility. (See, for example, "Eschatology and Feminism," throughout.) The source of

Ruether's near-silence on the nature of salvation or redemption is finally in her description of the divine as Matrix and transhistorical Other, whose dynamic relation to humankind is often one of shattering breakthrough and transformation rather than consummation and fulfillment. (See, for example, Hampson and Ruether, 16.)

148. "God is experienced as 'breaking into' existing social reality as judgment upon human claims to righteousness. . . . what are shattered are the ideological pretensions of dominant systems of power. . . . To say God 'shatters' such power does not mean God literally overthrows it as a substitute for human struggle against it. Rather, it means one is transported into a compelling experience of authentic divine justice in a way that reveals the utter hollowness of the claims to divine righteousness made by such systems of domination. One is also grounded anew in God's true mandate for creation that empowers one to struggle against demonic misuse of power." (Hampson and Ruether, 16.)

149. The quoted phrase is Wanda Warren Berry's (Wanda W. Berry, "Images of Sin and Salvation in Feminist Theology," *Anglican Theological Review* 60 [January 1978], 29). Vaughn notes that, for Ruether, "salvation is an ongoing process of conversion and the recovery of authentic creational life which cannot be done once and for all." (Vaughn, 157) After the death of individuals, Ruether believes, "our personal achievements and failures are gathered up and assimilated into the fabric of Being, to be preserved in eternal memory." (Ruether, "Eschatology and Feminism," 123. Compare Suchocki's understanding of eschatology, discussed in Chapter 9 of this book.)

150. Ruether, "Sexism and the Theology of Liberation," *Christian Century* 90 (Spring 1973): 1224; idem, *Sexism and God-Talk*, 255. Says Ruether, "liberation includes liberation from patriarchy; liberation means the creation of a new society and culture where women are fully valued, but not the creation of a new oppression of other groups whose value is discounted and unnoticed." (Hampson and Ruether, 20.) Further, as Vaughn notes, for Ruether salvation is a religious symbol of universal community: "it includes personal conversion and restored relations between dimensions of oneself, between individuals, between groups, and between humans and nature." (Vaughn, 155.) Identifying liberative transformation as ongoing accounts for the ever-present gap between the ideal and the actual and so may mitigate against despair, a familiar pitfall for those involved in struggles for change and liberation. (Ruether, *Sexism and God-Talk*, 237.)

151. Ruether, "Sexism and the Theology of Liberation," 1224; idem, *Sexism and God-Talk*, 255. See also Ruether, "Eschatology and Feminism," 121.

152. Ruether, *Sexism and God-Talk*, 113, 216. As Vaughn notes, individual salvation is found in the individual's participation in the history of creation. "The meaning of eternal life 'must be sought somehow in solidarity with the race, with the earth, and with the matrix that binds us together.' By the fact that we are participants in the universal community, we are saved. To the *extent* that universal community is achieved at particular moments throughout history, so too is salvation realized." (Vaughn, 156. Internal quote is from Ruether, "Beginnings: An Intellectual Autobiography," in *Journeys: The Impact of Personal Experience on Religious Thought*, ed. Gregory Baum [New York: Paulist Press, 1975], 34-56.)

153. Ruether, *Sexism and God-Talk*, 71; idem, *Liberation Theology*, 12.

154. Elisabeth Schüssler Fiorenza uses the term "option for our women selves" (*Bread Not Stone*, xv and passim) to indicate the form of conversion to the poor specific to feminist liberation theology. The subjugation of women involves the denial of the capacity for self-definition in favor of identity established by the dominant and internalized by the oppressed. Women's project under patriarchal domination necessarily involves the development of their own identity, autonomous from patriarchal definition.

155. Ruether, *Liberation Theology*, 12; idem, *Sexism and God-Talk*, 186.

156. For example, the development of the authentic female self entails exorcism of the internalized patriarchal definition of women as the inferior source of sin and evil, rather than identification with this projection.

157. Ruether, *Sexism and God-Talk*, 112-113.

158. Ibid., 186. White feminist discussions of self-sacrifice have in mind the coerced self-sacrifice of dominated individuals for the sake of the well-being of their dominators. Women in situations of multiple oppression distinguish between coerced self-sacrifice such as this and the voluntary sacrifice individuals make for the well-being of their communities, which are also dominated. See, for example, Mercy Oduyoye, "Churchwomen and the Church's Mission," in *New Eyes for Reading*, ed. John S. Pobee and Barbel von Wartenberg-Potter (Geneva, Switzerland: World Council of Churches, 1986), 68-80.

159. Ruether, *Sexism and God-Talk*, 136, 158.

160. Ruether, *To Change the World*, 21.

161. Ruether, *Disputed Questions*, 97.

162. "Although the complete realization of this hope transcends history, these new experiences of the presence of the Reign of God empower the community to shake free of the dead letter of past institutional expressions and envision new possibilities for creating the beloved community." (Hampson and Ruether, 16) Ruether notes that it is theologically necessary to acknowledge the possibility of approximation in history, or one denies the possibility of God's acting in history and giving all human existence over to the power of evil (Ruether, *To Change the World*, 22-23).

163. Ibid., 69.

164. Ibid., 40.

165. Ruether, *Sexism and God-Talk*, 91.

166. Ruether, *Disputed Questions*, 67; idem, *To Change the World*, 39. Thus no tradition can claim ultimate status, nor can any historical period (including the Biblical) (Idem, *Disputed Questions*, 39).

167. Ruether, *Sexism and God-Talk*, 71.

168. Ruether, *To Change the World*, 11.

169. Ibid., 68-69. See also Ruether, "Eschatology and Feminism," 121-122: "I have come to think of our task as creating a just, peaceable society as a continual process of finding sustainable balances in a web of relationships of humans to one another and to our fellow creatures of nature. . . . The Jubilee tradition of Hebrew scripture is my model for this continual work of renewal in every generation, as opposed to the quest for a final revolution that will set things right 'once-for-all.' . . . It is this shaping of the beloved community on earth, for our time and generation, to bequeath to our children, which is our primary capacity and task as finite, historical humans."

170. Ruether, *Sexism and God-Talk*, 266.

171. Jacquelyn Grant points out that Ruether modulates this Christological question over time. From an early focus on how Christology has been used to support social and theological systems of the domination of women, Ruether's critical focus shifts to the relation between soteriology and the dominant and dominating social order. Most recently, Ruether focuses on the liberation of Christology from patriarchy in order that it can serve the liberation of women. (Grant, *White Woman's Christ and Black Woman's Jesus*, 141f.) Grant's study was completed before Ruether published *Womanguides*, where

Ruether suggests that the male Christ must be surpassed by a WomanChrist.

172. The importance of women's experience arises precisely because women's identity and self-hood have been constituted in a context in which maleness is normative. To the extent that any savior presents a norm for human existence--as Christianity claims its savior certainly does--the normative character of maleness is intensified: to be human at all is to be male, and to be *redeemed* as a human or *authentically* human is to be male. (See Ruether's discussions of androgynous Christologies in *To Change the World* and *Sexism and God-Talk* for how even the most apparently egalitarian elements of the Christian tradition still enforce this notion.) The importance of women's experience is that it asserts against both these patriarchal norms the authenticity of female human existence as also normative.

173. See Ruether, *To Change the World*, 45-47.

174. Ruether, *Womanguides*, 112-113.

175. That is, as a male in patriarchal society, Jesus is privileged; but he is disprivileged as a Jew under Roman domination, and as a peasant in an urban-agrarian society where land is owned by some and worked by others.

176. Ruether "answered the Christology problem for white feminism by arguing that the fact that God in Christ became male is inseparable from the type of male he became." (Thistlethwaite, 95.) On this point, see also Grant, *White Woman's Christ, Black Woman's Jesus*, 143, and Weaver, 169.

177. Ruether, *Sexism and God-Talk*, 137-138.

178. Ibid., 137.

179. Remember, Ruether makes the same claim about the historical importance of Jesus' selection of women as exemplars: it is not their biological identity that matters, but the fact that their biological identity is socially constructed in the direction of their being dominated.

180. Ibid., 137.

181. Ibid., 69.

182. Ruether, *To Change the World*, 29.

183. Ruether, *Sexism and God-Talk*, 114. Ruether *in principle* supports the development of paradigms of liberation and salvation from women's experience. She remains unconvinced, however, by the concrete post-Jewish and post-Christian options presented by Naomi Goldenberg, Starhawk, Carol Christ, Mary Daly, and others. One of the most important questions Ruether raises is precisely that of particularity: if a male savior has only limited liberating value for

women, must not the same be said of any other redemptive figure, whose particularities necessarily include not only gender but race/ethnicity, class or caste, and other factors as well? As a historian, Ruether insists that any redemptive paradigm be developed in part through a "re-encounter" with historical sources as they are fruitful for understanding that paradigm for today.

184. See, for example, Ruether, "Feminism and Jewish-Christian Dialogue," throughout.

185. Indeed, Ruether has no interest in cleaving to Chalcedonian Christology. See Snyder, 91.

186. Tracy, *Analogical Imagination*, 215, 218.

187. Heyward, *Redemption of God*, 200; idem, *Our Passion for Justice*, 46 and 178.

188. Tracy, *Analogical Imagination*, 390.

189. Ibid., 311.

190. Ibid., 308-309.

191. Ibid., 314. Tracy's emphasis in this discussion is, characteristically, more on adequacy to Christian traditions (understood as ongoing in their development and interpretation) than on contemporary experience.

192. Ibid., 314-315.

193. Ruether, *Womanguides*, 112-113.

194. Ruether, *Sexism and God-Talk*, 114.

195. Ruether, *Womanguides*, 105.

196. Ruether, *Sexism and God-Talk*, 22-27.

197. See, for example, Ruether's reading of Amos 8: "In this context God is seen not as the one who represents the powerful, but one who comes to vindicate the oppressed. God's intervention in history is to judge those who grind the faces of the poor, those who deprive the widow and the orphan." (Ruether, *Sexism and God-Talk*, 25.)

198. Ruether, "The Future of Feminist Theology in the Academy," 710-711.

199. Ruether, *Womanguides*, 104.

200. Two examples should suffice here. Julian of Norwich and other mystics encountered Christ specifically through meditation on their and his suffering. And the thesis of Jacqueline Grant's *White Woman's Christ, Black Woman's Jesus* is precisely that white feminists have neglected the experience of African-American women of the presence of God through Jesus as the fellow-sufferer and Lord who will finally bring liberation.

201. Thus do Ogden and Hampson criticize Ruether. Hampson writes that Ruether is interested in Jesus' message, which is "held to concern the coming of the kingdom, the vindication of the poor and the creation of a just social order. The centre of her theology is the Christian vision. . . . But to be Christian is not simply to preach Jesus' message. It is also to proclaim a message about Jesus--and therein for a feminist lie all the problems." (For what these problems are, in Hampson's view, see my discussion in Chapter 2, above.) "But if Jesus of Nazareth is not thought to be unique, and the Christian story is just a myth, why, one must ask, should one who is a feminist choose to take up this particular myth when it is so male, and has central to it a male person who is held to be unique? . . . In which case why not jettison this religion which has been so harmful to women?" (Hampson, *Theology and Feminism*, 65-66.) For Ogden's critique, see "Problems for a Pluralistic Theology of Religion," 499-500.

Chapter 8

The Decisive Representation of Self-giving Love

A Feminist Christological Problem

In the preceding chapter, I discussed one of two models for Christology. The model of the iconoclastic prophet, as developed by Ruether, emphasizes proclamation of a new earth within history and a new heaven beyond it. This eschatological vision is given proleptic, partial form in the exemplary prophet, who manifests the general shape of the new humanity which is even now coming into being. What is less clear in this model or type is how the exemplary prophet also manifests the divine. Ruether's contention, as we have seen, is that any single historical exemplar can be only a partial and incomplete manifestation of both humanity and divinity.

In this chapter and the following three, I will discuss the other major model to be found in white feminist Christologies to date. The Wisdom-Logos model is found in various forms in the work of Patricia Wilson-Kastner, Marjorie Hewitt Suchocki, and

Carter Heyward. The Christologies presented here rest on the affirmation that Jesus is, for Christians, the full manifestation of both the divine and the human in history. He is the representation of divinely renewed humanity (Wilson-Kastner); the concrete actualization and vision of the life to which God calls us (Suchocki); the representation of the only liberating relationship a person can have with God (Heyward). This relationship between humanity and divinity has existed in principle from creation, is partially and potentially available to all in present history, and is promised as future transformation. In Jesus, Christians encounter this relationship in its full, actual, and concrete form. This model is drawn from the Logos-Wisdom strands of Christian theology, and modified to address the problems with use of this model both in a post-Enlightenment world and from a feminist perspective.

The Wisdom-Logos model of Christology appears to address with some facility a central dilemma for Christology, that is, how to indicate the relationship between elements which more readily seem to be either unrelated or in conflict. [1] Wisdom or the Logos as the self-expression and self-giving of God is incarnate in particular, concrete, and historical form as Jesus the Christ, showing how divine and human, eternal and temporal, universal and particular, creation and redemption are ultimately related. In other words, through Wisdom/the Logos, apparent dualisms are seen to be related as poles, the primary or originating one of which is, of course, the divine. The incarnate Wisdom/Logos reveals the very constitution of the universe; and that revelation moves the universe toward restoration and redemption.

However, Christologies that follow this model are notoriously beset with problems as well as possibilities, and in these same areas, as the history of Christology indicates from its earliest days. For example, precisely *how* humanity and divinity might be related in a concrete, particular, historical person is extremely difficult to articulate with full satisfaction, as the controversies leading up to and proceeding from the Council of Chalcedon make clear. Despite the fundamental assertion that humanity and divinity *are* related in Christ, the perceived incommensurability of divinity and humanity tends to force most (if not all) Christologies to over-emphasize one of the two poles or natures at the expense of the other. [2]

With the development of modern theologies, particularly since the Enlightenment, the problems associated with Wisdom-Logos Christologies have shifted. Modern thought's "turn to the subject" as existing in history rendered even less comprehensible the understanding of "person" and "nature" integral to classical Logos Christologies. And the valuation given to history as essential rather than accidental to truth and meaning itself came into direct and perhaps unresolvable conflict with the idealistic and static elements of classical thought. The related emphasis on the historical agency and responsibility of human persons in creating and ordering their existence challenged the classical understanding of God as the provider of an immutable order from creation. [3]

The severity of these problems with Logos Christologies is intensified when they are viewed from a feminist liberation perspective. Logos Christologies identify a past event as both ultimate and normative, often masking the historicity of and human participation in that event and de-emphasizing present and future experience and possibilities. This is of particular concern for feminist thought because of the long history of the suppression of women's agency and experience, and because of the androcentric bias and content of historical texts and traditions. Granting normative status to any past event implicitly if not explicitly at times serves to legitimize this suppression. [4]

Second, contemporary feminist analysis of philosophical and theological traditions directly criticizes the dualistic structures of thought enshrined in Logos Christologies, dualisms that persistently denigrate the female and so-called feminine characteristics and at the same time exalt the male and the so-called masculine. This fact is reflected in the language and concepts used to characterize these Christologies: the Logos is understood as mind (over against body), as rational ordering (rather than affective expression), as detached and disinterested even while involved in history. These static, stereotypically "masculine" attributes associated with the Greek Logos have subsumed and suppressed the more dynamic and "feminine" characteristics associated with the Hebrew Wisdom. This enshrining of essential dualisms means that even if a modern meaning can be given to the term "person," that meaning is most likely to be androcentric if not explicitly misogynist.

Further, the identification of the divine Logos of God with a male human being, Jesus, can be and has been used to deny the full participation of women in historical and ecclesiological existence, and to call into question their full humanity. [5]

In other words, despite the basic insight into relationality between diverse types of being which Wisdom-Logos Christologies may affirm, the problems associated with the development and history of effects of this insight are considerable, if not prohibitive. In the modern world and from a feminist perspective, these effects can be summarized under four headings: first, a profoundly static view of God, of the (hierarchical) order of the cosmos, and of "human nature" in classical Logos Christologies, over against a relentlessly dynamic view of the divine, of the evolution of the universe, and of human persons in modern and feminist thought; second, a dualistic view of fundamental relations (such as soul and body, divine and human, ideal and actual), over against the modern, feminist interactive, interdependent view; third, a traditional orientation toward a past, given, and "set" event, over against a contemporary emphasis on present experience and future fulfillment; and, fourth, a patriarchal identification of maleness as the idealized norm for both humanity and divinity, over against a feminist liberation insistence on the emergence of a full humanity where all persons are seen as equally created in the image of God.

In the face of these problems, some feminist Christian theologians such as Rosemary Radford Ruether have found in other alternatives for Christology more substance and promise than they believe are possible for even a feminist reconstruction of the Wisdom-Logos strands. However, other feminist Christian theologians, such as the three discussed in these four chapters, believe that the affirmation of relationality which is fundamental to both Wisdom and Logos traditions, together with the association of these traditions with embodiment or incarnation, justifies feminist liberation attempts to reformulate Christology using a Wisdom-Logos approach. But such a reformulation requires addressing each of these four problematic areas.

In these chapters, I will discuss three proposals for Christology in the Logos tradition, each of them from perspectives on Christology and theology as a whole which differ and even conflict significantly. For Wilson-Kastner, the overall pattern of Jesus' life, death, and resurrection shows him to be the representation of "a divinely renewed humanity," of the essentially relational character of God, and of the unity between divinity and humanity which has always been the case.[6] For Suchocki, the special revelation Christians find in Jesus is of humanity fully actualizing the possibilities offered by God within the limits of human existence. At the same time, Jesus is also a mirror in the world of God's harmony, "a concrete vision of the life to which God calls us."[7] For Heyward, Jesus' immediate and mutual relation with God is the full manifestation of "the *only* liberating relationship a person can have to God," a relationship that in principle always is and always has been possible for all human persons.[8] In other words, for all three, Jesus is himself the historical manifestation of the relation between God and humanity that has existed from creation, that is partially restored in the present, and that is promised to all as future transformation.[9]

However, each of these three theologians takes a different path to reach her key assertion, and this can obscure the essential structural similarities in their arguments. For example, Heyward claims that Jesus was "fully and only human, . . . exactly human, like us."[10] Only a careful examination of Heyward's understanding of the divine makes it clear how such a statement can fit into a Wisdom-Logos Christology. Or, from a different angle, Wilson-Kastner's insistence on beginning with humanity's unity rather than difference seems incompatible with feminist interest in women's experience as unlike men's. But study of Wilson-Kastner's epistemology indicates how experience is the medium through which the reality of relationality as both unified and diverse is known.   Suchocki's emphasis on the drive of existence toward harmony can appear to minimize the reality and importance of choice and conflict, until one attends with some care to the role of choice and decision in the generation of harmony.   Therefore, in order to indicate clearly the essential agreements in the Christologies presented in these chapters, I will discuss each author's work in some detail before venturing a comparison.

For, despite the differences in how their key assertions are developed and the overall theological contexts in which they are placed, the three Christologies discussed in these chapters are significantly similar in indicating the possibilities that a Logos-Wisdom approach holds for the development of a relatively adequate feminist Christology.   For Patricia Wilson-Kastner, Marjorie Hewitt Suchocki, and Carter Heyward, Jesus is *the* Christ *for us*, the one who definitively manifests the fullness of both humanity and divinity for Christians.   Indeed, the differences in these proposals, when put in conversation with each other, will enrich the Wisdom-Logos approach. Nevertheless, not all of the problems are susceptible to satisfactory resolution.   Finally, I will argue, these feminist reconstruals of Christology of the Wisdom-Logos type require interaction with the prophetic-messianic approach outlined in the previous chapter.

The Christology of Patricia Wilson-Kastner

Introduction

Patricia   Wilson-Kastner[11]   finds   three   challenges   facing Christian feminism. Radical feminists such as Mary Daly, Carol Christ, and Naomi Goldenberg (for example) judge Christianity to be antithetical to the liberation of women from patriarchy, because Christianity is inherently patriarchal and so will always "deny   women   a   whole   and   integrated   self-concept,   while obscuring for women the divine which is within them." [12]   That this feminist critique is justified is amply indicated by the second of Wilson-Kastner's challengers, doctrinal fundamentalists[13] who argue that while men and women may be spiritually equal, "in this world they belong to different spheres or worlds."[14] Wilson-Kastner's work is addressed to a third group of persons who find themselves positioned between these two views, admitting the justification of the feminist challenge while refusing to accede to the fundamentalist view. Both challengers pose the same problem: "Must [one] choose between Christianity and feminism?" The third group, Christian feminists, drawing on both other groups and their "own internal sense of rightness and equity," judge that Christian faith does in fact contribute to the liberation of women.[15] A clearer formulation of the interrelationship of Christianity and feminism is needed in order to explicate this third group's judgment.

In response to these three challenges, Wilson-Kastner proposes a reformist Christology thematized by a principle of wholeness and inclusivity. In this formulation, Christ is the re-presentation of the essential relational character of God and God's reconciling relation with creation. Wilson-Kastner identifies this as feminist in that it presents "the significance of Christ as embodying values and ideals which also are sought for and valued by feminists."[16] This reconciliation on the basis of shared ideals and visions involves a mutual corrective and transformation: Christianity's infidelity to God, which is manifest in its embrace of patriarchal distortions of essentials of Christian faith, can be corrected and transformed by feminism; and feminism's erroneous adoption and reversal of patriarchal values can be corrected and transformed by accurate formulations of Christian faith.

The Character of Human Existence

Wilson-Kastner finds significant commonalities and mutual interests shared by radical and Christian feminists. Both groups criticize the hierarchicalization of gender differences, the truncation of women's experience, and the profound patriarchalism of Christianity and other religions. The two types of feminism diverge most significantly, Wilson-Kastner believes, in their view of the very nature of humanity. Radical feminists, Wilson-Kastner believes, imply that humanity is inherently binary, male and female, with vastly different experiences of existence, which require vastly different epistemologies.[17] Christian feminists, by contrast, insist that humanity is essentially one, with socially based differences.[18] Yet both feminisms are engaged in a common quest for wholeness as a primary goal. The very fact of this common quest validates a basic human experience which is reflected in the Christian feminist viewpoint: the unity of humanity in all its apparent difference.

Wilson-Kastner believes that the division of genders is an indication of a more basic problem: the fragmentation of human existence, which is the opposite of and opposing force to integration toward wholeness. Fragmentation is part of the world in which human persons exist, a world that contains an element of "surd" and unintelligibility. Human knowledge, because partial, is also fragmentary. The variety, persistence, and profundity of fragmentation in the face of an inherent human desire and quest or drive for wholeness raises the question of the meaning of human existence: how is this struggle to be resolved? Moreover, while human participation in fragmentation shows no sign of decreasing over the course of history, the hopeful quest for wholeness is neither baseless nor delusory: "If the power of healing is not somehow already present among us, how can we know it?"[19] Theological anthropology has as one of its tasks the accurate description of this reality and of the vision of wholeness arising from it.

In feminism, Wilson-Kastner finds a helpful description of one kind of fragmentation: patriarchy, which feminism identifies as fundamental. Wilson-Kastner also finds, however, that despite their concern for wholeness, "contemporary feminists do not deal in any substantial way" with many other aspects of fragmentation, including how human persons, including women, contribute to this central human dilemma.[20]

Wilson-Kastner argues that patriarchy is one, albeit very damaging and significant, manifestation of the tendency of "a fundamentally good human nature" toward "self-destruction, harm toward others, self-deception, and even the twisting of the good into that which is less good and sometimes very harmful."[21] As feminism correctly and helpfully observes, patriarchal dualism takes the fundamental traits of all human beings and separates them along gender lines. Whereas all human persons are, ideally, "at one and the same time self-possessing and self-giving, self-centered and self-transcending," patriarchal dualism assigns the first characteristic of each pair to men and the second to women.[22] This fragments "the very core of human selfhood," preventing the wholeness of both women and men.[23] The ultimate expression of the severity of this fragmentation is, for Wilson-Kastner, the notion that humanity is in effect two species, rather than one.

And it is here that radical feminism falters, as does doctrinal fundamentalism, both of which insist that "male and female humanness is indeed radically different."[24] While fundamentalists assert that male and female humanness is "spiritually" equal, in this world they belong to separate, immutable orders.[25] Radical feminists posit a philosophical principle about inherent differences between men and women on the basis of a similar distinction between hypothetical unity and the concrete, historical differences that exist "in the reality of this world in which we actually live."[26] Wilson-Kastner suggests that, although there are important concrete differences in the two views' relative valuing of male and female humanness, *structurally* radical feminists make the same mistake to which they properly object in the fundamentalist position. Wilson-Kastner concludes, "To categorize human beings into male and female, prior to an assertion of their common humanity, invites sexism and oppression, whether of the male or female mode."[27] Further, any anthropology that in any way begins from the notion of two humanities by definition cannot accomplish the double task of combatting core fragmentation and enabling healing that will "transform and enable the entire person to become more whole and self-integrated."[28] Anthropologies that posit two humanities instead actively side with fragmentation in the struggle for wholeness.

Better, Wilson-Kastner insists, "to begin by assuming a common humanity," and proceed to a discussion of gender differences as one category among many within one humanity, a category rendered problematic precisely by the undue determinative emphasis given it. [29] On this score, it is Christian feminism which is representative of feminist insight, because Christian feminism reflects a more profound concern for wholeness. Christian feminism consistently preserves the essential feminist insight that women are fully human, and so humanity is one. That is, Christian feminism refuses to take the experience of one group out of many as its referent; it identifies fragmentation as detrimental to human existence, and wholeness as its fulfillment; and it expresses the profound hope that wholeness may overcome fragmentation. On this basis, Christian feminism can affirm and reconstruct its Biblical and theological traditions, which maintain even at their most sexist moments that humanity is unified in its essence before God. [30] At the same time, these traditions recognize that differences and diversity exist and have positive value. [31]

Wilson-Kastner's focus on the oneness of humanity develops a crucial, though often largely under-developed, constructive philosophical and epistemological insight from feminism: that women are indeed fully human. Wilson-Kastner criticizes feminism for failing to carry its own critique deep enough, and for accepting and even embracing the most essential dualism of all: between male and female as two forms of humanity. This acceptance is shown in feminism's beginning with the historical (and so limited) reality of gender difference, rather than with the ultimately real (and so achievable and in part already experienced) fact of unified human nature which is also diverse. Given Wilson-Kastner's epistemology, the starting point is important: how we construe and so understand reality has great significance for our participation in it. Beginning as a matter of principle with the unity of humanity thus is necessary in the ever-ongoing realization of one humanity--wholeness--within the historical actualities and limitations of human existence. [32]

Methodology for Understanding.

Wilson-Kastner's interest, then, is to develop a more comprehensive Christian feminist philosophical theology that integrates

> the feminist concern with wholeness . . . within the context of the theological affirmations about the unity of humanity and the fragmentation which we each experience in our individual selves and in corporate life of the human community--our world.[33]

Essential to this task is a feminist epistemology which adequately addresses the fact that men and women appear to differ in their ways of knowing. This epistemology must also address contemporary understandings of the relation between subject and object and the related necessity of modifying the Western intellectual world's preference for a "dualistic, scientifically oriented analysis of knowing" as normative.[34] Feminism's revaluing of the human as embodied, relational, and affective offers much assistance in this modification. Wilson-Kastner offers an epistemology responsive to this feminist vision, using the Christian philosophies of Bernard Lonergan and Teilhard de Chardin.

The epistemology that Wilson-Kastner develops indicates that humanity is one, though diverse. Wilson-Kastner contends that humans perceive the world as a differentiated whole in which the knower is fundamentally linked to the known organically, as it were.[35] Human perception itself indicates that the knower is a psychophysical reality whose mind is dependent on and linked to bodily existence.[36] Human experience always involves limitation, because humanity itself is limited by its own historical particularities and its constitutional finitude. Experience is a medium for apprehension of reality, providing data that must be submitted to reflection. In order to reflect reality fully and accurately, particular experience must be expanded to include the differing reality of others, which is to be apprehended with empathy and concern.[37]

Understanding is affective as well as rational, cumulative and relational (both socially and cognitively) rather than discrete and autonomous.[38] The human mind inherently seeks to integrate its diverse perceptions into a whole. Thus, knowing is a matter of integration as much as of distinction.[39] This inherent seeking after integration is self-transcendent, in that in seeking the whole, the knower is "attuned to the significance of the particular, the moment, the specific, and is also able to relate it to a growing comprehension of the whole."[40]

In other words, within human existence there is an actual dynamic relation between immanence and transcendence, which drives the search for a principle of wholeness that is both within, yet in some way other than, what is already known.[41] Theology as "the rational spelling-out and explaining of one's faith" indicates that this transcendent element is intrinsic to, yet in some ways different from, human reality, "which both apprehends and feels itself grasped by the divine, reaches new depths of itself and others, and enjoys the beauty of all in light of the Ultimate."[42] This transcendent element is re-presented as also immanent in the Christ; and its essentially relational character--which grounds human relationality--is expressed by the understanding that God is Trinity. Humanity's relationship with the rest of the cosmos is "founded on the very nature of God, whose life of interrelationship we are invited to share through Christ," that member of the Trinity who manifests the inherently relational nature of the divine while living "a human life."[43]

Wilson-Kastner's epistemology validates feminist analyses and visions that insist on the importance of the affective (as well as the rational), of embodiment, of relationality, and of integration over against the fragmenting distortions of patriarchal dualism.[44] Wilson-Kastner's own discussion thus complements the work of other feminists by noting forms of fragmentation found in the limits posed by natural existence, including destruction.[45] Wilson-Kastner also examines in detail how human choice contributes to both fragmentation and destruction by cooperating with ignorance (one form of fragmentation) and by willing "that which we ought not to do."[46] The contradiction between human cooperation with fragmentation and opposition to wholeness (both of which Wilson-Kastner designates as sinful or evil) and the profound, innate human desire for wholeness poses a problem of meaning. This problem in itself stimulates the search for wholeness and hope of its achievement: "If one chooses to assume that anything makes sense at all, the ultimate conclusion must be, I believe, that wholeness must in some sense triumph over fragmentation."[47]

Christology

For Christians, it is through the Christ as the Incarnation of God's love that the relation between God and the universe is brought most fully to expression, and the possibility of wholeness is made manifest.[48] Wilson-Kastner understands Christology to be the "theological and rational explanations of Jesus Christ" as "the focus or prism through whom God is known and interpreted to the Christian community." The term "the Christ" refers to "the historical figure of Jesus" *and* to "the living Christ of Word and Sacrament in the church throughout the ages."[49] It is the overall pattern of Jesus' life--the incarnation, passion, and resurrection--rather than his work and teachings, which is revelatory of the love of God that works toward reconciling wholeness.[50] This pattern makes it clear that "the most fundamental meaning of Christ for Christianity is that of reconciliation and inclusiveness."[51]

Critique.

Christian feminism acknowledges that the maleness of Jesus poses problems because emphasis on it has tended toward fragmentation. In Wilson-Kastner's view (and here she agrees with the radical feminists), this problem cannot be resolved by reference to "the outmoded patriarchy of the biblical writers."[52] Instead of reconstructing a feminist historical Jesus, Christian feminists must focus on a theological interpretation of Jesus as the Christ who is the decisive re-presentation of ultimate reality, explicitly authorizing authentic self-understanding.[53] Focus on the historical "concrete details" of Jesus' life--his maleness, the limitations of his knowledge, his "confinement to the first century in Palestine"--is a literalistic misapprehension of "the significance and meaning of Jesus Christ as a revelation of divine love."[54] "Jesus the Christ is the expression of God in *a* human life, not *the* human life."[55]

Once again, Wilson-Kastner is responding to two challenges. Contemporary doctrinal fundamentalism continues the development, begun during the first centuries of Christianity's history, away "*from* an egalitarian Jesus of the gospels who accepted women as human beings on a par with men, *to* an exclusivistic Christ, one who was portrayed by the church with increasing frequency as a figure of male excellence."[56] Associated ambivalent-to-negative attitudes toward physical life and a variety of philosophical developments combine to place great emphasis on the distance between the divine and the human, rather than on their relation.[57] Contemporary doctrinal fundamentalism, the heir to these developments, thus presents an exclusive Christ, not the loving redeemer of all, but the transcendent savior of a humanity which is normatively male.

Radical feminism, in acceding to the androcentric and misogynist emphasis on the maleness of Jesus, misses his significance as the love of God expressed through humility and self-emptying. Focus on Jesus' historical life and teachings tends to emphasize his "good will" and to ignore "the power of an energy which is the heart, core, and cohesive force of the universe."[58] In other words, in the Incarnation of God under the conditions of history, the power of God's love is made manifest within the limits of human existence. These limits include gender, and also location and ethnicity; but these do not therefore indicate something about the being of God. Feminism's mistake--again, most obvious in radical feminism--is in equating a set of historical particulars with the representation of ultimate reality. However, once it is understood that Jesus is "the living Christ" whose presence continues in Word and Sacrament, the importance of the historical Jesus, however reconstructed, diminishes.[59] Christology is a theological interpretation of who Jesus *is*, not who Jesus *was*.[60]

Construction.

The identification of the Christ as the re-presentation of ultimate reality in human history minimizes the importance of the maleness of the historical Jesus by emphasizing the Christ's function rather than Jesus' life.

> Christ is the human expression of God to us, and thus we must try to understand what God meant in Christ. Christ is also the inclusive revelation of God's intention for humanity. In Christ we see something of how a divinely renewed humanity acts in the world . . . As a human he shows us what human self-possession and self-giving are. Thereby Christ shows us the link between divine and human, the cosmos and its conscious inhabitants. [61]

With Ogden, Wilson-Kastner describes the Christ as the decisive re-presentation of ultimate reality who explicitly authorizes authentic self-understanding. [62] The elaboration of this understanding of the Christ is feminist "in understanding the significance of Christ as embodying values and ideals which also are sought for and valued by feminists": [63] wholeness, inclusivity, relationality. Thus, Wilson-Kastner believes, feminism's essential challenges are met, and met on terms also adequate to the experience of liberation claimed by Christian feminists.

That this is a Wisdom-Logos Christology is apparent when the three angles from which the Christ is understood are stipulated. The Christ is the revelation or re-presentation of a God whose "self-giving creativity"--an aspect of love--precludes any divine requirement of cosmic subservience.

> Christ as Logos draws our attention to the self-giving creativity of God, the eternal openness of God to the creation. . . . creativity is fundamental to the divine nature itself. . . . The Word does not call creation into being in order to rule over a subservient reality forced to do deeds for God's benefit. The divine Word speaks in order that a reality--a

potentiality--that is already contained within God may be brought to actuality. [64]

The Christ is the revelation of the unity among humanity on the basis of a common nature. [65] And the Christ is the link between the divine and the human and the rest of the cosmos. [66] That is, the Christ is the divine self-expression of the ordering of all relations within divinity itself and within the universe. In Wilson-Kastner's presentation, the Christ re-presents a set of dynamic relationships in which the affective, expressive, and rational all come into play. In this way, she has recovered many of the elements of the Wisdom strand that have been suppressed in classical Christology. [67]

Wilson-Kastner's Christology focuses on the incarnation, crucifixion, and resurrection of the Christ, rather than on Jesus' ministry and teachings. Through each of these three major events, the incarnate Christ reveals something about God and something about humanity.

Jesus as the Christ is the incarnation of the Word, the member of the Trinity who

> articulates divine creativity in all of its diversity, but centered through its unity in God. Multiplicity, diversity, and change are all characteristics contained in God's creativity, upholding and sustaining creaturely development and activity. [68]

The Incarnation is an extension of this sustaining creativity: it is part of and reveals what God has been doing from the beginning. Moreover, because the Incarnation is the entirely mutual unity of divine and human in the Christ, it means that God accepts the fragmented human condition into Godself. This acceptance also indicates God's affirmation of the goodness of all creation, including creation's freedom and integrity. [69]

At the same time, the Incarnation means that the human is always in relation to the divine, despite fragmentation and human responsibility for it. Human diversity and particularity are seen to be related to divine creativity rather than to human imperfection or fault. The Incarnation affirms that human goodness is more essentially human than is sin, because human life participates in the divine life. The unity of the human and the divine in the Incarnation begins a process of transformation, which is carried further in the Christ's Crucifixion.

The crucifixion of Jesus the Christ shows that God will not interfere in human freedom and maturation, which are implied by God's own freedom and creativity.[70] But this also means that God risks, indeed experiences, real rejection, even as humans do. The cross reveals divine acceptance of "the possibility of alienation, rejection, pain, and the disintegration of the very self of God," for on the cross, Jesus the embodiment of God is rejected not only by humans, but also by God.[71] This risk indicates the depth and persistence of the divine love, and the unbreakable unity of human and divine which underlies their difference.[72] But reconciliation and the restoration of fragmented unity require labor like that of birth-giving.[73] And they require purification.[74] In feminist terms, the reconciliation indicated in the crucifixion indicates that dualisms--between human and divine, between diverse aspects of human being and existence--have no place in a universe which is being redeemed.[75] Fragmenting dualisms are embraced and transformed in the crucifixion as reconciling event.

The crucifixion, then, shows God to be non-coercive, free and risk-taking, and engaged in creation, nurturance, reconciliation, and transformation. The crucifixion also shows humanity as sharing these qualities with God in the midst of the will to destruction that furthers fragmentation. The crucifixion is thus a vindication of these qualities' ongoing presence in human existence, and their possibilities as constructive, transforming forces in human history.[76] Human diversity is affirmed *in se*, rather than being a source of alienation or being "naturally" arranged hierarchically and dualistically.[77]

The crucifixion is not the final event of transformation or revelation, however. The resurrection of the Christ is the definitive overcoming of alienation in Jesus as one person, and is at the same time the promise that this overcoming will be extended to the entire cosmos. In the resurrection, humanity is shown to be transformed, for the Christ is *the* new human, the bearer in his own person of a humanity become what it truly should be, delivered from the seeds of its own destructiveness which it has nurtured and cherished. In Christ we are returned to God and ourselves, and begin the active process of returning to God in all areas of our lives. [78]

The resurrected Christ reveals redeemed humanity free of fragmentation, and part of the whole of creation rather than alienated from and destructive toward it. [79]

Christ is that unifier because he incorporates in the crucifixion the depths of the experience of fragmentation, and in the resurrection the transformation of that fragmentation into wholeness. The crucified and risen Christ richly expresses the dynamic movement toward wholeness which feminism seeks. [80]

The resurrection is the beginning of the end of fragmenting division and "the definitive step in the process of cosmic reconciliation." [81]

Salvation and Wholeness

God the Trinity.

To meet the challenges of both doctrinal fundamentalism and radical feminism, as well as Christian feminists' experience of God as the source of wholeness, Wilson-Kastner describes God as "at one and the same time holy, inexpressible, and greater than all that is, and also . . . One whom all creation resembles, and who is present in and to all creation." [82] This balanced formulation maintains the theological and anthropological tension between immanence and transcendence, which is lost in doctrinal fundamentalism's assertion of radical difference between the divine and the human. In that view, "humanity [is] perceived in terms of immanence alone, and the divine in terms of transcendence. Sin was the fundamental characteristic of humanity *in concreto*," and particularly of female humanity. [83]

The other challenger, radical feminism, abandons transcendence altogether, instead either resorting to a fully immanent conception of the Ultimate, or eliminating any notion of an Ultimate beyond the human. [84]

Wilson-Kastner proposes that understanding God as Trinity has great possibilities for Christian feminism precisely because such an understanding stresses the absolutely fundamental importance of relation. [85] To reflect on the Trinity is inherently to reflect primarily on relationality as a key quality of the divine. At the same time, this focus moves away from the problems of gender specificity. [86] The relation between the three persons of the Trinity can be helpfully understood as a dance-like exchange of energies within divinity, which is also directed outward toward the universe as its source of common life. [87]

Wilson-Kastner proposes that the most appropriate description of the fundamental self-revelation of God is love that is simultaneously self-giving, receptive, and expressive. [88] To say that God is love is to assert that the central dynamic of the universe itself is relational. [89] This love moves toward wholeness in opposition to fragmentation, and so gives meaning to human experience. [90] Moreover, the perception that the fundamental characteristic of that relationality is love militates against hierarchicalization within the Trinity, and for mutuality, harmony, and peace. [91] This love thus also has a positive moral value and end: it tends toward the expression and reception of the good.

The nature of love as "perfect openness . . . giv[ing] unreservedly of itself" relationally makes a profound connection between divinity and the universe: divinity invites the universe to share in God's own inter-relationality, both in relation to the divine and in relation with its constituent members. [92] And the nature of love as receiving means that the relation between God and universe is ideally harmonious and mutual. This is most evident in the capacity for freedom found in the divine and so in the human. Because love respects freedom, God refuses to interfere with human freedom, and risks human rejection. [93] At the same time, humans as the most free members of the universe have the particular attendant responsibility of representing the universe's love for God. [94]

One Humanity.

Wilson-Kastner's understanding of God as inherently and fundamentally relational grounds the fundamentally relational character of human being and existence.   The complexity and diversity of creation and of human existence are directed by love "toward healing the wounds caused by negativity and nurturing a diverse but united cosmos" where diversity is united in the same way that the three persons of the Trinity are one. [95] The human portion of creation is an important part of this dynamic of transformation.   And it is in relationality where transforming, integrating love is the essential dynamic that human persons are most fully like God.

The human person is self-conscious, self-focused, self-possessed, and at the same time self-transcendent, embodied and relational as well as autonomous. [96]   In other words, human persons are like what human persons perceive: they are both differentiated and integrated.   Human existence is continuous with its environment, not at odds with it.   "Humanity occupies a key position because of its ability to understand and to love, to acknowledge the created reality of the world, its participation in the world, and at the same time its innate affinity for the divine life." [97]   It is humanity's consciousness and freedom that uniquely suit the human to represent the divine in creation and the development of creation to the divine.   For human consciousness and freedom imitate the reality of the divine, but also are developments of characteristics found in other created beings as well as the human.   This means that human persons are most fully who they are meant to be when they are intentionally acting to foster inclusiveness, community, and freedom to choose the good, not only among humans, but throughout creation. [98]

In the Incarnation, crucifixion, and resurrection of Jesus the Christ, the realities of both human and divine are re-presented in the midst of human experience and existence.   This reality is one of wholeness and inclusivity, which is realized through a transforming process of reconciliation. These events reveal what God has always been doing, and who humanity has always been. At the same time, they are a definitive part of a process of transformation, and so are actually part of redemption, which is the reunification of the human and the divine in a dance of mutual love. This reunification lies ahead of us, never to be known in this life, but always to be longed for and sought. [99]

Summary and Evaluation

Wilson-Kastner's epistemology and Christology attempt to demonstrate the dynamic connection between unity and diversity, positing unity as the more absolute or fundamental of the two realities: what differentiates diversity from fragmentation is the relationship of diverse things to each other, i.e., unity that does not erase difference. In advancing a feminist rendering of transcendental Thomist epistemology and metaphysics, Wilson-Kastner endeavors to show how feminist criticism of patriarchal dualisms, based as it is in a vision of wholeness and integration, in fact points toward a relational view of the human and human knowing in which all persons are engaged in the same general processes of knowing, while not necessarily knowing the same things in the same way.

Wilson-Kastner's Christology then indicates what of ultimate value is to be known, and how that knowledge is available through the re-presentation of the ultimate in history through Jesus the Christ. The Christ means reconciliation and inclusiveness; and in the Christ human persons are met both by the revelation or self-expression of the divine and by entirely authentic human existence embodied in one person. The Christ shows the link between divine and human, the cosmos and its conscious inhabitants.

This is a Wisdom-Logos Christology in that the Christ is the revelation or re-presentation of a God of "self-giving creativity" and self-giving love, of a humanity that is unified in the structure of its existence but diverse in its experience, and of the overall relational structure of the cosmos as a whole. By emphasizing the dynamism of all these relations within as well as between each sort of being, Wilson-Kastner reconstructs the more static orientation of the Wisdom-Logos tradition. She attempts to show how basic polarities--finite and infinite, mental and bodily aspects of existence, and so on--are interactively rather than dualistically related. And her epistemology and metaphysics are grounded in the continuity rather than the disruption between past, present, and future. Finally, what is normative about Jesus as the Christ is neither his maleness nor any other historical particularity, but the overall pattern of his life, death, and resurrection--a pattern that shows how historical concreteness indicates transhistorical realities and processes. In sum, Wilson-Kastner has addressed each of the difficulties inherent in a feminist reconstruction of the Wisdom-Logos strand through her appropriation of contemporary transcendental Thomist theology and feminist thought.

The value of Wilson-Kastner's work toward a relatively adequate feminist Christology lies in her epistemology and in her reconstruction of a Logos Christology that reasserts the more dynamic and affective Wisdom elements evident in the first five centuries of Christianity's development. By weaving together a Lonerganian epistemology with feminist insights into the importance of bodily, aesthetic, and affective sensibilities in human experience, Wilson-Kastner develops a complex view of the human that emphasizes the common structures and processes of experience that unify its historic diversity. Again following Lonergan modified with feminist insight, she indicates how the Christ reveals the primordial connection between human experience and the divine life. The life, death, and resurrection of Jesus are one concrete and historical embodiment of this connection. Thus, the Christ reveals both the divine life and the fullness of authentic humanity which is established at creation, distorted by the fragmentation of sin, and promised as future fulfillment through restored unifying connection between humanity and divinity.

However, neither her epistemology nor her Christology are entirely satisfactory. Wilson-Kastner insists without faltering that how humans understand and construe their experience is actively formative of their existence. Thus, she argues, it is of the greatest importance to begin consistently with the assumption of one humanity. Then, it is the *structure* of human experience that may unify its content without suppressing irreducible differences. The significance and real fruitfulness of this point is, however, diminished by Wilson-Kastner's failure to address adequately the extent of the distortions associated with patriarchal domination, and, therefore, the extent of the fragmentation of actual lived human existence by constructs such as gender, race, and class. The force of feminist analyses of patriarchal dualisms is that the distortions of patriarchy *in fact do* jeopardize the unity of humanity, and simple re-assertion of unity will not restore it, particularly when fragmentation is enforced not just by ignorance but also by exertion of persuasive or coercive power. Attending to actual difference without minimizing its scope is a necessary part of the recovery of wholeness in existence as well as in theory. Wilson-Kastner moves too rapidly to unity, virtually brushing aside the difference difference makes. [100]

Nevertheless, the structural approach of her epistemology holds promise for indicating how humanity is one while still diverse. Wilson-Kastner's argument here would be stronger with more sustained evident inclusion of explicitly social categories. Still, her understanding of the human is, in principle, adequately complex to meet the case outlined in my discussion of experience in Part II.

Wilson-Kastner's Christology also has its problems. First, she is quite uninterested in grounding her portrayal of Jesus as the Christ in more than absolutely minimal historical concreteness. In part this comes from her quite orthodox insistence that the Christ is to be found in Word and Sacrament as well as in historical event, an insistence that goes far in meeting some of the difficulties of a more historicist approach such as Ruether's. Even so, Wilson-Kastner's lack of interest in the concrete aspects of Jesus' life and teaching diminish the significance of his concrete humanity and weaken possible connections between the quality of his life and the formation of the faithful life of his followers.

While Wilson-Kastner attends to all three areas that I have argued are necessary to a relatively adequate feminist Christology--tradition, contemporary experience, and future use--it is tradition that carries the greatest weight. Wilson-Kastner has engaged in the apologetic task of indicating how feminist Christianity is consistent with classical Christianity; and she has devoted considerable effort to identifying strands of Christian tradition that are fruitful for the elaboration of feminist Christian theology. However, in doing so, she often fails to address the androcentric biases of these traditions, and fails to explain how she has reconciled fundamental differences in the presuppositions of the materials she weaves together. [101] Thus, her use of tradition lacks the critical fullness necessary for adequacy for feminist Christian theology.

Second, as already noted, her theoretical treatment of experience (and so of contemporary experience) tends to minimize real historical differences in order to maintain the fundamental principle of the unity of humanity.

Third, Wilson-Kastner consistently indicates that the fullness of humanity and restored relation with God lie in the future. Her vision of the future, however, is largely continuous with the corporately oriented realized eschatologies of more traditional Christianity. Her discussions of reconciliation and unity focus on the return or restoration of humanity to lost relationship with God and each other, through which creation is healed. [102] Transformation, then, is a matter of reform, growth, and fulfillment, rather than radical destruction and reconstruction of historical existence. Again, Wilson-Kastner's presentation is limited by her reluctance to pursue fully the relentlessly critical aspects of feminist theology. Missing here is the rigorous social analysis and vision of Ruether and Heyward (for example).

For while Wilson-Kastner sketches the practical and ethical applications of her more speculative discussion, she does so within her major goal, which is to present feminist Christianity as still within the fold of mainline Christianity. Her argument is likely to be of greatest use within Christian reform movements that are seeking to incorporate feminism as part of liberal Christianity. Wilson-Kastner contributes to the more comprehensive liberation and transformation of Christian life and practice beyond patriarchy envisioned by Ruether and Heyward (for example) by taking what is essentially an apologetic stance on behalf of feminism toward mainline Christianity. Wilson-Kastner's work helps establish a meeting point between liberal and liberation perspectives in theology.

Finally, Wilson-Kastner presents what is, after all, a reformist Christology from above. What matters here is what God does through the Christ. And this is known to us not primarily through existential encounter, but through authoritative teaching (albeit by elements of Christian tradition whose values contemporary feminists share), and through Word and Sacrament as conveyed by the community that follows the Christ, the church. To put it another way, Wilson-Kastner's Christology, in both its sources and its content, stays firmly within reformist sacramental tradition. Its strength lies in showing how that tradition can legitimately and effectively be interpreted in feminist Christian terms.

Yet this reformist approach is quite fruitful, all the more so when it is linked to Wilson-Kastner's epistemology. Wilson-Kastner responds to the feminist challenge by indicating how Christianity can be understood as well as experienced as liberating. And given the mutually formative connection between understanding and experience which her epistemology espouses, this connection is of considerable importance: once one understands how Christianity can be liberating, one may (once again) experience it in this way. Thus, if Christian theology expresses the structure of the divine and the universe--and so of human existence--as relational in love, and so non-hierarchical, it also indicates how the divine is neither oppressive nor exclusive, and is, in fact, actively opposed to oppression and exclusion as forms of fragmentation of finally unbreakable unity. Therefore, patriarchal Christianity is itself a perversion, reflecting infidelity to God and to the essentials of Christian faith. More faithful is the feminist Christian understanding, which understands God as the self-giving One who nurtures and fulfills our yearning for reconciliation and wholeness.

Notes

1.   Wisdom (Heb. *Hokmah*, Gk. *Sophia*) in the Hebrew biblical tradition is the self-expression of God, associated with divine creative power and with the cultivation of human character and existence in accord with the divine. My interest here is primarily with Wisdom as the self-expression of God. On this, see Elizabeth A. Johnson, "Jesus, the Wisdom of God: A Biblical Basis for Non-Androcentric Christology," *Ephemerides Theologicae Lovanienses* 60 no. 4 (December 1985): 261-294; John L. McKenzie, "The Word of God in the New Testament," *Theological Studies* 21, no. 2 (June 1960): 183-206; Adela Yarbro Collins, "New Testament Perspectives: The Gospel of John," *Journal for the Study of the Old Testament* 22, no. 1 (1982): 47-53; and Leo D. Lefebure, *Toward a Contemporary Wisdom Christology: A Study of Karl Rahner and Norman Pittenger* (Lanham, MD: University Press of America, 1988). On the wise life, see R. B. Y. Scott, *The Way of Wisdom in the Old Testament* (New York: Macmillan, 1971).

The concept of the Logos (Word, mind) is drawn primarily from Greek thought, and in the development of early Christian theology is understood as the eternal self-expression or mind of God, which is the ordering and creative force of the cosmos, and is related to the Godhead as the spoken word is related to the whole person. The development of and variations within the Logos strand of Christian theology are extremely complex, and will not be discussed in detail here. See G. L. Prestige, *God in Patristic Thought* (London: SPCK, 1952); J. N. D. Kelly, *Early Christian Doctrines* (New York: Harper and Row, 1958); Aloys Grillmeier, *Christ in Christian Tradition*, vol. 1, *From the Apostolic Age to Chalcedon* (Atlanta: John Knox, 1975); and Jaroslav Pelikan, *The Emergence of the Catholic Tradition (100-600)*, vol. 1:   *The Christian Tradition: A History of the Development of Doctrine* (Chicago: University of Chicago Press, 1971).

2.   Of the feminist authors discussed in this book, Heyward is the one who gives the fullest explicit discussion of this particular problem. See Carter Heyward, *The Redemption of God: A Theology of*

Mutual Relation, 107-126, 189-192; idem, *Our Passion for Justice: Images of Power, Sexuality, and Liberation*, 211-221; idem, *Speaking of Christ: A Lesbian Feminist Voice*, ed. Ellen C. Davis (New York: Pilgrim Press, 1989), 16-20.

3.   As Gotthold Ephraim Lessing so sharply put it, an "ugly ditch" had opened between the present and the time of Christ: "Accidental truths of history can never become the proof of necessary truths of reason." ("The Proof of the Spirit and of Power," *Lessing's Theological Writings*, trans. Henry Chadwick [Stanford: Stanford University Press, 1956], 53.) On the challenges posed by modernity to Christology, see, for example, Walter Lowe, "Christ and Salvation," in *Christian Theology: An Introduction to its Traditions and Tasks*, ed. Peter C. Hodgson and Robert H. King (Philadelphia: Fortress Press, 1985); and Claude Welch, *Protestant Thought in the Nineteenth Century*, vol. 1 (New Haven: Yale University Press, 1972).

4.   On this problem, see Carol Christ, *Laughter of Aphrodite*; Gerda Lerner, *The Creation of Patriarchy*; and Rosemary Radford Ruether, *New Woman/New Earth, Sexism and God-Talk*, and *Womanguides*.

5.   See, for example, Rosemary Radford Ruether, *Sexism and God-Talk*, 122-126; Ruether, *To Change the World*, 45-49; Mary Daly, *Beyond God the Father*, 69-73; and Rita Nakashima Brock, *Journeys by Heart*, 54, 60-62.

6.   Wilson-Kastner, 91, 106-108.

7.   Marjorie Hewitt Suchocki, *God-Christ-Church: A Practical Guide to Process Theology* (New York: Crossroad, 1982), 129, 101. Hereafter referred to as *God-Christ-Church* 1982; I will refer to the second revised edition (New York: Crossroad, 1989) as *God-Christ-Church* 1989.

8.   Heyward, *The Redemption of God*, 200; *Our Passion for Justice*, 46, 178.

9.   On the relation between creation and eschatological redemption, see Heyward, *Our Passion for Justice*, 243-247 and related passages in *Redemption of God*; Wilson-Kastner, ibid., 51-52, 108; and Suchocki, *God-Christ-Church* 1982, 176ff.

10.   Heyward, *Redemption of God*, 31, 198.

11.   Patricia Wilson-Kastner is an Anglican scholar and priest whose training is in patristic theology. She has taught theology, ethics, and homiletics, and is currently serving as the rector of an Episcopal church in Connecticut. In addition to *Faith, Feminism, and the Christ* (my principal source here), she is the author of *Imagery for Preaching*

(Minneapolis: Fortress Press, 1989) and (with G. R. Kastner et al.) *A Lost Tradition: Women Writers of the Early Church* (Washington: University Press of America, 1981), as well as numerous articles.

12. Wilson-Kastner, 1. Wilson-Kastner's discussion of these authors focuses on Daly's argument in *Beyond God the Father* and *Gyn/ecology*, Christ's in *Womanspirit Rising* and *Diving Deep and Surfacing*, and Naomi Goldenberg's in *The Changing of the Gods*. Later arguments by these authors were still forthcoming at the time *Faith, Feminism, and the Christ* was written in 1983.

13. Wilson-Kastner uses the term *doctrinal fundamentalists* in order to preserve the possibility that doctrine properly understood supports--perhaps requires--a position like the one *Faith, Feminism, and the Christ* articulates.

14. Ibid., 2. Wilson-Kastner refers here to both Biblical and doctrinal fundamentalists. Overall, her major interest is in the arguments of doctrinal fundamentalists, particularly in the Episcopal, Orthodox, and Catholic churches as these have been involved in heated controversy over the ordination of women during the last two decades.

15. Ibid., 3, 1.

16. Ibid., 92.

17. Ibid., 11-16. Wilson-Kastner here follows the lead of Rosemary Radford Ruether.

18. Ibid., 19-20.

19. Ibid., 49-51.

20. Ibid., 50.

21. Ibid., 63.

22. Ibid., 61-62.

23. Ibid., 63

24. Ibid., 55.

25. Ibid., 2.

26. Ibid., 55.

27. Ibid., 56.

28. Ibid., 63.

29. Ibid., 56-57. Hampson criticizes Wilson-Kastner at exactly this point: "Nor does she have a sense for the impact which the fact that Christ has been seen as male and as part of the Godhead has had on the relations of women and men in western culture. It is as though, for her, Christ is beyond sex. The question with which we are concerned is not tackled." (Hampson, 60.)

30. Ibid., 57.

31. Wilson-Kastner points to the Pauline and Cappadocian use of the image of the Body of Christ, and the modern and contemporary renderings of the same insight in the form of emphasis on the cosmos as a living whole that exists in relationship to an ultimate, as theorized by Teilhard de Chardin and Alfred North Whitehead. (Ibid., 58-59.)

32. Affinities with F. D. Maurice's methodology on this point are apparent enough. See my discussion of Maurice in Chapter 3, above.

33. Wilson-Kastner, 65.

34. Ibid., 40.

35. Ibid., 41, 45.

36. Ibid., 45-46.

37. Ibid., 65. Consequently, "women's experience" may be *a* source for Christian feminist theology; but it cannot be *the* source if feminist theology is to give a more adequate account of reality than has the patriarchal theology it critiques. Tradition is epistemologically authorized as a source precisely because it provides an expansion of the apprehension of reality: it is outside of but not entirely unknowable to contemporary historical particularity. Theologically, tradition is a source because it is a formative part of the contemporary Christian community's experience of Christ as liberating. It is also a source of insight into emerging visions and ideas.

38. Ibid., 43, 46-47.

39. "Reality can 'make sense' only if the human person is animated in the wellspring of her or his conscious life by the urge to know the whole, and the mental equipment to constantly put all the events and perceptions of the whole into the perspective of totality the person seeks. . . . Within the human mind is a dynamic that seeks understanding of the whole of reality, not just bits and pieces." (Ibid., 44.)

40. Ibid., 47.

41. Ibid., 51. Theologically this principle is expressed as the Ultimate or God.

42. Ibid., 6.

43. Ibid., 125, 90.

44. In other words, feminism itself poses an epistemological challenge by disclosing the philosophical consequences of the fragmentation that is patriarchal dualism. (Ibid., 19.)

45. Ibid., 48.

46. Ibid., 49.

47.   Ibid., 51.   Hampson ignores all of this in her criticism of what she takes to be Wilson-Kastner's fideism.   But Hampson's own final position is derived from an epistemology very like Wilson-Kastner's.   See Hampson, *Theology and Feminism*, 61 and 162-175.

48.   Ibid., 91.

49.   Ibid., 7.   Because Christology is the rational explanation of an ongoing encounter, rather than a contemporary reconstruction of a historical/past event with ongoing significance, it is legitimate to reformulate it to express contemporary faith experience.

50.   Ibid., 91 and passim.

51.   Ibid., 5.

52.   Ibid., 4.

53.   Ibid., 92.   Wilson-Kastner draws heavily on Schubert Ogden, *The Point of Christology*, especially 82-83.

54.   Ibid., 90.   The essential error of the literalistic misapprehension is that it mistakes experience for the content of reality, instead of understanding experience as the medium through which reality is known and appropriated.   (*Ibid.*, 64; following Paul Tillich, *Systematic Theology*, vol. 1 [Chicago: University of Chicago Press, 1951], 40-46.)

55.   Ibid., 90.

56.   Ibid., 71; italics in the original.   Wilson-Kastner traces the historical development of androcentric and misogynist bias in Christology from Irenaeus' use of Adam-Christ/Eve-Mary parallels in *Proof of the Apostolic Preaching*. (Ibid., 80.)

57.   Ibid., 83.

58.   Ibid., 90.

59.   Clearly, Wilson-Kastner sees herself as an inner-Christian apologist rather than as an advocate for the legitimacy of philosophical theology in a secular world.

60.   Ibid., 91-92, again following Ogden, *The Point of Christology*, 82-83 and throughout.

61.   Ibid., 91.

62.   Ibid., 92.

63.   Ibid., 92.

64.   Ibid., 95.

65.   Ibid., 77.

66.   Ibid., 91.

67.   See Johnson, 261-294.

68.   Wilson-Kastner, 96.

69. Ibid., 96, 100. Among other sources, Wilson-Kastner here draws on Julian of Norwich's vision of Jesus the Word as Mother.

70. Ibid., 103-4.

71. Ibid., 105. Here Wilson-Kastner follows Moltmann in *The Crucified God*.

72. Wilson-Kastner deliberately begins her discussion of the crucifixion with reconciliation as unity rather than as self-giving, presumably in order to indicate that authentic self-giving is grounded in relation, rather than establishing it. This tacitly addresses the oft-voiced feminist critique of the use of self-giving and self-sacrifice to diminish and control the self-expression of women.

73. Ibid., 101-104. This image Wilson-Kastner draws from Julian of Norwich, who connects the motherhood of Jesus with the crucifixion.

74. Ibid., 98.

75. Ibid., 101.

76. Ibid., 106. Thus women's "steadfast love" is given constructive value as a historical force, without denying its problems.

77. Ibid., 99-100.

78. Ibid., 109. Note that while Jesus lives *a* (particular) human life (ibid., 90), as the Christ he is also *the* new human. That is, the ideal can be--must be--expressed in the particular.

79. Ibid., 111.

80. Ibid., 52.

81. Ibid., 107-108.

82. Ibid., 7.

83. Ibid., 84.

84. Ibid., 6f, 20ff.

85. Ibid., 122.

86. Ibid., 122, 127.

87. Ibid., 126-127, following both John of Damascus and Jürgen Moltmann.

88. "In perfect openness good gives unreservedly of itself (in traditional language, the Father), and this love is a perfect receiving of love (the Son, or Word). Love self-giving and love receiving relate to each other in mutual harmony, and to love which is the perfect expression of this divine love (the Holy Spirit)." (Ibid., 128.)

89. Ibid., 89.

90. Ibid., 5, 51.

91. Ibid., 123, 129.

92. Ibid., 125.

93. Ibid., 60.
94. Ibid., 125.
95. Ibid., 125, 129.
96. Ibid., 61.
97. Wilson-Kastner continues, "At the same time that each being in the world has its own integrity, each and every one finds its ultimate fulfillment in the service of God, according to one's own capacity." (Ibid., 59.)
98. Ibid., 131-133.
99. Ibid., 57.
100. This is also Hampson's criticism of Wilson-Kastner in *Theology and Feminism*, 60-61. On the importance to white feminist theology of the issue of difference, see especially Susan Brooks Thistlethwaite, *Sex, Race, and God*.
101. On this latter point, see the review of *Faith, Feminism, and the Christ* by Mary Knutsen, *Religious Studies Review* 12 no. 3/4 (July/October 1986), 197-202.
102. See Wilson-Kastner, 107-116, where her discussion of the resurrection promised to all, through Christ, is couched in the cosmic evolutionary terms of Gregory of Nyssa and Teilhard de Chardin.

Chapter 9

The Revelation of God
to Us

Introduction

Marjorie Hewitt Suchocki[1] criticizes classical theology because of two related, basic problems: androcentrism, and inadequacy to contemporary human experience. Suchocki takes to heart the post-Christian feminist analysis of Mary Daly and others, and restates it as a dilemma for Christian feminists: "if the question to be raised is, 'Can a woman be both feminist and Christian,' then it is precisely we women who identify ourselves as both who are in question. We do not simply raise the question; we are the question."[2] Suchocki's recognition of both the deep-rooted patriarchal character of Christianity and the positive power of Christianity experienced by Christian feminists leads her to reformulate Christian theology so that "the Christian and feminist visions can blend in transformation."[3]

The Christian feminist dilemma points to an even more compelling reason for reformulating classical theology: classical theology is inadequate to any contemporary experience because it reflects an obsolete mode of conceptualizing experience. The "Christian conviction that God is for us" must be expressed in the "common sense" of each era of human history, reflecting Christians' location in the world as much as their religious heritage and its Scriptural texts. And in our time, "the dominant understanding of the world"--the vernacular language, as it were--is inter-relational, relative, and processive. Christian theology must be expressed in these terms if it is to continue having a formative influence in "the 'real world' of everyday-ness."[4]

Constructively, then, Suchocki presents a feminist Christian reading of the process thought of Alfred North Whitehead that emphasizes relatedness; the creative interdependence of past, present, and future; and fundamental continuity between the human and the divine. Jesus is the Christ in that his "is the life which reveals the nature of God for us; this is the life which offers a concrete vision of the reality to which God calls us; this is the revelation of God to us for the sake of conforming us to that divine image."[5] Jesus manifests the nature of God as wisdom, power, and presence that is constant even in the most horrifying moments of existence. Jesus also reveals that and how God moves all existence toward harmony, which weaves together all the diverse elements of existence into unity.

The Character of Human Existence

Becoming and relationality are the keys to Suchocki's presentation of process thought. In process thought, being is always in the process of coming to be more fully through the creation of greater harmony and unity among increasingly complex and intense elements.[6] Being *is* becoming. This is true for all aspects of existence, not just humans.[7] Relationality is "constitutive of existence, and not simply accidental to it. . . . Relation pushes existence into being: once having become, that new being likewise demands relation to a future."[8] Relational interaction constitutes and completes individuals as they push out of themselves toward others, bringing about mutual modification or transformation as each seeks to conform the other to itself and at the same time adjusts itself to the other's uniqueness.[9] Individual existents come into being out of an immediate past composed of diverse events, choices, influences, and feelings that are related in the individual existent. These past occurrences are creatively unified and harmonized according to the individual's envisioned purposes. "Existence is a movement, a dance, of mutual enrichment: the many contribute the wealth of their experience to the becoming one, who in turn contributes to all successors."[10] The one emerges from the many; diversity is creatively harmonized into unity.[11] Change has positive value because it enables the drive of individuals toward completion and outside of themselves toward others.

The emergence of the present and the future from the past is made possible by two factors: a drive toward harmony that is inherent in existence as such, and the influence of novelty, which renders previously incompatible elements compatible by reshaping them.[12] The past cannot be repeated; it can, however, be appropriated as part of the individual's drive toward harmonious completion. Indeed, "The richness of the present is the degree to which it incorporates its past in a positive movement into the future."[13] The close connection between past, present, and future means that the present is bound or obligated to consider what type of future will desirably succeed it, and present fidelity to the past means openness to the future.[14]

What distinguishes human relational existence from some other forms of existence is the significance of reflective consciousness, which renders available to consideration and intentionality the many relations that constitute the individual. This particularly human quality does not ontologically separate humankind from other existents. Rather, it serves to illumine all existence, and to indicate to humans their continuity with the world around them.[15] And it gives to human existence an extra measure of responsibility, both to represent non-conscious existence and to shape human intentionality to reflect and continue the interdependence among all existents.[16]

That relation, internal and external, is the constitutive fact of the human means that theological anthropology must reflect in an integral manner the social aspects of humanity, including how individuals appropriate or internalize present and past social contexts, relations, and events. [17] The interdependent interaction between self and world has both just and unjust possibilities, depending on how an individual's agency is interwoven with corporate existence and activity. [18] Relational existence is relativized existence: understandings of the human good, the right or just, and the holy depend on the concrete and particular possibilities available within human existence. The human good is the movement toward harmony. [19] And the relationality of all existence means that "the welfare of all creates the welfare of each, and the welfare of each contributes to the welfare of all; such is the rhythmic movement of harmony." [20]

Suchocki identifies two ways in which the relationality that constitutes the human self can be denied: self-absolutization and self-depreciation. In both cases, the reality of relationality and the importance of others to the very being of the self are distorted and denied. [21] In the case of self-absolutization, one and only one existent is put at the center of existence, when all existents belong there. Self-depreciation is just the reverse: all but one existent are seen as at the center. [22] As they become habitual, these distorted views of reality become a form of bondage or imprisonment that can be broken only by outside intervention in the form of a novelty (or new occasion) that reasserts the importance and reality of relation either to self (in the case of self-depreciation) or to others (in the case of self-absolutization). [23]

Suchocki names these forms of distortion as sin. They, like all distortions, posit a condition contrary to reality; they "go against the grain of things," [24] and form habits that limit openness to other possibilities, past, present, and future. [25] In a universe understood in process terms, anything that mitigates against or actively prevents creative movement toward harmonious unity is sinful. Included, then, are not only distortion or imprisonment of the self and denial of others, but also restriction of access to a full range of possibilities (as is the case with oppressive social structures), fear of the future (as in the fear of death, for example), acceptance of an oppressive past (as in internalization of domination and oppression), and protection against novelty (as in habituation). [26] Concomitantly, resistance to any of these distorting tendencies is part of overcoming them, in that resistance provides the possibility of openness to new appropriations of reality. [27]

But overcoming the distortions of reality that are the prison of sin cannot be accomplished without assistance external to the sinful situation.

> The paradox is that while we ourselves built the prison, we built it with our own existence. Therefore we do not have the strength to break the prison down, and we are trapped by and in sin. Release must come from beyond ourselves in a counterforce to sin. We require a force in the past strong enough to counter the demonic, a force in the future that is stronger than death, and a force in the present that can enable us to live in the full interchange of relational existence. [28]

That is, human persons are agents responsible for the sin in their situation to the extent that they have chosen from a range of possibilities available to them, and made their choices part of themselves through the processes of internalization which form the self. But these same processes create limits on what responsible agents may effectively do to change their situations: they may think, feel, and act only from within limitation. New possibilities must be given them in order for them to respond to and act upon them. And they must choose to appropriate and utilize these possibilities.

The various forms of distortion of relationality constitute sin for Suchocki, because they deny reality and limit creative participation in it. There is an additional form of distortion of relationality which, in Suchocki's view, is not in and of itself sinful: loneliness. Loneliness presents the self with the threat of meaninglessness through devaluing of relations. This occurs because loneliness is actually a longing for relationality of a more profound sort than that which has been the case; it is a sense of contrast between what has been and is, and what might be.[29]

Suchocki describes loneliness as an intermediate layer between the relations of daily existence and "a deeper dimension to reality that has the power of judgment over loneliness."[30] This description suggests that one of the ways in which the self imprisoned by sin moves toward release from the bondage of distortions of relationality is through loneliness as the recognition of the limited character of the self's relations. That is, loneliness is a longing for release into a more profound, complex, intense reality. It is, in theological terms, the longing for God.[31]

Method for Appropriation

Suchocki's concern is to provide an explication of process thought interwoven with Christian theology that is adequate to contemporary experience. In the first instance, this means centering both form and substance in relatedness, in the manner sketched above. In the second, adequate contemporaneity requires showing how philosophical formulations may attend to pressing concerns such as injustice, massive human suffering, and encounter with "the other" in dialogues with other religions and worldviews, and in movements of liberation.

Indeed, in theology, contemporary experience, while profoundly shaped by Scripture and tradition, *must* be used to give "faithful expression" to "biblical understanding" of God, Christ, and other aspects of Christian faith in order to remain faithful.[32] The decisive advantage of process theology is precisely that it has a contemporary experiential base.[33] The decisive advantage of a feminist liberation reading of process thought is that it casts this experiential base in concrete terms drawn from the daily existence of the marginalized and silenced. This reading brings contemporary theology in line with the Biblical view of the relation between God and human existence understood always as communal.[34]

However, Suchocki believes that the primacy of contemporary experience as the basis for theology in no way negates or denigrates the importance of "biblical understanding" in Christian theology.[35] The relation of past, present, and future in process thought means that tradition (including Biblical tradition) and contemporary experience can be distinguished but not separated: they mutually shape each other. Present existents come into being on the basis of the past that precedes them. But they incorporate only some selected elements from the past: their very existence is an evaluative interpretation and appropriation of the past.[36] Further, *all* experience may provide hints or clues about the nature of the divine and of the whole of existence, since all experience receives its possibilities from God. "What God is for us, God is in the depths of the divine being. If God is presence, wisdom, and power for us in our human experience, then God is presence, wisdom, and power internally and everlastingly."[37] For Christians, experience is reflectively interpreted through the intensification of the image of God in human consciousness which occurs in and through Jesus.

Christology

Critique

In developing the Christological components of her theology, Suchocki recognizes the particular dilemma of Christian feminists, in terms similar to those used by Patricia Wilson-Kastner: "if the question to be raised is, 'Can a woman be both feminist and Christian,' then it is precisely we women who identify ourselves as both who are in question."[38] And the outcome of such questioning cannot be known in advance. "To parallel Daly's journey is to risk the question, to risk ourselves, for the genuineness of any question is that we do not know the answer."[39] On the one hand, Suchocki as a Christian feminist recognizes the validity of the feminist analysis of the deep-rooted patriarchal character of Christianity.

> If this brutal oppression of women is but the offspring of
> patriarchy, the child of Christianity, then can we as feminists
> align ourselves with this institution? Do we assent to the
> crimes by our assent to the criminal? . . . How can we
> follow, even transformatively, in a tradition which has not
> only perpetrated such horror, but dared to treat it as trivial?[40]

On the other hand, she argues that "It remains a fact that
feminists who are Christians have probably all experienced a
tremendous power for life, not death, through Christianity."[41]
"Two thousand years of history: yet we have emerged from that
history; it has yielded to its future, made space for the present."[42]

Suchocki addresses three points of Daly's critique: the
centrality of patriarchal dualism in Christianity; the history of
Christianity's brutal oppression of women; and the problematic
of a male savior for women's identity.   In none of these cases
does Suchocki deny the validity of Daly's claims against
Christianity.   Suchocki insists that patriarchy and its negative
historical   effects--its   contribution   to   disharmony--have
destructively distorted and curtailed women's identity, and so
their capacity to participate in the movement toward harmony.[43]
In response, she suggests ways in which Christianity might be
transformed to eliminate the core problems and serious distortions that Daly and others have identified.   This transformation
is a matter of unravelling and reweaving the fabric of Christianity; that is, of neither rending nor patching it.   Process
theology's emphasis on relationality and creativity or novelty
suits it for this task.

Suchocki argues that the incarnation is a signal instance of
novelty which provides an example of the harmony possible
between human and divine.   This example influences all
subsequent existence and so advances the lure of divine
harmony.   And, when Christology is cast in processive,
relational terms, the relationality rather than the maleness of
Jesus is central.   The primary characteristics of God can then be
understood in the relational terms of wisdom, presence, and
power.[44]   Finally, Suchocki recasts fidelity to Jesus the Christ
as   a   matter   of   a   process   of   appropriation   rather   than

characterological imitation, a focus on how "Christ lives in me" rather than a "Not I, but Christ" elimination of personal character.[45]

Construction

Christian faith's identification of Jesus with the incarnate one, the Christ, identifies the life of Jesus with "God with us," the immediate and full presence of God. This means that Jesus' life "is the life which reveals the nature of God for us; this is the life which offers a concrete vision of the reality to which God calls us; this is the revelation of God to us for the sake of conforming us to that divine image."[46] Such a claim has the effect of "lift[ing] all that we see in that revelation to ultimacy."[47] In other words, the incarnation of God in Christ is an intensification of the general revelation which enables existents to infer much of the creative and sustaining activity of God from the course of ordinary existence. The incarnation is also a special revelation of how the distortion of sin is broken by the God who is newly revealed and understood to be "God *for* us."[48]

The identification of Jesus with the Christ hinges on concrete aspects of his life. Suchocki highlights Jesus' historical location in a time of expectant concrete anticipation of the Reign of God and associated "purity," reform, and liberation movements and impulses. Suchocki notes that Jesus' own attitudes were continuous with these expectations, but made an advance beyond them; this advance is indicated by Jesus' inclusion of those considered impure in relation to the Kingdom: sinners, the marginalized and outcast, the handicapped, and even oppressors.[49] Jesus' relations are also reciprocal: he receives service as well as rendering it, affirming the "daily interdependence" of existence.[50] In this and other ways, Jesus reverses the prevailing social order, thereby both opening up possibilities for the inbreaking of God's reign and revealing the nature of God as love made evident in justice.[51]

Jesus' inclusive interactions with others manifest the relation between judgement and love: all those with whom Jesus comes into contact are challenged to be transformed, including those whose lives and choices are severely limited by their social and historical circumstances. [52] At the same time that Jesus challenges or calls specific people to abandon the familiar and risk the new, he also himself embodies the possibility and actuality of the new, which is to say that he provides both the hope and the reassurance needed by others to follow his example. [53]

Suchocki presents Jesus' cross and resurrection as continuous with his life: these also reveal the nature of God as one who feels every sin, every pain, and who transforms them. [54] Indeed, such revelation would seem to be the point of these events, in Suchocki's view. In Jesus' cross and resurrection, the depth, scope, and character of God's relation to other existents is made clear: God suffers as other existents suffer; but God's suffering cannot be rendered impersonal or indirect, since "God feels the effects directly, both as given and received. . . . what the theology of the cross expressed in process terms requires us to acknowledge is that God continues to love in *God's* pain." [55]

In other words, God's presence in human suffering is always fully co-present, mutual, and participatory. When this fact is seen in light of the movement of all toward increasing harmony and unity, the intensity and immediacy of the relation between presence, wisdom, and just power as primary attributes or characteristics of God are more evident. And it is this full evidence of the nature of God, which contributes to and directs the transformative process in the witnesses to Jesus' death and resurrection, that leads to the foundation of the church. [56] As Jesus' death is continuous with his life, his resurrection both confirms his life and transforms it. [57]

> Jesus expresses the nature of God through his life, cruci-
> fixion, and resurrection, taking the revelation progressively
> deeper until finally we are led, not simply to a description of
> God but to the mystery of God as God. And that mystery is
> inexhaustible love, manifested in a power that both confirms
> and transforms the world. [58]

In sum, Jesus as Suchocki understands him is legitimately designated the Christ, the incarnate one, because he meets in concrete form all the conditions included in this designation. His life and work are both continuous with and an advance upon his concrete situation. He reveals in plain form the nature of God, particularly through his work. His cross and resurrection indicate that he has fully adopted or actualized (without adaptation) the divine nature presented to him as possibility. And his existence contributes a new direction toward transforming all existence toward greater harmony. [59]

The designation of Jesus as the Christ indicates that he reveals fully the nature of both the human and the divine, but in different ways, in Suchocki's formulations. That is,

> Jesus manifested the divine nature in our history. In him the harmony of God is mirrored in the world, not dimly but in all its wonder for us. The depth of God, the intensity of divine beauty, the vortex of divine harmony, all receive expression in Jesus, making him the Christ, anointed with God's presence, manifesting God's presence in, to, and for the world. [60]

Through Jesus, his followers become more intensely aware of the presence and direction of God's love, and of God's openness to other existents; and his followers recognize both as inherent to God's ownmost nature. [61] At the same time, Jesus' followers become more intensely aware that their own "actions in accordance with love and justice are in conformity with the direction of the universe": [62] certain impulses, attitudes, and activities in human existence are validated or vindicated, and their meaning and importance definitively located within ultimate reality. This changes human self-constitution, because there is a change in how humans consider the nature of reality, and this change has profound effects on human action. [63]

In other words, Jesus offers us salvation in three ways. First, "Jesus is a counterforce to the demonic through the simple power of his presence in our past. Jesus is the alternative the demonic denies." [64] In process thought, this means there is an actuality in the past which provides a real possibility that would not otherwise be present; [65] the possibilities for human existence are unalterably changed. Second, the presence of God in Jesus indicates that God both endures all we endure, and is stronger than all that threatens us. This makes endurance possible for us, to a degree it was not possible before. Third, and following from the first two, Jesus offers salvation through the proclamation made about him by those subsequent to him. It is this offer which makes the first two offers of salvation present long after Jesus' ascension. [66]

Jesus embodies and so begins a new order; but he does not complete it. This work is left to those who follow him, albeit substantially influenced and directed by his presence. The work of the church as the body of those following Jesus is of extreme importance in carrying on Jesus' presence by both proclamation and action and so shaping the Reign of God. [67] The concrete reality of the Reign of and in God is always emergent, as God introduces new possibilities into historical existence, and as historical existents respond to those possibilities. Both the manifestations of God in history and the proclamation of humans about that manifestation will determine what God's Reign will be. [68]

Suchocki's Christology, in summary, understands the Christ to be the revelation and intensification of God understood as presence, wisdom, and the power of justice, manifested in full and concrete form in the life and person of Jesus.

> In Christ God's universal aim toward the good for all stands revealed. . . . In Christ we see not simply an abstract revelation of the nature of God as an absolute good viewed far off--to the contrary, in Christ we see God for us. God in goodness bends to our condition, fitting divine harmony to the human situation. In Christ we see the universal made relative. [69]

The incarnation fully reveals God as always fully present in existence--including in suffering--and present in a way that directs existence in love toward greater harmony. Suchocki's largely tacit contention is that this view meets the challenge of the feminist critique of Christology (understood as part of a more comprehensive, less clearly articulated critique coming from contemporary thought) by transforming the historical, damaging patriarchal character of traditional Christology through process theology's emphasis on relationality as fundamental to the structure of cosmic reality.

This transformation highlights human responsibility without diminishing divine power, in that it renders the relation between the human and the divine fully mutual. At the same time, the "otherness" of God is protected in process thought's understanding that God is the one fully actualized existent, while all other beings exist partly in potential and partly in actuality. God is thus the exemplar of all characteristics (such as presence, wisdom, and just power), an exemplar whose complete actualization of these qualities stands in stark contrast to their partial and distorted occurrences in uncompleted existents.

Finally, Suchocki's Christology presents Jesus as fully and definitively the Christ, the incarnate one. But this does not mean that the particular relation between divine and human which makes Jesus the Christ is exclusive to him. Rather, that relation is to lesser extent true between God and all existents, and Jesus' full manifestation of that relation intensifies it (at least potentially) in all existence subsequent to him. Jesus may, then, be said to be the definitive manifestation *for us* of the Christ, the incarnate presence of God who draws all toward increasingly harmonious and unified relation.

Salvation and Harmony

The God Who Is Presence, Wisdom, and Power

In Suchocki's view, God is intimately and immediately connected with all movement toward harmony. God surrounds and embraces all existence in every moment, and as both source and end "giv[es] us birth in every moment through the touch of the divine will for us." [70] The immediate presence of God in existence means that self-revelation of God's nature is integral rather than tangential to the divine: revelation makes clearer "the harmony that is God," so that the world can more easily adapt it to its own situation. [71] God is also the harmony that holds the universe together; but this is a matter of ongoing creation in response to the world, rather than an imposition of static order. [72]

Thus, "God integrates the feeling of the world within the context of harmony," unifying all possibilities and giving them different value according to their relation to the increase of harmony overall. [73] Given the intimacy and mutuality of the relation between God and the world, in order to create possibilities that may move toward integrative harmony, God *feels* the world; that is, God is fully and deeply involved in the world as it is, and profoundly comprehends and appropriates every moment of existence. [74] New possibilities emerge from this responsive feeling in God, with the aim of increasing harmony, unity, and value within finite existence. [75]

While it is the power of God that both creates and saves the world, precisely which world it is that will be saved depends on the world's response to God. That is, God presents the world with possibilities that aim toward greater harmony. But it is the world that receives, chooses from among, and adapts these possibilities, thereby forming the context that God feels in order to suggest new possibilities. [76] To this degree and in this way, the world has responsibility in its own salvation. [77] To put it another way, God is related to and turned toward the world as "pervasively present . . . , ultimate in wisdom, and . . . the power of justice." [78]

The unfailing, all-encompassing presence of God indicates God's faithfulness and guidance. [79] But the invariable, surrounding presence of God presents a paradox to consciousness: God seems to be hidden, because God is inseparable from God's own ongoing effecting of the world and response to human need. [80] Human loneliness--that alienation from daily life that springs from longing for deeper relation--strips away the veil of dailiness which hides God and opens to view the difference between God and the world. [81] Human sin also hides God by distorting and limiting appreciation for and appropriation of the possibilities for harmony that God provides. But God's constancy and the fidelity of God's presence, even in loneliness and the distortion of sin, are revealed in the presence of God with Jesus on the cross and the vindication of Jesus' life through the resurrection.

Suchocki's understanding of God as wisdom addresses God's relation to the temporality, perpetual perishing, and uncertainty associated with finite existence. [82] To say that God is wisdom is to say that God provides guidance for the future. [83] That is, wisdom is not just knowledge, but also the use to which knowledge is put through valuation and intention as it is integrated into the movement toward harmony. [84] To put it another way: the past is transformed through wisdom for the present and the future. [85] And what God knows of the future is only probable: the future is always contingent on what all existents and not just God make of the present. [86]

To speak of God as the power of justice is to address the value and direction of God's transformative integration of the world into the divine harmony beyond existence as we know it. [87] Redress of all evil and restoration of total well-being are not possible within the confines of finitude. [88] But neither are these deferred beyond the agency of injustice's victims. Justice can be approximated in history on the basis of human response to the divine presentation of possibilities for justice; but both are bound to contextual circumstances. [89] And evil and suffering are further transformed as they are taken up into the very existence of God.

God as presence, God as wisdom, and God as justice are one God, constituted by relational complexity and the complete harmony that is meant when the term *unity* is applied to a complex being. In other words, presence, wisdom, and justice are inseparably woven together. [90] Nor is this the only way to speak of God's inherent, ultimate relationality. God is the one existent whose life contains and transforms every other existent, an embracing reality whose way of being is nevertheless "totally different from anything in our experience." [91] "God is the supremely complex One" whose primordial or always-initial harmony and unity constantly issue in multiple possibilities, each of which is a direct address and invitation to the existent at whom it is aimed. And God is the even fuller harmony toward which existence moves and into which it is incorporated. [92]

Eschatological Harmony

In Suchocki's view, existence inherently but not uninterruptedly drives toward greater harmony and unity among increasingly complex and intense elements. [93] The human good is precisely this movement toward harmony. [94] "The foundations of the new world of God's reign are simply the foundations of the interdependence of love, working itself out as justice." [95] Movement toward the good is also movement toward the just, understood as the well-being of all. [96] But justice, harmony, and unity cannot be attained by human persons alone. Existence is limited because it is concrete. Therefore, the external introduction of novel impulses and opportunities is necessary for existence to be other than what it already is in any present moment. These impulses and opportunities come from God, and reflect the very nature of God. "Can the source be less than the call? Must not the source of such a call be itself a complex, intense harmony? And does not the movement of the world toward such qualities become revelatory of this?" [97]

The wisdom of God provides guidance and opportunities for the future. [98] That is, Wisdom is not just knowledge, but the use to which knowledge may be put through valuation, intention, choice, and action as God's aims and lures are integrated into the movement toward harmony. [99] Clearly, understanding God under the aspect of wisdom (rather than omniscience) illuminates the fact of human responsibility for the future. Although we can no longer believe that God knows in advance all that will happen, "We can trust God to offer redemptive possibilities, no matter what may transpire--but what it is that will have to be redeemed depends upon the activity of the world. . . . God invites us into a future that we must create in our own response to God." [100] Finally, the effect of God's wisdom on human existents is related to God's presence: in the midst of a universe of contingency and perpetual perishing, the fidelity of God (indicated by God's presence) and the wisdom of God (indicated by God's use of knowledge for guidance) combine to ground human trust and hope in transformation. [101]   God's   power toward justice provides the value and direction of the world toward the divine harmony. [102]   While justice can only be approximated within the confines of finite existence, there is nevertheless an imperative toward justice in the fact that the future probability of justice depends on present attempts to approximate it. [103] The encouragement to follow this imperative is provided by the realization that "To work for justice is to work with the dynamics of reality. . . . Further, inasmuch as the mode of justice that is seen relative to any situation is a mode that is suited to the world through the creative ordering of God, then that mode of justice is truly achievable." [104]

Even when justice is not approximated in history, evil and injustice are transformed eschatologically without being erased. To make this process clear, Suchocki gives the detailed example of a medieval woman unjustly burned as a witch. [105] God is present with the woman throughout her life and death, "co-experiencing" her entire existence, including the humiliation, terror, and pain of her death.   All this is taken up and transformed into the divine harmony which is God, where she is co-present with God.   "She knows herself as God knows her; she knows herself as she could have been, and as she is." [106]

Also taken up into God is the judge most responsible for the woman's death. In his copresence with God, he is also copresent with the woman he burned; he feels her pain as she felt it. And he experiences "God's feeling of her as a judgement of wrath against himself for what might have been if he had only responded positively toward God's aim for himself for an alternative mode of action and being." [107] For the woman, presumably, being in God is an experience of "a wonderful degree of freedom"; but for the judge, it is hell. [108]

But is the woman's agony redressed? Only in the sense that in her full copresence with God she moves beyond her suffering and so transforms it and is transformed. [109] In other words, even in God there remain both the hard edges of tragedy and a "mighty center of goodness, love, holiness, and joy," a center of profound, primordial harmony. The tragedy is not erased; but movement is inexorably into the center. And that, finally, is justice: the fulfillment of all existence.[110] "There is a home in God, a home for the whole universe. In that home, multiplicity finally achieves unity; fragmentation is embraced in wholeness." This is "the reign of God which is the reign *in* God which is God."[111]

Summary and Evaluation

Suchocki's theology, in summary, understands the Christ to be the full and concrete revelation for Christians of God as presence, wisdom, and the power of justice. God is always fully present in existence (including in suffering) in a way that directs existence in love toward greater harmony. Within its overall theological context, Suchocki's Christology transforms traditional Christology by emphasizing the fundamental importance of relationality in the structure of cosmic reality. This means that, while Jesus is fully and definitively the Christ for Christians, others may to lesser extent also see manifest in him the relation between divinity and humanity; and the effects of his embodiment of the harmonious relation between humanity and divinity extend throughout human history. In this sense, the singularity of Jesus lies in the fullness of his incarnation of divine harmony, rather than in the uniqueness of its appearance. All existence may be brought into harmony and unity with the divine in the future toward which God draws the world.

Although Suchocki does not name it as such, her Christology is of the Wisdom-Logos type.[112] That is, Jesus is the incarnation of the presence, wisdom, and power of God, for Christians the decisive or full manifestation of the divine. The life of Jesus "is the life which reveals the nature of God for us; this is the life which offers a concrete vision of the reality to which God calls us; this is the revelation of God to us for the sake of conforming us to that divine image."[113] Jesus is the manifestation of the fullness of human existence and the possibilities of God which are always offered; and that manifestation moves our existence toward its fulfillment in redemption even as it provides an exemplary vision of what lies ahead. In his life, death, and resurrection, Jesus reveals both divinity and humanity. Christians find in this revelation the source of their decisive understanding of all that is ultimate. Others may find this revelation exemplary as well, even without designating it as decisive or complete.

As I indicated in the opening section of the last chapter, casting contemporary Christology along the lines of the Wisdom-Logos strand of tradition faces four challenges. These challenges are related to the contemporary emphasis on dynamism rather than stasis; to the feminist interest in overcoming dualistic construals of basic polarities; to a global problematic arising from the idealization of Jesus' historical particularities; and to contemporary concern for the present and future as well as for the past. Suchocki's casting of Christology in both process and feminist terms attempts to address each of these problems.

Process theology begins from the presupposition that all existence--including and especially divine existence--is dynamic, interactive, and fundamentally relational. Thus, any Christology constructed from this perspective will see the Christ as revealing this dynamism and relationality. In Suchocki's case, Jesus' response to those around him is the manifestation of the responsiveness of God, who always provides the possibilities for movement toward harmony that are appropriate to each existent in each moment of existence. Suchocki's eschatology further indicates that how historical existents respond to God's initiative determines what God will be able to offer next, albeit within the primordial movement of the divine toward greater harmony.

This emphasis on interaction and responsiveness between existence and its creator breaks the dualisms of which feminism is critical by highlighting the unbreakable connection between humanity and divinity, which are nevertheless understood to differ from each other. Where humanity (as the representative form of existence) is finite and limited, God is infinite. Where humanity with all existence is caught in perpetual perishing, nothing perishes in the divine life. Yet this means not that human and divine are ultimately separated, but rather that human existence is appropriated in all its fullness in the greater fullness of divine existence.

When differences are related as poles of each other rather than as opposites--that is, when they are distinguishable but not separable--in this way, then the relation between the particular and the whole is one of partial exemplification or manifestation with general relevance for all experience, but with special, intensified relevance in particular contexts.   That is, Jesus is potentially an exemplary figure for all who encounter him; but for Christians he is the decisive figure. This is the case because Christians live in a context significantly influenced by all that influenced Jesus himself, a context which ever afterward also reflects his presence. The idealization here, then, is of *all* his particularities, but only insofar as those are appropriated in the movement toward harmony taking place in contemporary existence.   In this context, then, what stands out is the fundamental significance of Jesus' relationality as a manifestation of the relationality of God.

Finally, and again by definition for process theology, past, present, and future are related in continuity and contrast, with the lure of the future bearing the strongest weight. The past *shapes* the future through the way present existence appropriates the past in its response to the possibilities extending toward the present. But the past can be neither repeated nor completely lost. The fundamentally dynamic approach of process theology ensures that no established order or event can legitimately remain immutable.

Suchocki's feminist process theology, then, meets the challenges presented to a contemporary casting of the Wisdom-Logos strand. The strength of her presentation lies, first, in its comprehensiveness and coherence: there is no area of theological reflection that is neglected or minimized. And each area is consistently connected to the others. Second, her emphasis on normative relationality as one of mutual responsiveness guided by a general principle of creativity suggests how the distortions, fragmentations, and destructiveness of historical existence may be transformed without their effects being suppressed. [114] It is relationality *of a particular sort* that is of highest value.

The weaknesses of Suchocki's presentation lie in two areas. First, while Suchocki's frequent use of concrete examples helpfully concretizes the abstract principles and processes she presents, these examples seem, most often, to be not actual lived experiences that move deductively toward this formulation of theology, as much as typical and typological examples that exemplify inductive conclusions already reached. [115] In other words, Suchocki's recourse to experience is first and foremost to a philosophical category, and only then to concrete historical existence. For feminist theology, this is problematic precisely because philosophical categories have been formed and formulated in patriarchal culture, which marginalizes and discounts the actual historical existence of significant portions of the human race, particularly women. For this and other reasons, women's concrete historical experience as both oppressed and liberated, expressed in women's own voices, is an important plumbline for feminist liberation theology, one against which categories as well as claims may be evaluated. In revising *God-Christ-Church* to incorporate narratives and analyses of lived human experience, Suchocki herself seems to have recognized the importance of such evaluation.

Second (and for reasons related to the first point), Suchocki's careful attempt to formulate justice as an eschatological category that may be realized partially in the present falls short of being fully satisfying, however philosophically satisfactory it may be.

Suchocki rightly insists that the establishment of justice cannot fully redress the suffering of victims. Her unusually detailed discussion of the fulfillment of all existence, not only in this life but in "the life of the world to come," establishes the continuity between history and transhistory, a continuity that hinges as much on the "dangerous memory" of tragic suffering as it does on the establishment of harmony and justice. But her account of the transformation of evil and the hell experienced in this process by its perpetrator rings more true than does her discussion of the fulfillment and satisfaction that transform the victim. It seems likely that this is because a detailed discussion of human repentance can be based on historical experience, while a discussion of complete redress and fulfillment after tragedy is of necessity speculative. Here, where Suchocki has recourse primarily to the extension of her fundamental principles, the credibility of her discussion falters because its very detailed character exceeds the limits of experience. Yet Suchocki insists that the benefit of a process approach is that it expresses the "common sense" and "'real' everydayness" of our time.[116]

These deficits are minor, however, particularly in relation to the cogency and clarity of Suchocki's presentation taken overall. For the essential relatedness and responsiveness of each to all and all to each comes through strongly and persuasively. Suchocki's feminist-process thought does indeed show how the "Christian conviction that God is for us" stands forth clearly when God is understood to be actively and continuously responsive to the tragedies and creativity of human existence.

Notes

1.   Marjorie Hewitt Suchocki, a Methodist scholar, is the Ingraham Professor of Theology at the School of Theology in Claremont, where she trained in process theology. In addition to the works cited here, she is also the author of numerous articles on process theology, and a contributor to the contemporary development of theological education through a variety of fora.

2.   Suchocki, "The Challenge of Mary Daly," 307.

3.   Ibid., 315.

4.   Suchocki, *God-Christ-Church* 3; cf. 1989, 2. Suchocki's theology is clearly and explicitly of the process school, which she attempts to render comprehensible to a lay audience, and applicable to practical theological concerns.

5.   Ibid. 1982, 101; cf. 1989, 98.

6.   Ibid. 1982, 53; cf. 1989, 45. Intensification is accounted for in process thought through the combination of accumulation and multiplication of experiences, a combination which is inherent in the passing of time and the positive fact of novelty.

7.   Ibid. 1982, 10; cf. 1989, 12.

8.   Ibid. 1982, 9-10; cf. 1989, 11.   To put it another way, "in the process model the individual presupposes the community." (Ibid. 1982, 130)

9.   Ibid. 1982, 14; cf. 1989, 238-239.

10.   Ibid. 1982, 31; cf. 1989, 25.

11.   Ibid. 1982, 8; cf. 1989, 9.   But note that not all past occurrences or occasions are selected; existence is as much a matter of "perpetual perishing" as it is of immortality through continuity.

12.   On the drive toward harmony/ completion, see *God-Christ-Church* 1982, 12-18; on novelty, 19. Cf. 1989, 237-244; on novelty, 245. The positive valuation of novelty in process thought accounts in part for the ready willingness of Suchocki and other process theologians to incorporate the insights of feminist and other liberation theologies and the dialogue between the religions into their discussions. See, for example, *God-Christ-Church* 1982, 195, and Marjorie Hewitt Suchocki, "In Search of Justice: Religious Pluralism from a Feminist Perspective," in *The Myth of Christian Uniqueness: Toward a Pluralistic Theology of Religions,* ed. John Hick and Paul F. Knitter (Maryknoll, NY: Orbis Books, 1987), 149-161.

13.   *God-Christ-Church* 1982, 31; cf. 1989, 24-25.

14.   Ibid. 1982, 137; cf. 1989, 143.

15.   Marjorie Suchocki, "Weaving the World," *Process Studies* 14 (Summer 1985), 80.

16.   *God-Christ-Church* 1982, 53-55; cf. 1989, 45-47.

17.   "[W]e are not responsible for a past we did not create, and we cannot avoid that past.   Inexorably, we feel its weight.   Our responsibility lies in what we do with the past." (*God-Christ-Church* 1982, 107; cf. 1989, 108.) Further, "insofar as there is assent to that past, there is responsibility for perpetuating that past." (Ibid. 1982, 24; cf. 1989, 18.)

18.   "The many for the one, and the one for the many: these are the dynamics that allow each instance of injustice, but they are also the dynamics that make redress of the injustice possible." (*God-Christ-Church* 1982, 88; cf. 1989, 83.)

19.   Ibid. 1982, 85; cf. 1989, 81.

20.   Ibid. 1982, 54-55; cf. 1989, 46-47.

21.   Ibid. 1982, 32; cf. 1989, 26.

22.   The feminist critique has long insisted that self- depreciation rather than self-absolutization is the predominant form of distorted relationality for women.   The diminished capacity for freedom in women is occasioned in patriarchal social and psychological structures

and attitudes by the identification of self-sacrifice as a virtue, particularly for women. (See *God-Christ-Church* 1982, 31; cf. 1989, 25.) I take it, then, that Suchocki is providing an account of a basic form of human fallibility--distortion of the self-in-relation--which has two major forms, the appearance of which is related to the social location and psychological formation of individuals.

23.   Ibid. 1982, 32; cf. 1989, 26.

24.   Ibid. 1982, 33, 49; cf. 1989, 27, 40.

25.   Ibid. 1982, 33; cf. 1989, 26.

26.   Ibid. 1982, 24-26; cf. 1989, 18-19.

27.   Ibid. 1982, 24; cf. 1989, 18.

28.   Ibid. 1982, 33; cf. 1989, 27.

29.   Ibid. 1982, 57, 61; cf. 1989, 49, 53.   Suchocki carefully distinguishes loneliness from aloneness.

30.   Ibid. 1982, 58; cf. 1989, 50.

31.   Ibid. 1982, 59; cf. 1989, 51.

32.   Ibid. 1989, 4; cf. 1982, 5.   Suchocki attempts to formulate most of her discussion on the basis of general revelation, that is, "simply through the dynamics of existence as we consider the world around us . . . without direct recourse to biblical revelation." (Ibid. 1982, 93; cf. 1989, 87.)   This sets the stage for interaction with non-Christian worldviews.   It also allows her to designate as "special revelation" not only Jewish and Christian Scripture, but also any indication of the nature of the divine which breaks through human-produced distortions of existence. (Ibid. 1982, 56; cf. 1989, 48.)   Because *God-Christ-Church* is directed toward audiences for whom such breakthroughs come from Biblical materials, these are the sources upon which Suchocki draws.   However, Suchocki's argument suggests that a case could be made that, in principle, other sources are possible, providing that they are revelatory *for those who are using them*.   Cf. Ruether (in *Sexism and God-Talk* and *Womanguides*) on additional sources for feminist Christian theology.

33.   Ibid. 1982, 5; 1989, 5-6.   I am not sufficiently acquainted with process thought to assess Suchocki's rendering of it here.   The major area where her reading may be open to dispute has to do with the nature of God, and the extent to which God differs from all other existents.   Suchocki indicates that God always begins from satisfaction, while all other existents move toward it. (Ibid. 1982, 37ff.   See also Marjorie Hewitt Suchocki, *The End of Evil: Process Eschatology in Historical Context* [Albany: State University of New York Press, 1988]).   According to at least one critic, this is a violation of a basic

process tenet, that God is the exemplar *of*--rather than the exception *to*--all rules. (Philip E. Devenish, review of *God-Christ-Church* in *Theological Studies* 44 [March 1983]: 146.) It should be noted, however, that Suchocki indicates that this reversal completes rather than violates her model (*God-Christ-Church* 1982, 37); and affects the primordial and not the consequent nature of God, who therefore is still to be seen as "becoming" as well as "being." (Ibid. 1982, 40.) Moreover, in addition to keeping the model logically coherent, this reversal also provides an account of the experience of God as potential as well as actual.

Suchocki also concurs with what appears to be another major development beyond Whitehead: the notion of subjective immortality, which accounts for the continuation of individuals as such in the life of God, after the completion or satisfaction of individual existence. See *The End of Evil*, 81-86, and related footnotes. (I am indebted to David Tracy for clarification of this point.)

34.   *God-Christ-Church* 1989, 88-89, 93. In a review of *God-Christ-Church* 1982, Carter Heyward questions the book's adequacy as feminist liberation theology, because, in Heyward's view, Suchocki does not give women's concrete lived experience epistemological privilege. (Carter Heyward, "An Unfinished Symphony of Liberation: The Radicalization of Christian Feminism among White U. S. Women," *Journal of Feminist Studies in Religion* 1, no. 1 [Spring 1985], 99-118.) Unlike Heyward, I read Suchocki as presenting a clearly feminist reading of process thought: I find Suchocki's other published writings and her consistent use in both editions of *God-Christ-Church* of examples from the experience of oppressed and marginalized women and men as such sufficient evidence of her feminist liberation commitments. *God-Christ-Church* shows the considerable affinities between the two perspectives even while it strengthens the liberation orientation which others have argued is inherent in process theology. (See particularly John B. Cobb, Jr., *Process Theology as Political Theology* [Philadelphia: Westminster, 1982]). One of the things that distinguishes the 1989 revision of *God-Christ-Church* from the earlier version is Suchocki's rendering even more explicit the connection between her process theology and struggles for liberation.

35.   The 1989 revision of *God-Christ-Church* makes more explicit use of the Scriptural elements which were often left implicit in the 1982 edition, as well as bringing more to the fore the liberation-theological elements of Suchocki's formulations.

36.   Further, theology is always dependent on "special revelation" for all its work: "Special revelation, or the understanding of God as given through scripture, is prior to general revelation, providing the key whereby we name our interpretation of God in the world as 'revelation' in the first place." (*God-Christ-Church* 1989, 87; cf. 1982, 93.)

37.   Ibid. 1982, 213; cf. 1989, 227.

38.   Suchocki, "The Challenge of Mary Daly," 307.

39.   Ibid., 31.

40.   Ibid., 314.

41.   Ibid., 316.

42.   Ibid., 314. Also important for Suchocki are the women who precede contemporary feminists, whose positive experiences with Christianity should be forgotten no less than their negative ones.

43.   Ibid., 311-313; *God-Christ-Church* 1982, 197.

44.   These counter not only the traditional designation of God as Father, Son, and (male) Holy Spirit, but also the view of God as absent, all-powerful (and so unempowering of others), and unjust, a view which is both implicit and explicit in the feminist critique of traditional Christian theology. (See my discussion of Carter Heyward's work, below.) Suchocki also indicates that the traditional designations of God as gendered cannot be taken seriously in process thought, because gender is part of composite identity, while God's identity is always fully actualized; i.e. not composite. (*God-Christ-Church* 1982, 103; cf. 1989, 100.)

45.   Ibid. 1982, 130-133; cf. 1989, 133-137. cf. Suchocki, "The Challenge of Mary Daly," 311.

46.   Ibid. 1982, 101; cf. 1989, 98.

47.   Ibid. 82, 101; cf. 1989, 98.

48.   Ibid. 1982, 93-94. The quote is from *God-Christ-Church* 1989, 1; italics in the original.

49.   Ibid. 1982, 96-98; cf. 1989, 92-95. The 1989 edition consistently uses the term *Reign of God* instead of Kingdom of God.

50.   Ibid. 1982, 98; cf. 1989, 101.

51.   Ibid. 1989, 93, 97.

52.   Suchocki refers particularly to the anointing woman in Luke's Gospel and to the Pharisee Simon. Ibid. 1982, 98; cf. 1989, 94-95.

53.   Ibid. 1982, 100-101; cf. 1989, 97.

54.   Ibid. 1982, 105-109; cf. 1989, 105-110. "The cross is the crowning manifestation of love in the life of Jesus."

55.   Ibid. 1982, 109-110, italics in the original; cf. 1989, 109-110.

56.   Ibid. 1982, 111; cf. 1989, 112.
57.   Ibid. 1982, 112; cf. 1989, 112.
58.   Ibid. 1989, 117.
59.   Ibid. 1982, 95-96; cf. 1989, 91.
60.   Ibid. 1982, 129; cf. 1989, 132.
61.   Ibid. 1982, 102, 110; cf. 1989, 99, 101.
62.   Ibid. 1982, 102; cf. 1989, 98.
63.   Ibid. 1982, 120; cf. 1989, 124.
64.   Ibid. 1982, 117; cf. 1989, 118.
65.   Ibid. 1982, 101; cf. 1989, 97.
66.   Ibid. 1982, 117; cf. 1989, 119.
67.   "The fullness of christology waits upon the church, as God mediates the benefits of Christ to the world.   This appropriation of Christ is the ongoing completion of christology. . . ." (Ibid. 1982, 125; cf. 1989, 130.)   The church carries on Jesus' presence by both proclamation and action.   Thereby, it shapes God's Reign as present and future in both possibility and actuality.   Jesus as the Christ provides "the revealed guidelines reinforcing for us the sense of God's directions, and the trust that God will be ever-adapting the application of these criteria through the surety of guidance at the very base of our existence." (Ibid. 1982, 194.)
68.   Ibid. 1982, 119; cf. 1989, 123.
69.   Ibid. 1982, 152; cf. 1989, 170.
70.   Ibid. 1982, 66; cf. 1989, 60.
71.   Ibid. 1982, 55; cf. 1989, 47.   It is quite coherent (if not necessary) to this understanding of the relation of God and world that there be multiple revelations, because of the multiple situations found in the world. (Ibid. 1982, 199f.)   It is also possible that there is more than one ultimate principle as well.   See Ibid. 1982, 154 n., following John Cobb's discussion in "Buddhist Emptiness and the Christian God," *Journal of the American Academy of Religion* 45, no. 1 (1977): 11-25.   Cf. Suchocki, "In Search of Justice: Religious Pluralism from a Feminist Perspective."
72.   Ibid. 1982, 43, 192; cf. 1989, 253-254, 191.
73.   Ibid. 1982, 41, 38-39; cf. 1989, 252, 249-250.
74.   Ibid. 1982, 66, 109; cf. 1989, 59-60, 110.
75.   Ibid. 1982, 67, 94; cf. 1989, 60-61, 88-89.
76.   "[T]he primordial vision is like a beam of light, containing all color within it--but as potential, not actual.   God's aim is then like a prism, reflecting the light to the world.   However, the colors in the light do not become visible, thus really revealing light, until they meet

with the actuality of the world . . . . When the light is finally reflected, it reveals not only its source, but that which it touches as well. If we follow the metaphor, God's light is revealed through the actuality of the world. Just as light reveals the nature of the objects that hold it, even so the actualization of God's initial aims in the world reveals the shape of the world. That means that the revelation of God is . . . always twofold. God and the world are seen through the same light." (Ibid. 1982, 50.)

77. Ibid. 1982, 191.
78. Ibid. 1982, 56; cf. 1989, 47.
79. Ibid. 1982, 67; cf. 1989, 60.
80. Ibid. 1982, 44; cf. 1989, Appendix.
81. Ibid. 1982, 63-65; cf. 1989, 56-59.
82. Ibid. 1982, 69; cf. 1989, 62.
83. Ibid. 1982, 78; cf. 1989, 73.
84. Ibid. 1982, 75; cf. 1989, 69. Suchocki's description of God as wisdom is a reconstruction of the classical doctrine of God's omniscience, which is incomprehensible in our time because of contemporary recognition that temporality renders existence uncertain and identity (human and divine) dynamic. Where God's omniscience guaranteed human security, God's wisdom guarantees human trust. (Ibid. 1982, 70-72; cf. 1989, 63-65.)
85. Ibid. 1982, 77; cf. 1989, 72-73.
86. Ibid. 1982, 76; cf. 1989, 71.
87. Ibid. 1982, 76; cf. 1989, 70. With her understanding of God as justice, Suchocki reconstructs the classical doctrine of God as omnipotent, on the understanding that the significance of that view was to indicate that God is the source of "the power of hope against despair." To say that God is all-powerful is to say that "God is the source of the vision and reality" of transformation toward justice. (Ibid. 1982, 82-83; cf. 1989, 78.) Note, then, that Suchocki defines justice as the interlocked well-being of the one and the many, understood as creative movement toward a full, rich unitive harmony.
88. The only way it can be claimed that redress and restoration are achieved in finite existence, Suchocki finds, is by both scaling down or otherwise limiting the definition of justice, or ignoring the fact that injustice often crushes its victims so that reparation is impossible. (Ibid. 1982, 79-81; cf. 1989, 74-77.)
89. Ibid. 1982, 87; cf. 1989, 82-83.
90. Ibid. 1982, 216; cf. 1989, 230.
91. Ibid. 1982, 214; cf. 1989, 228.

92. Ibid. 1982, 214-216; cf. 1989, 228-229.

93. Ibid. 1982, 53; cf. 1989, 45-46. Intensification is accounted for in process thought through the combination of accumulation and multiplication of experiences, a combination which is inherent in the passing of time and the positive fact of novelty.

94. Ibid. 1982, 85; cf. 1989, 80.

95. Ibid. 1989, 97. On this theological basis, Suchocki proposes as "the fundamental criterion of value and the focus of dialogue and action among religions," justice understood as well-being that knows no boundaries. For her discussion of this proposal, its problems and possibilities, see "In Search of Justice: Religious Pluralism from a Feminist Perspective."

96. "Justice is the well-being of a society: a society has well-being when its members find that the society helps them develop their humanity, through which each member enriches the other. Interdependence and reciprocity are involved, together with a valuation of the diversity of talent and ability in human existence." (Ibid. 1982, 79; cf. 1989, 74.) See also "In Search of Justice: Religious Pluralism from a Feminist Perspective," throughout.

97. Ibid. 1982, 53; cf. 1989, 44.

98. Ibid. 1982, 78; cf. 1989, 72-73.

99. Ibid. 1982, 75; cf. 1989, 69.

100. Ibid. 1982, 78; cf. 1989, 73.

101. Ibid. 1982, 76, 83; cf. 1989, 70, 78.

102. Ibid. 1982, 76; cf. 1989, 70. Remember that Suchocki defines justice primarily as the interlocked well-being of the one and the many. Cf. "In Search of Justice: Religious Pluralism from a Feminist Perspective."

103. Ibid. 1982, 87; cf. 1989, 82.

104. Ibid. 1982, 89; cf. 1989, 83.

105. The discussion that follows summarizes *God-Christ-Church* 1982, 176-189; cf. 1989, 199-216. Suchocki uses an example from the past to indicate that historical changes do not effect justice for previous victims. "Five million women living in a world of justice and mutuality make no difference to that one woman's experience of fire, agony, and death. She feels no affirmation of her existence and no redress of the crime, no matter how fervently women five centuries later decry the evil of witch burning. Justice for the many does not answer the requirement of justice for her. Without 'the life of the world to come,' her unredeemed experience stands as a finality of

injustice, mocking the power of God's justice. Without resurrection, justice cannot be complete." (Ibid. 1982, 176-177; cf. 1989, 200.)

106. Ibid. 1982, 184; cf. 1989, 210-211. It is important to note that in a process view, the woman is still who she is. What transformation means here is not obliteration of her previous existence, but a recasting of it in two regards. First, the sequentiality of temporal existence is abolished; she feels herself as joyful child and terrorized woman simultaneously. Second, she understands herself as God understands her; that is, completely, and in the context of all else that God understands, which is to say of the entirety of existence, of what has been possible for it, and of what remains possible for it. That is, she understands how she has contributed to the whole of existence.

107. Ibid. 1982, 186; cf. 1989, 212.

108. "[I]nsofar as one's own use of freedom is in conformity with the nature of God, one will experience God as heaven; insofar as one's freedom is against the nature of God, one will experience God as hell." (Ibid. 1982, 187; cf. 1989, 214.)

109. "It does not now appear what we shall be, but we shall nevertheless be transformed, reconciled with all creation in the depths of God in a justice that is inexorable love." (Ibid. 1982, 210; cf. 1989, 224.)

110. Ibid. 1982, 189; cf. 1989, 215. While Suchocki's explanation of the woman's vindication is brief, her discussion of the judge's redemption is more detailed. (Ibid. 1982, 188-189; cf. 1989, 214-215.) The judge is redeemed in part by the woman he burned, because he experiences her transformation as if it were his own.

It would seem that the experiential adequacy of this discussion of justice hinges on valuing eternity (integration into God) over temporality. That is, the woman's temporal (and so relatively brief) suffering is requited by her eternal presence in harmony with God. Her lost possibilities are not returned to her, although she does participate in redeeming the judge and all other existents. What is significant about Suchocki's view is that the experience of the victim is neither denigrated nor obliterated, either of which gives the executioner a posthumous victory. (See my discussion of Fackenheim, above.) Instead, the victim's experience is fully felt by all existence because it is fully felt by God. Her suffering is not without meaning. And it is not the last word about her existence.

111. Ibid. 1989, 216; italics in the original.

112. See the section "A Feminist Christological Problem" in Chapter 8.

113. Ibid. 1982, 101; cf. 1989, 98.

114. See, again, her discussion of the eschatological transformation of historical evil in *God-Christ-Church* 1982, 176-189; cf. 1989, 199-216; and my discussion of her views, above.

115. Cf. Heyward, "An Unfinished Symphony of Liberation: The Radicalization of Christian Feminism among White U. S. Women," 99-118.

116. *God-Christ-Church* 1982, 3; cf. 1989, 1.

Chapter 10

Christ, Mutuality, and Justice

Introduction

Carter Heyward[1] proposes a theology of mutual relation in which the original and fundamental relatedness of all being is liberated and redeemed in history through the recreation of mutuality and justice. In this theology, Christ manifests a dynamic, intimate, and immediate relational harmony between humanity and divinity, a harmony that has always been possible. The Christ is the re-presentation of "the *only* liberating relationship a person can have with God."[2] This relation can be seen through re-imaging an exemplary figure, who embodies this unique relation of the human and the divine: Jesus. It can also be seen in courageous and compassionate justice-making, exemplified by Jesus and by others. For liberating relation is grounded in mutuality and justice, characteristics of the divine life in which all creation participates.[3]

The Character of Human Existence

Concrete, embodied, historical experience of relation is the essential fact of human existence, Heyward contends. [4]

> Relation is where it all begins, . . . We come into this world connected, related, to one another--by blood and tissue, history, memory, culture, faith, joy, passion, violence, pain, and struggle. The lines of continuity between and among us are visible/invisible, sturdy/fragile, inviting/frightening, delightful/sad, occasions for celebration/remorse, depending on which connections we know best, or seek, or acknowledge, or explore. To be related is essentially good, but not all relationships are good. [5]

Difference and plurality are givens of historical human existence: We are "different from one another, yet connected [at] the very root of our humanness." [6] The difficult dilemma of differentiation and connection (or how the person can be a self-in-relation)[7] may be resolved through polarization, which turns difference or differentiation into separation and individualistic identity, masking the importance of connection. This dualistic casting of relation is at the foundation of patriarchal thought and social organization. [8] While this solution distorts, denies, or diminishes the importance of relationality, dualism cannot abolish relationality: Relation always remains constitutive of human existence.

Heyward emphasizes that relationality is a dynamic, interactive process, funded by a creative desire for connection. Heyward refers to this drive as *dunamis*, the power in relation, erotic power.[9] *Dunamis* is generative, free, unmediated and uncontrolling, self-attributed and self-authorizing, and most fully found in relations characterized by mutuality and justice. [10]

> Mutuality is sharing power in such a way that each participant in the relationship is called forth more fully into becoming who she is--a whole person, with integrity. . . . Justice is the shape of mutuality in our life together, in our societies and relationships. . . . Justice is the actual shape of love in the world. [11]

Dunamis makes relation or connectedness possible. All humans are powerful because all are in relation. The necessary social structuring of human existence ought to derive from and be released by relational *dunamis*; that is, social structures ought to be just, not seeking to suppress or eradicate the constitutive power of the *dunamis* that resides in each and every human being.[12]

Relation is nothing less than the ground of being, both foundational and ultimate. Faith identifies God as the source of the power in relation. In faith one discovers both the essential connectedness of all existence, and the power to transform brokenness into mutual participation that moves toward the unity of all aspects of be-ing despite forces of domination and destruction.[13] The task of theology is to articulate those faith experiences of liberation and redemption that arise from concrete transformative struggles for justice and mutuality, or right-relation.[14]

However, radical reconstruction of theology is necessary if it is to take on this task adequately. Theology, as an element and instrument of culture, reflects and participates in patriarchal domination with its misogynist attitudes, unjust structures, and damaging effects. But the problem for theology reaches beyond the specific social and psychological subjugation of women to Christianity's undervaluing of humanity as less good and less important than divinity.[15] This disparity in value is the result of a foundational dualism that sets the human and the divine in opposition to and fundamental alienation from each other, rather than seeing the divine as the source, movement, and force of all existence and transformation, whether or not humans recognize this to be the case.[16]

In its tendency to identify the human condition as one of loneliness, separation, division, and estrangement, orthodox Christian thought has seen God as an omniscient, omnipotent, and perfect "wholly other" who is paradigmatically alone and above the universe "He" has created. God is able to save individual human persons from *their* estrangement only by removing them from their human condition into a "higher," isolated state like God's own.[17] A theology that defines God as the perfect, lone source of all power and the only source of deliverance (understood as salvation *from* human existence) also denies human responsibility and agency in the fostering of human well-being. [18]

In Heyward's view, the Holocaust is the signal event that indicates the severity of the dualistic negation of human existence and human experience. [19] The Nazi program of dehumanizing and destroying the Jews sought not only to obliterate entirely its victims' actual relations, but also to negate the very capacity for relation in those who continued to live. [20] The Holocaust, far from being an accidental aberration, was "the evil effect of a domination-submission motif constructed socially in the theological likeness of a dominating deity who overcomes, and negates, human relation and human choice." [21] The Holocaust and other events of massive unjust suffering are the outcome of the deeply embedded, pervasive concealment in Western civilization and philosophy of the essential and finally unbreakable connectedness of all things with each other in and through the power of relation which is God. [22]

The Praxis of Relational Co-operation

What is needed? The recovery or re-membering of the truly human--the human as relational--and the death of this false, dominating, and isolated "God." [23] In contrast to the dominant theologies of the Christian tradition that begin with separation, isolation, and alienation, Heyward contends that all theology must be grounded in and informed by the concrete human experience of just, mutual relation as revelatory of the power of God and constitutive of human existence. [24] For justice or right-relation is the concrete manifestation of the being of God in history, "the pattern of the Sacred in our life together." Right-relation is God's logos or complete self-expression. [25] Without justice, truly mutual relation or interconnectedness is not possible, which means that true human being is not possible. [26]

On this basis, Heyward proposes the concrete, experiential "love of neighbor as self--*rather than* love of God" understood abstractly and ahistorically--as "*the* norm for Christian life and theology."[27] This normative love of neighbor or "praxis of relational cooperation"[28] reflects and is informed by "faith in a just god/ess" whose justice is the concrete expression of divine love,[29] manifest in relations characterized by mutuality and justice. These two base points shape each other in an ongoing process of mutual questioning, reflective articulation, action toward justice, and mutual criticism.[30] Lived experiences in struggles for justice serve as the data against which claims about divine power are tested, evaluated, criticized, and re-formulated.[31] Faith experiences serve as a source for the evaluation and formulation of other experiences, and for judgments that lead to action.[32]

Authority, then, is redefined as neither external nor internal, residing neither in texts or traditions nor in privatized subjective experience, but in the evocation and further generation of a connectedness which already in some form exists, and which we know "when we are related rightly."[33] The authoritative sources for a relational theology based in *praxis* are, therefore, as rich and various as life itself: they include fantasy, the imagination, artistic and poetic expression, and emotional and bodily life as well as rational processes and formulations.[34] They also include the traditional texts of Christian theology--but only when those texts inspire "us to envision and embody justice and to resist domination, subordination, violence, and greed."[35]

Grounding all in concrete, lived relation that moves toward mutuality and justice dissolves a number of significant human dilemmas, Heyward contends. The well-being of the individual is seen as integrally and necessarily related to the well-being of the community, rather than in competition with it.[36] Human responsibility to and for life on the earth is made apparent and compelling by asserting human connection with other "earth creatures" and the earth itself as a given, rather than as something that must be established.[37] And historical existence--rather than transcendence above it--is seen to be the context from which and because of which "our faith, our will, and our works emerge."[38] Hierarchical dualisms give way to co-operation and co-creative activity in which thought, feeling, and action are seen as integrally related. Isolation gives way to "the possibilities of love" that is just.[39] In this transformation is the redemption of humanity--and the redemption of God who is the power of relation.[40]

Christology

Critique

Christology ought to articulate the essential connection or relation between the human and the divine, in Heyward's view.[41]   But this connection is distorted and concealed by traditional Christologies' incorporation of the basic dualism that supposes that in human experience, "'humanity' and 'divinity' signify two discrete, objective 'qualities' of what we can know and love, and that we come to know these qualities as polarities, or opposites. There can be no shared ground between the two. What we humans are, God is not, and vice versa."[42]   In traditional Christologies, God is understood as infinitely superior to and so infinitely separated from humankind, as dominant and dominating, the sole real actor in a drama of redemption where the overcoming of human choice is necessary to establish human good.[43] In this drama, human persons are able to choose only their own alienation from God and each other; they cannot choose their own redemption and liberation.[44] In other words, traditional Christology begins from an assumption that humanity and divinity are metaphysical opposites as well as moral opponents.[45]

In Heyward's understanding, "The centrality of Jesus' place in Christianity has resulted from a mis-conception of Jesus as a divine person rather than as a human being who knew and loved God."[46] Jesus' "spiritual accomplishments" as "a divine Savior" are more significant than "the spiritual possibilities of concerted human commitment."[47] The human Jesus of Nazareth is traditionally pictured as having few mutual relations, that is, relations from which he derives any understanding or growth. He is pictured primarily as dissimilar from other human persons;

his characteristics are not found in them.[48] In few of his relations does Jesus seem to have choices to make. Even his relation to God is traditionally characterized by essential rather than voluntary unity.[49] Thus, if mutuality, choice, and responsibility are constitutively human, there is a question as to whether Jesus is human at all.[50] This essentially docetic Christology reinforces the opposition between human existence and an impassive God who is finally "completely useless to us" because totally separate and wholly other from us, and completely unaffected by us.[51]

Classical Christological formulations, Heyward argues, are also ideologically laden *against* the liberation (or historical redemption) of the powerless, and *for* the continued historical power of the dominant.[52] The divinity of Christ and his consequent Lordship justify the dominating rule of those who are understood to be re-created in his sovereign image. At the same time, the passive suffering and exemplary obedience of the human Jesus justify the submissiveness (both externally forced and internally accepted) of the majority of his followers and those who do not recognize him as Lord at all.[53] All this is given the sanction of an immutable, ordering deity, masking the formative significance of human activity in history and the possibility of human modification.[54]

Enlightenment and contemporary Christologies which focus on the Jesus of history react against the static, ahistorical elements of the classical "Christ of faith" Christologies from above. But Christologies based in the Jesus of history also perpetuate the notion of a God above history; and, tacitly, they often "simply name as 'divine' whatever they admire in Jesus, which seems moreover to reflect whatever they admire in themselves."[55] And, because these "Christologies from below" fail to recognize the extent to which this is the case, they perpetuate and legitimate the same structures of oppression, injustice, and exclusiveness as do "Christologies from above."[56]

While Heyward is not unsympathetic to many of the factors that led to traditional formulations of Christology, she judges that their historical consequences render them not only worthless but also damaging today. Until their dualistic foundation is rooted out, the related problems of the value of human historical experience and existence cannot be adequately addressed. Heyward's conclusion: Christologies based in classical views are dead, although they continue to wield power. [57]

Corrective: The Liberating Relation with God

Christology must shift its ground to the interaction of the human and divine as this interaction is grounded in a praxis of relational co-operation. [58] Heyward's Christology understands the relation between the human and the divine as one of dynamic, intimate, and immediate relational harmony such that the divine and the human can be neither identified nor contrasted. [59] By "Christ," then, Heyward means this cooperative interaction, [60] a unique kind of relation with God rather than a single, unique person. Christology can provide an articulation of this relation by focusing on its concrete manifestation within human experience. This unique kind of relation can be seen through re-imaging an exemplary, historical figure who fully embodies this unique relation of the human and the divine: Jesus. [61] And it can be seen through "justice-making with compassion, courage, and integrity, which can be interpreted as either 'human' or 'divine' and is, in fact, both at once." [62] These two sources for contemporary Christology are related because of the life of justice-making and mutuality lived by the historical figure whom Christians recognize the Christ.

In order to disclose this life, Heyward re-images Jesus. [63] She presents what Jesus *did* as the basis of understanding who he *was*, thereby keeping Christology firmly grounded in the struggles, ambiguities, and particularities of history (and the historical study of Jesus), rather than in abstraction, idealization, or speculation about "inner states." [64] Heyward retains the particularities of the activity of Jesus of Nazareth, including both his refusal to portray himself as the Messiah and his direction of his own attention to God as the power in relation inherent in all human persons. [65]

She also draws on contemporary relational experience that has been formed by the "encouragement" Christians receive from "the Jesus-figure" in relation to their other relations; by the long and ongoing history of the use of images of Jesus to warrant and sanctify both privilege and oppression; and by pressing movements of empowerment and liberation which both reflect and require the power in relation which is God.[66] Use of contemporary experience is warranted by the fact that the incarnational possibility of which Jesus is a paradigm is inherent in *all* human beings.[67]

Christology then becomes an ongoing process of imaging and re-imaging on the basis of the interaction between concrete historical activities associated with a particular figure from the past whose spirit is with us,[68] and our encounters with each other and our participation in the praxis of relational justice.[69] The resulting image is thus historically concrete, although governed by contemporary terms.

Jesus' relations with God and with other human persons have three essential characteristics: intimacy ("the centering of relation in the depth of human being"), immediacy (the unmediated "sense of power in present relation"), and passion (sustaining and "bearing up" of human life).[70] As each and all of Jesus' relations exhibit these relations, the presence and power of God in Jesus is made manifest.

For Heyward, Jesus' relations with the ordinary people around him--especially those whom he heals--particularly manifest not only human empowerment by the divine, but also the immediate and intimate character of human relations. Jesus can heal the woman with the issue of blood (Mark 5:25-34) because he knows her intimately and immediately,[71] and because "he knows himself as a human being who, like all human beings, is seeking to touch and be touched, move and be moved, heal and be healed."[72] This meeting and touching at the deepest, fullest level of human relationality empowers the woman, enabling her to heal herself as she claims her own power in relation (what Mark calls her faith).[73] This relational *dunamis* extends even to the overcoming of death itself (Mark 5:35-43), in that *dunamis* and faith in it deny that death has the power to overcome relation. [74]

In Heyward's discussion, Jesus' relations with his followers and disciples present another aspect of his manifestation of the power in relation. Jesus' followers recognize his authority for what it is: *dunamis* rather than *exousia*, relational power rather than authority. Thus, when he asks them who they think he is, the disciples' reply "You are the Christ" means "you are someone in whose way of being I see power, the power of justice, right-relation. . . . you can help us see the power, love the power, claim the power, use the power" [75]--the power of friendship, of love in deep and intimate mutual relation. [76]

The accounts of Jesus' baptism and his relation to the God he called *Abba* indicate the depth and extent of the mutuality between Jesus and God as "Jesus grows *with* God in love" beyond absolute dependence on God into voluntary and mutual interdependence. [77] *And* Jesus facilitates God's growth by bearing God into the world in Jesus' own human activities and relations:

> In Jesus, we see that the human-divine relation is so intimate
> . . . and so immediate . . . that Jesus' choice to co-operate
> with the power that moves him into relation and keeps him
> there is his choice to do God's activity . . . in the world. By
> God, with God, for God, Jesus claims his own authority of
> possibility in the world. By Jesus, with Jesus, through Jesus,
> God acts. [78]

The intimacy and immediacy of Jesus' relation with his *Abba* become overtly passionate when Jesus encounters situations and persons who would restrict or deny mutuality and *dunamis*, as in his relations with institutionalized religion and politics. Here, Jesus manifests *dunamis* over against authoritarian and institutional *exousia*, radicalizing the Jewish covenant, for example, by insisting on and demonstrating "the intimacy and immediacy of God's activity through human *dunamis*. . . . God is here, God is now. God is not simply in the memory of mighty acts or in the hope for salvation." [79]

While Jesus could not have been surprised by the outcome of his challenges to social and religious institutions, his experience of the power in relation gives him angry courage, which Heyward sees as the alternative to doubt, depression, and despair.[80] The God manifest in Jesus' passion--in his angry courage and his painful suffering--is "an indignant power, a power with a sharp edge that cuts into the possibility of accommodation with any relation that is less than just, or right. Jesus' anger feeds his sense of authority and is fed by his power in relation."[81] Jesus' death shows that this God is also a power that can be broken as relations are broken and the power of God is destroyed in the world.[82] But Jesus' death does not destroy his relation to his followers; it further empowers them, giving them the courage and the vision to make their lives like his own.

> Following Jesus' death, his friends came to life. What began between Jesus and those who loved, and were loved by, him, continues among these lovers of humanity. What was initiated by the passionate investment of one person in relation to others is carried on among these people in relation.[83]

Jesus, as Heyward re-images him, manifests "the immediate and intimate dimensions of relation" which characterize that harmony between the human and the divine which is possible for all human persons. Jesus shows us "ourselves as we are meant to be," and shows the divine to be the power in all right relation.[84] This Jesus is "fully and only human, . . . exactly human like us."[85] It is his very humanity that shows that Christ is "the love relation between the human and the divine, manifest in human life that is lived in right-relationship with God."[86] Jesus is but one example of this harmony that exists at least in potential in and between all persons, and that is fulfilled through on ongoing process of constant, mutual empowerment involving God and God's people.[87]

Heyward does not deny Jesus' divinity: he is divine as well as human in living deeply into his own power in relation, which is God.[88] What Heyward *does* deny is that Jesus *alone* is both divine and human.[89] For Christians, the life of Jesus is paradigmatic of what it means for humans to stand with the

Sacred and with each other in the struggle for right-relation.[90] It is imperative, therefore, that Christians take this paradigm seriously as a full human being, living a particular life in particular historical circumstances. Only by doing so "can we discern in what he did the divine spirit moving with and in and through him."[91] Heyward's focus on Jesus as "fully and only human,"[92] then, is designed as a corrective to the denigration of humanity contained in the dualisms of traditional Christian theology.[93] Jesus is *human* brother, revealer, and model or paradigm; and these human relations with him encourage us to approach

> one another in the *particular spirit we believe was revealed with such power, grace, and courage in the life of Jesus*: a particular way of engagement marked by openness to those who are "different," willingness to risk on behalf of our commitments, efforts to stand our ground without possessing it, and, most importantly, relentless faith in a God whom we, like Jesus, have met and come to know as the source and constant resource of love, which--in this world--is always actualized in justice.[94]

In Jesus we see realized the present realm of God *and* the prolepsis of what is yet to come. And this manifests not some messiah who is other than human persons involved in fully human relations, but ourselves--who we are, and who we are meant to be(come), and what it means to know and love a God of justice.[95]

Jesus continues to manifest both the divine and the human, in that he represents to both human and divine what the relation between the two most truly is. Jesus manifests "the *only* liberating relationship a person can have with God,"[96] a relation of intimate and immediate love which enlivens and empowers, engendering a passion for justice as the "actual shape of love in the world."[97] In this relation, embodied by Jesus, humanity is in a relation of active cooperation with divinity, where the two are neither identified nor contrasted.[98] For Christians, Jesus is the complete manifestation of this way of being which is Christ. He shows "God's activity in conjunction, partnership, friendship with humanity: human and divine being in a single act. *We see in Jesus that this is the way it has been all along. . . .* It did not begin with Jesus of Nazareth."[99] That is, Jesus reveals and manifests the very constitution of human being as always related to the divine.

The completeness of this manifestation is something new in the history of divine and human interaction, but, as the manifestation of true human being, the relation itself cannot be unique for all time.[100] However, Jesus, in completely manifesting Christ, is doing the work of redemption in the world in a new way. Jesus brings into human history concrete evidence of the essential human relation to God. And he does so in a way that involves a radical shift in consciousness,[101] and that, through voluntary mutual relation, empowers that shift in others. Thus, he contributes in a signal way to the fulfillment of divine and human relation in history. This is his redemptive work. But it is not work that Jesus completes: it is work that he hands over to others throughout his life and upon his death.

Heyward, then, has reconstructed rather than rejected the Christology of two natures in one person of classical Christian theology. What she does reject, and emphatically so, are the classical claims about the unique and once-for-all character of the Christ. For Heyward, "Christ" is a title that refers to Jesus, but not only to him. It refers to a way of being in the world and in relation that all persons may participate in and bear, although not all do.[102] All persons are empowered to bring to pass in the present the future which is longed for as the fulfillment of just and right relation.[103] The presence of God in all intimate and immediate relations intending justice is modeled by Jesus; but it is also evident in the lives of many other humans, only some of whom we can remember by name.[104]

For Heyward, then, Christ is "a way of being in which God's being and human being are experienced as one."[105] Being in Christ makes it clear that it is not necessary to place the divine and the human in relation; *they are always already in relation.*

[I]n Christ we perceive what we believed to be "divine" (out there, far away) and what we believed to be "human" (us,

here, now) together in one reality. In Christ, God and
humanity are, in a single glance through a glass darkly,
perceived to be in unity. The dualism is shown for what it
was all along: a delusion. [106]

How does Jesus save?   By incarnating--manifesting in
embodied existence--"the *only* liberating relationship a person
can have to God." [107]   Through Jesus we learn who we are
meant to be, and this is why we call him the Christ. [108] Does
only Jesus save? No. Redemption is accomplished by divine
and human interaction, embodied in many persons, in history.
Jesus, fully and decisively for Christians, shows that this
interaction is always already possible; and that it is at the same
time not yet completely actual or realized.

Christic Power

While Jesus may manifest the only liberating relation a person
can have with God, he is not the only one to do so; and the
limitations associated with identifying one person as savior
makes even more pressing the need to shift the ground on which
Christology is constructed. While Heyward has yet to work out
fully how she believes this shift may be accomplished, she has
offered some suggestions or possibilities for developing a
feminist liberation christology that addresses these and other
problems. [109]

As we have seen, for Heyward the Christ is the incarnation or
embodiment of the relational power whose source is God but
which is possible in every relationship. "Christic power," in
Heyward's recent thought, is the relational power that liberates
existence from wrong-relation and for right--mutual and just--
relation. [110] Christology is Christian reflection on this power,
and on the "christological sensibilities" it releases; that is, on the
"experiences, beliefs, and images of who or what 'Christ' is, or
may mean," for the reflector. [111]

Heyward sees christic power in specific persons--"Socrates,
Sappho, Sojourner Truth, [Martin Luther] King, [Jr.], [Camillo]
Torres, Mother Theresa, and countless other women and men in

history . . . " [112]--and in specific moments of human existence--in "'the exchange of glances heavy with existence' . . . ; or in refusing to live any longer with 'someone's feet upon our necks' . . . ; or in the vision of a promised land in which we are 'free at last'. . . ." [113] She also sees christic power in Christa, the "image of redemptive womanpower" presented by the artistic representation of Christa, a crucified female Christ. [114]

Heyward believes that Christa may inspire and empower new christological reflection. Christa "can represent for christian women precisely what the church has crucified with a vengeance, and what we must now raise up in our lives: *the erotic as power and the love of God as embodied by erotically empowered women.*" [115] In Christa, Christian women may recognize their own sufferings, not as automatically redemptive, but as a consequence of the misogynist and erotophobic sin of others and a call for resistance. [116]

And Christa can represent these possibilities in a way that the traditional male Christ figures cannot, because that male Christ "has become a living symbol of our humiliation, suffering, and death at the hands of christian men." [117] The image of Christa also stands in radical *dis*continuity with the misogynist aspects of Christianity, and discloses women's suffering and humiliation as both the result of "men's sin against women" and the ground of women's resistance. [118] At the same time, for Heyward the image of Christa has some continuity with the image of Jesus as an embodiment of relational power, insofar as Jesus' passion and unjust suffering are the outcome of conflict between the desire for relation and the destruction of it. [119]

Christa, Heyward thinks, is a "transitional image" which may disclose new ways to grow into and express mutual, just relation. Like Jesus, Christa is not the only image of christic power. Her name is one more powerful, efficacious, and encouraging name for the concrete power in relation which is God, and which Christians recognize as the source, ground, inspiration, and movement toward right-relation, that is, toward mutuality and justice as inseparable. That power is embodied, for Christians, in Jesus, certainly, but also in other paradigmatic figures, some of them historical, some of them imaginative. The importance of these paradigmatic figures is their ability to inspire and empower contemporary struggles for mutuality and justice. Their truth lies in their relation to the fruits of those struggles.[120]

The Redemption of God

God as Relational Power

While Heyward's project hinges on demonstrating the essential connective unity between the human and the divine, she does not collapse the two.

> God, or the power of love, is the power of right relation, righteousness, or justice. God is the doing of justice. . . . God is not the relation itself; nor is God identifiable in a static way with a particular "person" or "party" in the relationship (though from time to time God's presence may be especially clear in the relational presence of a particular person).[121]

When God is the power in relation, the human and the divine are by definition "co-subjects, co-operating, co-creating . . . a constellation of relation in which God is nothing other than the resource of relational *dunamis*, unable to be wholly contrasted or identified with any one person in time or place."[122] At the same time, the divine is not contained in the human: we experience the power of God as "a cosmic, mysterious, unifying principle moving not only in our lives, but beyond our lives, relating each and all of us to God's own way of being in the universe."[123]

In naming God as the power in relation, be-ing itself, Heyward construes God as a living, processive force rather than as a static entity.[124] God's own inherent "dynamic relationality" spills out into the relations that exist "as well as [the relations] between God, Jesus, and the rest of us."[125] God's relation to us creates us, endows us with relational power, and sustains and enlivens by being the connecting bond in all relation.[126] The power that is God is good, just, loving, creative, and free, enabling these same qualities in all other beings by working in, through, and between them, in their relations. [127] God as the power in relation always drives toward justice, which is necessary to the very existence of relation. [128]

Further, because God is the power in relation, "God is who God is (Exodus 3:14) in relation to creation. Without creation, without humanity, our God-in-relation does not exist." [129] This means that God is affected by human existence and activity, that is, by actual human relations. God understood as power in relation is strengthened by human co-operation, and God suffers when humans suffer. In the dehumanization and destruction of victims in death-camps, and in the crippling and distortion of the human relational possibility of the subjugated and marginalized, the very existence of God is affected as actual relations are destroyed or crippled. [130] Similarly, it is accurate to speak of God's redemption, as human existence and activity and human relations are redeemed by transformation. [131]

God's transcendence, then, does not consist in God's being above or beyond the human. [132] Instead,

> God's transcendence is experienced in the constancy of God's "crossing over" between us and among us. . . . Divinity drives us, yearns for us, moves in us and by us and with us in the coming to know and love ourselves as persons fundamentally in relation, not alone. [133]

This means that God is always present to us, but we realize this only to the extent that we are able and willing to engage the power of relation which God is. [134]

> [W]hereas it is true that without God we are nothing, it is also true that we are never without God. This means that we are ever able to dip into the infinitely deep wellsprings of justice and act together to shape the realm of God, which even now we may glimpse whenever we notice the fruits of love in our common life. [135]

The qualitative difference between human and divine is found in the notion that the power that is God is limitless in depth, scope, constancy, and goodness, always available, always creative, always coming into being, "the source and constant resource of good in our lives." [136] Human power, by contrast, is limited in all these areas, as well as misdirected. The power of God provides "radical re-encouragement" in the face of human restriction and distortion. [137] But it does so because of the essential connection between the human and the divine.

The Mutuality of Love and Justice

When the human and the divine are understood as always already connected, human persons are understood to be co-operative agents with God, with each other, and with the world that is itself an expression of God's relationality. Co-operation and participation reflect an authentic comprehension of what the human is and how it is constituted. [138] This full humanity, characterized by deep and powerful active engagement in relation to others and to the world, participates in the power of incarnation; in fact, it incarnates God in the world. [139]

The world is an ambiguous place, an arena of conflict as well as positive relation, of sin and evil (non-relation or destructive relation) as well as grace and goodness (right-relation); and humans know good and evil and have the power to effect them. [140] Injustice is a social fact and a sin that breaks relation and so separates the human from God. [141] The Holocaust; the oppression of women, homosexuals, the poor, and persons of color; human alienation from and exploitation of the natural world: each of these indicates the unjust consequences of misunderstanding, fear, and distortion of the power of relation in concrete social structures and situations. All of these disclose the extent to which the miscasting of mutual interdependence into hierarchical terms has affected the life of the cosmos itself. [142] And so the life of God.

All persons, then, are called into question--prophetic but compassionate judgment--on the basis of our participation in interstructured structural injustice, and are called to the renunciation of unjust relations and privilege, and to resistance.[143] We cannot not sin. We can, however, engage in a conscious, ongoing struggle to transform situations and structures of injustice and to create right-relation.

For Heyward, redemption is experienced in precisely this struggle. This means, further, that liberation or redemption is not a state that can be achieved. It is an ongoing journey through time, always "in dissonant tension with counterforces."[144] Mutuality and justice are unfulfilled "in this world." Yet they draw us forward, because we already know them in part, "through intimations and glimpses, intuitions and relationships."[145] This movement is at the same time creative and redemptive: "our power draws us into our beginnings--into the heart of our creation/ creativity, into our relatedness."[146]

Summary and Evaluation

Using relationality as the ground of all reflection gives Heyward a theology in which creation, liberation, and redemption are intimately and immediately linked. In the midst of the ambiguities and tensions of human existence, this link is manifested and partially realized for Christians through "christic power," concretely evident decisively in Jesus and in other paradigmatic figures--including Christa--who manifest a similar full humanity in mutual relation with the divine power. It is the human relation with the divine which creates, sustains, and enlivens human existence in the world. And it is this relation which draws us forward into a liberating and redemptive future in which justice and mutuality are fulfilled. "God is our relational matrix (or womb). God is born in our relational matrix. God is becoming our relational matrix."[147] For Christians, christic power forms the connection with the divine. Christic power forms "the *only* liberating relation a person can have with God."[148]

This power is not knowable separate from concrete existence. It is found in "the praxis of relational co-operation," which

Christians recognize in part because they recognize it even more fully embodied or manifest in their experience of Jesus. He shows "God's activity in conjunction, partnership, friendship with humanity: human and divine being in a single act. *We see in Jesus that this is the way it has been all along.*"[149] This experience empowers relational co-operation, moving those engaged in it toward liberation and redemption that effect the transformation of the world and the redemption of the God who is intimately and immediately engaged with that world.

Heyward's Christology, then, indicates how Jesus manifests full humanity and full divinity in one, concrete historical existence. For Christians Jesus is the incarnation of christic power. But the very nature of both humanity and divinity precludes identifying him as the *only* such manifestation or incarnation. The relation between full or authentic humanity and divinity incarnate and manifest in Jesus is the same human-divine relation possible for all persons, but not actual. The actualization or full embodiment of this same relation by other persons depends on their claiming this same relation with the divine, something they are inspired and empowered to do by the example of Jesus, by other human exemplars, and by their own "praxis of relational co-operation."

It is the way Heyward understands relationality that makes Jesus more than a merely human exemplar. Because Jesus' relation with God is *fully* mutual, Jesus incarnates in history the divine power itself. That power enlivens all his relations, showing them to be also relations empowered by the divine. This mutual empowerment is redemptive as well as paradigmatic.

Heyward is attempting to formulate an incarnational Christology which is fully historical or concrete, and which is directly accountable to struggles for liberation. In this attempt, she sets Christian traditions--understood through the fully critical approach of a feminist liberation hermeneutics of suspicion--in dynamic relation with contemporary experience in struggles for liberation and with a vision of a fully liberated future. The occasional imprecisions of her formulations--her early statement that Jesus is "fully and only human . . . like us"[150] for example--are the result of her commitment to remain as concrete and praxis-based as possible. They do not indicate a basic renunciation of the central Christian affirmation that it is in Jesus that Christians experience the full manifestation of the divine. Her ongoing identification of persons other than Jesus as also exemplary or paradigmatic of christic power is an attempt to clarify how divine power is manifest also in others, in those to whom Jesus was related historically and in those who are inspired by Jesus. [151] This same affirmation is reflected in her references to the Spirit which is found in Jesus and which continues in those who follow him. [152] Having recently identified the dualistic foundations of the modern interest in the Jesus of history, Heyward is now trying to develop a nondualistic basis for Christology. This aspect of her work continues. [153]

Heyward's is a Wisdom-Logos Christology in its focus on christic power as manifestation and actualization of that mutuality, love, and justice that characterize "the only liberating relationship a person can have with God." [154] In the mutual and just relations which Jesus shared with his friends and followers, and in the struggles for mutuality and justice in which other exemplary figures have been fully engaged, human persons encounter the embodiment of divine power. This encounter, mediated through the concrete lives of these paradigmatic figures, transforms human life by evidencing and encouraging the inherent possibility of every human person's ever fuller embodiment of this same power. [155]

Heyward's use of dynamic relationality as her central model or paradigm establishes a high degree of continuity between things more often seen as dualistically related. That is, the power of being connects divinity and humanity: Individuals may and do differ considerably one from another, but each is relationally connected by the power that is God to the divine power and to all other beings. The grounding importance of being as relational also connects humanity with nature, love with justice, and so on. At the same time, historical contexts pose limits and demands that require very concrete active response; but the shape of that response comes from the fundamental fact of relationality as embodied or manifest in mutuality, love/justice, and cooperation. [156]

Nevertheless, historical existence also obscures, distorts, perverts, and attempts to destroy relationality. Thus, the power of God is encountered sometimes as judgment: as "an indignant power, a power with a sharp edge . . . "; [157] as harsh and offensive prophetic speech and action; [158] in the fractures and disconnections inherent in historical limitation; and in eruptions in individual lives lived in a structurally unjust society. [159] This judgment is coupled with compassion--"bearing with *in spite of* radical difference and conflict" [160]--and so, even in difference and conflict, reveals that dynamic relationality cannot, finally, be destroyed.

Heyward's contribution, then, lies in her relentless emphasis on relationality that is mutual and just as the power of being, that is, as God. This focus on the dynamic connection between individuals allows for a range of difference and change that is limited only by the necessity of maintaining or regaining mutual relation. The focus is on the connection between things. Consequently, the obduracy and opacity of individuality is to varying degrees bracketed or suppressed in Heyward's work. While Heyward conscientiously gives multiple, diverse examples of modes of connection, the light shines primarily on their commonalities.

It is only as Heyward modifies her key category, relation, with the qualities of mutuality, justice, and cooperation that the full dynamism of her core insight emerges. Relation as such brings into focus the importance of connection and the fact that all selves are indeed always selves-in-relation. But the distinction between just and unjust relations indicates how the quality of relation which constitutes those selves is always mutable, dynamic, and dependent on both the individuals and the contexts that are connected.

Heyward's discussions evidence two other weaknesses. The first is the unsystematic character of her work. The situational basis of much of her published work leads her to adopt significantly different rhetorical strategies that shape her proposals to the interests and locations of her many and varying audiences.[161] Therefore, it is often difficult to determine the precise meaning of even some of her most central statements, such as her claim that Jesus is "fully and only human." While Heyward's work may excite the imagination, it can frustrate analysis as well.

Second, the role of tradition in Heyward's work is unclear. She claims that tradition is useful only insofar as it helps us understand ourselves and our relation to God.[162] She also seems to suggest that the gaps of history opened by time and by oppression are too great to be bridged except imaginatively.[163] For Heyward, it is both contemporary experience and the envisioned just future which are determinative. Even so, and particularly in her more analytic work, it is clear that some aspects of Christian theological tradition shape her thought profoundly, often implicitly; yet she is less than forthcoming about the reasons that prompt her to select one strand rather than another.[164] A clearer explication of her use of tradition would be helpful.

These difficulties in Heyward's proposals result from the fact that she is attempting to formulate a new and comprehensive paradigm for theological reflection. Therefore, she must at one and the same time develop a new language to be used alongside an older, less effective language to convey her insights. And since, as we have seen, language and experience are socially constructed, the emergence of a new paradigm is neither smooth nor consistent. While it must be recognized that Heyward's strengths lie not in systematic or precise thought, these deficits are more than balanced, in my judgment, by the creativity and evocative energy of her constructive proposals. Heyward's intensely poetic approach allows one to touch, if not to express, the fullness and the strength of the liberating relationship between human and divine that she finds in Jesus' and others' embodiment of christic power.

Notes

1. Carter Heyward is professor of theology at Episcopal Divinity School in Cambridge, MA, and one of the first eleven women ordained to the priesthood in the Episcopal Church. Of her own work she writes, "Increasingly, I understand my vocational 'part' to be that of a healer. I write this book to help heal splits in my own, as well as our corporate, body." (*Touching Our Strength: The Erotic as Power and the Love of God* [San Francisco: Harper and Row, 1989], 5.) I am grateful to Carter for our collegial relationship since 1974, and for her encouragement and her willingness to converse with me about her work. She kindly provided me with copies of a number of essays prior to their publication, and also spoke and corresponded with me a number of times, responding to my questions about her writings and encouraging the development of my own position.

2. Heyward, *Redemption of God*, 200; italics in original. Heyward conceives of the 1989 *Touching Our Strength* as "a companion piece to and development of" the 1982 *The Redemption of God*. (*Touching Our Strength*, 159 n. 2.)

3. Ibid., 3-4, 6, and passim; idem, *Touching Our Strength*, 22, 74, and passim.

4. Heyward, *Redemption of God*, 2-3. Relationality is the "metaphysics of all that is created" and "our ontological (essential) state." (Heyward, *Touching Our Strength*, 12.)

5. Heyward, *Touching our Strength*, 192-193.

6. Ibid., 14.

7. See Heyward, *Redemption of God*, 16. "A 'person' emerges from within a relational matrix, or womb. There is no such thing as simply an 'individual' person, separate from others. Our lives are connected--spiritually, politically, economically, psychologically. To be a person is to be related." (Heyward, *Touching Our Strength*, 191.) Heyward's understanding of the person or self-in-relation is influenced by Martin Buber; by the object-relations psychology of W. Ronald Fairbairn, Alice Miller, and Donald W. Winnicott; and by the work of the Robert S. and Grace W. Stone Center for Developmental Services and Studies at Wellesley College. See *Touching Our Strength*, "Introduction" and related footnotes, for Heyward's most complete published discussion of the self-in-relation.

8. Ibid., 185. In a context where the tendency to individualism is exaggerated--such as patriarchal culture--human particularities must be subjected to self-critical reflection and dialogue with others whose

particularities differ. This is a major point of The MudFlower Collective's *God's Fierce Whimsy* (New York: Pilgrim Press, 1985), much of which Heyward wrote out of the Collective's work together. See also "An Unfinished Symphony of Liberation: The Radicalization of Christian Feminism among White U. S. Women," throughout; and Heyward, *Speaking of Christ*, 22.

9.   Ibid., 40-49; idem, *Our Passion for Justice*, passim. Heyward defines the erotic as "our desire to taste and smell and see and hear and touch one another. It's our yearning to be involved--all 'rolled up'--in each other's sounds and glances and bodies and feelings. . . . *the erotic is the sacred/godly basis of our capacity to participate in mutually empowering relationships.*" (Heyward, *Touching Our Strength*, 187; italics in the original.)

10.   *Dunamis* is also present in wrong-relation: "There is right relation, . . . relation in which all parties are empowered to be more fully who they are as persons (or creatures) in relation. There is wrong relation, that which is literally perverse, "turned around" from its own possibility, distorted. . . . Wrong relation is the root of evil in our life together. Its causes are myriad, though fear of our humanness . . . plays a primary role in precipitating and cementing wrong relation." (*Heyward, Touching Our Strength*, 193.)

11.   Heyward, *Touching Our Strength*, 191, 190.

12.   Power in relation is also expressed as *exousia*, socially constructed authority which exercises control and is liable to distorted and unjust expression, as human relations are distorted and unjust. (Heyward, *Redemption of God*, 41.) It is, however, false to designate *dunamis* as "good power" and *exousia* as bad: the difference is one of kind rather than of value.

13.   Heyward, *Redemption of God*, 58. Heyward self-consciously draws on the work of Paul Tillich and Mary Daly here. She is also substantively influenced at this point by philosophers of the new physics. (Ibid., xxiv n. 13; Conversation, Winter 1988.)

14.   "Theology, the study of God, can be defined in various ways. I define it as critical, creative reflection on the patterns, shape, and movement of the Sacred in our life together, and I go further: The pattern of the Sacred in our life together is justice. The shape of God is justice. The movement of the Holy in our common life is toward justice. The justice of God is both with us now and coming." (Heyward, *Touching Our Strength*, 22.)

15.   Heyward, *Our Passion for Justice*, 185, 216.   Heyward believes that the devaluing of humanity has been seen as a necessary concomitant to the recognition of the power of the divine.

16.   Heyward, *Speaking of Christ*, 14; idem, *Touching Our Strength*, 24, 30, 189, and passim. Cf. Heyward's paraphrasing of F. D. Maurice, who has influenced her greatly: "whereas it is true that without God we are nothing, it is also true that we are never without God. This means that we are ever able to dip into the infinitely deep wellsprings of justice and act together to shape the realm of God, which even now we may glimpse whenever we notice the fruits of love in our common life." (Heyward, *Speaking of Christ*, 24.) Maurice writes, "Apart from Him, I feel there dwells in me no good thing; but I am sure that I am not apart from Him, nor are you. Nor is any man." (*Theological Essays* 1957, 67.; quoted by Heyward, op. cit., 90 n.2.)

17.   Heyward, *Redemption of God*, 1. On this basis, Heyward critiques the claims of liberal theologians (e.g., Paul Tillich) for seeing both God and themselves as "being above it all," that is, neutral and disengaged from human existence, human struggles, and human yearning for justice. (Heyward, "Heterosexist Theology: Being Above It All." *Journal of Feminist Studies in Religion* 3 no. 1 (Spring 1987), 34.) Heyward observes that all theology is done out of situations of concrete praxis, whether or not the theologian recognizes this; there is no such thing as objectivity, or neutrality, or disengagement. (Heyward, Our *Passion for Justice*, 224, and passim.) Further, from Heyward's feminist liberation perspective, conflict and struggle with what is sinful involve first not individual choice (as liberal theology claims), but often involuntary involvement with structures that shape and limit the possibilities and actualities of individual choice. (Heyward, "Heterosexist Theology," 35.) Against liberal idealism, Heyward argues that human well-being is not individual or spiritual, but tied up with bodily existence and survival, and with relation with other humans and all living things. (Heyward, Our *Passion for Justice*, 174.)

18.   Ibid., 130. The importance of historical existence is further minimized by the positing of another time and place when reality rather than appearance will be manifest. This also contributes to tendencies to abdicate and deny responsibility. (Ibid., Chap. 4.)

19.   Ibid., 74.

20. Ibid., 80-81. Of great, even determinative, influence on Heyward's decision to ground all in the human is the post-Holocaust Jewish thought of Elie Wiesel: with Wiesel, Heyward is deeply distressed by the manner in which theology and culture have devalued the human in the name of religion, and used this devaluation to break human relationality and so human existence utterly. In this light, Heyward's proposals can be seen as an effort to take seriously Wiesel's profound concern for humanity and human evil without agreeing with his agnosticism. See *Redemption of God*, 73-107 and 179-185.

21. Ibid., 89.

22. Ibid., 77.

23. Ibid., Prologue. Heyward sees moves in precisely this direction throughout the history of Christianity, but most hopefully in aspects of the later thought of Dietrich Bonhoeffer, in the American left of the 1960s and in "death of God" theology, and in contemporary movements toward and theologies of liberation throughout the world. She also traces the roots of a theology of mutual relation to Biblical Judaism and its definition of righteousness as right-relation, and in the thought of Martin Buber and Elie Wiesel.

24. Ibid., 1-2; idem, *Our Passion for Justice*, 184.

25. Heyward, *Touching Our Strength*, 22, 74. Heyward relates justice to the being of God through the doctrine of the Trinity. (Ibid., 23, 189.)

26. Heyward, *Our Passion for Justice*, 167; idem, "An Unfinished Symphony," 109, 114ff. (esp. 116).

27. Ibid., 227; "An Unfinished Symphony," 102. In Heyward's view, the two great commandments of love of God and love of neighbor are interchangeable, indivisible, and inseparable. (Heyward, *Redemption of God* 1-2, emphasis in the original; ibid., 44, 48.)

28. Heyward, *Speaking of Christ*, 21.

29. Throughout her work, Heyward draws on the Jewish and Christian Biblical notions of right-relation (*hesed*) to show the connection between justice and love, a connection which is rooted in the righteousness of God, who is both just and loving. (Heyward, *Redemption of God*, 3; idem, *Touching Our Strength*, 190-191.) Theologically, it is imperative to understand that *God* is on the side of the victims, never disengaged, bipartisan, or value-free. (Heyward, *Our Passion for Justice*, 193-194.)

30. Heyward, *Our Passion for Justice* 227-229. Heyward's critique of theological and political liberalism includes evaluation of liberal claims that insights and analyses have universal applicability,

and so normative status. Heyward argues not only that this claim masks the socio-historical rootedness and so contingency of analytical insight and constructive position; it also blocks the possibility of the dialogue and change necessary to both mutual relation and corporate justice. (Heyward, "Heterosexist Theology," throughout.) Heyward here is explicitly following Gutierrez. Cf. Heyward, *Redemption of God*, 205-208; and idem, *Our Passion for Justice*, 107-111. On the complexity and ambiguity of any human situation, see *Redemption of God*, 164-166; *Our Passion for Justice*, 29 and 76, and passim.

31.   Ibid., 78 and passim. Heyward's theological formulations reflect her involvement in various reform and liberation movements. Much of the published work used here--many of the essays in *Our Passion for Justice* and *Speaking of Christ* and the appendices of *The Redemption of God*--were written as sermons or addresses presented in situations of liberating *praxis*. See also Heyward's autobiography, *A Priest Forever: The Formation of a Woman and a Priest* (New York: Harper and Row, 1976), for reflection on her experience as one of the first eleven women ordained to the priesthood in the Episcopal Church, before the legalization of such ordinations.

32.   Of her own religious experience Heyward writes, "[T]he women's liberation effort called me into the heart of the Christian faith I had professed from childhood, and, for the first time, I looked straight into the eyes of my sisters and brothers and met there the compelling eyes of God. . . . Washed, cleansed, and made new by the power of God, many of my sisters and I knowing full well the extent of our own brokenness and participation in sins of lovelessness, selfishness, and arrogance, made a common commitment to spend the rest of our lives in efforts to build a world both more fully human and fully divine, . . ." *Our Passion for Justice*, 155.

33.   Heyward, *Touching Our Strength*, 73-75. Therefore, the question to be asked is "Does it help us realize more fundamentally our connectedness with one another and hence the shape of our own identities as persons-in-relation?"

34.   Expressing this relational praxis theologically involves re-naming and re-imaging experience in language expressive of that experience. (Heyward, *Redemption of God* 13.) In this area Heyward is particularly influenced by the work of Mary Daly, Adrienne Rich, Audre Lorde, and Alice Walker, to all of whom she refers frequently. A major and explicit source for Heyward as a feminist theologian, and a major focus of her constructive interest, is the fact of human embodiment and sensual and sexual experience.

(Heyward, *Our Passion for Justice*, 228; and idem, *Touching Our Strength*, throughout.)

35.   Heyward, *Touching Our Strength*, 81.   Like Elisabeth Schüssler Fiorenza, Rosemary Radford Ruether, and others, Heyward has concluded that "The bible is not a word of God when it is used to justify structures and dynamics of unjust power relations. . . . No text is sacred that is used to abuse, violate, or trivialize human and other earthcreatures. The christian bible is holy only insofar as we who read, study, preach, or teach it do so in a spirit of collaborative, critical inquiry steeped in collective struggle for radical mutuality between and among us all on the earth." (81-83.)

36.   Heyward, *Redemption of God*, xviii; idem, *Our Passion for Justice*, 16 and 237.

37.   Heyward, *Our Passion for Justice*, 166 and passim.

38.   Ibid., xvi.

39.   Heyward, *Redemption of God*, xix.

40.   Heyward, *Our Passion for Justice*, xvi. See the Prologue to *The Redemption of God* for Heyward's own poetic presentation of both her critique and her vision. Heyward is neither naively romantic nor idealistic, however. Human and divine activity take place wholly within the complexities and ambiguities of history. And it is from history that all vision arises. Thus "the vision is not pure" or final; and it has the limitations that are found in its social and historical context. (Heyward, *Our Passion for Justice*, 71.)

41.   Heyward, *Redemption of God*, 36.

42.   Heyward, *Touching Our Strength*, 14. Heyward traces this problem to neo-Platonic idealism, with its "dualistic image of the divine (that is, 'good') life in relation to the (not so good) creation, including human experience: God is above, we are below; God is infinite, we are finite; God is all-powerful, we are impotent; God is universal, we are particular. Whatever we are, God is *not*, and it is hard to see the good (god) in such a 'low' opinion of humanity." (Carter Heyward, "Can Anglicans be Feminist Liberation Theologians and Still be 'Anglican'?" in *The Trial of Faith: Theology and the Church Today*, ed. Peter Eaton [Wilton, CT: Morehouse-Barlow, 1988], 41-42.)

43.   Heyward, *Redemption of God*, 34. Heyward's critique of Christology emerges in stages. The first is emphasized in *The Redemption of God*. The second, which more fully incorporates a sociology-of-knowledge approach, is found in the later essays in *Our Passion for Justice*, especially in "Must Jesus Christ Be a Holy

Terror? Using Christ as a Weapon Against Jews, Women, Gays, and Just About Everybody Else" (211-221). The third emerges in the essays in *Speaking of Christ*, in which Heyward begins to chart the course for her future elaboration of Christology. (Conversations, 1988)

44.   This view further reinforces human tendencies toward passivity, inaction, and denial of responsibility by indicating that ordinary human persons are incapable of acting effectively on their own behalf in matters of ultimate concern. *(Heyward, Redemption of God*, 53, 168, 198, and throughout.)

45.   Heyward, *Speaking of Christ*, 14. Christology is then "the study of how Christians understand these opposites, humanity and divinity, joined in the person of Jesus, thereby making him the Messiah or Christ to whom Hebrew Scriptures refer."

46.   Heyward, *Redemption of God*, 32.

47.   Ibid., 54, 63, 89. Heyward finds problematic the shift of focus from the God whom Jesus proclaimed to Jesus himself as that God or the Son of that God because this shift masks the redemptive and liberating message itself: that human persons have power in relation and are called and enabled to use it in the world. (Ibid., 126ff. and throughout; idem, *Our Passion for Justice*, 13.) The orthodox view, Heyward contends, is quite the opposite of the one held by Jesus himself, who focused on God and the power of God reflected in mutual human relations. (Heyward, *Our Passion for Justice*, 13.)

48.   Brushing aside his similarities to other persons denies the possibility that persons other than Jesus have also lived fully in the power in relation that is God. (Heyward, *Redemption of God*, 164.) Further, Heyward argues, the conjunction of Jesus' relational isolation and the claim that he is the once-for-all, unique Savior and exemplar minimizes all human particularities not found in Jesus himself. (Ibid., 199-200.)

49.   Ibid., 4, 198. In this book (which attempts to answer the question "to what extent are we responsible for our own redemption in history?"), Heyward puts great emphasis on the voluntary character of all relations, including those between God and Jesus, and God and human history.

50.   Ibid., 39.

51.   Ibid., 7. Note the similarity here to the critique of classical theism rendered by Charles Hartshorne, Schubert Ogden, Marjorie Hewitt Suchocki, and other process theologians.

52. Specifically: maleness is emphasized over the activity of the one man Jesus (Heyward, *Redemption of God*, 196; idem, *Our Passion for Justice*, 212.); the oppressed and marginalized are lured into complicity with their own oppression (rather than empowered for liberation) by ideologies which connect present suffering with future reward (idem, *Our Passion for Justice*, 216ff.); and the claims to full humanity of non-Christians, especially Jews, are negated, thereby causing or colluding with events of mass dehumanization and destruction like the Holocaust (idem, *Redemption of God*, 89, 196; idem, *Our Passion for Justice*, 211ff.).

53. Heyward, *Redemption of God*, 126.

54. Heyward, *Our Passion for Justice*, 215-216.

55. Heyward, *Speaking of Christ*, 17. Heyward, again, is following Maurice, who writes that theology which attempts to "work up from earthly ground" forms "abstractions called 'god,' in which 'God' becomes anything, everything, and nothing." (Maurice, *Theological Essays* 1957, 81; quoted in Heyward, *Speaking of Christ*, 17.)

56. Heyward, *Speaking of Christ*, 18. For example, Heyward finds, Bonhoeffer continues the devaluation of humanity, while Moltmann perpetuates the domination of the human by an over-valued divinity. Sobrino does both. Soelle makes Christ her God and thus maintains the view that Jesus is divine rather than human. (Idem, *Redemption of God*, 211-215.) Indeed, Heyward now judges that her own earlier analyses and constructions--such as those in *Redemption of God*--are inadequate for precisely the same reasons. (Conversation, September 1988; idem, *Speaking of Christ*, 16.)

57. Ibid., 14.

58. Ibid., 21; conversation, winter 1988. In other words, Christology must begin from the connection or relation of the human to the divine, rather than from separation. On this point, Heyward is influenced by F. D. Maurice, who argued that, while human beings may separate themselves from God, God establishes and continues to be related to humanity. Failure to recognize this "essential fact" continues the sin of separation. See, for example, Maurice's *Theological Essays* 1957, 67, and his interpretation of the Book of Job in the same volume ("On the Sense of Righteousness and the Need for a Redeemer.")

59. Heyward, *Redemption of God*, 17, 39; idem, *Our Passion for Justice*, 29, 42.

60.   Heyward, *Our Passion for Justice*, 29; idem, "Can Anglicans Be Feminist Liberation Theologians?", 39.

61.   Heyward's process of re-imaging is similar in method and outcome to Ruether's re-encounter with the Jesus of the Synoptic Gospels (discussed in Chapter 5, above). For Heyward, this approach is mandated by the necessity to break through the dualisms and distortions present in classical texts and traditions, and by the theological contention that the divine-human relation which Jesus embodies is possible for all persons.

62.   Heyward, *Speaking of Christ*, 21.

63.   "To image is not to 'imagine' or 'fantasize' in the popular sense of creating reality in one's mind. Rather, imaging is a process of exploring and expressing something about reality--namely, about a relation that we know already between ourselves and that which we image." (Heyward, *Redemption of God*, 26.)

64.   Heyward, *Redemption of God*, 34. (This is also more consistent with the Jewish tradition, Heyward thinks; op. cit., 3.) For her re-imaging, Heyward relies most heavily on the Gospel of Mark, both because it seems to be the earliest of the Gospels, and also because it accords most fully with her own experience. (Heyward, *Redemption of God*, 35.)

65.   Ibid., 49, 202; idem, Our Passion for Justice, 217.

66.   Ibid., 31, 169. The task is this: "Our christology becomes an image of our relational experience, just as, I believe, incarnation was an image of Jesus' relational experience." (Ibid., 31 and 34.) Heyward's emphasis on present experience enables a recovery of the Judaic understanding of God, as revealed in God's acts, as a God of righteousness and justice who is "'in-carnate' in right relation between divine and human and among humans." (Ibid., 8.) In turn, this recovery is part of forming solidary relations between Jews and Christians.

67.   Ibid., 31. Indeed, this is precisely what has been done in the traditional images of the incarnation, which is "an image of Jesus' relational experience" of God and other human persons.

68.   Heyward, *Our Passion for Justice*, 28. Heyward is convinced that the gaps in historical existence are crossed by the human spirit expressed in events. Historical disjunctions can set us free from past patterns of wrong relation, and they can help us focus our attention on the present. Thus, recognizing that we cannot be like Jesus in any literal way empowers us to see incarnation as something that always goes on, in the present. As important, in Heyward's view, is

that recognition of the gaps and ruptures in history presents an accurate image of the human situation of tension, ambiguity, conflict, and dissonance as much as of harmony and continuity. (Idem, *Redemption of God*, 36; idem, *Our Passion for Justice*, 29, 76.)

69. Ibid., 221.

70. Heyward, *Redemption of God*, 44, 49, 54f.

71. Heyward insists that both *intimate* and *immediate* be understood etymologically, that is, as "inmost" and "direct and unmediated," without sentimental or private connotations. (Idem, *Redemption of God*, xxv n. 13.)

72. Heyward, *Redemption of God*, 45.

73. Ibid., 46-47. See also thematically related stories at Mark 7:24-30, 9:17-29, 10:52, and 11:22-23.

74. Ibid., 51-52.

75. Ibid., 36, interpreting Mark 8:27-29.

76. Interestingly, Heyward does not discuss the ways in which Jesus' followers attempted to turn his and their *dunamis* into *exousia*, as would seem to be the case particularly in the remainder of the confession of Peter at Caesarea Philippi (Mark 8:32-33), in the case of the exorcist who is not a follower of Jesus (Mark 9:38-41), or in the attempt by the sons of Zebedee to secure high position in the coming realm of God (Mark 10:35-45). Nor does she discuss the betrayal and desertion by many of Jesus' followers at the time of his arrest and death. In other words, Heyward does not discuss how Jesus' relations with his disciples provide multiple instances of the ambiguity and tension which Heyward herself contends attend many attempts to incarnate *dunamis* in a world which fears it and which instead resorts to unjust *exousia* and to denial of relation. And part of Jesus' human experience, his ongoing passion, is life within exactly these ambiguities. (Ibid., 56.)

77. Ibid., 37, 38.

78. Ibid., 39.

79. Ibid., 42, 54-57. Heyward construes Jesus' urgent preaching of the imminent inbreaking of God's reign as "motivated by a sense of the power in present relation to effect the coming realm of God." (Ibid., 50.)

80. Ibid., 56-57.

81. Ibid., 55-56.

82. Ibid., 56.

83. Ibid., 59.

84. Heyward, *Our Passion for Justice*, 17.

85.   Heyward, *Redemption of God*, 31, 198; also 47. Therefore, what Jesus did (and in that sense who he was) "may be instructive in our understanding of the power in relational experience." (Ibid., 33.) Heyward's statement that Jesus is fully and only human prompts Hampson to note that "If this is all she thinks, she surely cannot be considered Christian." (Heyward, *Theology and Feminism*, 63.)

86.   Heyward, *Our Passion for Justice*, 18.

87.   Ibid., 178.

88.   That is, when God is the power in all just and mutual relation, and this is what is meant by the word *God*, humanity is divinized by participation in such relations. Jesus is therefore fully divine, because his relations are fully just and mutual. Yet this potential resides in all human persons simply because they are human. This view hinges on understanding the human person as constructed as a self precisely by relationality. This, I take it, is Heyward's point in her discussions of the self-in-relation in *Speaking of Christ* and *Touching Our Strength*.

89.   Ibid., 17. Heyward distinguishes between labelling Jesus as uniquely divine for all time, and calling him the Christ. The former designation blocks dialogue and solidarity with persons of non-Christian (and especially Jewish) and post-Christian beliefs. The latter--that Jesus is the Christ *for Christians*--identifies the experiential particularity that is one of the pre-conditions for dialogue. (Ibid., 215-219.)

90.   Heyward, *Speaking of Christ*, 23.

91.   Ibid., 23.

92.   Heyward, *Redemption of God*, 31, 198.

93.   Ibid., 197. Hampson misses this point in her criticism of Heyward (Hampson, *Theology and Feminism*, 63). Recall Heyward's argument that the dualistic view of the relation between humankind and God works to overshadow and denigrate human being in order to protect the power of God. (See especially *The Redemption of God*, 1ff., which I have discussed under "The Character of Human Existence," above.)

94.   Heyward, *Our Passion for Justice*, 221; emphasis in the original.

95.   Heyward, *Redemption of God*, 163.

96.   Ibid., 200; italics in the original.

97.   Heyward, *Touching Our Strength*, 190.

98.   Heyward, *Redemption of God*, 42; idem, "Can Anglicans be Feminist Liberation Theologians?", 39.

99.   Heyward, *Our Passion for Justice*, 178; emphasis mine.

100. In addition to which, Heyward notes, there can be no monopoly on relational *dunamis*, that is, on God. (Heyward, *Redemption of God*, 47.)

101. Heyward, *Our Passion for Justice*, 17.

102. "Everyone can incarnate God. . . . Everyone can, but not everyone does." (Heyward, *Redemption of God*, 47.)

103. Heyward, *Redemption of God*, 49.

104. Ibid., 33; idem, *Our Passion for Justice*, 254-255 and passim.

105. Heyward, *Our Passion for Justice*, 29.

106. Ibid., 46. See also 28 for a slightly different version of the same formulation.

107. Heyward, *Redemption of God*, 200; italics in original.

108. Ibid., 36, 163; idem, *Our Passion for Justice*, 17. Jesus' own "restraint from making or accepting magnanimous claims for himself has enabled us to discover that we are, like him, simply human, and are, like him, able to affect the course of events in the world." (Heyward, *Redemption of God*, 202.)

109. Heyward expects to have worked these suggestions out more fully within the next five years. (Conversation, September 1988.)

110. Heyward, *Speaking of Christ*, 21-22.

111. Ibid., 10.

112. Heyward, *Redemption of God*, 33.

113. Heyward, *Our Passion for Justice* 87. The internal quotes are from, respectively, Elie Wiesel, Sarah Grimke, and Martin Luther King, Jr.

114. Heyward, *Touching Our Strength*, 114.

115. Ibid., 115; italics in the original. For Heyward's definition of the erotic, see note 9, above.

116. Ibid., 115-116. "[H]er body signals a crying need for woman-affirming (nonsexist), erotic (nonerotophobic) power that, insofar as we share it, will transform a world that includes our own most personal lives in relation." (Ibid., 114.)

117. Ibid., 116.

118. Ibid., 116-117.

119. See Heyward's interpretation of the passion and crucifixion in *The Redemption of God*, 53-58.

120. Heyward, *Speaking of Christ*, 22; idem, *Touching Our Strength*, 117-118.

121. Carter Heyward and Margaret Craddock Huff, "Digging Foundations for Anglican Ecclesiology: A Feminist Liberation Perspective" (unpublished paper presented to the Conference of Anglican Theologians, 1988), 7; used by permission.
122. Heyward, *Redemption of God*, 43.
123. Heyward, *Our Passion for Justice*, 16.
124. Heyward, *Redemption of God*, throughout; idem, *Our Passion for Justice*, 12. God may be spoken of as if God were an entity or existent, as human beings are; but it is more appropriate, in Heyward's view, to speak of God as a dynamic or a process. The affinities between Heyward's thought and various versions of process theology are evident. However, Heyward refuses to define her work as process theology because she finds that process thought begins from speculation and uses speculative abstractions to thematize the concrete. See Heyward, "An Unfinished Symphony of Liberation," 108ff.
125. Heyward, *Touching Our Strength*, 189. See also idem, *Speaking of Christ*, 24.
126. Heyward, *Redemption of God*, 6-8. Or, "From a trinitarian perspective . . . , we may try to envision, on the basis of our experience, God in three images: God is our relational matrix (or womb). God is born in our relational matrix. God is becoming our relational matrix." (Idem, *Touching Our Strength*, 23.)
127. Heyward, *Our Passion for Justice*, 45, 141. God is related voluntarily: power in relation includes the capacity to choose and to will effectively and lovingly (and so always interdependently). (Idem, *Redemption of God*, 40.)
128. Ibid., 98. Heyward refers to justice as "the logos of God." (Idem, *Touching Our Strength*, 74.) One of the effects of the divine power is to equalize (rather than abolish) human power, which may mean overthrowing human structures and attitudes that block or counteract the drive for justice. (Idem, *Redemption of God*, 202.)
129. Heyward, *Redemption of God*, 9 and passim.
130. Ibid., 9, 40, and passim; idem, *Our Passion for Justice*, 254-55. Because God is the power in relation, rather than a separable entity, God's ability to act depends on human choice, and on human good will.
131. Ibid., 163ff.
132. By naming as God the power in relation, Heyward has reformulated the classical theological distinction between immanence and transcendence, an idea derived out of unjust use of power to dominate and suppress and so of little benefit and often great harm.

Her formulation of transcendence as "crossing over" retrieves from the distorted, hierarchicalized view the immediate forcefulness and limitlessness of the power that is God. It thereby eliminates both damaging power relations attached to the previous formulation, and false division of God into what can be experienced and what remains mysterious. (Heyward, *Our Passion for Justice*, 244-245.)

133. Heyward, *Our Passion for Justice*, 166.

134. "*If* we love, God comes and makes a home with us. God's life with us is contingent upon our love, our opening our lives, lifting up our hearts, saying what we must, doing what we can, sharing what we are and have. . . . The point is, God has taken the initiative, and God's initiative is our birthright. . . . Insofar as we are lovers of human and created life, bearers of compassion and courage, justice-makers, visionaries, and workers for a better world, *it is we ourselves who do these things by the power of the One Spirit who has called us to this life together*. . . . It is in our cooperation with a God who is love and who acts in history though us, that we may find the peace that the Spirit, in Her Wisdom, has made available to us from the beginning." (Heyward, *Speaking of Christ*, 54-55; italics in original.)

135. Heyward, *Speaking of Christ*, 24. Heyward is here paraphrasing F. D. Maurice, who writes, "Apart from Him, I feel there dwells in me no good thing; but I am sure that I am not apart from Him, nor are you. Nor is any man." (Maurice, *Theological Essays* 1957, 67; quoted in Heyward, op. cit., 90 n. 2.)

136. Heyward, *Touching Our Strength*, 190.

137. Heyward, *Our Passion for Justice*, 118.

138. "Simply because we are human, we are able to be co-creative agents of redemption. Our vocation is to take seriously the creative character of who we are--both in relation to one another (humanity) and to the power of relation itself (God). . . . The redemption of the world--of human and divine life, ourselves and the transpersonal bond among us--is dependent upon our willingness to make love/justice in the world. In so doing, we co-operate with each other and with God in a process of mutual redemption--that is, in the deliverance of both God and humanity from evil." (Heyward, *Redemption of God*, 2.)

139. Heyward, *Redemption of God*, 163ff. and passim; idem, *Our Passion for Justice*, 124.

140. Ibid., 151-152.

141. Heyward, *Our Passion for Justice*, 187, 206.

142. Heyward's analysis here draws heavily on liberation theology and Ruether's discussion of the interstructuring of oppression and its victim-blaming ideology of sin. Heyward's own elaboration focuses in greater detail on the effects of oppression on the oppressed; that is, on the ways in which the concrete realities of oppression are internalized as self-denigration, self-blame, self-hatred, depression, and acceptance of powerlessness. For the subjugated in general, "the most deadly of our sins is not the deed we do, or fail to do, but rather the denial of ourselves as God's harvest." (Ibid., 251; emphasis in the original.) For women as women in patriarchal cultures, the greatest separation from God--the greatest sin--"has always been our failure to take ourselves seriously as strong, powerful, autonomous and creative persons." (Ibid., 3.)

143. Ibid., xiv, 205. On these grounds, it is imperative, in Heyward's view, that white Christian feminists engage themselves in the struggle against white racism and anti-Semitism. See Heyward, "An Unfinished Symphony of Liberation," 113; and *God's Fierce Whimsy*, of which Heyward was the principal compiler.

144. Ibid., 180.

145. Heyward, *Touching Our Strength*, 91.

146. Ibid., 92.

147. Ibid., 23.

148. Heyward, *Redemption of God*, 200; italics in original.

149. Heyward, *Our Passion for Justice*, 178; emphasis mine. Note the similarity to Maurice and to other Logos Christologies.

150. Heyward, *Redemption of God*, 31, 198. Heyward's attempt in this claim in *Redemption of God* was also to focus on the Jesus of history rather than the Christ of faith, while still preserving an incarnational theology. She has subsequently recognized the misleading characteristics of this statement and the dualisms that are embedded in it. (Idem, *Speaking of Christ*, 13-18; conversation, September 1988.)

151. Heyward, *Touching Our Strength*, 116.

152. See, for example, Heyward, *Speaking of Christ*, 19.

153. Ibid., 15; conversation, September 1988.

154. Heyward, *Redemption of God*, 200.

155. Jesus is not, for Heyward, the total or final manifestation of christic power. Rather, "his relationship to God was uniquely and singularly the *only* liberating relationship a person can have to God." (Heyward, *Redemption of God*, 200; italics in the original). Because of differences in historical context and the shape of mutuality possible

in differing contexts, other exemplars bring into view other aspects of this same liberating relationship. Some, but not necessarily all, of these may then be seen as christic when Christians "re-image" Jesus. That is, historic figures such as Sojourner Truth, Dietrich Bonhoeffer, and Oscar Romero, as well as more imaginative figures such as Christa, disclose liberating relationship in ways which are recognizable in part because of their resemblance to the liberating relationship seen in Jesus. At the same time, they make yet more evident some aspects of Jesus' liberating relationship with humanity and God, and disclose other possibilities present in this kind of relationship.

156. The fact that this relational power must be concrete in history prevents its ever being characterized as static--one of the drawbacks of the Logos tradition, recall. Precisely because being is grounded in *power* rather than in substance, it is always dynamic, always empowering. And when being is so understood, what it creates is also inherently dynamic.

157. Ibid., 55.

158. See especially Heyward's 1981 sermon "Judgment," in Heyward, *Our Passion for Justice*, 200-210.

159. On the former, see Heyward, *Touching Our Strength*, 145-148. On the latter, see Heyward, *Our Passion for Justice*, 208.

160. Heyward, *Our Passion for Justice*, 207.

161. Both her published anthologies--*Our Passion for Justice* and *Speaking of Christ*--exhibit a wide range of genres and language use, as well as the development of her thought over a period of time.

162. Heyward, *Redemption of God*, 34.

163. Ibid., 25-35.

164. See, for example, Heyward, *Redemption of God*, 14-15. For example, Heyward's longtime interest in and appropriation of the work of F.D. Maurice is quite evident in her teaching and her conversations, but is acknowledged in print only recently, in the some of the essays published in *Speaking of Christ*.

Chapter 11

Wisdom-Logos Christology in Feminist Perspective

In the preceding three chapters, I have discussed at length the Christologies of three white feminist theologians, setting those Christologies within the overall framework of their thought. Each of these theologians presents a Wisdom-Logos theology, which understands the Christ as in some sense the one who definitively manifests for Christians the fullness of both humanity and divinity. Whether understood as the representation of "a divinely renewed humanity" that is in unity with God (Wilson-Kastner),[1] as "the revelation of God to us" (Suchocki),[2] or the full manifestation of "the *only* liberating relation a person can have to God" (Heyward),[3] Jesus is himself the historical manifestation of the relation between God and humanity which has existed from creation, which is partially restored in the present, and which is promised to all as future transformation.[4] These are Wisdom-Logos Christologies in that Jesus as the Christ is the self-expression of God, incarnate in concrete, historical form. The Christ is also the manifestation of the fullness of humanity. In one person, the fundamental relation between divinity and humanity is revealed; and that revelation moves the universe toward redemption.

As I indicated at the beginning of Chapter 8, a primary advantage of Wisdom-Logos Christologies is that they establish a structural relationship between elements that have significant differences from each other, most importantly between the human and the divine. In these three authors, that connection is established by the fact of relationality itself.[5] It is because God is primarily relational--not primarily autonomous--that all existence must be understood in relational terms. But different approaches are used to characterize God's relationality.[6] For Wilson-Kastner, the relations of self-giving love unify the Trinity. This same quality of relation is recapitulated in the structures of human diversity, which are themselves unified in part historically and ultimately eschatologically through reconciliation and inclusiveness. For Suchocki, the universe is constituted dynamically, and its essential movement is toward the creation of a harmony in which the historical and finite are appropriated into the eternal and ongoing divine creativity and harmony. Heyward's understanding of the divine as the dynamic and forceful power in relation undergirds her insistence that relation is not just constitutive of existence; relationality is the very nature of existence. Divinity and humanity, then, are inherently inseparable, although they are distinguishable on the basis of their scope and their consistency of actualization of just and mutual love. The Christ, for all three, is the revelation of the essential reality and importance of relation in human existence.

Human relationality is an image of God's, cast along the same lines of self-giving love, creativity, and dynamic power. But the reality of human limitation and of sin as distortion requires that each of these images of God's relationality be modified so that distortions can be corrected, healed, and redeemed. Thus, the divine self-giving love that Wilson-Kastner invokes requires of humans movement toward wholeness and inclusivity, in which self-giving is integrally related to creativity and receptivity. For Suchocki, divine creativity requires of humans a balance or tension between appropriation and novelty, that is, between appreciation and adoption of what is, and movement toward new and often disturbing possibilities. The dynamic power that is central to Heyward's approach drives humans always toward mutuality, love, and justice; and human persons--so prone to use power coercively--must set mutuality, cooperation, and justice always in front of themselves.

The life, death, and resurrection of Jesus reveal or manifest the character of ultimate relationality. For Wilson-Kastner, divine relationality is most apparent in the death of Jesus on the cross, where God's self-giving love embraces alienation and "painful diversity." [7] Jesus' resurrection reveals this embrace as transformative and redemptive. At the same time, in his free acceptance of rejection, abandonment, and death, Jesus embodies human hope that tragedy can be healed; his human love is both strong and accepting. [8] Jesus' resurrection as "*the* new human" vindicates his vision of what humanity truly ought to be, "delivered from the seeds of its own destructiveness which it has nurtured and cherished." [9] The resurrection also shows forth the unity of humanity in this resurrected one who represents all of humanity. [10]

For Suchocki, the fullness of humanity is seen in Jesus' inclusive, reciprocal, and transforming relations with others, relations that are continuous with but expansive beyond acceptance of the Reign of God as it was breaking in in his time. [11] His death is continuous with this life. His resurrection both confirms his life and transforms it. [12] At the same time, the inclusive and transformative characteristics of his life and death are shown by the resurrection to be a manifestation of the full scope of God's presence and participation in all of human existence, including suffering. The resurrection also shows that God's inexhaustible love transforms existence toward a greater harmony that is part of the divine harmony. [13]

For Heyward, Jesus fully embodies the intimacy, immediacy, and passion of the divine-human relation, and this is apparent in his healing, empowering, and justice-making relations with others. Jesus shows the power of this right-relation, and this manifestation encourages others to embrace relational power and find it in themselves. [14] His death brings his followers to a life like his, life in which the divine love for humanity is expressed through struggles for justice, mutuality, and cooperation as "the actual shape of love in the world." [15]

For all three theologians, what Jesus *is* is an indication of what all human persons have the potential to *become*. This potential is originally constituted in God's creation of humanity in the divine image. But the fullness of redeemed humanity still lies in the future: it remains for other humans to actualize this inherent potential in themselves. In this they are aided by Jesus understood as the Christ. But Jesus is not only a model or paradigm of human possibility. The life, death, and resurrection of Jesus are God's action in human existence: "God living a human life," "God with us," "God's being and human being . . . experienced as one." [16] God's concrete but full presence in history accomplishes a change. It is the life, death, and resurrection of Jesus that forcefully and transformatively represent and reveal what God intends humanity as a whole to be.[17] Humanity is already redeemed in that full human existence has been concretely embodied in Jesus. "The resurrection marks the beginning of the suffusing of humanity in the divine life and light." [18] Human existence is creatively advanced toward more inclusive and pervasive harmony, and that advance is available for future appropriation. [19] Jesus newly manifests "God's activity in conjunction, partnership, friendship with humanity: . . . the way it has been all along." [20] Because of the particular relation of humanity and divinity in Jesus the Christ, all future human possibility is moved in the direction of unity, harmony, and right-relation. That is, human existence is moved by God toward final redemption.

It is the foundational significance of relationality understood in dynamic and processive terms which addresses and (in my judgment) overcomes the problems I have identified with classical Wisdom and Logos Christologies. First, all that is, is dynamic rather than static, because relationality itself is dynamic. That is, how relationality is actualized varies with social and historical particularities, yet the structure of relation remains the same. Wilson-Kastner's epistemology shows how human experience is common in its structures, operations, and drives, but is diverse and varied in its phenomena. Suchocki indicates that all existence is made up of dynamic processes of adoption and adaptation, or creativity and appropriation, which may move toward harmony; and these processes by definition involve difference, choice, and interaction in which multiple, always-changing variables are involved. Heyward directs attention toward mutuality, cooperation, and love/justice as the fundamental characteristics of the divine power that enlivens all relations, thereby indicating a common direction or impetus found (but not necessarily grasped) in each differing historical moment. In sum, the fact that for each of the three the most fundamental characteristic of being is a continuing dynamic means that all other aspects of being will be in some measure continuously dynamic as well. [21]

This emphasis on dynamic connection works toward the healing of the dualisms whose importance has been decisively identified by Ruether: because the emphasis is on connection, varying elements can, in principle, be distinguished even while they remain connected. The divine and the human, for example, are connected through the quality of relationality; but the divine differs significantly and determinatively from the human in that God is the prime and unsurpassable example of relationality in its fullest measure--as self-giving (Wilson-Kastner), as creative (Suchocki), and as justly and lovingly powerful (Heyward). Likewise an eternal and universal quality (rather than entity) is expressed within temporal and particular history without being exhausted at any given moment. This quality begins all that is, and its dynamic character provides the force that moves history from creation to redemption and establishes the qualities which characterize redemptive completion or fulfillment.

Therefore, dynamic connection also characterizes the range of possible relations between past, present, and future, and so between the sources and norms of tradition, experience, and envisioned future. The past is a contributor to the present, providing the background out of and against which the present and future are seen. At the same time, the present provides both perspective on the past and the elements out of which a differing future can be imagined. Further, it is the general shape of the future that is desired--unity, harmony, just mutuality--which shapes how both past and present will be understood.[22] The past does not represent an ideal or idealizable moment that has been lost and must be recovered. It does give to the present and the future resources for their shape and direction. But how these resources will be used is ultimately determined both by the fundamental dynamic itself and by how actors in history will choose to use all the resources and possibilities available to them.

The emphasis on relational qualities that are reshaped in every age carries over into the treatment of Jesus as the human incarnation of God. The quality of Jesus' relationships manifests the divine relationality as it is historically embodied. Self-giving, creative response and appropriation and just mutuality are human characteristics, found decisively in this one historical figure who is (like all human persons) a member of groups characterized by gender, race, class, nationality, and so on.

Jesus' being male has revelatory importance only because of the meaning of maleness in patriarchal history and culture. The fact that Jesus' relations with others were self-giving, inclusive, reciprocal or mutual, cooperative, and just stands against the patterns and conventions of patriarchy, which operate to the benefit of men of dominant groups and to the detriment of women and other marginalized persons. Jesus' relations are, therefore, all the more revelatory of the possibility of full humanity for all. At the same time, these relations reveal the nature of God as also self-giving, inclusive, and just, thereby removing the possibility of divine sanction for patterns of domination and suppression. In other words, it is what Jesus makes of the meaning of maleness that undoes the distortions of gender that are central to patriarchy.

These feminist Wisdom-Logos approaches to Christology, in sum, address and resolve the problems with classical Wisdom and Logos Christologies primarily by emphasizing dynamic relationality and the processes of connection as the most fundamental characteristics of the divine, and so of the universe which the divine continuously creates and sustains. But to what extent does this feminist retrieval of the Wisdom-Logos strand approach adequacy?

These Wisdom-Logos Christologies focus on Jesus the Christ as the manifestation of the fullness of both divinity and humanity in one person, and as the proclamation of the future relation of the human and divine promised to all of humanity. As I indicated in Chapter 5, a typology of manifestation and proclamation describes the dialectically related expressions of human encounter with the divine, an encounter which is experienced as both participation in and distanciation from the whole. The pole of proclamation focuses on encounter with the divine as radically other, an encounter of intensification and defamiliarization. The pole of manifestation correlates with the intensification of participation, where the sacred is sensed to be the radically immanent, immediately powerful, and always present ground. [23] Within the manifestation type, Christologies tend to emphasize fundamental trust in humanity, history, and cosmos, where God is present as love. The Christ is then understood to be the incarnate manifestation or self-expression of the divine itself; and the kind of human existence which is manifested in the Christ is understood to be always already possible. [24] When this paradigm is transformed by liberating praxis, prophetic social-historical action and eschatological urgency are grounded in the essential giftedness of existence and in incarnation as manifestation. [25]

In the Christologies discussed in the preceding three chapters, Jesus the Christ is not only the human exemplar of a new humanity. He is also the self-expression of the divine relationality manifest as self-giving love, harmonious integration of possibility, and just mutuality. The incarnation of God in Jesus manifests the present possibilities for wholeness, harmony, and reconciliation through a variety of authentic hopes and promises given through the gracious presence of the divine. In these ways, Jesus embodies the relation between humanity and divinity--a relation which is potentially possible for all human persons simply because they are human. [26] Because this incarnation is an act of God in history, it works a transformation in history, moving history as a whole toward actualization of a now-fully revealed always-present possibility. But it is the present where redemption can--and so must--be partially experienced.

The centrality of Jesus the Christ and the location in the past of the decisive manifestation of both the divine and the human present potential problems for this type of Christology, even in the dynamic feminist-liberation retrieval these authors achieve. The centrality of a single figure, no matter how construed, mitigates against a thoroughgoing focus on relationality, in that it is always *Jesus* who represents the fullness of relation. Even when--as in the case of the hemorraghing woman (Mark 5:25ff.)--an individual's faith makes her well, it is *Jesus* who is not only the instrument of healing, but also the source of it. [27] To this extent, Rita Nakashima Brock's criticism of the largely tacit hero-worship of Christian feminist Christologies holds. [28]

Further, focus on a single figure as the decisive manifestation of both divinity and humanity, even when relativized, also tends toward negating the possibility of other authentic manifestations, within and outside Christianity. All three authors are well aware of this problem. In each case, the shift in Christological emphasis away from the maleness of Jesus to the quality of his human relations provides a framework for addressing the truths of other religions and other religious experiences. Each author, in slightly different ways, makes two affirmations that are significant here. The first affirmation concerns historical particularity, which all three authors see as importantly shaping how divine activity is encountered in the midst of human existence. The other affirmation is found in the insistence of all three authors that Jesus is the Christ *for Christians*; others need not make this affirmation. Further, all three authors suggest at least one criterion that may be used to evaluate the authenticity of any possible manifestation. For Suchocki and Heyward, justice may and must be used as a measure, a position whose problems Suchocki has discussed explicitly. [29] For Wilson-Kastner, the criterion is self-giving. Still, each approach would benefit from further exploration of the possibility that even their carefully considered discussions may presume a universal norm which is in fact tradition- or experience-specific.

As I have already noted, the emphasis on a decisive manifestation in the past is problematic for any feminist Christology that draws significantly on present reality. Given the extent to which the mediation of patriarchy has been decreased and new encounters with the divine are part of contemporary women's experience, feminist theology must be open in principle to receiving what is genuinely both new and revelatory in those encounters. Among the authors discussed in these four chapters, the possibility of inadequacy on this score is most apparent in the work of Patricia Wilson-Kastner, whose discussions make the least use of concrete elements of contemporary women's experience. On the other hand, Heyward's recent reflections on the symbol of Christa when taken together with her re-imaging of Jesus through contemporary experience indicate the fruitfulness of placing a past manifestation in relation to a present one. The difference here would seem to lie in the use of concrete contemporary experience as a primary source for reflection.

But the major problem area for feminist Wisdom-Logos theologies' emphasis on the pole of manifestation is this pole's traditional focus on continuity and orderly procession from past to present to future. [30] But in these feminist retrievals of the Wisdom-Logos structure, continuity is maintained, in the first place, by the fundamental formal importance of dynamic relationality, rather than of static forms. Materially, each of these three theologians emphasizes continuity with historically marginal movements whose thrust toward liberation and transformation manifests the presence of the divine in suppressed, silenced, and marginalized traditions. In other words, these three theologians are adamant that the historical dominance of a particular socio-cultural order does not establish it as the *divine* order, whatever its beneficiaries may claim.

Nevertheless, in contrast to the proclamation type, manifestation-type Christologies such as these can tend to downplay radical interruption and otherness. As Tracy notes, the divine is encountered in the intensification of distanciation as well as participation. And it is this distanciation that is proclaimed by prophetic voices and disruptive events. [31] It is precisely *dis*continuity and *re*ordering that are necessary for the radical transformation that these Wisdom-Logos Christologies urge. The situation of massive and sustained domination and dehumanization in the midst of which women and others struggle for liberation requires interruption and disruption as well as continuity with the liberating forces and traditions already manifest in that situation. An emphasis on the pole of manifestation brings to light and strength those liberating forces and traditions. But it cannot by itself provide the assurance of domination's disruption by a power in some manner outside it. Nor can a manifestation emphasis readily provide sufficient motivation for interrupting these historical patterns from within history. For this, proclamation is needed. And movements of interruption, such as contemporary movements for liberation and their associated theologies, provide rich and compelling evidence of the force of proclamation in these dissonant, ambiguous situations.

In these three theologies, proclamation is the key to continuity across disrupting gaps of history and experience. In Wilson-Kastner's work, the premise is that her manifestation Christology will be of interest to those who have already accepted the proclamation that Jesus is the Christ; [32] the whole orientation of her work, then, is apologetic rather than evangelical. Suchocki states clearly that the proclamation of the Church is essential for the transmission of the experience of faith from one generation to the next. [33] For Heyward, Christian proclamation is necessary to bridge the dissonances, ambiguities, and gaps that fill history. But for genuine encounter to take place, the "Jesus story" must be re-told in contemporary terms, whether or not those terms are continuous with the tradition. [34]

In these three theologies, the prophetic, proclamatory pole is most apparent in the use all three authors make of justice as a judgment on the past and as the plumbline against which the present is judged and the future envisioned. For Suchocki and Heyward particularly, justice is an eschatological category which can and must be approximated in the present, but which will be fully realized only in the future.

Suchocki's detailed discussion of eschatology makes especially clear that judgment on the basis of justice continues into the transhistorical future: the fact of unjust suffering in the past is not obliterated through redemption. It is, rather, transformed. And the agent of transformation is God. For, as Suchocki indicates, God's taking up of all existence into the harmony of the divine life includes an element of judgment, in which the possibilities curtailed and cut off by injustice are revealed as valuable, and their loss is felt as tragic by the perpetrator of injustice as well as by its victims. [35]

In Heyward's discussions, justice and judgment are exercised by human persons empowered by the divine, which is manifest as an "indignant power" which will make no peace with oppression.[36] The justly empassioned both proclaim and manifest this side of God. This is particularly the case in Jesus' passion, in which his proclamatory words and actions against injustice manifest one element of his liberating relation with God, and so indicates that our passion for justice also partakes of that kind of relation. [37]

The theologies of Wilson-Kastner, Suchocki, and Heyward emphasize the presence in historical existence of elements of creation that are being fulfilled as part of redemption: the present possibilities for wholeness, harmony, and reconciliation; a variety of authentic hopes and promises; the gracious presence of the divine. The imperative force of struggles for liberation comes primarily from the fact that it is the present where redemption can--and so must--be partially realized. This location of the imperative in the present derives from a Christological focus on the re-presentation of both the fullness of divinity and the fullness of humanity which has already happened in Jesus the Christ.

However, the centrality of one figure in the past who is the decisive manifestation of both the divine and the human presents major problems that are not entirely resolved in these theologies as they attempt to draw significantly on present reality, where radically new encounters with the divine occur, and where long-standing and deeply rooted patterns of domination and dehumanization are not easily dismantled. The approaches of

Heyward, Wilson-Kastner, and Suchocki, then, make important contributions *toward* a feminist Christology, but are not alone sufficient to the task of feminist Christology. It remains for me to indicate how the strengths of both manifestation and proclamation types can work together toward a more nearly adequate feminist Christology.

Notes

1.   Wilson-Kastner, *Faith, Feminism, and the Christ*, 91, 106-108.

2.   Suchocki, *God-Christ-Church* 1982, 101; cf. 1989, 98.

3.   Heyward, *Redemption of God*, 200.

4.   On the relation between creation and eschatological redemption, see Heyward, *Our Passion for Justice*, 243-247 and related passages in *Redemption of God*; Wilson-Kastner, *Faith, Feminism, and the Christ*, 51-52, 108; and Suchocki, *God-Christ-Church* 1982, 176ff.

5.   The primary metaphors used by each author come from different areas of theological reflection, and each selection is characteristic of the method of each author.   Wilson-Kastner's reformist commitments lead her to classical views of the Trinity made newly   accessible   by   contemporary   transcendental   Thomist epistemology. Suchocki's concern for casting classical theology in the "common sense" language of her own time prompts her to approach divine relationality through the human experience of becoming as a relational process.   Heyward's commitment to healing the wounds caused by oppression and encouraging struggle for liberation conceives of the divine as a dynamic power which infuses and energizes all that exists. To put it another way, Wilson-Kastner places great emphasis on reconstructing tradition; Suchocki seeks to formulate theology in terms of contemporary experience philosophically understood; and Heyward begins with concrete historical situations laden with conflict between a present which is both oppressive and liberative and an envisioned liberated future.   When viewed together, these three approaches indicate rich possibilities for a feminist theology in which

the connections between tradition, contemporary experience and modes of reflection, and movement toward the longed-for future interact.

6. It should be noted that these differences are to some extent a matter of emphasis: all three approaches are found in each of the three authors.

7. Wilson-Kastner, *Faith, Feminism, and the Christ*, 99.

8. Ibid., 106.

9. Ibid., 109.

10. Ibid., 110.

11. Suchocki, *God-Christ-Church* 1982, 96-98.

12. Ibid. 1982, 112.

13. Ibid. 1982, 95-96, 129.

14. Heyward, *Redemption of God*, 36 and passim.

15. Heyward, *Touching Our Strength*, 190. The treatment of Jesus' resurrection varies considerably among these three authors. Wilson-Kastner characteristically presents the most traditional reading: Jesus' earliest followers encounter the risen Christ, and these encounters are the core of their and all subsequent Christian proclamation. (Wilson-Kastner, *Faith, Feminism, and the Christ*, 107-108.) Suchocki and Heyward understand the resurrection in more contemporary terms. For Suchocki, the immediacy of the resurrection is "hidden in God," but its results are apparent in the transformations of existence. The resurrection leads from description of God to "the mystery of God as God." (Suchocki, *God-Christ-Church* 1989, 115-117.) For Heyward, Jesus' resurrection takes place in his followers: they "come alive" after his death and continue the "passionate investment . . . in relation to others" which he had begun. (Heyward, *Redemption of God*, 59.)

16. Wilson-Kastner, *Faith, Feminism, and the Christ*, 90 (quoting William Temple); Suchocki, *God-Christ-Church* 1982, throughout; Heyward, *Our Passion for Justice*, 29.

17. See Ogden, "'The Reformation that We Want,'" for the importance of this distinction; and also "Problems for a Pluralistic Theology of Religions," 505.

18. Wilson-Kastner, *Faith, Feminism, and the Christ*, 109.

19. Suchocki, *God-Christ-Church* 1982, 120.

20. Heyward, *Our Passion for Justice*, 178.

21. These varying approaches to relational dynamism imply a continuum of normative treatments of the problems of difference, conflict, and disruption. Wilson-Kastner subsumes difference and conflict under unity, whereas Heyward attempts to preserve both

difference and disruption as an inherent part of mutual relationality. Suchocki's focus on harmony allows for difference, but envisions a final resolution into harmony of the conflicts which difference as such engenders. On the importance of difference in white feminist theologies, see Thistlethwaite, *Sex, Race, and God*.

22. As I have noted above, the three authors differ here on the weight given to past, present, and future, or tradition, experience, and vision, with Wilson-Kastner being the most explicitly appreciative of the classical Christian tradition and Heyward the least. Suchocki's emphasis on the conjunction of past and future in each and every immediate moment means that her primary emphasis is less on the importance in their own time of specific distant historical movements and ideas, and more on how they are perceived and appropriated *now*.

23. Tracy, *Analogical Imagination*, 215, 218.

24. Ibid., 330-331.

25. Ibid., 390.

26. Busk, 211. Cf. F. D. Maurice, *The Gospel of St. John* (London: Macmillan, 1867), 297.

27. See, for example, Heyward, *Redemption of God*, 45ff.; and Brock, *Journeys by Heart*, 82ff. In her public addresses, Schüssler Fiorenza refers to this as *kyriocentrism*. Hampson would argue that such is unavoidable as long as feminists use the Bible.

28. Brock, *Journeys by Heart*, 65; contrast *ibid.*, 82ff. (following Elisabeth Schüssler Fiorenza). For feminist Christology this problem is particularly acute, because that figure has been used to legitimate certain elements of subjugation which have been of particular damage to women. (See particularly Daly, Hampson, Christ, and Brock on the maleness of Jesus and on traditional understandings of self-sacrifice, discussed in Chapter 2, above.)

29. Suchocki, "In Search of Justice: Religious Pluralism from a Feminist Perspective."

30. See Ruether, *Sexism and God-Talk*, 125f; idem, *Womanguides*, 23f.

31. Tracy, *Analogical Imagination*, 209 and passim.

32. Wilson-Kastner, *Faith, Feminism, and the Christ*, 1ff.

33. Suchocki, *God-Christ-Church* 1989, Chapter 13, "One, Holy, Apostolic Church."

34. Heyward, *Redemption of God*, 36; cf. idem, *Our Passion for Justice*, 29 and 76.

35. Suchocki, *God-Christ-Church* 1982, 176-189; cf. 1989, 199-216.

36. Heyward, *Redemption of God*, 55-56.
37. Heyward, *Speaking of Christ*, 21.

Chapter 12

The Re-presentation of Resistance and Transformation

Summary of the Study

Christology is the critical and reflective attempt to express in appropriate and credible terms the Christian witness that the true relation between the divine and the human (and so the true nature of both divine and human) is definitively manifest in Jesus of Nazareth whom Christians call the Christ. This book has focused on one important area of the contemporary Christological discussion, contemporary Christian feminism. Here the familiar post-Enlightenment problems of the relation of history to transcendence are sharpened and intensified by the historical and ongoing use of Christology to justify and perpetuate the patriarchal domination of women and the suppression and marginalization of women's experience.

Christology poses a problem for white Christian feminists from two directions: feminist criticism and traditional Christianity. Both traditionalist Christians and post-biblical feminists judge that Christology and feminism are incompatible because Christianity's patriarchal orientation and commitment are inherent in the religion itself. In contradiction to this stands Christian feminist experience, which indicates that Christianity moves ambiguously toward liberation--the goal of post-biblical feminists--*and* contributes to the continuation of patriarchal domination--which traditionalists support.

As I indicated in Chapter 2, Biblical and doctrinal traditionalists argue that the subordination of women to men in Christian thought and practice and in Western culture are both acceptable and normative, because they originate in the divine will. On this view, in seeking to overthrow patriarchy, feminism seeks to overthrow social arrangements that are divinely established, revealed, and sanctioned. Feminism and Christianity are thus unalterably opposed.

Post-biblical feminism, in contrast, while agreeing with the traditionalists that Christianity is inherently and essentially patriarchal, argues that this character is a reflection not of divine desire, but of human production. Both post-biblical and Christian feminist critics identify three aspects of Christology that are problematic for feminism: the implicitly and explicitly androcentric and patriarchal character of Christological symbolism; the location of women's identity and salvation outside women's existence and experience; and the contribution of the moral exemplarity of Christ to women's subjugation and devaluation. These critics argue that traditional Christology is patriarchal in its focus on the male child of a father God. Further, the identification of Jesus as the unique, once-for-all savior makes Christianity structurally both hierarchical and exclusive, not only of women, but of other marginalized peoples as well. Finally, Christology lifts up an exemplar who is a self-sacrificing victim, whose passivity and willingness to suffer have been and are being used to reinforce women's acceptance of their own domination. These critics conclude that women must seek their liberation and healing elsewhere, in their own experience. The challenge issued by feminist critics to Christology is finally comprehensive, if not conclusive. This analysis taken as a whole challenges Christian feminists either to show that Christianity's core symbolism does not have the effect its critics claim, or to transform the core itself.

Christian feminist theologians have taken up the latter aspect of this challenge. Together, feminism and Christian faith and practice have brought Christian feminists to recognize the multitudinous ways in which Christianity has contributed to women's subjugation. But Christian feminist experience is more complex and ambiguous than that: it also recognizes that Christianity, like feminism, has taught women to hope and struggle for liberation and transformation. Therefore, Christian feminists are engaged in attempts to reconstruct Christology and the whole of Christianity so that the freedom that Christianity proclaims can be actualized in the lives of women.

If this is to be done--if the challenge is to be met--then feminist Christologies must be constructed so that the Christ is understood in a way that fosters rather than diminishes the realization of women's authentic human potential. This cannot be done without addressing the ambiguous history of effects of Christology. Further, feminist Christologies must use women's experience to express the meanings of the terms *freedom* and *salvation*, and attend to the possible future effects of such a construal.

Thus far, two types of constructive proposals have emerged in white feminist theological consideration of Christology. Each type takes with utmost seriousness the feminist critique of Christology, and recognizes the need for feminist theological reconstruction that addresses the breadth and depth of the problematic. Each also emphasizes one pole of human encounter with the divine, which can be characterized as manifestation and proclamation, which intensify both participation and distanciation. The prophetic, iconoclastic bent of Rosemary Radford Ruether's Christology is of the proclamation type, while the Wisdom-Logos Christologies of Patricia Wilson-Kastner, Marjorie Hewitt Suchocki, and Carter Heyward are of the manifestation type. These white feminist Christologies both illustrate and modify this typology. One modification is an increased emphasis on the mediation of the ordinary, of everyday existence. Another, related modification comes through the primacy of liberating praxis, which transforms everyday existence and provides new sources for theological reflection and construction.

When the intensification of particular experience tends toward participation, the sacred is sensed to be radically immanent and immediately powerful, the enveloping ground which is always already present. The human self is understood as participating in a sacred cosmos, and is divinized by participatory contact with the sacred. Within this type, Christologies tend to emphasize fundamental trust in humanity, history, and cosmos, where God is present as love and existence is gifted. The Christ is understood to be the incarnation or manifestation of the true nature of both human and divine. And the kind of human existence manifested in the Christ is understood to be possible for other humans as well. In the contemporary period, this understanding builds on the Wisdom and Logos strands of the Bible and of church traditions, reconstructing these strands to reflect post-Enlightenment understandings of history, the transcendent, the human person, and human experience.

When the intensification of particularity tends toward nonparticipation, the sacred or divine is encountered as a power that shatters and defamiliarizes. The human self is ambiguous, both finite and limited. Christ's prophetic-eschatological message and cross are emphasized, disclosing the need for reform, for refusal to comply with the structures and forces of sin, and for conflict or struggle against the present human condition. The focus here is on the fact that the life commanded by Christ is not yet actualized, at least in part because of human nonacceptance of the divine reality and love. In the contemporary period, this strand recovers and reconstructs Biblical and traditional understandings of the divine interruption of human history, prophetic judgment on human pretensions, and eschatological fulfillment of divine promises.

In Rosemary Radford Ruether's proclamation Christology, Jesus is an iconoclastic, messianic prophet who, by his words, actions, life, and death, shatters the old order and proclaims a new heaven and new earth in which idolatrous dualisms (or schisms) are overcome. This model of redeemed humanity is characterized by mutual and just servanthood directed toward the whole of creation. God/ess is the matrix and inspiration of this liberating transformation; the Shalom of God/ess brings all the disparate aspects of existence into harmony. The spirit of Jesus the prophet of God/ess draws others into lives of liberating struggle and transformation. Thus the proclaimed new existence lives on, however partially, in those who take this prophetic model as exemplary. However, the full realization--the full manifestation--of the promised existence lies in the future, which is prefigured in proleptic, anticipated form in the prophetic Jesus and "in the form of our sister."

In showing the liberating face of God/ess, Jesus is the Word of God that proclaims and points to the fullness of God but is not itself the full self-expression of the divine. Jesus thus is the prophet of the One who is to come. Jesus is the Christ, then, in that he discloses the new humanity that is coming into being, and proclaims the Reign of the One who is to come. But, according to Ruether, he is not the only Christ, even for Christians. The Christ is known wherever the new humanity appears, and wherever the face of God/ess as liberator is shown.

What is particularly Christ-like about Jesus, what particularly shows the liberating face of God/ess, is Jesus' *kenosis* of patriarchy. This emptying-out of the power of patriarchal attitudes and privileges begins the process of healing the dualisms which must be transformed into polarities as part of both the new humanity and the Shalom of God/ess. In principle and effect, Jesus ends the old humanity and prefigures the new. But he does not *himself* embody the fullness of the new humanity. Other Christs are yet to come, for the Christ is fullness within historical conditions, complete authenticity in the midst of finite existence, unswerving devotion to the source and power of history *as* the source and power of history. The Christ stands as one who points beyond the self, beyond the human, to the true God who is the ground and power of all.

Ruether's emphasis on the humanity of Jesus is deliberate. Ruether is convinced that any attempt to render the transcendent in terms appropriate to the historical and finite alone will only serve to continue the same difficulties that she has been at some pains to identify and analyze. The fullness of God, Ruether concludes, remains beyond history, not fully poured out into history. It is the *Word* of God, the *spirit* of God, or the liberating *face* of God/ess that is present in history, and within the limits of historical forms and existence. Jesus' proclamation of God/ess and his authentically human life and death point accurately to where God/ess is to be found: at the source of earthly existence, and beyond it.

The Christologies presented by Patricia Wilson-Kastner, Marjorie Hewitt Suchocki, and Carter Heyward are of the manifestation type. In these reconstructions of the Wisdom-Logos tradition, Jesus manifests and incarnates the fullness of both humanity and divinity, in a relationship that has existed in principle from creation, is partially available to all in the present, and is promised to all as future transformation. In one person, the fundamental relation between divinity and humanity is revealed; and that revelation moves the universe toward redemption.

In these Christologies, relationality is taken to be a primary characteristic of God, whether as self-giving love that unifies the Trinity, as creative and harmonizing dynamism, or as dynamic and forceful relational power. And because God is relational, all existence is constituted relationally, and is always already related to the divine. But the limitations inherent in being human and the distortions, fragmentations, and alienations that are a consequence of sin make necessary a manifestation of relationality beyond that found in creation itself. The Christ is that manifestation.

God's self-giving creativity and unifying love are manifest in Jesus' love that embraces alienation and moves toward reconciliation. God's complex and creative harmony is revealed through Jesus' inclusive, reciprocal, and transforming relations with others. And God's just and loving power are manifest in the intimacy, immediacy, and passion found in all Jesus' relations. For all three theologians, Jesus is constituted as a person by these relations, and their qualities reflect his relation with God. Jesus' relationality reveals a potential shared by all human persons simply because they are human. By manifesting the full realization of this relationality in concrete history, Jesus reveals its importance in human existence. This potential is originally constituted in God's creation of humanity in the divine image. But the fullness of humanity still lies in the future, as humans actualize this inherent potential in themselves. In this they are aided by Jesus' model.

But Jesus is not only "the new human," the model or paradigm for Christians of human possibility. The life, death, and resurrection of Jesus are God's actions in human existence. They forcefully and transformatively represent and reveal what God intends for humanity as a whole. They are the self-expression of God's intention for humanity as a kind. Because of the particular relation of humanity and divinity in Jesus the Christ, all future human possibility is moved in the direction of inclusive and pervasive unity, harmony, and right-relation. That is, through Jesus, human existence is moved by God toward a final redemption which is prefigured even now.

These four Christologies have in common their agreement with and appropriation of a core critique of patriarchy as dualistic and pervasive. Second, all insist on the central, constitutive role of human relationality to all theological and ethical formulations. Third, all agree that visions of liberating and redemptive historical possibilities and of future, transhistorical redemption arise in the context of historical struggles for liberation, nurtured by exemplary or paradigmatic figures in both the present and the past. Fourth, all agree on the importance of women's experience as a corrective to patriarchal distortion and as a source for new constructive proposals. That is, these Christologies rely on an interpretation of who Jesus *is* in contemporary feminist experience, emphasizing Jesus' egalitarian relations with others, his identification with the lowest of the low (many of whom are women), his renunciation of any form of domination, his new understanding of service as mutual empowerment, and his trust in God. They also view his death as the consequence of a life of mutuality and justice in a historical situation characterized by systems of domination, and they cast his resurrection as the vindication by God of such a life.

These common analyses and motifs, as well as the differences of approach and emphasis, provide the foundation for a conversational encounter between these two types of Christology. As I indicated in Chapter 3, conversation which is rigorously both mutually appreciative and mutually critical is the appropriate method for feminist theology, with its focus on the relational, diverse, and often conflictual character of human existence. Such conversation recognizes that every position presents some indispensable elements of the truth, but none is possessed of the whole. Different emphases arising from different interpretations of historical circumstances bring to light important principles or insights; but failure to see particularities in a larger context also leads proponents to miss the value of others' insights. Dialogue that brings to light both commonalities and differences in a "feast of contradiction" can yield a richer understanding of Christology in which both commonalities and differences interact generatively.

What, then, might a conversation between these two different approaches to the feminist Christological problem generate?

As I indicated at the close of Chapter 7, Ruether's powerful emphasis on the prophetic and eschatological elements of Christology provides real drive, force, and grounding to the desire and need for liberation and transformation. God/ess' continual shattering of the distortions of human history points toward the regrounding of all in an original generative matrix that continuously transforms history and also moves existence toward a new, as yet only glimpsed fulfillment beyond history. The *kenosis* of patriarchal domination proclaimed and embodied by Jesus is followed by the appearance of the Christ "in the form of our sister," the new humanity which emerges out of the struggle for liberation from domination. This forceful dialectic of denunciation and annunciation moves toward the healing of dualisms and the restoration of polarities and tensions inherent in finite existence.

Ruether's rejoining of criticism and hope and of history and transcendence in dialectic (rather than dualized) relation renders the struggle for authentic human existence realistic, ever filled with conflict, partial resolution, and new vision. Ruether's emphasis on the future as well as the past is particularly helpful to those whose presence and participation have been largely distorted, suppressed, and silenced in records of the past. The possibility and promise of a radically transformed future inspire those burdened not only by the unjust conditions of contemporary existence, but also by the further injustice of having no rooting in a heritage of full humanity. The power of such a future new heaven and new earth is evident in Ruether's own rendering of her vision:

> The scales begin to fall from our eyes, and all around us we see miracles. . . . The harmony is still there, persisting, supporting, forgiving, preserving us in spite of ourselves. . . . To return Home: to learn the harmony, the peace, the justice of body, bodies in right relation to each other. The whence we have come and whither we go, not from alien skies but here, in the community of earth. Holy One, Thy Kingdom come, Thy will be done on earth. . . . [1]

This strong emphasis on the momentarily glimpsed and partially manifest future stands in contrast to the greater emphasis on the present in the Wisdom-Logos approach. The theologies of Wilson-Kastner, Suchocki, and Heyward emphasize the presence in historical existence of elements of creation which are being fulfilled as part of redemption: the present possibilities for wholeness, harmony, and reconciliation among differing elements that retain their diversity; a variety of authentic hopes and promises disclosed in communities and relationships of struggling and justice-making mutuality; the gracious presence of the divine as wisdom and power embracing all existence in every moment and taking it up into a transformed complex harmony. In the fully human life of Jesus, the Christ is manifest as the embodied re-presentation of the divine's ongoing and unbreakable relation with all the exigencies and travails of history. In the Christ, the relation between human and divine which has always been possible is fully present and manifest, transforming the present and making it the locus of the partial realization of a redemption whose fullness is promised in the future.

Yet, as I argued in Chapter 11, this emphasis on the present whose import is understood through a decisively paradigmatic figure from the past risks downplaying the depth and extent of distortion even as it may mask the interruptive power of a God who breaks in unexpectedly from the future. Furthermore, emphasis on a single decisive figure may compromise the importance of the very human relationality which is so central to these Christologies. Here, Ruether's emphasis on the prophetic and apocalyptic stands in corrective tension with the inaugurated eschatologies of Wilson-Kastner, Suchocki, and Heyward. Indeed, Heyward's characteristic emphases on struggle that begins to create a just future, and on paradigmatic figures like Christa who are in crucial ways dissimilar to Jesus, can be taken as a deliberate attempt to make just such a corrective. [2]

At the same time, the emphasis on manifestation and participation with the divine encountered in the present, which is found in the Wisdom-Logos Christologies, serves as a corrective to Ruether's over-emphasis on the humanity of Jesus and the partiality of his embodiment of the new humanity. As I have argued, Ruether's emphasis on the kenotic action of the divine is primarily prophetic: Jesus empties out the power of patriarchy. But he does not "empty out" divinity into full and present self-expression in a human life. In this second sense, the Wisdom-Logos Christologies provide a fuller reconstruction of the idea of kenosis, the self out-pouring or full expression of the divine. For these Christologies emphasize the incarnation of the fullness of divinity as well as humanity in the person, life, death, and resurrection of Jesus. They also--and importantly for feminist theology--empty out any significance to Jesus' maleness; for here he is the decisive re-presentation of the only God who saves, not the self-emptying of a merely patriarchal deity whose repentance of his own domination is revealed by a prophet. That is, for Wilson-Kastner, Suchocki, and Heyward, only in distorted human imaginings is God the tyrannical monarch of Ruether's Prologue to *Sexism and God-Talk*.

For the Wisdom-Logos approach, in the Christ God is fully self-expressing and self-giving, gracing the distorted and downtrodden aspects of subjugated human existence with a full presence which is nevertheless Other. Even the particularities of human existence that have been used to justify domination--such as the maleness of Jesus and his self-sacrificial death for the healing and reconciliation of others--are laden with the creative, transforming love characteristic of the divine. Thus it is not only a prophetic exemplar but also the very presence of God which urges humans not to "Lord it over" one another (in Ruether's paradigmatic phrase). Rather, by active and manifest divine as well as human example, humankind is engaged in "the only liberating relation one can have with God."

But what of the persistent ability of humanity to turn any view of God into an idol, to distort any relation whatsoever into one of domination? If the Christ is the full or complete representation of both divinity and humanity, how is theology to safeguard against the tendency to conceal the propensity for dehumanization and domination which feminism has so carefully unmasked in patriarchal religion? Here, the inaugurated eschatology of the Wisdom-Logos approach needs the powerful corrective of the more apocalyptic view of Ruether, where new revelations of both new humanity and the fullness of divinity lie in the transhistorical future, and where prophetic iconoclastic figures appear time and again to shatter human pretensions. Ruether's prophetic-iconoclastic Christs--Jesus and the expected WomanChrist, for example--deliberately point ahead to yet another one who is to come. And the Spirit who indwells the followers of Christ enables hope for and recognition of that one's in-breaking. All historical manifestations are relativized. Only the divine is absolute, and only beyond history. When no Christ is understood to be the only and final or complete embodiment of both humanity and divinity, both human and divine are set free for fuller expression of the range of possibilities inherent in both, different modes of being.

This brief comparison of the two approaches studied in this book illustrates the necessity of feminist theologies' maintaining a generative tension between them. As Ricoeur and Tracy have demonstrated, the tension between manifestation and proclamation is present throughout the Christian tradition taken as a whole, although individual theologians emphasize one pole over the other. What this present discussion indicates is the necessity of maintaining this tension in contemporary and future constructions in order to address with relative adequacy certain problems that are perennial in Christian thought, and no less pressing on feminist theology than on other contemporary theologies.

The tension between the two approaches is fundamentally dialectic, generating new possibilities. I wish now to sketch one of these possibilities, drawing on the many components of the preceding chapters of this book.

A Constructive Sketch

I am proposing here that a relatively adequate feminist Christology can be elaborated around the core affirmation that for Christians, Jesus is the Christ because he is the manifestation of the transformation of humanity in the struggle to resist dehumanization, *and* he is the definitive re-presentation of only God who saves. [3] In the Christ, redemption of all existence is accomplished in principle, but it will be actualized only fully in the future. Thus, the incarnation of God in Jesus the Christ is simultaneously revelation of what has always been the case, vindication of this enduring if concealed and distorted reality, and promise and prophecy of its greater future fulfillment.

Before elaborating these statements, a brief recapitulation of the criteria for evaluating them is worthwhile. In Chapters 3 and 6, I proposed three criteria under which feminist Christology must strive for adequacy: Christian tradition, contemporary women's experience in the struggle for liberation from domination, and future use in projects of domination and liberation. I argued that feminist theology understands tradition in a broadened sense, including suppressed and marginalized traditions where the experience and participation of women may be disclosed. I further argued that the term "women's experience" might helpfully be understood both as a corrective to patriarchal domination and as a source and norm for constructive formulations. Finally, I argued that, given the depth and extent of the effects of patriarchal domination on thought and practice, accountability to an envisioned liberated future further safeguards against lingering, often hidden elements of androcentrism and misogyny. This safeguard operates through projection of the use of particular approaches, arguments, and formulations in future projects of liberation and domination.[4] The assessment of relative adequacy of my proposal, then, hinges on its ability to meet all three of these criteria in its elaboration of the indispensable Christian affirmation that in Jesus in whom Christians recognize the Christ, the human and the divine are intimately related, and their authentic characters are definitively manifest.

Schubert M. Ogden has persuasively argued that in the Christ, Christians see their own authentic existence as well as the existence of God.[5] That is, in the Christ, what it means to be fully human is decisively disclosed, and movement toward that full humanity is encouraged and enabled. Thus, the revelation of Christ addresses fundamental questions of human existence. For those marginalized and subjugated by systems and structures of domination, questions of the meaning of human existence arise directly and intensely from situations of massive unjust suffering and through pervasive structures and systems whose purpose seems to be not only death but dehumanization. Movement toward and recognition of authentic existence entails not only becoming *fully* human; first and foremost, it involves becoming human at all.

Feminist analyses of the effects on women of being patriarchy's "other" have exposed the multiple ways in which women's formation, function in the world, and sense of self have been distorted, curtailed, and diminished by the pressure to adhere to patriarchal and androcentric norms that construct Woman as deviant from the ideal human. Thus, the movement toward authentic existence for women in patriarchy involves an "option for our women selves"[6] or a conversion to the female self, what Ruether has called "the resurrection of the authentic self"[7] or the emergence of full humanity in and for women.

In Chapter 4, I argued that the problem of the patriarchal distortions of women's experience can be addressed effectively by developing a relational description of human experience. On this view, human consciousness is constructed by the interaction of the multiple factors--inherited and current--which make up human existence, and which are interpreted and appropriated by the human subject through linguistic, symbolic, and traditional structures that mediate the subject's engagement with these elements. The subject's agency within her situation reconstructs both the situation itself and her consciousness of it. Consciousness, that is, is "a process . . . , a particular configuration of subjectivity, . . . produced at the intersection of meaning with experience."[8] Therefore, when either meaning or experience changes--as both do with changes in their constituent parts--consciousness itself changes. Specifically feminist meaning or experience breaks the silences and suppressions that are a consequence of patriarchy, affecting tradition and contemporary experience alike. This breakage transformatively allows a mending or reconstruction of meaning, experience, and consciousness.

This breaking and reconstructing is properly understood as an act of resistance, that is, of the maintenance and re-creation of humanity in the midst of massive and pervasive dehumanization. In the struggle against the fragmentation, distortion, and domination that characterize much of human existence, human persons may be forced or coercively persuaded to participate in and collude with what distorts and limits their existence. Nevertheless, they may know both that they are unnecessarily afflicted[9] and that they have the capacity to participate in the alleviation of their affliction and the transformation of its causes. The dehumanized are also able to participate in the creation of more humane possibilities for themselves and/or others.[10]

When understood from the perspective of the victims of dehumanization who were and are also agents of mending, resistance is seen as part of a dialectical movement from domination to transformation. It is this movement which discloses authentic human existence. In such circumstances, the question of the authenticity of existence under subjugation is answered by the experience of resistance, wherein the maintenance of a shred of humanity transformatively moves the human person toward the recreation of full humanity. The fact that some--indeed, perhaps many--are unable to resist force or coercion renders acts of resistance more valuable, in that they open up possibilities for others and provide a "dangerous memory" that helps continue the process of mending and transformation.

Resistance to dehumanization thus discloses and develops previously unrecognized aspects of human being in history, and generates hope for further transformation, not only for the resisting victims, but also for those who remember them. Through resistance, thought and practice that are ruptured by the effects of domination are mended. Thus, resistance and reflection on it reconstitute human being as such, even in the midst of massive unjust suffering. Further, as resistance mends and motivates the human capacity to engage the very conditions of existence, resistance reveals anew the connection of human being to ongoing history and the transcendence toward which humanity strives.

Resistance, then, is one of the elements that constitutes human being itself. The phenomenon of resistance as I have developed it also reconnects existence with transcendence, in that it is the victims' sense that they are "under orders to live" that spurs them to confront the powers that would destroy them.[11] These "orders" spring from human subjectivity itself; but they also manifest an Other who is present and who draws near to those who claim their humanity even in the face of death-dealing domination.[12] The experiential conviction that "my Redeemer lives, and in my flesh I shall see God,"[13] that "God knew what it was like to be a woman who was raped,"[14] that victims are "under orders to live"--this conviction witnesses powerfully to the unbreakable relation between humanity and the divine, a relation whose continuation is desired and sought on both sides. For when a shred of humanity is maintained and mending becomes possible, what is disclosed is the resistance of divinity itself to ruptures of the connection between history and transcendence--ruptures that are consequences of domination.[15]

For Christians, the resistance of both humanity and divinity to domination is decisively manifest and recognized in Jesus the Christ. In Christ, Christians find the dialectic movement from domination through resistance to transformation both vindicated in history and connected directly with the existence of God. Taken as a unity, Jesus Christ's life of active and transformative identification with the marginalized, his consequent death, and the vindication of his life and death manifested in the resurrection together reveal the possibilities of similar life for other persons, and vindicates its historical actualities. [16]

Jesus lived in a time of concrete anticipation of the Reign of God. His own "lively expectation of the coming of God's kingdom" as an historical era of peace and justice [17] was built on the expectations of renewed relation with God held by the many messianic groups in Roman-dominated Palestine. But Jesus' vision diverged from these views in its emphasis on the Reign of God as already manifest in the midst of human struggles for personal and social survival, wholeness, and healing. [18] In words and deeds, Jesus proclaimed God's Reign as a Jubilee, the "conquest of human historical evil; the setting up of proper conditions of human life with God and one another here on earth within the limits of mortal existence." [19] Jesus refused to portray himself as the Messiah, and he directed attention toward God as the source of healing and vision now, and of fulfillment in the future. [20]

In his own relations with those around him, Jesus directed his attention to relations of domination and subjugation, resisting the dehumanizing actuality of these relations by living a life characterized by mutual regard and cooperation. He included the most despised and marginalized in his circle of friends and followers, giving and receiving healing, service, and instruction in these relations and affirming "the daily interdependence of existence" [21] and the necessity of response to the just claims of others. [22] His intimate and immediate engagement with others empowered them to heal and free themselves, and thereby to enter more fully into the human community and into their own humanity.

Jesus addressed the roots of systems of domination by providing the downtrodden with an example of resistance to and transformation of hierarchical power into mutual cooperation. He thereby worked against that internalization of power which leads to reversal of unjust relations rather than to their transformation.[23] His lifting up of the lowest and their social roles as exemplary models proclaims a radical redefinition of leadership as mutual service, in which none are masters and all serve each other.[24] Jesus also relentlessly criticized "the love of prestige, power and wealth that causes people to seek domination and lord it over each other,"[25] and encouraged those in positions of power and wealth to renounce their privileges for the benefit of the poor and marginalized.[26]

In his inclusive interactions with others, Jesus challenged even those whose lives and choices were severely limited by socio-historical circumstances to risk engagement, resistance, and transformation. Jesus' own engagement with both the dominant and the marginalized appealed to humanity's goodness, thereby affirming that that goodness is more essential than sin. This affirmation, even in the midst of dehumanization, encourages the desire for redemption, and encourages confidence in the presence of God's redemptive power.[27]

Jesus' life, then, manifests and proclaims the actuality and possibility of authentic humanity that engages the conditions of human existence and actively and effectively resists their dehumanizing elements at individual and social-systemic levels. Jesus also embodied the healing of humanity through transformation of existing circumstances, thereby bringing into being a new consciousness of the power of mutual cooperation to overcome dehumanization and unjust suffering. In himself, Jesus embodied the possibility and actuality of the new, thereby changing the experience of those around him. This embodiment also provides both the hope and the reassurance needed by others in order to follow his example.[28] Therefore, Jesus' advocacy and embodiment of the transformative reversal of prevailing social roles opens up further possibilities for the inbreaking of God's reign in the context of human existence. Thus, Jesus' life vindicates and re-presents the fullness of authentic humanity.

This vindication and re-presentation manifest the presence and power of God in human life. The transformative qualities of Jesus' relations with others reveal that God is love made evident in justice.[29] That this love heals and raises up the lowly is shown in Jesus' embrace of the marginalized, which manifests God's presence with the suffering and the dominated in their struggle for survival. Jesus' involvement in liberating relations with the dehumanized reveals God's transformative power toward human fulfillment.[30]

The mutually cooperative qualities of Jesus' relations with others reveal God's continuously creative responsiveness in "eternal openness" to creation.[31] Jesus' willingness to meet the desires and needs of others with challenging or comforting words, healing connection, and empowering actions manifests God's wise and provident engagement with the vagaries and happenstances of human existence.[32] Jesus' teachings, particularly in the parables, proclaim the involvement of God in the ordinary as creative source, sustaining energy, and transforming power. Thus, Jesus manifests "the only liberating relationship a person can have with God."[33]

God's love is also manifest as judgment in Jesus' call to repentance and to the renunciation of the privileges of power and wealth embedded in systems of domination.[34] Jesus' resistance to the exercise of authority for its own sake, in both social and religious arenas, manifests God's freedom and power to break through human pretensions and destroy human idols in order to make all things new. Jesus' resistance also reveals divine power as self-giving rather than domination. Thus, Jesus' life manifests the nature and presence of the only God who sets us free.[35]

Jesus' incarnation of the divine--his "personification of God's own self in creative and saving involvement with the world"[36]-- reveals the divine as self-expressive and self-giving, coming into creation in the multiple forms of love, wisdom,[37] and just power. God's love can be seen to be the self-expression of God's being, which is inherently relational and so directed outward.[38]

The Word does not call creation into being in order to rule over a subservient reality forced to do deeds for God's benefit. The divine Word speaks in order that a reality--a potentiality--that is already contained within God may be brought to actuality. [39]

The self-expression of God in Jesus extends this creativity, revealing what God has been doing from the beginning. [40] In this way, Jesus manifests and reveals the only God there is. [41]

The meaning of Jesus' life is confirmed in his death and vindicated in his resurrection. Jesus' own suffering and death are the outcome of a just life lived in resistance to an unjust world. They are a pouring out of self for the sake of others, consistent with the model of serving leadership given in his life. In voluntarily continuing on a course which would likely lead to disaster, Jesus remained faithful to the marginalized in whose company he lived and taught, and to his prophetic and iconoclastic vision of God's Reign. In suffering an ignominious and agonizing death, Jesus maintained his solidarity with the suffering and with victims of domination.

Jesus' suffering and death also reveal the nature of God as one who feels every sin, every pain, and who transforms them. [42] God suffers as other existents suffer; "God feels the effects directly, both as given and received. . . . God continues to love in *God's* pain." [43] God's presence in human suffering is always fully copresent, mutual, and participatory. Jesus' death shows that God is a power that can be broken as relations are broken and the power of God is destroyed in the world. [44] Jesus thus re-presents the God who is relentlessly present in the midst of human tragedy.

Jesus' resurrection proclaims that death is not the final word about human existence and God's transforming involvement with it. As Jesus' death is continuous with his life, his resurrection both confirms his life and transforms it. [45] In the resurrection, humanity is shown to be transformed, for the risen Jesus

is *the* new human, the bearer in his own person of a humanity become what it truly should be, delivered from the seeds of its own destructiveness which it has nurtured and cherished.

In Christ we are returned to God and ourselves, and begin the
active process of returning to God in all areas of our lives. [46]

The resurrected Christ reveals redeemed humanity free of
fragmentation, and part of the whole of creation rather than
alienated from and destructive toward it. [47]   At the same time,
in the resurrection, God definitively resists and overcomes the
evil consequences of sin, and promises that this mending will be
extended to the entire cosmos. The resurrection of Jesus reveals
the power of God's love to be as strong as death.

Jesus' death and resurrection work a transformation in his
followers. They become more intensely aware that their own
"actions in accordance with love and justice are in conformity
with the direction of the universe." [48] Mutual cooperation and
service among human persons, resistance to domination, and
struggle for transformation are validated or vindicated, and their
meaning and import are definitively located as part of ultimate
reality. Through Jesus' death and resurrection, human self-
constitution is therefore changed. [49]

Jesus embodies and begins a new order; but he does not
complete it. As Suchocki puts it, Jesus' life "is the life which
reveals the nature of God for us; this is the life which offers a
concrete vision of the reality to which God calls us; this is the
revelation of God to us for the sake of conforming us to that
divine image." [50] Jesus shows us "ourselves as we are meant to
be." [51] That is, Jesus manifests the very constitution of human
being as always related to the divine. Those who follow Jesus
are called to embrace and actualize this reality in lives of
resistance, liberation, and transformation. Such lives also
manifest "God's activity in conjunction, partnership, friendship
with humanity." [52] That is, they manifest "Christ in the form
of our sister" and brother. [53] The concrete reality of the Reign
of God is always emergent, as new possibilities emerge in human
existence, and as human experience and consciousness respond
to these possibilities. Thus, Jesus' life, death, resurrection, and
experienced presence in the lives of his followers disclose "the
paradoxical power of an always-already Love who is the final

reality who even now, even here touches our always-already, not-yet humanity." [54]

For Christians, then, Jesus is the Christ in that he is the decisive re-presentation of authentic humanity and the personification in history of the divine self. In Biblical and traditional terms, Jesus is both Wisdom and Logos, the self-outpouring of the divine in human reality. As such, he prophetically and eschatologically embodies the movement of creation toward the divine, and the divine movement toward creation. That is, Jesus' manifestation of the liberating and saving relation between humanity and divinity is also a proclamation of the future into which creation is being moved by divine initiative and human response. Through Jesus the Christ, Christians recognize their own authentic existence in relation to God, and so are encouraged to see themselves and others as continuously re-created in the form of the Christ. Yet, under the finite conditions of historical existence, the fullness of that re-creation always lies ahead, in the promised future in which God reigns in a new and renewed creation of harmony, peace, and justice.

I have sketched a Christology that shows a clear preference for the Wisdom-Logos strand of Christian tradition, but that emphasizes resistance to domination on the part of both humanity and divinity in order to maintain the necessary tension between elements of manifestation (characteristic of the Wisdom-Logos strand) and the emphasis on proclamation which characterizes the prophetic and eschatological approach. I wish to emphasize that this is a preliminary sketch only. A fully developed proposal must await further study in a number of areas. Here, I have yet to draw on Biblical and historical research; to do so would both modify and expand the sketch I have presented. Nor have I set this proposal fully in the context of other discussions of Christology by revisionist and liberation theologians. Both these avenues must be pursued before the proposal I have offered can be fully subjected to evaluation on the criteria of adequacy which I have proposed. However, I would hypothesize that the beginning formulation I have offered here as the product of a conversation between contemporary white feminist theologians is constructed from elements which in principle meet those criteria. I will conclude this work with a brief examination of one other area of emerging Christological formulation in order both to begin to broaden the conversation and to provide a brief test of the adequacy of my proposal at this stage of its development.

Broadening the Conversation: Womanist Christologies

The intent of white feminist theory and practice has been the liberation of all women into full humanity. However, in reality, that intent has been distorted and limited by white feminists' historical[55] and ongoing failure to engage systematically the interstructuring of race and class with gender upon which much feminist theory insists.[56] That is, white feminist theologians have ignored the differences difference makes in the experience of Black and white women. Grant, for example, notes that

> Slavery and segregation have created such a gulf between these women, that White feminists' common assumption that all women are in the same situation with respect to sexism is difficult to understand when history so clearly tells us a different story.[57]

In theology, white feminists have formally defined patriarchy as a "pyramidal system and hierarchal structure of society in which women's oppression is specified . . . in terms of race and class . . . ."[58] But white feminists' studies have often focused primarily if not exclusively on the struggle against male domination. In Christology, this has led to a focus on the maleness of Jesus and whether or not a male savior can save women. Yet, as Jacquelyn Grant argues, this focus does not take into account the liberation concerns of African-American women, who face subjugation not only on the basis of gender, but also on the basis of race and class.[59] In this sense, white feminist theology is not only ethnocentric, but also racist: it has presumed both to speak for all women while listening only to the experience of white women; and it has sought to define the rules and agenda for the struggle against sexism in a way which both ignores and suppresses the just claims of women of color and perpetuates the racist orientation of the dominant culture. [60]

African-American womanist theologians have recognized and criticized the generally tacit racism of much white feminist theology in the course of articulating theology from their perspective of double and often triple jeopardy within systems of domination. [61] If white feminist theology is to maintain its commitment to the full humanity of all women, the voices of womanist theologians must be heard and heeded. [62]

In emerging womanist thought, [63] three theologians--Delores S. Williams, Jacquelyn Grant, and Kelly D. Brown--have formally and publicly engaged Christology. Their work is still in preliminary form, entailing critical studies of white feminist and African-American male theological constructions as one element of the context from which womanist Christologies are emerging. Yet it must be emphasized that the womanist critique is most directly shaped by African-American women's historical and contemporary experience of Jesus as the Christ; and it is this experience which prompts the womanist critique of the formulations of those who claim to base their Christologies in women's or African-American experience. [64] In this concluding section, I will briefly examine the preliminary proposals of these womanist theologians.

Delores S. Williams follows Alice Walker's use of the term *womanist* in outlining the sources and tasks of womanist theology. [65] The concept "womanist" describes African-American women's "affirm[ation of] themselves as *black* while simultaneously owning their connection with feminism and with the Afro-American community, male and female." [66] Womanist theology draws on cultural codes that are "female-centered and . . . [that] point beyond themselves to conditions, events, meanings, and values that have crystallized in the Afro-American community *around women's activity* and formed traditions" such as mother-daughter advice, hospitality, and nurturance. [67]

> These cultural codes and their corresponding traditions are valuable resources for indicating and validating the kind of

data upon which womanist theologians can reflect as they bring black women's social, religious, and cultural experience into the discourse of theology, ethics, biblical and religious studies.[68]

Along with feminist theological hermeneutics of suspicion, retrieval, and reconstruction, these cultural codes and traditions form an interpretive framework through which such sources as Scripture,[69] "female slave narratives, imaginative literature by black women, autobiographies, the work by black women in academic disciplines, and the testimonies of black church women"[70] are appropriated by womanist theologians. Womanist theology also uses this framework to draw on black theologies and the theologies of other suppressed and marginalized groups.[71]

Williams identifies two religious traditions within the African-American Church. One (articulated by James Cone, Gayraud Wilmore, and other black male theologians) focuses on liberation. Here, men have the authoritative roles in liberation struggles. The normative principle is the liberating activity of God in Jesus Christ; and liberation provides the interpretive principle through which all traditions are understood. Williams argues that the Biblical paradigm of the Exodus--so central for black male liberation theology--ignores crucial aspects of African-American women's experience: sexual exploitation, surrogacy, homelessness, and the conflicts between women and men and between women and women.[72] In other words, as Kelly Brown has written, "although Black [male] theologians claimed to write from the vantage point of the total Black experience, Black women were 'invisible' in Black theology."[73]

For example, in her study of the symbol of the Black Christ which emerged in the context of the Civil Rights and Black Power movements of the 1960's, Brown judges that none of the three interpretations of the Black Christ

spoke to the multi-dimensionality of the Black community's oppression. They imaged Christ in such a way that ignored the historical and personal experiences of more than half of the Black community--Black women. None of the three interpretations of the Black Christ as liberator of the oppressed seemed to be even remotely aware that Black women suffer not only under the yoke of racial oppression but also gender exploitation. [74]

Brown believes that the particular, multidimensional oppression of African-American women has not been taken into account by black theology for complex historical and cultural reasons.[75] First, the ideological structure of racism means that African-American men have historically been oppressed in their particularity as *men*.[76] Black theology therefore has been appropriately concerned with the reconstruction of African-American manhood. Second, the African-American community--men and women alike--have internalized sexist values; and these values have been reflected in African-American struggles against racism as well as in the Black Church. [77]

> Whereas the symbol [of the Black Christ] was adequate for disclosing the *particularity* of Christ's liberating ministry as it related to the Black community, it was not adequate for disclosing the *universality* of Christ's liberating ministry *within* the Black particularity. . . . it addressed Black people's experience in a White racist society, but it failed to address Black people's experiences within the Black community. [78]

Williams identifies a second strand of religious tradition in the black church, a strand that is woman-centered, and that focuses on women's struggle for survival and quality of life for themselves, their children, and their community. [79] The experiences of African-American women are appropriately thematized using the Biblical image of wilderness. In this strand, the story of Hagar is central, both in the present experience of African-American women and throughout the history of African-American Christianity. [80]

Williams' use of a wilderness model illuminates four issues in African-American culture: survival and quality of life; motherhood and social processes; [81] surrogacy; and homelessness and other economic realities. For Williams, it is surrogacy that particularly thematizes the experience of African-American women. Defining surrogacy as standing in the place of someone else, and doing what someone else is supposed to do, Williams describes the various forced and coerced surrogacy roles which African-American women have been expected to fill. Williams emphasizes that African-American women were at times able to use these roles for the benefit of their own communities and well-being. But surrogacy has also contributed to African-American women's subjugation in sexist and racist culture. [82]

For Williams, the figure of Hagar provides a paradigm that draws on the experience of surrogacy and suggests its ambiguities and its potential for transformation. Hagar discovers and draws on resources in herself for her survival and that of her child; and her use of these resources moves her toward liberation. But, in contrast to the liberation theology of African-American male theologians, the emphasis here is on Hagar's initiative, rather than on the intercession of God. And--as even the brief discussion of this section makes clear--in contrast to the white feminist liberation paradigm, the womanist model emphasizes survival as well as freedom.

Given African-American women's experience of multi-dimensional struggle against sexism, racism, and classism, with its concrete manifestations in poverty, coerced surrogacy, and threat to survival, how might womanist theology reconstruct Christology?

Jacquelyn Grant provides a sketch for womanist Christology by beginning from the concrete historical and contemporary experience of African-American women in church and society. Grant's womanist approach views Scripture through the interpretive lens of experience, employing a hermeneutics of suspicion and retrieval. Constructively, she describes Jesus as the co-sufferer whose persecution and crucifixion resemble in their severity the persecutions and crucifixions of African-American women, who are the lowest of the low in a patriarchal system in which gender, race, and class are inter-related. [83] Jesus is the one who empowers the weak in their struggles for survival and dignity. [84] This Jesus means freedom from concrete oppression. That is, the Christ is a political messiah, one who identifies with the lowly of his own and of any day, and one whose "resurrection brings the hope that liberation from oppression is immanent." [85] Grant argues that this womanist vision of Christ is one of true universality, in that it encompasses, affirms, and transforms the existence of the least, and thereby moves all humanity toward wholeness. [86]

Following Grant's analysis, Kelly Brown notes that "the tri-dimensional oppression of sexism, racism and classism" faced by African-American women means that "A womanist understanding of Christ is more than a combination of the Black Christ and the 'feminist' Christ." [87] Brown proposes that womanist Christology must "confront the interpretations of Jesus which have aided and abetted the oppression of Black women, and affirm Black women's faith that Jesus has identified with them in their struggles to be free." [88]

That is, Brown argues, womanist Christologies must critically confront the concrete ways in which the proclivity of the Black Church to equate the male Jesus with God has prevented Black Christian women from "see[ing] themselves in Christ and Christ in themselves." [89] Emphasis on the maleness of Jesus has also contributed to the continued refusal of some branches of the Black Church to ordain women, and to ongoing emphasis on female submission in both church and home. [90] Therefore, for womanist Christology as for white feminist Christology, "the relationship between the biological [and other historical] particularities of the historical Jesus and the universal qualities of the Christ of faith" must be engaged and reconstructed on the basis of women's experience--here, specifically Black women's experience. [91]

Constructively, womanist Christologies "must affirm Black women's faith that Jesus supports them in their struggles to survive and be free." [92] Jacquelyn Grant argues that this affirmation can build on the "egalitarian Christology" which affirms the wholeness of Christ, who "died for the woman as well as the man" and so is "a whole Saviour [not] a half Saviour." [93] Brown argues that these two constructive components may combine in a liberation approach, which "will stress that God did become incarnate in Jesus, but the significance of the incarnation is not found in what Jesus looked

like. Rather it is found in Jesus' ministry to the oppressed.[94]
This liberation approach shifts identification of Christ from
"inextricable connection" to the historical Jesus, to "inextricable
identification"

> with those engaged in concrete activity to sustain and liberate
> the socially oppressed. The essential characteristic of Christ
> is that he/she is identified with a particular suffering
> community in its struggle to survive and be free. . . . Jesus
> does not have exclusive claims on being God incarnate, on
> being the Christ. Christ is only exclusive to those engaged in
> concrete efforts to sustain and liberate historically oppressed
> peoples.[95]

Such a Christ is present in multidimensional, but not single-
dimensional, struggles against racism, sexism, and classism.
Further, this Christ becomes present through the struggles of
particular communities for survival and freedom in which the
oppressed seek Christ, in the compelling faith that Christ is "a
sustainer and liberator of the oppressed." [96]

In her constructive work toward a womanist Christology,
Delores Williams argues that Jesus is, for Christians, the
ultimate surrogate figure, and through him surrogacy takes on a
sacred aura. But, Williams argues, womanist theologians must
critically examine the surrogacy aspects of traditional doctrines
of redemption to discover whether the image of a surrogate God
can be salvific for African-American women, or if it does not
instead reinforce the acceptance of the exploitation that
surrogacy brings. Related questions include the role of God the
Father in determining the redemptive character of the surrogacy
role; the question of whether Jesus' surrogacy was coerced by
God the Father; and the place of the cross, which, in the Black
Church, may be a powerful symbol of the raising up of
abandoned men. [97]

Williams sketches a proposal for reconstructing Christology so
that it addresses the profound ambiguity of surrogacy in the
experience of African-American women. Williams suggests that,
rather than coming to die (as some traditional views of
atonement suggest), God comes into the world to model the

perfect form of a life of mutual relation, which humankind has not seen before. Redemption, on this model, is participation in this model of life. The cross may be part of this life, but is not central to it. Williams' shift from a Christology of the Cross to one of the Incarnation, as I understand it, attempts to recover the positive elements of surrogacy--self-giving for the sake of the community on a model of mutuality--while eliminating the negative elements of overt and covert coercion, exploitation, and degradation.[98]

These preliminary statements of a womanist approach to Christology have in common their emphasis on the importance of survival as well as of freedom or liberation. They view Jesus as the fellow sufferer who lived and died in identification with the lowest of the low, who, in this time and place, are African-American women burdened by sexism, racism, and classism. Jesus' resurrection vindicates the suffering of "the least," and is a compelling source of hope in concrete struggle. These emerging womanist Christologies are also strongly incarnational. That is, Jesus is the incarnation of God (not merely a proclaimer of God) who, in his identification with the least, manifests God's presence and liberating and saving activity. Jesus means freedom; and God is the ultimate provider of the freedom Jesus represents.

There are a number of clear affinities with the white feminist Christologies which I have studied in this book, and with the constructive proposal I have begun to develop. Both womanist and white feminist Christologies have a liberation bent: the freedom which Jesus the Christ means is found in concrete form in history, and comes into being in the course of human struggle against structures of domination. Like Wilson-Kastner (and with similarities to Suchocki), Grant emphasizes Jesus' whole humanity as representative of the wholeness of humankind. But, unlike Wilson-Kastner and Suchocki, Grant focuses constantly on Jesus' concrete particularity, and especially on his identification with the poor.[99] Like Ruether, Grant and Brown address the significance of the interstructuring of gender, race, and class oppression; but, unlike Ruether, they consistently attend to matters of race and class. Like Heyward, Williams emphasizes the ambiguity of historical experience and the importance of human initiative and mutuality. But more consistently than Heyward, Williams acknowledges the ambiguities of all relations. Like Wilson-Kastner, Suchocki, Heyward, and myself, Grant, Brown, and Williams have all identified Jesus as the Christ because of his manifestation of the liberating God. But the three womanist theologians connect this manifestation more directly with the presence of God in ongoing suffering. I have thematized women's experience under the rubric of resistance as the maintenance of a shred of humanity in situations of massive dehumanization. Grant, Brown, and Williams render resistance more comprehensively through the endurance of African-American women in centuries-long situations of many degrees and nuances of dehumanization.

These affinities and differences in womanist and white feminist Christologies provide the ground upon which a rich conversation has already begun. The recent (and often yet-unpublished) work of Heyward, Thistlethwaite, Cannon, Williams, and others demonstrates some of the generative potential of this conversation. But there remains much room for expansion of dialogue. For example, the increasingly comprehensive and complex examination of the ambiguities of Scripture and tradition found in white feminist theologies has yet to emerge in womanist theology; and from such emergence womanist theology stands to benefit. On the other hand, the womanist critique of white feminists' ignoring of the importance of race and class in the criticism and construction of experience and theology has much to teach white feminist thought. Through this conversation, as well as the individual constructive proposals that foster it, together womanist and white feminist theologies testify that, via the Christ as manifestation of authentic humanity and present divinity, Christian women may yet discover that "humanity has been a holy thing, though each [one] felt [herself] to be unholy. . . . In Him it is proved that [humanity] is meant to have [our] dwelling with God." [100]

Notes

1.   Reuther, *Sexism and God-Talk*, 266.
2.   See, for example, *Speaking of Christ*, 22; *Touching Our Strength*, 114f., 116-118; *Redemption of God*, 33 and passim; *Our Passion for Justice*, passim.
3.   My use of the phrase "for Christians" and "definitive" as qualifiers is a deliberate safeguard against the tendency toward the supersessionism often found and correctly criticized in Wisdom-Logos Christologies. See, for example, Baum's Introduction to Ruether's *Faith and Fratricide*.
4.   It is worth noting that this criterion has an ethical dimension in holding the theologian accountable for the likely use of her own work. This dimension is consistent with the oft-articulated feminist commitment to engaged scholarship, that is, scholarship which serves the liberation of the marginalized, rather than assuming distance from concrete praxis.
5.   Ogden, *The Point of Christology*, passim.
6.   Schüssler Fiorenza, *Bread Not Stone*, xv. See also the work of Carol Gilligan, and other works cited in Chapter 4.
7.   *Sexism and God-Talk*, 71.
8.   de Lauretis, "Feminist Studies/Critical Studies," 8.
9.   In distinction to pain, Dorothee Soelle defines affliction as involving physical, psychological, and social suffering. With Simone Weil, Soelle contends that "'There is not really affliction unless there is social degradation or the fear of it in some form or another.' The degradation shows itself in the isolation that accompanies affliction." (Dorothee Soelle, *Suffering*, trans. Everett R. Kalin [Philadelphia: Fortress Press, 1975], 13-14. The internal quote is from Simone Weil, "The Love of God and Affliction," *Waiting for God*, trans. Emma Craufurd with an introduction by Leslie A. Fiedler [New York: G. P. Putnam's Sons, 1951], 119.)
10.   In the future, I hope to do more work on the concrete aspects of the development of consciousness, attending in particular to how participation and nonparticipation in oppressive structures shape reflection and action. The problem of collusion is, I believe, a pressing but difficult one: theological interpretations of victims' involvements with the systems that contribute to their dehumanization must always make a way between "blaming the victim" and perpetuating dehumanization by denying victims the capacity for responsibility. As I have indicated in Part II, I find the work of Emil

Fackenheim and of numerous historians of African-American and women's history helpful and suggestive.

11. Fackenheim, 217 and passim; quoted and discussed in Chapter 5.

12. See my discussion of Maurice's interpretation of Job in Chapter 6: Job's resistance to his friends' understanding of his situation drives him to the conviction that his redeemer lives and will be present to him in the flesh.

13. Job 19:25.

14. Ruether, "The Future of Feminist Theology in the Academy," 710-711.

15. Recall my discussion of Fackenheim in Chapter 5.

16. In this paragraph and those that follow, I am relying on the Biblical studies of Schüssler Fiorenza, Ruether, Heyward, and Suchocki. I take this work to be trustworthy in light of studies in sociological, redactional, and rhetorical criticism, such as Gerd Theissen, *Sociology of Early Palestinian Christianity*, trans. John Bowden (Philadelphia: Fortress, 1978); Burton L. Mack, "All the Extra Jesuses: Christian Origins in the Light of the Extra-Canonical Gospels," in *Semeia* 49 (1990): 169-176; George W. E. Nikelsburg, "The Genre and Function of the Markan Passion Narrative," in *Harvard Theological Review* 73 no. 1-2 (1980): 153-184; and Mary Rose D'Angelo, "Women in Luke-Acts: A Redactional View," in *Journal of Biblical Literature* 109 no. 3 (1990): 441-461. For a more traditional historical-critical study of "the earliest witness," see Willi Marxsen, "Christology in the New Testament," in *Interpreters Dictionary of the Bible: Supplementary Volume* (Nashville: Abingdon, 1976), 146-156; and idem, *The Beginnings of Christology*, trans. Paul J. Achtemeir and Lorenz Nieting (Philadelphia: Fortress, 1979). I am grateful to Dr. Elizabeth Waller for her continuing assistance in Biblical studies. The fuller elaboration of my proposal will of course entail further Biblical research.

17. Ruether, *Faith and Fratricide*, 248. Cf. Heyward, Suchocki.

18. Cf. Suchocki, *God-Christ-Church* 1982, 96-98; cf. 1989, 92-95.

19. Ruether, *To Change the World* 14-15; idem, *Sexism and God-Talk*. Cf. Heyward, *Redemption of God*, 42, 54-57, and passim. See Luke 4:18-19.

20. Heyward, *Redemption of God*, 49, 202.

21. *God-Christ-Church* 1982, 98; cf. 1989, 101.

22. See Mark 5:25-34 and 7:25-30.

23. Hence the importance of Ruether's central Gospel passage: "But Jesus called them to him and said, "You know that the rulers of the Gentiles lord it over them, and their great ones are tyrants over them. It shall not be so among you; but whoever would be great among you must be your servant, and whoever wishes to be first among you must be your slave; just as the Son of Man came not to be served but to serve, and to give his life a ransom for many." (Mt. 20:25-28, NRSV)

24. "By becoming servant of God, one becomes freed of all bondage to human masters. Only then, as a liberated person, can one truly become 'servant of all,' giving one's life to liberate others rather than to exercise power and rule over them." (Ruether, *Sexism and God-Talk*, 121.)

25. Reuther, *To Change the World*, 15; Idem, *New Woman/New Earth*, 64f. Cf. Matt 20:25-27.

26. See, for example, Matthew 19:16-30.

27. Wilson-Kastner, Suchocki, Heyward; cf. Maurice on Job, discussed in Chapter 6.

28. *God-Christ-Church* 1982, 100-101; cf. 1989, 97.

29. Heyward, *Redemption of God*, 39 and passim.

30. On the importance of survival and fulfillment for the oppressed, see the works of the womanist theologians discussed in the final section of this chapter.

31. Wilson-Kastner, *Faith, Feminism, and the Christ*, 95.

32. Suchocki, "God as Wisdom," Chapter 7 of *God-Christ-Church*.

33. Heyward, *Redemption of God*, 200. Cf. Schubert M. Ogden, *The Point of Christology*, 122f.

34. Cf. Heyward and Suchocki, passim.

35. Ogden, *The Point of Christology*, 127ff.

36. I.e., Jesus as Wisdom incarnate. See Elizabeth A. Johnson, "Jesus, the Wisdom of God: A Biblical Basis for Non-Androcentric Christology," *Ephemerides Theologicae Lovanienses* LXI no. 4 (Dec. 1985): 272.

37. On God's wisdom, see Suchocki, *God-Christ-Church*, Chapter 7, "God as Wisdom." See also Johnson, *op. cit.*; and Adela Yarbro Collins, "New Testament Perspectives: The Gospel of John," *Journal for the Study of the Old Testament*, Issue 22 (Feb. 1982): 47-53.

38.　Cf. Ogden on God's boundless love (*Point of Christology*, 118f); Ruether's emphasis on God's *kenosis*; and Heyward's, Wilson-Kastner's, and Suchocki's explicit statements to this effect.

39.　Wilson-Kastner, *Faith, Feminism, and the Christ*, 95.

40.　This construal is consistent with the Hebrew word *dabar*, usually translated *word*, which signifies "to drive, to get behind and push." See John L. McKenzie, S. J., "The Word of God in the Old Testament," *Theological Studies* no. 2 (June 1960): 191. Adela Yarbro Collins notes that, in the Gospel of John, "The Logos includes more than the person, life and teachings of Jesus. It is an order and a power in all reality. The implication is that God may be known through the Logos even apart from Jesus." (Collins, 49-50)

41.　Ogden, *The Point of Christology*, passim.

42.　*God-Christ-Church* 1982, 105-109; cf. 1989, 105-110. "The cross is the crowning manifestation of love in the life of Jesus."

43.　*God-Christ-Church* 1982, 109-110, italics in the original; cf. 1989, 109-110.

44.　*Redemption of God*, 56.

45.　*God-Christ-Church* 1982, 112; cf. 1989, 112.

46.　Wilson-Kastner, *Faith, Feminism, and the Christ*, 109. Note that while Jesus lives *a* (particular) human life (*Ibid.*, 90), as the Christ he is also *the* new human. That is, the ideal can be--must be-- expressed in the particular.

47.　Wilson-Kastner, *Faith, Feminism, and the Christ*, 111.

48.　*God-Christ-Church* 1982, 102; cf. 1989, 98.

49.　*God-Christ-Church* 1982, 120; cf. 1989, 124.

50.　*God-Christ-Church* 1982, 101; cf. 1989, 98.

51.　*Our Passion for Justice*, 17.

52.　*Our Passion for Justice*, 178.

53.　Ruether, *Sexism and God-Talk*,

54.　Tracy, *Analogical Imagination*, 332.

55.　See, for example, the critiques by Bell Hooks in *Ain't I a Woman?* and *Feminist Theory: From Margin to Center*; Angela Y. Davis, *Women, Race and Class*; Barbara Hilkert Andolsen, *Daughters of Jefferson, Daughters of Bootblacks: Racism and American Feminism*; Elizabeth Fox-Genovese, *Within the Plantation Household: Black and White Women of the Old South*; and Susan Brooks Thistlethwaite, *Sex, Race, and God*.

56.　See, for example, Ruether's discussion in Chapter 5 of *New Woman/New Earth*, "Between the Sons of White and the Sons of Blackness: Racism and Sexism in America."

57. Grant, *White Woman's Christ, Black Woman's Jesus*, 195-196. As Ruether writes in *New Heaven/New Earth*, "In a real sense, any women's movement which is *only* concerned *about sexism and no other form of oppression, must remain a women's movement of the white upper class, for it is* only this group of women whose *only* problem is the problem of being women, since, in every other way, they belong to the ruling class." (125)

58. Schüssler Fiorenza, *Bread Not Stone*, 5.

59. Grant, *White Woman's Christ, Black Woman's Jesus*, 209-210.

60. Following Brenda Eichleberger, Grant identifies five racist components in white feminism: neglect of class issues, resulting in an emphasis on fulfillment rather than on survival; stereotypical negative imagery of Black women; lack of knowledge about Black women's existence; co-optation of women of color to serve a white agenda; and neglect of the importance of family life in suppressed communities. (Grant, *White Woman's Christ, Black Woman's Jesus*, 200-201.) Susan Thistlethwaite accurately notes, "White feminist theology is racist because it has assumed the prerogative of naming the world for black women on the basis of white women's definitions of experience." (*Sex, Race, and God*, 101.)

61. As womanist thinkers note, African-American women are situated at the bottom of hierarchies of gender, race, and class, being among the poorest of the poor in the United States. In addition to the womanist theologians discussed here, see also the works of Bell Hooks, Angela Y. Davis, and Paula Giddings.

62. Ruether, Heyward, Thistlethwaite, and Letty Russell are among the white feminists who have sought to listen carefully to the experience and theology of women of color.

63. In recent years, numerous sessions at the Annual Meetings of the American Academy of Religion have addressed womanist theology. These include the Afro-American Religious History Group, the Womanist Approaches to Religion and Society Consultation, and the Women and Religion Section. In addition, there are numerous ongoing working groups of womanist theologians, and a series of major symposia offered by the Women's Theological Center in Boston.

64. "Black male and White feminist theologians have failed to address Black women's concerns in their theologies, and . . . Black women's theological expressions are derived from the unique struggle of Black women to survive and be free." (Brown, "'Who Do They Say that I Am?'," 184.)

65.   Delores S. Williams, "Womanist Theology: Black Women's Voices," in *Weaving the Visions: New Patterns in Feminist Spirituality*, Judith Plaskow and Carol P. Christ, eds. (San Francisco: Harper and Row, 1988), 179-186. Williams and other womanists draw on the definitive essays in Walker's 1983 collection of essays, *In Search of our Mother's Gardens*.

66.   Williams, "Womanist Theology," 179; italics in the original. It should be noted that Williams, Jacquelyn Grant, and Kelly Brown identify the primary context of womanist theology as the African-American--rather than the women's--community. The reasons for this are of a complexity which I cannot address here. Suffice it to say that principal among them is racism itself, which has allowed white feminists to claim, tacitly or explicitly, normative status for their own experience. On this, see Jacquelyn Grant, *White Women's Christ and Black Women's Jesus*, 195ff. (Grant's book is the published version of her doctoral dissertation, "The Development and Limitations of Feminist Christology: Toward an Engagement of White Women's and Black Women's Religious Experiences" [PhD dissertation, Union Theological Seminary, 1985].) Williams argues that the relational focus of white feminist theology will not be adequate until "it make[s] an analysis of women's relational history integral to any discussion of women's oppression so that the oppression of women at the hands of other women is not overlooked." (Brown, 189, summarizing Delores S. Williams, "Women's Oppression and Life-Line Politics in Black Women's Religious Narratives," *Journal of Feminist Studies in Religion* (Fall 1985): 59-71.)

67.   Williams, "Womanist Theology," 180.

68.   Williams, "Womanist Theology," 180; italics in the original.

69.   See, for example, Renita J. Weems, *Just a Sister Away: A Womanist Vision of Women's Relationships in the Bible* (San Diego: LuraMedia, 1988).

70.   Williams, "Womanist Theology," 180.

71.   On the use of Native American traditions in womanist theology, see Susan Brooks Thistlethwaite, *Sex, Race, and God*, 104-105. On the modifications made in black and feminist theologies by womanist theologians, see the sources cited in this section, and Katie Geneva Cannon, "The Emergence of Black Feminist Consciousness," in *Feminist Interpretation of the Bible*, Letty M. Russell, ed. (Philadelphia: Westminster Press, 1985), 30-40; and idem, *Black Womanist Ethics* (Atlanta: Scholars Press, 1988), passim.

72.   "The Use of Scripture in Womanist Theology," lecture in Feminist and Womanist Theologies course, Colgate-Rochester Divinity School/ Bexley Hall/ Crozer Theological Seminary, Rochester, NY, February 27, 1990.

73.   Brown, 178-179. Brown here is summarizing the analysis of Jacquelyn Grant in "Black Theology and the Black Woman," in *Black Theology: A Documentary History, 1966-1979*, Gayraud S. Wilmore and James H. Cone, eds. (Maryknoll: Orbis, 1979), 418-433.

74.   Brown, 165. The three interpretations of the Black Christ which Brown studies are the literal version of Albert Cleage, the generic or universalist approach of J. Deotis Roberts, and the ontological interpretation of James Cone. Brown believes that Cone's approach is the most nearly adequate of these three, but falls short in its incorporation of the experience of African-American women.

75.   Using the concept of "kairos" developed by Paul Tillich, Brown argues that, although the Black Christ served an "essential function during the time that it emerged,

. . . the 'kairos time' had not arrived for a Christ that pointed more directly to the particularity of Black women's oppression." (Brown, 176.)

76.   Ruether notes that the construction of white femaleness and black femaleness as opposites of each other not only affected women's roles and identity, but also "required the suppression of the rights of the black male as husband, father, and householder." (*New Woman/New Earth*, 117.)

77.   Brown, 168-179. Among white feminist theologians, Rosemary Ruether discusses the oppression of Black men in *New Woman/New Earth*.

78.   Brown, 176-177; italics added. That is, the symbol of the Black Christ is not complex enough to deal with the fact that "Black men . . . [are] the oppressed in relationship to the White community, but [are] the oppressors in relationship to Black women."

79.   On the importance of survival, see also Katie G. Cannon, *Black Womanist Ethics* (Atlanta: Scholars Press, 1988), which identifies and develops the virtues of "the woman farthest down," i.e., women oppressed on the basis of race and class as well as gender.

80.   On the Hagar story, see Williams' doctoral dissertation, "A Study of Analogous Relation Between African-American-Women's Experience and Hagar's Experience: A Challenge Posed to Black Liberation Theology." Ph.D. diss., Union Theological Seminary, 1983.

81.   Williams contends that it is Hagar's motherhood that upsets Sarah, rather than racial differences between them. That is, focus on the reproductive roles of women in patriarchy helps illuminate the conflicts between women, particularly when surrogate nurturance is involved. See the further discussion of surrogacy, below.

82.   Williams, "Use of Scripture in Womanist Theology"; idem, "Black Women's Surrogacy Experience and Christian Notions of Redemption," in *Beyond Patriarchy*, Paula Cooley and William Eaken, eds. Maryknoll: Orbis, forthcoming. Delivered in lecture form, February 27, 1990, Colgate-Rochester Divinity School/Bexley Hall/Crozer Theological Seminary, Rochester, NY.

83.   Grant, *White Woman's Christ, Black Woman's Jesus*, 212-213.

84.   Ibid., 214.

85.   Ibid., 215-216. Here, Grant follows African-American male liberation theologians.

86.   Ibid., 217-218.

87.   Brown, 192.

88.   Brown, 193.

89.   Brown, 195.

90.   Brown, 194. See also Grant, *White Woman's Christ, Black Woman's Jesus.*

91.   Brown, 194; see idem, 196-198 on the scandal of particularity.

92.   Brown, 195.

93.   Grant, *White Woman's Christ, Black Woman's Jesus*, 219. The latter quotes are from Jarena Lee, *Religious Experiences and Journal of Mrs. Jarena Lee* (Philadelphia: n.p., 1849), 15-16, quoted in Grant, *White Woman's Christ, Black Woman's Jesus*, 219; and Brown, 196.

94.   Brown, 198.

95.   Brown, 199.

96.   Brown, 200, interpreting the story of the Syro-Phoenician woman.

97.   Ibid.

98.   Ibid.

99.   Thistlethwaite, 101-102; cf. Grant, *White Woman's Christ, Black Woman's Jesus*, 232.

100.   Maurice, *The Epistle to the Hebrews*, 29-30.

Bibliography

Berry, Wanda W.   "Images of Sin and Salvation in Feminist Theology." *Anglican Theological Review* 60 (January 1978): 25-54.

Bettenson, Henry, ed.   *Documents of the Christian Church*, 2d ed. Oxford: Oxford University Press, 1963.

Brock, Rita Nakashima.   "And a Little Child Will Lead Us: Christology and Child Abuse." In *Christianity, Patriarchy, and Abuse: A Feminist Critique*, ed. Joanne Carlson Brown and Carole R. Bohn, 42-61. New York: Pilgrim Press, 1989.

_____.   "Beyond Jesus the Christ: A Christology of Erotic Power."   Paper presented to the Currents in Contemporary Christology Section of the American Academy of Religion, November 1987.

_____.   "The Feminist Redemption of Christ." In *Christian Feminism: Visions of a New Humanity*, ed. Judith L. Weidman, 55-74. San Francisco: Harper and Row, 1984.

_____.   "A Feminist Consciousness Looks at Christology." *Encounter* 41, no. 4 (1980): 319-332.

_____.   *Journeys by Heart: A Christology of Erotic Power*. New York: Crossroad, 1988.

Brock, Rita Nakashima.   "Power, Peace and the Possibility of Survival." In *God and Global Justice: Religion and Poverty in an Unequal World*, ed. F. Ferre and R. Mataragnon, 17-35. New York: Paragon House, 1985.

Brown, Kelly Delaine.   "'Who Do They Say that I Am?': A Critical Examination of the Black Christ." Ph.D. diss., Union Theological Seminary, 1988.

Buber, Martin. *I and Thou*. Translated by Walter Kaufmann. New York: Charles Scribner's Sons, 1970.

Busk, Michael C.   "F.D. Maurice's Trinitarian Theology: An Historical and Constructive View." Ph.D. diss., University of Chicago, 1984.

Cannon, Katie Geneva. *Black Womanist Ethics*. Atlanta: Scholars Press, 1988.

_____. "The Emergence of Black Feminist Consciousness." In *Feminist Interpretation of the Bible*, ed. Letty M. Russell, 30-40. Philadelphia: Westminster Press, 1985.

Carr, Anne E.   "Is a Christian Feminist Theology Possible?" *Theological Studies* 43 (June 1982): 279-297.

_____. *Transforming Grace*. San Francisco: Harper and Row, 1988.

Cashdollar, Charles D.   *The Transformation of Theology, 1830-1890: Positivism and Protestant Thought in Britain and America*. Princeton, NJ: Princeton University Press, 1989.

Cauthen, Kenneth.   *Systematic Theology: A Modern Protestant Approach*. Lewiston, Ont: Edwin Mellen Press, 1986.

Christ, Carol P.   "Embodied Thinking: Reflections on Feminist Theological Method." *Journal of Feminist Studies in Religion* 5, no. 1 (Spring 1989): 7-16.

Christ, Carol P. *Laughter of Aphrodite: Reflections on a Journey to the Goddess*. San Francisco: Harper and Row, 1987.

_____. "The New Feminist Theology: A Review of the Literature." *Religious Studies Review* 3 (1977): 203-212.

_____. "Reflections on the Initiation of an American Woman Scholar into the Symbols and Rituals of the Ancient Goddesses." *Journal of Feminist Studies in Religion* 3, no. 1 (1987): 57-66.

_____. "Spiritual Quest and Women's Experience." In *Womanspirit Rising: A Feminist Reader in Religion*, ed. Carol P. Christ and Judith Plaskow, 228-245. San Francisco: Harper and Row, 1979.

_____. "Why Women Need the Goddess: Phenomenological, Psychological, and Political Reflections." In *Womanspirit Rising: A Feminist Reader in Religion*, ed. Carol P. Christ and Judith Plaskow, 273-287. San Francisco: Harper and Row, 1979.

Christ, Carol P., and Judith Plaskow, ed. *Womanspirit Rising: A Feminist Reader in Religion*. San Francisco: Harper and Row, 1979.

Christensen, Torben. *The Divine Order: A Study in F.D. Maurice's Theology*. Leiden: E.J. Brill, 1973.

_____. The Origin and History of Christian Socialism: 1848-1854. Aarhus: Universitetsforlaget, 1962.

Clark, Elizabeth, and Herbert Richardson, eds. *Women and Religion: A Feminist Sourcebook of Christian Thought*. New York: Harper and Row, 1977.

Collins, Adela Yarbro. "New Testament Perspectives: The Gospel of John." *Journal for the Study of the Old Testament* 22, no. 1 (1982): 47-53.

Cooey, Paula M., Sharon A. Farmer, and Mary Ellen Ross, eds. *Embodied Love: Sensuality and Relationship as Feminist Values*. San Francisco: Harper and Row, 1987.

Daly, Mary. *Beyond God the Father: Toward a Philosophy of Women's Liberation*. Boston: Beacon Press, 1973.

_____. *The Church and the Second Sex*. With a New Feminist Postchristian Introduction. New York: Harper Colophon Books, 1968 and 1975.

_____. *Gyn/Ecology: The Metaethics of Radical Feminism*. Boston: Beacon Press: 1978.

D'Angelo, Mary Rose. "Women in Luke-Acts: A Redactional View." *Journal of Biblical Literature* 109, no. 3 (1990): 441-461.

de Lauretis, Teresa. *Alice Doesn't: Feminism, Semiotics, Cinema*. Bloomington, IN: Indiana University Press, 1984.

_____, ed. *Feminist Studies/Critical Studies*. Bloomington, IN: Indiana University Press, 1984.

Devenish, Philip E. "Review of *God-Christ-Church*." *Theological Studies* 44 (March 1983): 145-147.

Douglass, Jane Dempsey. "Women and the Continental Reformation." In *Religion and Sexism: Images of Women in the Jewish* and Christian Traditions, ed. Rosemary Radford Ruether. New York: Simon and Schuster, 1974.

Dunfee, Susan Nelson. "Christianity and the Liberation of Women." Ph.D. diss., Claremont Graduate School, 1985.

Fackenheim, Emil. "The Commanding Voice of Auschwitz." In God's Presence in History: Jewish Affirmations and Philossophical Reflections, 71-93. New York: New York University Press, 1970.

_____. *To Mend the World: Foundations of Future Jewish Thought*. New York: Schocken Books, 1981.

Fulkerson, Mary McClintock. "Review of Rosemary Radford Ruether, *Womanguides*." *Journal of the American Academy of Religion* 54 (Fall 1986): 607-608.

Geertz, Clifford. *The Interpretation of Cultures: Selected Essays.* New York: Basic Books, 1973.

Grant, Jacquelyn. "Black Theology and the Black Woman." In *Black Theology: A Documentary History, 1966-1979*, ed. Gayraud S. Wilmore and James H. Cone, 418-433. Maryknoll: Orbis, 1979.

_____. "The Development and Limitations of Feminist Christology: Toward an Engagement of White Women's and Black Women's Religious Experiences." Ph.D. diss., Union Theological Seminary, 1985.

_____. "Subjectification as a Requirement for Christological Construction." In *Lift Every Voice: Constructing Christian Theologies from the Underside*, ed. Susan Brooks Thistlethwaite and Mary Potter Engel, 201-214. San Francisco: Harper and Row, 1990.

_____. *White Women's Christ and Black Women's Jesus: Feminist Christology and Womanist Response.* Atlanta: Scholars Press, 1989.

Grillmeier, Aloys. *Christ in Christian Tradition.* Vol. 1: *From the Apostolic Age to Chalcedon.* Translated by John S. Bowden. Atlanta: John Knox, 1975.

Hall, Robert T. "The Unity of Philosophy, Theology, and Ethics in the Thought of Frederick Denison Maurice." Ph.D. diss., Drew University, 1967.

Hampson, Daphne. *Theology and Feminism.* Oxford and Cambridge: Basil Blackwell, 1990.

Hampson, Daphne, and Rosemary Radford Ruether. "Is There a Place for Feminist in a Christian Church?" *New Blackfriars* 68, no. 801 (January 1987): 7-24.

Heyward, Carter. "Can Anglicans be Feminist Liberation Theologians and Still be 'Anglican'?" In *The Trial of Faith: Theology and the Church Today*, ed. Peter Eaton, 27-50. Wilton, CT: Morehouse-Barlow, 1988.

Heyward, Carter. "Heterosexist Theology: Being Above It All." *Journal of Feminist Studies in Religion* 3 (Spring 1987): 29-38.

_____. *Our Passion for Justice: Images of Power, Sexuality, and Liberation*. New York: The Pilgrim Press, 1984.

_____. *A Priest Forever: The Formation of a Woman and a Priest*. New York: Harper and Row, 1976.

_____. *The Redemption of God: A Theology of Mutual Relation*. Washington: University Press of America, 1982.

_____. *Speaking of Christ: A Lesbian Feminist Voice*, ed. Ellen C. Davis. New York: Pilgrim Press, 1989.

_____. *Touching Our Strength: The Erotic as Power and the Love of God*. San Francisco: Harper and Row, 1989.

_____. "An Unfinished Symphony of Liberation: The Radicalization of Christian Feminism among White U.S. Women: A Review Essay." *Journal of Feminist Studies in Religion* 1 (Spring 1985): 99-118.

Heyward, Carter and Margaret Craddock Huff. "Digging Foundations for Anglican Ecclesiology: A Feminist Liberation Perspective." Paper presented to the Conference of Anglican Theologians, 1988. Used by permission.

Hooks, Bell. *Ain't I A Woman: Black Women and Feminism*. Boston: South End Press, 1982.

_____. *Feminist Theory: From Margin to Center*. Boston: South End Press, 1984.

Houghton, Walter E. *The Victorian Frame of Mind, 1830-1870*. New Haven: Yale University Press, 1957.

Johnson, Elizabeth A. "Jesus, the Wisdom of God: A Biblical Basis for Non-Androcentric Christology." *Ephemerides Theologicae Lovanienses* 60, no. 4 (December 1985): 261-294.

Kelly, J.N.D. *Early Christian Doctrines*. New York: Harper and Row, 1958.

Keohane, Nannerl O., Michelle Z. Rosaldo, and Barbara C. Gelfin, eds. *Feminist Theory: A Critique of Ideology*. Chicago: University of Chicago Press, 1982.

Knutsen, Mary M. Review of *Faith, Feminism, and the Christ*. *Religious Studies Review* 12, no. 3/4 (July/October 1986): 197-202.

_____. "'This Terrible Battle for Meaning': A Critical Interpretation of Mary Daly's Radical Feminist Critique of Christianity." Unpublished paper, University of Chicago, Chicago, 1982.

Lefebure, Leo D. *Toward a Contemporary Wisdom Christology: A Study of Karl Rahner and Norman Pittenger*. Lanham, MD: University Press of America, 1988.

Lerner, Gerda. *The Creation of Patriarchy*. New York and Oxford: Oxford University Press, 1986.

Lessing, Gotthold Ephraim. *Lessing's Theological Writings*. Translated by Henry Chadwick. Stanford: Stanford University Press, 1956.

Lorde, Audre. "The Master's Tools Will Never Dismantle the Master's House." In *Sister Outsider: Essays and Speeches*, 110-113. Freedom, CA: The Crossing Press, 1984.

Lowe, Walter. "Christ and Salvation." In *Christian Theology: An Introduction to its Traditions and Tasks*, ed. Peter C. Hodgson and Robert H. King, 222-248. Philadelphia: Fortress Press, 1985.

Mack, Burton L. "All the Extra Jesuses: Christian Origins in the Light of the Extra-Canonical Gospels." *Semeia* 49 (1990): 169-176.

MacKinnon, Catharine A. "Feminism, Marxism, Method, and the State: An Agenda for Theory." In *Feminist Theory: A Critique of Ideology*, ed. Nannerl O. Keohane et al., 1-30. Chicago: University of Chicago Press, 1982.

McKenzie, John L., "The Word of God in the New Testament," *Theological Studies* 21, no. 2 (June 1960): 183-206.

Maurice, Frederick, ed. *The Life of F.D. Maurice, Chiefly Told in His Own Letters*. New York: Charles Scribner's Sons, 1884.

Maurice, Frederick Denison. *Christmas Day and Other Sermons*. London: Macmillan, 1892.

————. *The Doctrine of Sacrifice: deduced from the Scriptures*. London: Macmillan, 1879.

————. *The Epistles of St. John: A Series of Lectures on Christan Ethics*. London: Macmillan, 1867.

————. *The Epistle to the Hebrews: Being the Substance of Three Lectures Delivered in the Chapel of the Honourable Society of Lincoln's Inn, on the Foundation of Bishop Warburton, with a Preface Containing a Review of Mr. Newman's Theory of Development*. London: John W. Parker, 1846.

————. *The Gospel of St. John*. London: Macmillan, 1867.

————. *The Kingdom of Christ: or Hints to a Quaker Reflecting the Principles, Constitution, and Ordinances of the Catholic Church*. 3 vols. London: Darton and Clark, 1838.

————. *The Kingdom of Christ: or Hints to a Quaker Reflecting the Principles, Constitution, and Ordinances of the Catholic Church*. 1842 ed. 2 vols. London: Macmillan, 1883.

————. *Moral and Metaphysical Philosophy*. 2 volumes. London and New York: Macmillan, 1890.

————. *The Patriarchs and Lawgivers of the Old Testament*, second series. London: Macmillan, 1877.

————. *The Religions of the World and their Relations to Christianity Considered in Eight Lectures founded by Hon. Robert Boyle*. 5th ed. London: Macmillan, 1877.

Maurice, Frederick Denison. *Sermons Preached in Lincoln's Inn Chapel*. New ed. 6 vols. London and New York: Macmillan, 1891-92.

_____. *Social Morality*. London: Macmillan, 1869; new ed. 1893.

_____. *Theological Essays*. With an Introduction by Edward F. Carpenter. From the second edition (originally published in 1853). London: James Clarke & Co. Ltd., 1957.

_____. *Theological Essays*. Third edition. London: Macmillan, 1871.

_____. *The Unity of the New Testament*. 1st American ed. Boston: Lee and Shephard, 1879; London: Macmillan and Co., 1884.

_____. "The Use of the Word Revelation in the New Testament." In *Present-Day Papers on Prominent Questions in Theology*, second series, ed. Alexander Ewing, 1-47. London: Strahan and Co., 1871.

_____. *What is Revelation? A series of Sermons on the Epiphany; to which are added letters to a student of theology on the Bampton lectures of Mr. Mansel*. Cambridge: Macmillan, 1859.

Marxsen, Willi. *The Beginnings of Christology*. Translated by Paul J. Achtemeir and Lorenz Nieting. Philadelphia: Fortress, 1979.

_____. "Christology in the New Testament." In *Interpreters Dictionary of the Bible: Supplementary Volume*, 146-156. Nashville: Abingdon, 1976.

Moltmann, Jürgen. *The Crucified God: The Cross of Christ as the Foundation and Criticism of Christian Theology*. Translated by R.A. Nilson and John Bowden. New York: Harper and Row, 1974.

MudFlower Collective. *God's Fierce Whimsy*. New York: Pilgrim Press, 1985.

Newman, Paul W. *A Spirit Christology: Recovering the Biblical Paradigm of Christian Faith*. Lanham, MD: University Press of America, 1987.

Newsome, David. *Two Classes of Men: Platonism and English Romantic Thought*. London: J. Murray, 1974.

Nikelsburg, George W. E. "The Genre and Function of the Markan Passion Narrative." *Harvard Theological Review* 73, no. 1-2 (1980): 153-184.

Ogden, Schubert M. *Faith and Freedom: Toward a Theology of Liberation*. Nashville: Abingdon, 1979.

_____. *On Theology*. San Francisco: Harper & Row, Publishers, 1986.

_____. *The Point of Christology*. San Francisco: Harper and Row, 1982.

_____. "Present Prospects for Empirical Theology." In *The Future of Empirical Theology*, ed. Bernard E. Meland, 65-88. Chicago: University of Chicago Press, 1969.

_____. "Problems in the Case for a Pluralistic Theology of Religions." *Journal of Religion* 68, no. 4 (1988): 493-507.

_____. *The Reality of God*. San Francisco: Harper and Row, 1977.

_____. "'The Reformation that We Want,'" *Anglican Theological Review* 54 (October 1972): 260-273.

Pelikan, Jaroslav, *The Emergence of the Catholic Tradition (100-600)*. Vol. 1, *The Christian Tradition: A History of the Development of Doctrine*. Chicago: University of Chicago Press, 1971.

Pellauer, Mary. "The Religious Social Thought of Three U.S. Woman Suffrage Leaders: Toward a Tradition of Feminist Theology." Ph.D. diss., University of Chicago, 1980.

Petersen, William Herbert. "Frederick Denison Maurice as Historian: An Analysis of the Character of Maurice's Unsystematic Theology, Attempting to Disclose a Method Capable of Reconciling Secular and Ecclesiastical Historiography." Ph.D. diss., Graduate Theological Union, 1976.

Pfleiderer, Otto. *The Development of Theology in Germany since Kant, and its Progress in Great Britain since 1825.* Translated under the author's supervision by J. Frederich Smith. London: Swan Sonnenschein and Co., 1890.

Plaskow, Judith. *Sex, Sin, and Grace: Women's Experience and the Theologies of Reinhold Niebuhr and Paul Tillich.* Lanham, MD: University Press of America, 1980.

Prestige, G.L. *God in Patristic Thought.* London: SPCK, 1952.

Prickett, Stephen. "Coleridge, Newman, and F. D. Maurice: Development of Doctrine and Growth of the Mind." *Theology* 76 (July 1973): 340-349.

Prickett, Stephen. *Romanticism and Religion: The Tradition of Coleridge and Wordsworth in the Victorian Church.* Cambridge and New York: Cambridge University Press, 1976.

Reagon, Bernice Johnson. "Coalition Politics: Turning the Century." In *Home Girls: A Black Feminist Anthology,* ed. Barbara Smith, 356-368. New York: Kitchen Table: Women of Color Press, 1983.

Ruether, Rosemary Radford. "Beginnings: An Intellectual Autobiography." In *Journeys: The Impact of Personal Experience on Religious Thought,* ed. Gregory Baum, 34-56. New York: Paulist Press, 1975.

_____. "Christian Origins and the Counter Culture." *Dialog* 10 (Summer 1971): 193-200.

_____. *Disputed Questions: On Being a Christian.* Nashville: Abingdon, 1982.

Ruether, Rosemay Radford. "Eschatology and Feminism." In *Lift Every Voice: Constructing Christian Theologies from the Underside*, ed. Susan Brooks Thistlethwaite and Mary Potter Engel, 111-124. San Francisco: Harper and Row, 1990.

_____. *Faith and Fratricide: The Theological Roots of Anti-Semitism*. With an Introduction by Gregory Baum. New York: Seabury, 1974.

_____. "The Female Nature of God: A Problem in Contemporary Religious Life." In *God as Father*, ed. Johannes-Baptiste Metz and Edward Schillebeeckx; Eng. lang. ed. Marcus Lefebure, 61-66. Edinburgh: T. & T. Clark, 1981.

_____. "Feminism and Jewish-Christian Dialogue: Particularism and Universalism in the Search for Religious Truth." In *The Myth of Christian Uniqueness: Toward a Pluralistic Theology of Religions*, ed. John Hick and Paul F. Knitter, 137-148. Maryknoll: Orbis Books, 1987.

_____. "Feminism and Religious Faith: Renewal or New Creation?" *Religion and Intellectual Life* 3 (Winter 86): 7-20.

_____. "Feminist Interpretation: A Method of Correlation." In *Feminist Interpretation of the Bible*, ed. Letty M. Russell, 111-124. Philadelphia: Westminster Press, 1985.

_____. "Feminist Theology in the Academy: How Not to Reinvent the Wheel." *Christianity and Crisis* 45 (March 4, 1985): 57-62.

_____. "The Future of Feminist Theology in the Academy." *Journal of American Academy of Religion* 53 (Dec 1985): 703-713.

_____. "The Liberation of Christology from Patriarchy." *Religion and Intellectual Life* 2 (Spring 1985): 116-128.

_____. *Liberation Theology: Human Hope Confronts Christian History and American Power*. New York: Paulist Press, 1972.

Ruether, Rosemary Radford, *New Woman/New Earth: Sexist Ideologies and Human Liberation*. New York: Seabury, 1975.

_____. "Re-contextualizing Theology." *Today* 43 (April 1986): 22-27.

_____, ed. Religion and Sexism: Images of Women in the Jewish and Christian Traditions. New York: Simon and Schuster, 1974.

_____. "Review of Elisabeth Schussler Fiorenza, *In Memory of Her.*" *Horizons* 11, no. 1 (Spring 1984): 146-150.

_____. *Sexism and God-Talk: Toward Feminist Theology*. Boston: Beacon Press, 1983.

_____. "Sexism and the Theology of Liberation." *Christian Century* 90 (Spring 1973): 1224-29.

_____. *To Change the World: Christology and Cultural Criticism*. New York: Crossroad, 1983.

_____. *Womanguides: Readings Toward a Feminist Theology*. Boston: Beacon Press, 1985.

Ruether, Rosemary Radford, and Herman J. Ruether. *The Wrath of Jonah: The Crisis of Religious Nationalism in the Israeli-Palestinian Conflict*. San Francisco: Harper and Row, 1989.

Saiving, Valerie. "The Human Situation: A Feminine View." In *Womanspirit Rising: A Feminist Reader in Religion*, ed. Carol P. Christ and Judith Plaskow, 25-42. San Francisco: Harper and Row, 1979. Originally published in *The Journal of Religion* 40 (April 1960):100-112.

Schillebeeckx, Edward. *Jesus: An Experiment in Christology*. Translated by Hubert Hoskins. New York: Vintage Books, 1981.

Schüssler Fiorenza, Elisabeth. *Bread Not Stone: The Challenge of Feminist Biblical Interpretation*. Boston: Beacon Press, 1984.

Schüssler Fiorenza, Elisabeth. *In Memory of Her: A Feminist Theological Reconstruction of Christian Origins*. New York: Crossroad, 1983.

Scott, R.B.Y. *The Way of Wisdom in the Old Testament*. New York: Macmillan, 1971.

Snyder, Mary Hembrow. *The Christology of Rosemary Radford Ruether: A Critical Introduction*. Mystic, CT: Twenty-third Publications, 1988.

Soelle, Dorothee. *Suffering*. Translated by Everett R. Kalin. Philadelphia: Fortress Press, 1975.

Spelman, Elizabeth V. *The Inessential Woman: Problems of Exclusion in Feminist Thought*. Boston: Beacon Press, 1988.

Suchocki, Marjorie H. "The Challenge of Mary Daly." *Encounter* 41 (1980): 307-317.

_____. *God-Christ-Church: A Practical Guide to Process Theology*. New York: Crossroad, 1982.

_____. *God-Christ-Church: A Practical Guide to Process Theology*, 2d rev. ed. New York: Crossroad, 1989.

_____. "In Search of Justice: Religious Pluralism from a Feminist Perspective." In *The Myth of Christian Uniqueness: Toward a Pluralistic Theology of Religions*, ed. John Hick and Paul F. Knitter, 149-161. Maryknoll, NY: Orbis Books, 1987.

_____. "Weaving the World." *Process Studies* 14 (Summer 1985): 76-86.

Theissen, Gerd. *Sociology of Early Palestinian Christianity*. Translated by John Bowden. (Philadelphia: Fortress, 1978).

Thistlethwaite, Susan Brooks. *Sex, Race and God: Christian Feminism in Black and White*. New York: Crossroad, 1989.

Tracy, David. *The Analogical Imagination: Christian Theology and the Culture of Pluralism*. New York: Crossroad, 1981.

_____. *Plurality and Ambiguity: Hermeneutics, Religion, Hope*. San Francisco: Harper and Row, 1987.

Vaughn, Judith. *Sociality, Ethics, and Social Change: A Critical Appraisal of Reinhold Niebuhr's Ethics in the Light of Rosemary Ruether's Work*. Lanham, MD: University Press of America, 1983.

Walker, Alice. *The Color Purple*. New York: Washington Square Press, 1982.

Weaver, Mary Jo. *New Catholic Women: A Contemporary Challenge to Traditional Religious Authority*. San Francisco: Harper and Row, 1988.

Wedgwood, Julia. *Nineteenth Century Teachers and Other Essays*. London: Hodder and Stoughton, 1909.

Welch, Claude. *Protestant Thought in the Nineteenth Century. Volume I, 1799-1870*. New Haven: Yale University Press, 1972.

Welch, Sharon D. *A Feminist Ethic of Risk*. Minneapolis: Fortress, 1990.

Williams, Delores S. "Black Women's Surrogacy Experience and Christian Notions of Redemption." In *Beyond Patriarchy*, ed. Paula Cooley and William Eaken. Maryknoll: Orbis, forthcoming. Delivered in lecture form, February 27, 1990, Colgate-Rochester Divinity School/Bexley Hall/Crozer Theological Seminary, Rochester, NY.

_____. "A Study of Analogous Relation Between African-American-Women's Experience and Hagar's Experience: A Challenge Posed to Black Liberation Theology." Ph.D. diss., Union Theological Seminary, 1983.

_____. "The Use of Scripture in Womanist Theology," lecture in Feminist and Womanist Theologies course, Colgate-Rochester

Divinity School/ Bexley Hall/ Crozer Theological Seminary, Rochester, NY. February 27, 1990.

Williams, Delores S. "Womanist Theology: Black Women's Voices." In *Weaving the Visions: New Patterns in Feminist Spirituality*, ed. Judith Plaskow and Carol P. Christ, 179-186. San Francisco: Harper and Row, 1988.

_____. "Women's Oppression and Life-Line Politics in Black Women's Religious Narratives," *Journal of Feminist Studies in Religion* (Fall 1985): 59-71.

Wilson-Kastner, Patricia. *Faith, Feminism, and the Christ*. Philadelphia: Fortress Press, 1983.

Young, Pamela Dickey. *Feminist Theology/Christian Theology: In Search of Method*. Minneapolis: Fortress Press, 1990.

Index of Principal Authors